PRIVACY AND IDENTITY PROTECTION

# CONSUMER PROTECTION

## RECALLS, DATA SECURITY AND CONGRESSIONAL ISSUES

# PRIVACY AND IDENTITY PROTECTION

Additional books and e-books in this series can be found
on Nova's website under the Series tab.

PRIVACY AND IDENTITY PROTECTION

# CONSUMER PROTECTION

## RECALLS, DATA SECURITY AND CONGRESSIONAL ISSUES

RALF SCHAEFER
EDITOR

snova
New York

**Library of Congress Cataloging-in-Publication Data**

ISBN: 978-1-53615-876-2

*Published by Nova Science Publishers, Inc. † New York*

# CONTENTS

# PREFACE

Consumers, manufacturers, and auto dealers use publicly available auto recall information differently. Chapter 1 addresses: how consumers and industry stakeholders use such information and how easy to use do consumers find the auto recall areas of NHTSA.gov, among other objectives. Ticket pricing, resale activity, and fees for events vary. Chapter 2 review issues around online ticket sales including what is known about online ticket sales, consumer protection issues related to such sales, and potential advantages and disadvantages of selected approaches to address these issues.

The Telephone Consumer Protection Act of 1991 (TCPA) regulates robocalls. A robocall, also known as "voice broadcasting," is any telephone call that delivers a prerecorded message using an automatic (computerized) telephone dialing system, more commonly referred to as an automatic dialer or "autodialer." Chapter 3 addresses robocalls that are both illegal under the TCPA and intended to defraud, not robocalls that are defined only as illegal. Chapter 4 addresses FTC's role and authorities for overseeing Internet privacy, stakeholders' views on potential actions to enhance federal oversight of consumers' Internet privacy, and breaches of personally identifiable information. Chapter 5 provides a brief overview of federal regulation of Wells Fargo and a timeline of key events involving the company since the scandal's disclosure. It then discusses a few relevant policy issues, including consumer protection and corporate governance, and highlights recent instances of congressional oversight of the bank.

Chapter 6 summarizes measures FTC has taken to enforce consumer reporting agencies (CRA) compliance with requirements to protect consumer information, measures CFPB has taken to ensure CRA protection of consumer information, and actions consumers can take after a breach. Chapter 7 examines issues related to federal oversight of CRAs. This chapter discusses measures FTC has taken to enforce CRA compliance with requirements to protect consumer information, measures CFPB has taken to ensure CRA protection of consumer information, and actions consumers can take after a breach. Chapter 8 reviews gender-related price differences for consumer goods and services sold in the United States. Chapter 9 summarizes P.L. 115-174 as enacted and highlights major policy proposals of the legislation.

Chapter 1 - The number of vehicles affected by safety defect recalls increased sharply in recent years—from nearly 13 million in 2011 to over 51 million in 2016. Once a defect is identified, auto manufacturers are required to send written notification to vehicle owners by mail. NHTSA also aims to enhance awareness of auto recalls by providing information on its website, NHTSA.gov. The Fixing America's Surface Transportation Act includes a provision requiring GAO to study the use of publicly available safety recall information. This chapter addresses: (1) how consumers and industry stakeholders use such information and (2) how easy to use do consumers find the auto recall areas of NHTSA.gov, among other objectives. To understand consumers' use of auto recall information and to test website usability, GAO conducted 12 focus groups with 94 consumers who had a recall. Focus groups were held in six locations selected for population and geographic variation. GAO identified key website usability practices and requested an evaluation by website usability professionals. GAO reviewed statutes, regulations, and NHTSA documents, and interviewed industry stakeholders—including 10 manufacturers selected based on sales market share and other factors.

Chapter 2 - Tickets for concerts, theater, and sporting events can be purchased—typically online—from the original seller (primary market) or a reseller (secondary market). Some state and federal officials and others have raised issues about ticketing fees, the effect of the secondary market on ticket prices, and the transparency and business practices of some industry participants. Event ticketing is not federally regulated. However, federal legislation enacted in 2016 restricts bots (ticket-buying software). Also, the Federal Trade Commission (FTC) has taken two enforcement actions related to deceptive marketing by ticket sellers under its broad FTC Act authority. GAO was asked to review issues around online ticket sales. This chapter examines (1) what is known about online ticket sales, (2) consumer protection issues related to such sales, and (3) potential advantages and disadvantages of selected approaches to address these issues. GAO focused on concert, theater, and major league sporting events for which there is a resale market. GAO analyzed data on fees, ticket volume, and resale prices from a variety of sources; reviewed the largest ticket sellers' websites and purchase processes; and reviewed federal and state laws and relevant academic literature. GAO also interviewed and reviewed documentation from government agencies; consumer organizations; ticket sellers; venue operators; promoters and managers; sports leagues; and academics (selected for their experience and to provide a range of perspectives).

Chapter 3 - The Telephone Consumer Protection Act of 1991 (TCPA) regulates robocalls. A robocall, also known as "voice broadcasting," is any telephone call that delivers a prerecorded message using an automatic (computerized) telephone dialing system, more commonly referred to as an automatic dialer or "autodialer." Robocalls are popular with many industry groups, such as real estate, telemarketing, and direct sales companies. The majority of companies who use robocalling are legitimate businesses, but some are not. Those illegitimate businesses may not just be annoying consumers—they may also be trying to defraud them. The Federal Trade Commission (FTC) and Federal Communications Commission (FCC) regularly cite "unwanted and illegal robocalls" as their number-one complaint category. The FTC received more than 1.9 million complaints filed in the first five months of 2017 and about 5.3 million in 2016. The FCC has stated that it gets more than 200,000 complaints about unwanted telemarketing calls each year. These statistics, as well as complaints to congressional offices, have spurred Congress to hold hearings and introduce legislation on the issue in an effort to protect consumers. Congressional policymakers have proposed a number of changes to existing law and regulations to address the problem of illegal robocalls under the TCA, many of which are intended to defraud. These changes would, for example, expand the definition of what a robocall is, increase penalties for illegal spoofing, and improve protection of seniors from robocall scams. As yet, none of these proposals has become law. On August 19, 2016, a 60-day Robocall "Strike Force" convened, culminating in the testing of a Do Not Originate (DNO) Registry to stop unwanted calls from reaching customers. The intent of the registry is to block fraudulent calls before they can reach a consumer. With the FCC's permission, the Strike Force performed a trial of this concept. The trial was considered a success by the Strike Force and the FCC, reducing calls associated with one particular scam by about 90% in the third quarter of 2016. In November 2017, the FCC promulgated rules on the creation and use of the DNO Registry. The new rules explicitly allow service providers to block calls from two categories of number: (1) numbers that the subscriber has asked to be blocked, such as "in-bound only" numbers (numbers that should not ever originate a call), and (2) unassigned numbers, as the use of such a number indicates that the calling party is intending to defraud a consumer. Notwithstanding the efforts above, based on their long history, scammers appear determined to continue their attempts to defraud consumers. Robocalls make these efforts easier. The FTC asserts that law enforcement on its own cannot completely solve the problem of robocalls. Technological solutions, including robust call-blocking technology, likely will also be required. The DNO Registry, a technology solution that has been proven to significantly decrease robocalls, is supported by most stakeholders, but concerns remain with legitimate telemarketers who fear it may negatively impact them. The FCC intended to address these concerns in 2018. The impacts of the FTC initiatives on fraudulent robocalls, and the resulting impacts in the telemarketing industry, may continue to be oversight issues for Congress. In the 115th Congress, three hearings have been held, and 13 bills aimed at curtailing robocalls and protecting consumers have been introduced. Most of these bills are focused on the larger issue of spoofing, as well as curtailing robocalls for debt collection and politically oriented messages; two bills are aimed at protecting seniors from predatory robocalls intended to defraud them.

Chapter 4 - This is an edited, reformatted and augmented accessible version of the United States Government Accountability Office Testimony Before the Permanent Subcommittee on Investigations, Committee on Homeland Security and Governmental Affairs, U.S. Senate, Publication No. GAO-19-427T, dated March 7, 2019.

Chapter 5 - Wells Fargo Bank, N.A., is a large federally chartered depository bank. It is a subsidiary of Wells Fargo and Company, a bank holding company (hereafter, Wells Fargo or the Bank). Wells Fargo is the fourth largest bank in the United States with $1.9 trillion in assets at the end of 2018. In 2016, a scandal involving Wells Fargo creating fake accounts—which may have harmed more than 2 million consumers—increased scrutiny of the bank by Congress, financial regulators, and the public. Since the scandal was revealed to the public, certain of Wells Fargo's business practices have continued to raise concerns relating to consumer protection and corporate governance, leading to additional congressional oversight and interest. This chapter provides a brief overview of federal regulation of Wells Fargo and a timeline of key events involving the company since the scandal's disclosure. It then discusses a few relevant policy issues, including consumer protection and corporate governance, and highlights recent instances of congressional oversight of the bank.

Chapter 6 - CRAs collect, maintain, and sell to third parties large amounts of sensitive data about consumers, including Social Security numbers and credit card numbers. Businesses and other entities commonly use these data to determine eligibility for credit, employment, and insurance. In 2017, Equifax, one of the largest CRAs, experienced a breach that compromised the records of at least 145.5 million consumers. This statement is based on GAO's February 2019 report on the CRA oversight roles of FTC and CFPB. This statement summarizes (1) measures FTC has taken to enforce CRA compliance with requirements to protect consumer information, (2) measures CFPB has taken to ensure CRA protection of consumer information, and (3) actions consumers can take after a breach.

Chapter 7 - CRAs collect, maintain, and sell to third parties large amounts of sensitive data about consumers, including Social Security numbers and credit card numbers. Businesses and other entities commonly use these data to determine eligibility for credit, employment, and insurance. In 2017, Equifax, one of the largest CRAs, experienced a breach that compromised the records of at least 145.5 million consumers. GAO was asked to examine issues related to federal oversight of CRAs. Among other things, this chapter discusses (1) measures FTC has taken to enforce CRA compliance with requirements to protect consumer information, (2) measures CFPB has taken to ensure CRA protection of consumer information, and (3) actions consumers can take after a breach. GAO reviewed relevant laws, documentation related to CRA examinations, and policies and practices of selected CRAs; and interviewed representatives of regulatory agencies, CRAs, consumer and industry groups, and Attorneys General from four states with consumer reporting requirements.

Chapter 8 - Gender-related price differences occur when consumers are charged different prices for the same or similar goods and services because of factors related to gender. While variation in costs and consumer demand may give rise to such price differences, some policymakers have raised concerns that gender bias may also be a factor. While the Equal Credit Opportunity Act and Fair Housing Act prohibit discrimination based on sex in credit and housing transactions, no federal law prohibits businesses from charging consumers different prices for the same or similar goods targeted to different genders. GAO was asked to review gender-related price differences for consumer goods and services sold in the United States. This chapter examines, among other things, (1) how prices compared for selected goods and services marketed to men and women, and potential reasons for any price differences; (2) what is known about price differences for men and women for products not differentiated by gender, such as mortgages; and (3) the extent to which federal agencies have identified and addressed any concerns about gender-related price differences. To examine these issues, GAO analyzed retail price data, reviewed relevant academic studies, analyzed federal consumer complaint data, and interviewed federal agency officials, industry experts, and academics.

Chapter 9 - Some observers assert the financial crisis of 2007-2009 revealed that excessive risk had built up in the financial system, and that weaknesses in regulation contributed to that buildup and the resultant instability. In response, Congress passed the Dodd-Frank Wall Street Reform and Consumer Protection Act (P.L. 111-203; the Dodd-Frank Act), and regulators strengthened rules under existing authority. Following this broad overhaul of financial regulation, some observers argue certain changes are an overcorrection, resulting in unduly burdensome regulation. The Economic Growth, Regulatory Relief, and Consumer Protection Act (S. 2155, P.L. 115-174) was signed into law by President Donald Trump on May 24, 2018. P.L. 115-174 modifies Dodd-Frank provisions, such as the Volcker Rule (a ban on proprietary trading and certain relationships with investment funds), the *qualified mortgage* criteria under the Ability-to-Repay Rule, and enhanced regulation for large banks; provides smaller banks with an "off ramp" from Basel III capital requirements—standards agreed to by national bank regulators as part of an international bank regulatory framework; and makes other changes to the regulatory system. Most changes made by P.L. 115-174 can be grouped into one of five issue areas: (1) mortgage lending, (2) regulatory relief for "community" banks, (3) consumer protection, (4) regulatory relief for large banks, and (5) regulatory relief for capital formation. Title I of P.L. 115-174 relaxes or provides exemptions to certain mortgage lending rules. For example, it creates a new compliance option for mortgages originated and held by banks and credit unions with less than $10 billion in assets to be considered qualified mortgages for the purposes of the Ability-to-Repay Rule. In addition, P.L. 115-174 exempts certain insured depositories and credit unions that originate few mortgages from certain Home Mortgage Disclosure Act reporting requirements. A number of Title II provisions provide regulatory relief to community banks. For example, banks with under $10 billion in assets are exempt from the Volcker Rule, and certain banks that meet a new *Community Bank Leverage Ratio* are exempt from other risk-based capital ratio and leverage ratio requirements. Title III enhances consumer protections in targeted areas. For example, it subjects credit reporting agencies (CRAs) to additional requirements, including requirements to generally provide fraud alerts for consumer files for at least a year and to allow consumers to place security freezes on their credit reports. In addition, it requires CRAs to exclude certain medical debt from veterans' credit reports. Title IV alters the criteria used to determine which banks are subject to *enhanced prudential regulation* from the original $50 billion asset threshold original set by Dodd-Frank. Banks designated as *global systemically important banks* and banks with more than $250 billion in assets are still automatically subjected to enhanced regulation. However, under P.L. 115-174 banks with between $100 billion and $250 billion in assets are automatically subject only to supervisory stress tests, while the Federal Reserve (Fed) has discretion to apply other individual enhanced prudential provisions to these banks. Banks with assets between $50 billion and $100 billion will no longer be subject to enhanced regulation, except for the risk committee requirement. In addition, P.L. 115-174 relaxes leverage requirements for large custody banks, and allows certain municipal bonds to be counted toward large banks' liquidity requirements. Title V provides regulatory relief to certain securities regulations to encourage capital formation. For example, it exempts more securities exchanges from state securities regulation and subjects certain investment pools to fewer registration and disclosure requirements. Title VI provides enhanced consumer protection for borrowers of student loans. For example, it requires CRA to exclude certain defaulted private student loan debt from credit reports. Proponents of P.L. 115-174 assert it provides necessary and targeted regulatory relief, fosters economic growth, and provides increased consumer protections. Opponents of the legislation argue it needlessly pares back important Dodd-Frank protections to the benefit of large and profitable banks.

In: Consumer Protection
Editor: Ralf Schaefer

ISBN: 978-1-53615-876-2


*Chapter 1*

# AUTO RECALLS: NHTSA SHOULD TAKE STEPS TO FURTHER IMPROVE THE USABILITY OF ITS WEBSITE*

*United States Government Accountability Office*

## ABBREVIATIONS

| | |
|---|---|
| CY | calendar year |
| DOT | Department of Transportation |
| FAST Act | Fixing America's Surface Transportation Act |
| FY | fiscal year |
| GPRA | Government Performance and Results Act of 1993 |
| GSA | General Services Administration |
| MSA | Metropolitan Statistical Area |
| NHTSA | National Highway Traffic Safety Administration |
| NPRM | Notice of Proposed Rulemaking |
| OCCI | Office of Communications and Consumer Information |
| VIN | vehicle identification number |

* This is an edited, reformatted and augmented version of United States Government Accountability Office; Report to Congressional Committees, Publication No. GAO-18-127, dated December 2017.

## Why GAO Did This Study

The number of vehicles affected by safety defect recalls increased sharply in recent years—from nearly 13 million in 2011 to over 51 million in 2016. Once a defect is identified, auto manufacturers are required to send written notification to vehicle owners by mail. NHTSA also aims to enhance awareness of auto recalls by providing information on its website, NHTSA.gov.

The Fixing America's Surface Transportation Act includes a provision requiring GAO to study the use of publicly available safety recall information. This chapter addresses: (1) how consumers and industry stakeholders use such information and (2) how easy to use do consumers find the auto recall areas of NHTSA.gov, among other objectives. To understand consumers' use of auto recall information and to test website usability, GAO conducted 12 focus groups with 94 consumers who had a recall. Focus groups were held in six locations selected for population and geographic variation. GAO identified key website usability practices and requested an evaluation by website usability professionals. GAO reviewed statutes, regulations, and NHTSA documents, and interviewed industry stakeholders—including 10 manufacturers selected based on sales market share and other factors.

## What GAO Recommends

GAO recommends that NHTSA determine a completion date for its website consolidation effort and take interim steps to improve the usability of NHTSA.gov by addressing the website usability difficulties GAO identified. The Department of Transportation concurred with the recommendations.

## What GAO Found

Consumers, manufacturers, and auto dealers use publicly available auto recall information differently. For example, the 94 consumers in 12 focus groups that GAO conducted used this information to decide whether to repair their vehicles. These consumers overwhelmingly cited safety risk and convenience as the two most influential factors they considered. Most consumers reported a preference for receiving recall notification by at least one electronic means, such as by email or text message, in addition to mail. However, only 7 of 94 consumers reported receiving electronic notifications, suggesting a gap between the industry's auto recall notification practices and consumers' preferences. (See Figure). In response to a mandate in law, in September

2016, the National Highway Traffic Safety Administration (NHTSA) issued a proposed rule that, if finalized, would require manufacturers to notify consumers about auto recalls by electronic means in addition to mail.

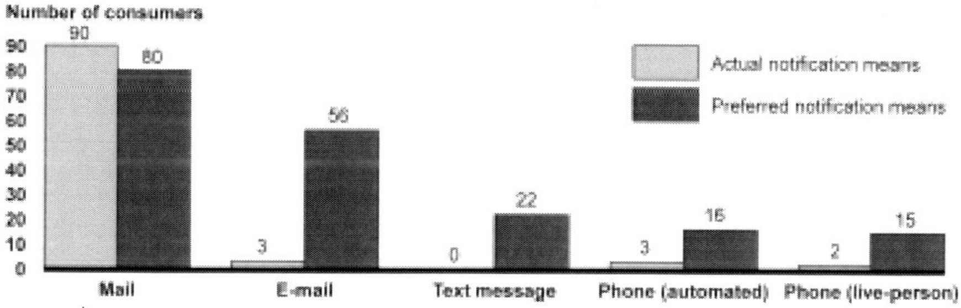


Source: GAO. | GAO-18-127.

How Consumers Who Participated in GAO's Focus Groups Actually Received and Preferred to Receive Auto Recall Information.

Most consumers in GAO's focus group website usability tests found the auto recall areas of NHTSA's website—NHTSA.gov—easy to use; however, some consumers experienced difficulties when asked to complete auto recall related tasks. For example, when consumers attempted to search for recalls affecting their specific vehicles, some found the search results confusing, leading them to question the accuracy of the results. Similarly, some consumers were hampered in searching for recalls by their vehicles' year, make, and model because the website did not always display model options using plain language. GAO found that the auto recall areas of NHTSA.gov do not always reflect federal and industry key website usability practices, and that an independent evaluation conducted by website usability professionals at GAO's request identified similar issues. NHTSA is in the process of consolidating its websites and plans to conduct a website usability study of NHTSA.gov with consumers after the consolidation is complete. However, the agency has not determined a completion date for the consolidation effort—an essential step for organizations to effectively guide their information technology efforts. Without establishing a completion date and taking interim steps to improve the usability of NHTSA.gov, consumers will likely continue to experience difficulties, which may limit the effectiveness of the website's primary means of providing consumers with information about recalls affecting their vehicles.

December 4, 2017

The Honorable John Thune
Chairman

The Honorable Bill Nelson
Ranking Member
Committee on Commerce, Science, and Transportation
United States Senate

The Honorable Greg Walden
Chairman

The Honorable Frank Pallone
Ranking Member
Committee on Energy and Commerce
House of Representatives

The number of vehicles affected by safety defect vehicle recalls (auto recalls) has increased dramatically in recent years—rising from nearly 13 million in 2011 to over 51 million in 2016. This increase is driven in part by several large-scale recalls, such as the ongoing recall of 34 million vehicles with defective Takata air bag inflators that have caused at least 13 deaths and more than 220 injuries in the United States.

Auto recalls seek to address a wide variety of safety risks, such as wiring system problems that may result in vehicle fires or windshield wiper assemblies that fail to operate properly. When safety defects are identified, auto manufacturers are required to notify consumers and remedy (repair) the problem without charge. The National Highway Traffic Safety Administration (NHTSA) monitors the percentage of defective vehicles that manufacturers ultimately remedy (completion rates). However, according to NHTSA's Strategic Plan 2016–2020, auto recall completion rates are unacceptably low, leaving vehicles with potentially deadly safety defects on the road.[1] In calendar year 2014—the latest year for which data are complete—67 percent of recalled light vehicles had been remedied. NHTSA aims to enhance the public's awareness of auto recalls and improve completion rates by, for example, providing information on its website, NHTSA.gov.

The Fixing America's Surface Transportation Act (FAST Act) requires GAO to study the use of publicly available safety recall information.[2] This chapter addresses the following objectives: (1) How do consumers and industry stakeholders use publicly available auto recall information? (2) How easy or difficult to use do consumers find the auto recall areas of NHTSA.gov? (3) What steps, if any, has NHTSA taken to raise consumer awareness about auto recalls and how has NHTSA evaluated the effectiveness of these steps?

---

[1] National Highway Traffic Safety Administration, *The Road Ahead: National Highway Traffic Safety Administration Strategic Plan 2016-2020* (October 2016).

[2] Pub. L. No. 114-94, § 24103(b), 129 Stat. 1312, 1702 (Dec. 4, 2015).

For purposes of this chapter we define publicly available auto recall information to include information on the auto recall areas of NHTSA.gov, such as examples of notification letters that manufacturers mail to consumers. This chapter focuses on safety defect vehicle recalls affecting passenger vehicles that are initiated when a defect in a vehicle or vehicle equipment creates an unreasonable safety risk, as determined by NHTSA or a manufacturer.[3]

To inform the first two objectives, we conducted 12 focus groups with new and used vehicle owners who had experienced an auto recall in the last 24 months. Each focus group was split into two sessions: (1) a discussion session to explore participants' thoughts, experiences, and preferences about auto recall information and (2) a session to test the usability of the auto recall areas of NHTSA.gov. We conducted focus groups at six locations across the country to provide population and geographic dispersion, with each group including 7 or 8 consumers for a total of 94 participants. Half of the focus groups were comprised of consumers who had completed the repair and the remaining half included consumers who had not completed the repair. We selected focus group participants based on age, income, gender, education level, race, and ethnicity to ensure we collected a range of perspectives.

- We evaluated transcripts of each focus group session using systematic content analysis to identify how consumers used auto recall information and to evaluate how easy or difficult consumers found the auto recall areas of NHTSA.gov to use.[4]
- We also analyzed participants' responses to the questionnaires we administered for each session to quantify responses regarding how consumers used auto recall information—including how they received and preferred to receive auto recall notifications—and participants' assessments of NHTSA.gov's usability while performing certain auto recall tasks on the website.

Since we did not select a representative sample of participants, the results of our focus group analyses are not generalizable to all vehicle owners.

---

[3] NHTSA is responsible for overseeing two types of recalls: compliance and safety defect recalls. Compliance recalls are initiated when vehicles are determined to be noncompliant with applicable Federal Motor Vehicle Safety Standards, as identified by NHTSA or a manufacturer. They represent a relatively small percentage of total vehicle recalls—about 16 percent in calendar year 2016, according to NHTSA's *2016 Annual Recall Report*. We did not examine compliance recalls, nor did we examine car seat (e.g., child safety seat), tire, and other equipment (e.g., vehicle accessories and after-market equipment such as lighting, trailer hitches, and bike racks) recalls, as these products have different consumer notification requirements. We did not review *Technical Service Bulletins*. Passenger vehicles include cars, pickup trucks, sport utility vehicles, large passenger vans, and minivans, but exclude other vehicles, such as motorcycles, recreational vehicles, and commercial trucks.

[4] Because the transcripts did not include a unique identifier for each focus group participant, we conducted our analysis of focus group session discussions at the group level.

To determine how industry stakeholders use auto recall information, we interviewed representatives from 10 auto manufacturers, selected based on each manufacturer's sales market share, place of ownership, and experience with auto recalls, collecting a range of perspectives on how manufacturers use auto recall information. We also interviewed four franchised dealerships and three independent auto dealerships across the country. The results of these interviews are not generalizable to all auto manufacturers and dealerships, but provide insights about how some industry stakeholders use auto recall information. To understand NHTSA's role in the auto recall process as well as that of other stakeholders, we also interviewed NHTSA program officials, industry groups, and consumer associations, among others.

To evaluate how easy or difficult consumers find the auto recall areas of NHTSA.gov to use, we first analyzed guidance documents from NHTSA and other federal agencies to identify key website usability practices. For example, we analyzed the General Services Administration's (GSA) and the Department of Health and Human Services' *Research-Based Web Design & Usability Guidelines*, which includes quantified, peer-reviewed guidelines intended to help federal agencies improve the design and usability of their information-based websites.[5] In addition, we reviewed federal standards for internal control related to communicating quality information externally.[6] During our usability testing sessions, we asked consumers to attempt to complete auto recall tasks—the primary means NHTSA.gov provides for consumers to access information about auto recalls affecting their vehicles—and discuss their experiences. We then compared consumers' experiences with the usability of the website against these practices. To corroborate the results of our usability testing sessions, we also requested that five website usability professionals from GSA's Federal User Experience Community conduct an independent evaluation of the auto recall areas of NHTSA.gov.[7]

To determine any steps NHTSA has taken to raise consumer awareness about auto recalls and how NHTSA evaluates the effectiveness of any steps, we reviewed relevant statutes, regulations, and agency documents, such as NHTSA's strategic planning and performance reports. We reviewed performance management practices as provided in the Government Performance and Results Act of 1993 (GPRA), the GPRA Modernization Act of 2010, and standards for internal control in the federal government to identify any opportunities for improvement.[8] We also interviewed responsible agency officials and discussed NHTSA's public awareness efforts during interviews with industry

[5] GSA and the Department of Health and Human Services, *Research-Based Web Design & Usability Guidelines* (Washington, D.C.: August 2006). GSA also offers website usability evaluation services to federal agencies. The Department of Health and Human Services manages usability.gov, a website where the federal government has published ways to assess a website's usability and, in partnership with GSA, issued guidance and best practices for designing federal websites.

[6] GAO, *Standards for Internal Control in the Federal Government*, GAO-14-704G (Washington, D.C.: September 2014).

[7] GSA's Federal User Experience Community is comprised of federal program managers, subject matter experts, designers, and developers with expertise in website usability.

[8] GAO-14-704G.

stakeholders (described above). We analyzed the results of these interviews along with the focus group discussions to identify perspectives on the effectiveness of NHTSA's public awareness steps. See appendix I for more information on our objectives, scope, and methodology, including the organizations we interviewed for this engagement.

We conducted this performance audit from October 2016 to December 2017 in accordance with generally accepted government auditing standards. Those standards require that we plan and perform the audit to obtain sufficient, appropriate evidence to provide a reasonable basis for our findings and conclusions based on our audit objectives. We believe that the evidence obtained provides a reasonable basis for our findings and conclusions based on our audit objectives.

## BACKGROUND

Safety defect vehicle recalls (auto recalls) are initiated when a defect in a vehicle or vehicle equipment creates an unreasonable safety risk, as determined by NHTSA or a manufacturer.[9] After a recall is initiated, manufacturers are required to provide written notification to vehicle owners via First-Class Mail within 60 days[10] and remedy the defect.[11] Franchised dealers—which sell or lease an auto manufacturer's new vehicles—perform the recall remedy.[12]

Before manufacturers send recall notification letters to affected vehicle owners, NHTSA reviews draft letters and envelopes to ensure they include required information about the safety defect. Required information includes, among other things, a clear description of the safety defect, an evaluation of the risk to vehicle safety, and a statement that the manufacturer will remedy the defect without charge.[13] See appendix II for an example of a notification letter.

---

[9] NHTSA does not categorize recalls according to the degree of safety risk they pose.

[10] 49 U.S.C. § 30118; 49 C.F.R. § 577.7.

[11] 49 U.S.C. § 30120(a). Manufacturers have three options for remedying the defect – repair, replacement, or refund. In the case of a vehicle recall, the manufacturer may choose to repair the vehicle at no charge; replace the vehicle with an identical or similar vehicle; or refund the purchase price in full, minus a reasonable allowance for depreciation.

[12] Independent dealers—which sell only used vehicles—and independent repair facilities are not generally authorized by manufacturers to perform auto recall remedies. Franchise dealers may also sell used vehicles from other manufacturers. According to NHTSA officials, current law does not require auto dealers to repair auto recalls in used vehicles on their lots prior to sale, or taxi and ride-sharing services to repair auto recalls in vehicles being used to transport customers.

[13] In June 2011, we reported on options NHTSA had to improve the safety defect recall process. See GAO, *Auto Safety: NHTSA Has Options to Improve the Safety Defect Recall Process*, GAO-11-603 (Washington, D.C.: June 15, 2011). We discuss steps NHTSA has taken to address these options later in this chapter.

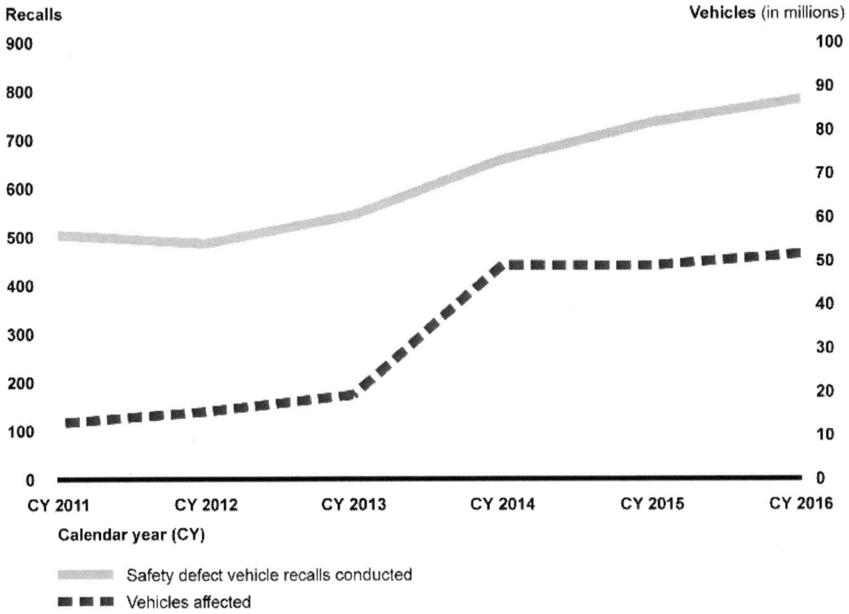


Source: National Highway Traffic Safety Administration. | GAO-18-127.

Figure 1. Number of Safety Defect Vehicle Recalls and Vehicles Affected from Calendar Years 2011 through 2016.

The number of vehicles affected by safety defect vehicle recalls has increased dramatically since 2011 (see Figure 1). The increase reflects, in part, several large-scale recalls. For example, in 2014, General Motors initiated a recall of over 8 million vehicles with faulty ignition switches. Similarly, according to NHTSA in 2014 and 2015, some passenger vehicle manufacturers began recalling Takata air bag inflators, recalls that have grown to include approximately 34 million vehicles and 19 auto manufacturers. For the Takata recall, NHTSA issued various orders and established a Coordinated Remedy Program under which the agency oversees the supply of remedy parts and risk-based prioritization of vehicles for repair, and manages related recalls with the assistance of an Independent Monitor.[14] The Independent Monitor assesses compliance with the applicable orders issued by NHTSA and makes recommendations aimed at enhancing the remedy program.

According to NHTSA's Strategic Plan 2016–2020, this unprecedented recall activity encouraged the agency to improve its system for identifying and addressing defective vehicles. For example, the plan states that NHTSA's "vision is to achieve a 100-percent completion rate for every recall by improving communication at every level, at every step of the way." Thus, according to the plan, NHTSA and the auto industry have committed to identifying and implementing effective strategies to inform consumers of safety

[14] The Independent Monitor is not counsel to or an agent of the United States or any other government, although it operates under the supervision of NHTSA. See http://www.takatamonitor.org/faqs. According to NHTSA officials, about 44 percent of Takata air bag inflators had been remedied as of September 2017.

defects and envision that their coordination will bolster recall efforts to improve completion rates.

NHTSA reported that annual completion rates for passenger vehicle recalls have remained relatively flat, ranging from 63 to 67 percent between calendar year 2011 and calendar year 2014.[15] See appendix III for completion rates by vehicle component and vehicle type. In part, to improve communication and encourage consumers to complete repairs, NHTSA and manufacturers provide auto recall information to the public on their websites. For example, certain motor vehicle manufacturers are required to allow consumers to search a vehicle's recall remedy status on the Internet using the vehicle identification number (VIN).[16] NHTSA also provides publicly available auto recall information on its website, including examples of recall notification letters.

In December 2016, NHTSA began consolidating its websites into NHTSA.gov to provide a single access point for its auto recall content. One of these websites, safercar.gov, was once NHTSA's primary method of communicating auto recall information to consumers; however, the agency is in the process of moving this information to NHTSA.gov. NHTSA's Strategic Plan 2016–2020 states that the agency wants NHTSA.gov to be a comprehensive user-friendly platform that serves as the premier source of vehicle safety information by, for example, improving the website's search capabilities.[17] NHTSA also aims to encourage consumers to use its website's auto recall information through its communications program.

NHTSA's Office of Communications and Consumer Information (OCCI) is the primary office responsible for implementing the agency's public communication efforts. OCCI intends to increase public engagement with the agency's information through its social media channels, such as Instagram, Twitter, and Facebook. The amount OCCI obligated to support the agency's auto recall efforts has increased from nearly $.5 million in fiscal year 2011 to about $2.5 million in fiscal year 2016.[18] According to NHTSA officials, these obligations supported various efforts, including public awareness campaigns, an auto recall hotline, advertising agencies, exhibits at auto shows, and NHTSA's mobile application.

---

[15] National Highway Traffic Safety Administration, *Report to Congress: "Vehicle Safety Recall Completion Rates Report"* (May 2017). NHTSA's latest available annual completion rate counts (as of July 1, 2016) include recalls issued between 2010 and 2014 in which the manufacturer reported the recall's completion status for at least five quarters after the remedy program became available. Recalls that had not reached this maturation point— including recalls filed in 2015—were not counted.

[16] 49 C.F.R. § 573.15. Requirements apply to manufacturers that have manufactured for sale, sold, offered for sale, introduced or delivered for introduction in interstate commerce, or imported into the United States 25,000 or more light vehicles or 5,000 or more motorcycles in the current calendar year or the prior calendar year. The VIN is a 17- character number that uniquely identifies a vehicle.

[17] The FAST Act directs NHTSA to implement current information technology, web design trends, and best practices that will help ensure that motor vehicle safety recall information available to the public on its website is readily accessible and easy to use, including by improving the organization, availability, readability, and functionality of the website. Pub. L. No. 114-94, § 24103(a), 129 Stat. 1312, 1702.

[18] An "obligation" is a definite commitment that creates a legal liability of the government for the payment of goods and services ordered or received. GAO, *A Glossary of Terms Used in the Federal Budget Process*, GAO-05-734SP (Washington, D.C.: September 2005).

# AUTO RECALL INFORMATION USE VARIES, AND MOST CONSUMERS IN FOCUS GROUPS PREFERRED ELECTRONIC RECALL NOTIFICATIONS IN ADDITION TO MAIL

## Consumers in Our Focus Groups Primarily Considered Safety Risk and Convenience when Using Auto Recall Information to Make Repair Decisions

As part of our focus group discussion sessions, consumers selected safety risk and convenience as the two most influential factors they considered when using auto recall information to decide whether to complete repairs.

- *All factors considered*: During each session, we first asked consumers to describe all the factors they considered.[19] Across the sessions, consumers shared a wide variety of factors including availability of a loaner vehicle, time to schedule and complete the repair, safety risk, and other factors. For example, some consumers had not yet repaired their vehicles because they were "just waiting" for parts to become available. Other consumers considered their previous customer service experiences at the franchised dealership or the distance they would need to travel to complete the repair. For example, one consumer at our rural focus group location told us it would take roughly 2 hours to reach the dealership's repair shop.
- *Most influential factors considered*: After the discussion of all factors, we then asked each consumer to select the single most influential factor they considered. Consumers in the sessions overwhelmingly selected safety risk and convenience as the two most influential factors (see Table 1).

**Table 1. Most Influential Factors Selected by Consumers in Our Focus Groups when Deciding Whether to Repair Recalled Vehicles with Safety Defects**

| Most influential factor | Consumers who completed repairs | Consumers who did not complete repairs | All consumers |
|---|---|---|---|
| Safety risk | 30 | 19 | 49 |
| Convenience | 12 | 15 | 27 |
| Parts availability | 0 | 8 | 8 |
| Dealer customer service | 1 | 1 | 2 |
| Repair without charge | 2 | 0 | 2 |
| Other[a] | 2 | 4 | 6 |
| Total | 47 | 47 | 94 |

Source: GAO. | GAO-18-127. [a]Other factors include dissatisfaction with dealer-proposed solutions, non-safety related consumer preferences, and forgetting about the recall.

[19] For more information about how we conducted our focus groups, see appendix I.

### *Safety Risk*

More than half of consumers in our focus group discussion sessions selected safety risk as the most influential factor they considered when making repair decisions. They told us that their perception of the risk influenced whether or not they repaired their vehicle. For instance, some consumers stated that they completed repairs immediately, because the risks "sounded serious" or that they considered the defect a "safety concern." Conversely, some consumers said they did not complete the repairs because the defect "didn't sound very urgent."

| **Focus Group Participant's Comment** |
|---|
| "[A cover under the hood of the car] could come loose and spark a fire, cause electrical damage. So, I had that fixed right away." |
| Source: GAO. \| GAO-18-127 |

While each recall notification letter is required to include an evaluation of the risk to vehicle safety reasonably related to the defect, consumers in our focus group sessions shared mixed opinions about the quality and clarity of safety risk information included in the notification letter they received.[20] For example, some consumers told us the letter's safety risk information seemed vague. For instance, one consumer told us the letter's description of the safety defect did not clearly state the chances of an increased risk of injury and so he "had to figure out [the risk] on his own." In addition, some consumers commented that the safety risk information could be more prominent in the notification letter, that the letter could emphasize the severity of the risk, or that the letter could describe the risk in simpler language. However, other consumers stated the notification letter they received adequately described the recall's safety risk. In June 2011, we recommended that NHTSA modify the requirements for defect notification letters to include additional information to obtain readers' attention.[21] In 2013, NHTSA responded to our recommendation by requiring manufacturers to include the statement "IMPORTANT SAFETY RECALL" at the top of auto recall notification letters.[22]

### *Convenience*

Consumers in our focus group discussion sessions selected convenience as the second most influential factor they considered in making repair decisions. While some consumers described the "hassle" of the repair and being "too busy" to schedule and fix the defect, other consumers told us they repaired their vehicles more easily because, for example, they could take advantage of previously scheduled service appointments to also

[20] 49 U.S.C. § 30119(a)(2), 49 C.F.R. § 577.5(f).
[21] See GAO-11-603.
[22] 78 Fed. Reg. 51,382, 51,422 (Aug. 20, 2013) (codified as amended at 49 C.F.R. § 577.5(b)).

repair the defect. Also, some consumers in our sessions stated that the letter or notification they received could better address the inconvenience of the recall, for example by including better estimates of how long repairs might take. In addition, some consumers recommended the letter include options for scheduling needed repairs.

| Focus Group Participant's Comment |
|---|
| "I don't want to be without a car for half the day or stay [at the dealership] with my kids all day." |
| Source: GAO. \| GAO-18-127 |

As we discuss later in the report, NHTSA officials told us they continue to work with auto manufacturers to identify ways to encourage consumers to complete needed repairs, while representatives from some manufacturers we met with described specific steps they have taken to address some of the inconveniences consumers may experience in completing repairs. For example, one manufacturer facilitated a pilot program for a third-party service provider in conjunction with dealers to repair vehicles at the owner's home or place of work, while another manufacturer told us they work with individual dealers to hold events specifically for recall repairs when consumers can come in to have repairs performed after normal business hours.

## Industry Stakeholders' Use of Publicly Available Auto Recall Information Varies

Industry stakeholders' use of auto recall information varies because these stakeholders play different roles in the auto recall process. Auto manufacturers are primarily responsible for providing auto recall information to the public and others, including NHTSA and auto dealers. Franchised dealers are responsible for performing the recall remedy for manufacturers and therefore use manufacturer-provided information for that purpose. Specifically, all of the franchised dealers we interviewed told us they identify recalls on new vehicles in their inventory primarily by accessing auto recall information through internal manufacturer databases.[23] These franchised dealers may also use information from third-party providers or publicly available auto recall information on NHTSA's website to identify recalls affecting used vehicles.

Independent dealers—which are not generally authorized by manufacturers to perform recall remedies—may use publicly available auto recall information to identify open

[23] Manufacturers are required to provide notification of safety-related defects to dealers to whom a motor vehicle was delivered. 49 U.S.C. §§ 30118(c), 30119(d)(4); 49 C.F.R. § 577.13.

recalls.[24] Specifically, 2 of the 3 independent dealers we met with told us they use NHTSA's VIN look-up tool to search for open recalls affecting vehicles in their inventory before selling them to consumers.[25] However, these dealers told us that the current design of the tool takes too much time to use, because it requires users to search each VIN individually. For example, one dealer told us each search took about 15 seconds to perform, resulting in significant time and cost because the dealership has tens of thousands of vehicles in its inventory. These dealers told us being able to search multiple VINs in a single search (i.e., VIN-batch search) could save them time or money.

Representatives from the Alliance of Automobile Manufacturers stated they—in coordination with other industry stakeholders—are working with a third-party provider to develop a search tool that would address this concern by enabling VIN-batch searches for use by government agencies, such as state departments of motor vehicles, and commercial entities. The group anticipates the tool will be available in the first half of 2018.

## Most Consumers in Our Focus Groups Prefer to Receive Recall Notification by Electronic Means in Addition to Mail

**Focus Group Participant's Comment**

"I would want every option possible...Send me an e-mail. Send me a text...Warn me in any way you can."

Source: GAO. | GAO-18-127

Although the vast majority of consumers who participated in our focus group discussion sessions reported a preference to receive auto recall notification by mail, most preferred to receive notifications by at least one additional electronic means such as e-mail, phone calls, and text messages.[26] Eighty of the 94 consumers in our sessions reported a preference for receiving notification by mail, and all but 4 reported actually receiving mailed notification (see Figure 2).[27] However, 69 of the 94 consumers in our

[24] Independent dealers sell only used vehicles; they do not have a franchise agreement with manufacturers to sell their new vehicles.

[25] In June 2011, we recommended that NHTSA create a VIN search function on its website to provide vehicle owners with specific information about whether their vehicle is involved in a recall. See GAO-11-603. In August 2014, NHTSA launched its VIN look-up tool for consumers.

[26] As part of the questionnaire administered to consumers in our focus groups, consumers were asked to report the ways they preferred to be notified. In responding, participants could report more than one preference.

[27] We previously reported on challenges that exist to identifying and notifying vehicle owners about auto recalls due to inaccurate mailing addresses, among other challenges. See GAO-11-603.

sessions also reported a preference for receiving recall notification by electronic means, but only 7 reported actually receiving at least one type of electronic notification. This result suggests a gap between industry recall notification practices and notification preferences for most consumers in our focus groups, especially for younger consumers who were more likely to report a preference for notification by electronic means. For complete results of the questionnaire we administered to consumers for the discussion session, see appendix IV. As we discuss later in this chapter, in September 2016, NHTSA issued a Notice of Proposed Rulemaking (NPRM) that proposes to require auto manufacturers to notify consumers about auto recalls by electronic means in addition to First-Class Mail.[28] NHTSA officials told us the agency is working with the administration on NHTSA's regulatory portfolio and priorities, including this rulemaking.

Some manufacturers told us they use additional methods to reach consumers, including notifying consumers by electronic means and translating recall information into Spanish.[29] For example, representatives from one manufacturer told us they always notify consumers by e-mail before sending out the required First-Class Mail letter notification. These representatives told us using multiple recall notification means resulted in higher recall completion rates.

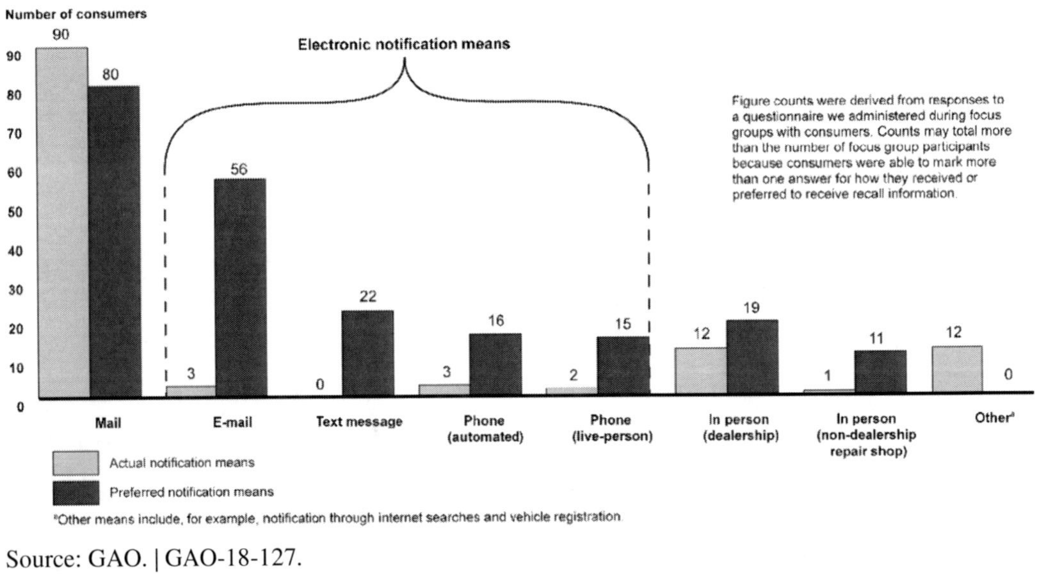


Source: GAO. | GAO-18-127.

Figure 2. How Consumers in Our Focus Groups Received and Preferred to Receive Auto Recall Notifications.

---

[28] *Update Means of Providing Recall Notification*, 81 Fed. Reg. 60,332 (Sept. 1, 2016). The FAST Act directs NHTSA to issue such a rule. Pub. L. No. 114-94, § 24104(a), 129 Stat. 1312, 1703.

[29] Notification letters sent to vehicle owners whose address is in the Commonwealth of Puerto Rico are required to be written in both English and Spanish. 49 C.F.R. § 577.5(a). As part of this chapter, we asked manufacturers about their efforts to translate auto recall notifications into other languages, including Spanish.

In addition, eight of the remaining nine manufacturers told us they use supplemental electronic means notification on a case-by-case basis—generally using additional means to improve recall completion rates—while four manufacturers stated they consider safety risk severity when deciding when or how to use additional notification means for individual recalls. Also, representatives from 3 of the 10 manufacturers we spoke with told us they translate the entire mailed notification letter into Spanish.

## MOST CONSUMERS IN FOCUS GROUPS FOUND THE AUTO RECALL AREAS OF NHTSA.GOV GENERALLY EASY TO USE, BUT SOME EXPERIENCED DIFFICULTIES

### Usability Testing with Consumers Found the Auto Recall Areas of NHTSA's Website Generally Easy to Use

In late 2016, NHTSA launched its redesigned NHTSA.gov website, including the auto recall areas consumers assessed during our testing sessions. According to responses to a questionnaire we administered during our testing sessions, 78 of the 94 consumers found the auto recall areas of NHTSA.gov either "somewhat" or "very easy" to use (see Figure 3). See appendix V for complete participant responses to the questionnaire we administered to each consumer.

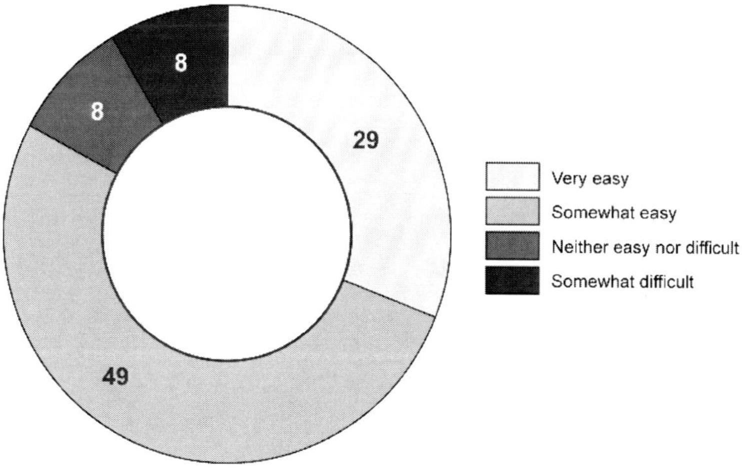


Source: GAO. | GAO-18-127.

Note: The scale consumers used to rate ease of use also included "Very difficult" as an option; however, no consumers in our focus groups chose this option.

Figure 3. How Easy or Difficult to Use Were the Auto Recall Areas of NHTSA.gov for Consumers Who Participated in Our Focus Groups.

**Focus Group Participant's Comment**

"[The NHTSA.gov homepage] is easy to get around even for people who aren't that tech savvy."

Source: GAO. | GAO-18-127

**National Highway Traffic Safety Administration's (NHTSA) Website Strategy**

"When consumers need information, the first place they typically turn is to the Internet. [NHTSA.gov is intended to be] a comprehensive, user-friendly platform that will serve as the premier source of traffic and vehicular safety information."

Source: NHTSA Strategic Plan 2016-2020. | GAO-18-127

To inform the development of the redesigned website, NHTSA worked with a contractor to conduct a usability study in 2015 to evaluate users' reactions to the agency's websites, including NHTSA.gov. According to agency officials, NHTSA implemented several changes based on the findings from the usability study, including:

- the creation of a dedicated "recalls" area of NHTSA.gov, and
- the ability for users to access the VIN look-up tool in three different ways—on the homepage, in the "recalls" area, and through direct links either in a NHTSA e-mail for subscribers or from an external website.

In addition, NHTSA officials told us that Department of Transportation (DOT) and NHTSA staff meet as needed to discuss the website and consider improvements. For example, the officials said they monitor user searches for the relevance and accuracy of results and adjust the search software to better assist users in finding auto recall information. Officials also told us the agency collects a variety of other information about how visitors use NHTSA.gov, including how visitors access the website, and makes adjustments accordingly. For instance, NHTSA incorporated responsive web design as part of the agency's ongoing consolidation effort—meaning the site is optimized for viewing on desktop, tablet, and mobile devices.[30] In addition to monitoring searches and how visitors access NHTSA.gov, NHTSA officials told us they collect and consider online survey data to make website improvements and use web-analytic software to monitor, for example, where visitors choose to exit the website. Officials stated that such

---

[30] Desktop computers, including laptop computers, were used for the usability testing sessions we conducted with consumers as well as the usability evaluation we requested from website usability professionals. According to an April 2017 NHTSA.gov report, 59.5 percent of visitors accessed the site via a desktop computer, 35 percent via a mobile device, and 5.5 percent via a tablet.

monitoring activities have allowed NHTSA to identify and correct problems with NHTSA.gov.

We did not directly evaluate the accessibility of the auto recall areas of NHTSA.gov to ensure the ability of people with physical or mental disabilities to use the website.[31] However, NHTSA officials provided us with an overview of several steps the agency takes to ensure NHTSA.gov complies with website accessibility requirements. For example, according to officials, NHTSA subscribes to a service that provides monthly accessibility scans of the agency's websites.

## Consumers in Our Focus Groups Identified Opportunities to Improve the Usability of Certain Auto Recall Tasks on NHTSA's Website

While most consumers in our usability testing sessions generally found the auto recall areas of NHTSA's website easy to use, some consumers experienced difficulties completing tasks we asked them to perform (see Table 2). Specifically, during each testing session we asked participants to perform tasks using the primary means NHTSA.gov provides for consumers to access information about auto recalls affecting their vehicles:

- searching for auto recalls using their vehicle's VIN;
- searching for auto recalls using their vehicle's year, make, and model; and
- locating NHTSA's auto recall notification e-mail subscription service.

**Table 2. How Easy or Difficult Did Consumers Who Participated in Our Focus Groups Find Performing Auto Recall Tasks on NHTSA.gov, by Number of Consumers**

| Task | Very easy | Somewhat easy | Neither easy nor difficult | Somewhat difficult | Very difficult |
|---|---|---|---|---|---|
| Search for recall using vehicle identification number | 76 | 12 | 3 | 1 | 2 |
| Search for recall using vehicle year, make, and model | 62 | 16 | 3 | 10 | 3 |
| Find Recall Notification E-mail System sign-up | 34 | 32 | 15 | 8 | 5 |

Source: GAO. | GAO-18-127.

---

[31] When federal agencies develop, procure, maintain, or use electronic and information technology, they are required to make this technology accessible to people with disabilities. For additional details about accessibility requirements, see appendix I.

In addition, an evaluation we requested to corroborate the results of our consumer usability testing, identified similar issues. As discussed below, consumers experienced these difficulties because the auto recall areas of NHTSA.gov do not always reflect federal and industry key website usability practices, which describe standards and guidelines for making websites easy to use.[32] Following such practices can assist agencies in creating quality websites while providing the flexibility necessary to meet organizational needs. Website usability is particularly important for agencies, such as NHTSA, that are responsible for conveying safety information to the public. Federal standards for internal control state that agencies should communicate quality information externally and select appropriate methods for communicating with the public.[33]

**Focus Group Participant's Comment**

"I found my car [using the VIN look-up tool]. But it said zero recalls. So to me, that could mean, okay, I fixed it and you guys marked it out, or you guys can't find my recall."

Source: GAO. | GAO-18-127

### *Recall Search Using VIN*

While most consumers in our usability testing sessions found searching for recalls by VIN somewhat or very easy, some consumers found the search results did not provide the information they were seeking. When we asked consumers to perform VIN searches, they generally found the VIN look-up tool easy to use—88 of 94 consumers found searching with a VIN either somewhat or very easy. But some consumers experienced difficulties performing this task. Specifically, some consumers who had had their vehicles repaired expected to find the completed recall on the search results page. However, they were confused because the page is designed to display only open (i.e., unrepaired) recalls, not completed (i.e., repaired) recalls—leading these consumers to question the accuracy of the results. In addition, the evaluation conducted by website usability professionals found that, when an error occurred during a VIN search, the error message was too difficult to locate on the search results page. The evaluation recommended the error message have greater weight and more prominence on the page.

Federal key website usability practices state that agencies should ensure that results of user searches provide the precise information being sought, and in a format matching users' expectations. When users are confused by search results, or do not immediately find what they are searching for, they become frustrated and may abandon the search or the website entirely. Since NHTSA launched the VIN look-up tool in August 2014, the

[32] To identify key website usability practices, we reviewed and analyzed relevant guidance documents from NHTSA and other federal agencies. For additional details on how we identified these key practices, see appendix I.

[33] GAO-14-704G.

number of VIN searches performed has increased (see Figure 4). According to NHTSA officials, major increases occurred in mid-2015— when the Takata air bag inflator recalls were announced—and in early 2017, when NHTSA made the VIN look-up tool search function available on NHTSA.gov and displayed it prominently on the website. Ensuring the usability of NHTSA's VIN look-up tool is particularly important because it is the only way on NHTSA.gov for a consumer to determine whether their specific vehicle has an open safety recall.

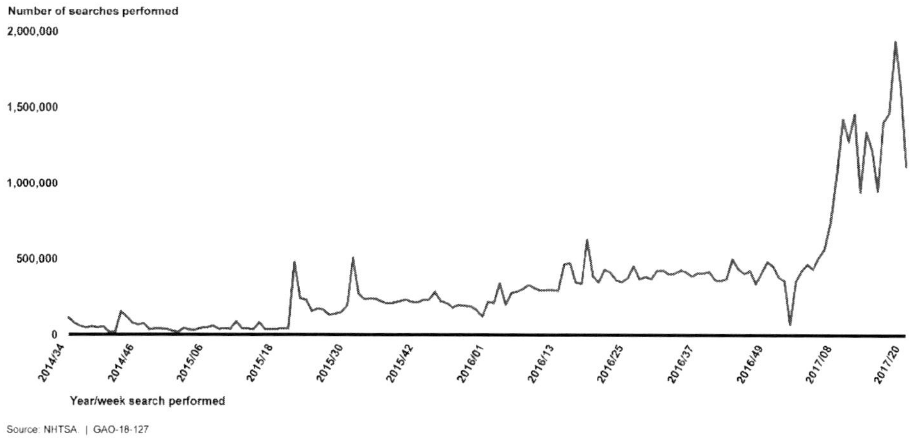


Source: NHTSA. | GAO-18-127.

Figure 4. Number of Auto Recall Searches by Vehicle Identification Number on the National Highway Traffic Safety Administration's (NHTSA) Websites, Weekly from August 2014 through May 2017.

### *Recall Search Using Vehicle Year, Make, and Model*

Some consumers' vehicle year, make, and model searches were hampered by the information required to conduct an accurate search, as the content on the website is not always in plain language. We asked consumers to perform a recall search using their vehicles' year, make, and model, and 78 of 94 consumers found the task to be either somewhat or very easy. However, some consumers found that they did not know enough information about their specific vehicles to feel confident that they were searching for the correct vehicle. For example, a year, make, and model search for a 2009 Toyota Tacoma may ask the consumer to choose among vehicle options, including "2009 TOYOTA TACOMA REGULAR CAB W/SAB RWD/AWD."[34]

**Focus Group Participant's Comment**

"The acronyms weren't spelled out...I don't know what they stand for."

Source: GAO. | GAO-18-127

[34] "RWD/AWD" stands for "rear-wheel drive/all-wheel drive."

Acronyms such as “W/SAB”— which stands for “with side air bags”—may be confusing to consumers. Federal key website usability practices state that federal agencies should write website content using plain language, so website visitors can easily find and use what they need.

### *Recall Notification E-mail System Sign-Up*

Some consumers suggested improvements to make the Recall Notification E-mail System Sign-Up easier to locate on the homepage. NHTSA first made its Recall Notification E-mail System Sign-Up available in March 2008.[35] Of the 94 consumers in our testing sessions, 66 found it either “somewhat” or “very easy” to find the Recall Notification E-mail System Sign-Up—making this the least easy of the three tasks we asked consumers to perform. Specifically, several consumers said the Recall Notification E-mail System Sign-Up should include a clearer description, be easier to find, and be located at the top of the homepage (see Figure 5). These improvements are particularly important because some consumers in our focus group sessions told us that the ability to sign up for auto recall e-mail notifications was the most useful part of the auto recall areas of NHTSA.gov.

**Focus Group Participant’s Comment**

“I think [the Recall Notification E-mail System Sign-Up is] poorly placed. I had to scroll to find it. I had to search for it. You want [it] at the top [of the page].”

Source: GAO. | GAO-18-127

The website evaluation conducted by website usability professionals recommended that NHTSA streamline its homepage with more of a focus on primary website tasks. The evaluation also found that users must move through too many pages to sign up for recall e-mails.

Federal key website design and usability practices state that agencies should put important items closer to the top of the page, where users can better locate the information. Key practices also state that agencies should design their websites so users can successfully complete the most common tasks in the fewest number of steps.

The website usability difficulties that consumers in our focus groups experienced may be due to the fact that NHTSA has not studied the website’s usability since the agency redesigned NHTSA.gov in late 2016 and, therefore, may have been unaware of these difficulties prior to our review.

---

[35] According to NHTSA, the system had 273,312 active subscribers as of May 31, 2017. Of the 94 consumers who participated in focus groups we conducted, 1 indicated having signed up for alerts from a government website.

NHTSA plans to conduct a website usability study with consumers after the consolidation effort, discussed above, is complete.

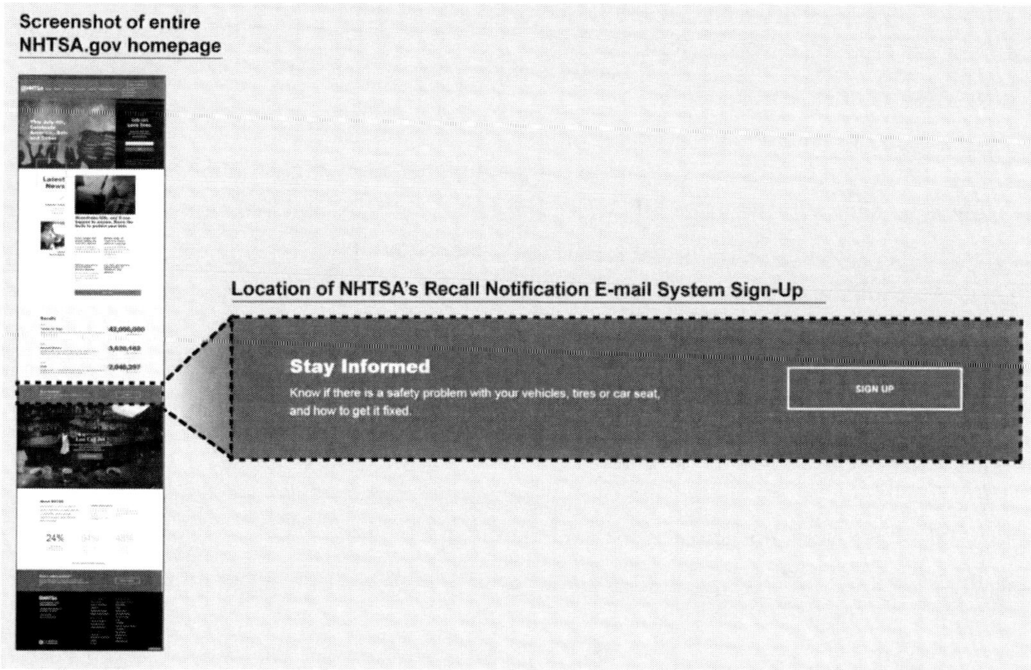


Source: NHTSA, 28 June 2017. Web. | GAO-18-127.

Figure 5. Location of the National Highway Traffic Safety Administration's (NHTSA) Recall Notification E-mail System Sign-Up Task on NHTSA.gov's Homepage.

However, NHTSA could not provide a general time frame for conducting the study because it has not yet determined when the consolidation effort will be complete.[36] We have previously reported that it is essential for organizations to effectively guide their information technology efforts by establishing timelines to complete them, among other strategic planning best practices.[37] Without establishing a completion date for its website consolidation effort, the website usability difficulties we identified may persist and limit the effectiveness of NHTSA's primary means of providing consumers with safety recall information about their vehicles on NHTSA.gov.

---

[36] As noted previously, the FAST Act requires NHTSA to make certain improvements to its website. Pub. L. No. 114-94, § 24103(a), 129 Stat. 1312, 1702.

[37] GAO, *Federal Motor Carrier Safety Administration Needs to Strengthen Its Strategic Planning and Oversight to Modernize Legacy Systems,* GAO-17-488 (Washington, D.C.: Jul. 13, 2017) and *Library of Congress: Strong Leadership Needed to Address Serious Information Technology Management Weaknesses*, GAO-15-315 (Washington, D.C.: Mar. 31, 2015).

# NHTSA Has Initiated Activities to Raise Consumer Awareness about Recalls, but It Is Too Early to Evaluate the Agency's Efforts

## Public Awareness Campaign

In January 2016, NHTSA launched a national advertising campaign encouraging consumers to check for open recalls using the agency's VIN and year, make, and model look-up tools. Through March 2017, NHTSA spent about $1 million on its *Safe Cars Save Lives* campaign, which sponsors advertisements on Google, Facebook, and other media platforms. For example, Google might place NHTSA's advertisement above other search results, when a consumer typed certain keywords— such as "recall," "airbag recalls," or "safercar.gov"—into the search.

NHTSA evaluated the campaign's effectiveness by monitoring website traffic performance reports to determine how frequently consumers clicked on NHTSA-sponsored advertisements and ultimately searched for open recalls using the agency's look-up tools. NHTSA also compared results across media platforms and adjusted the campaign's strategy to improve performance. For example, NHTSA optimized advertisements on mobile devices, since mobile-device users performed more recall searches than other users. According to NHTSA data, the awareness campaign resulted in consumers performing 1.1 million recall searches through March 2017—a cost of about $0.90 per search. Agency data indicate that this cost generally decreased as NHTSA improved the campaign's strategy. Agency officials told us NHTSA plans to spend another approximately $1.8 million on *Safe Cars Save Lives* from September 2017 through September 2018 due to the campaign's effectiveness in raising the public's awareness about auto recalls.

## Pilot Program with States

NHTSA began implementing a mandated 2-year pilot grant program intended to evaluate the feasibility and effectiveness of informing consumers about open auto recalls during state vehicle registration.[38] In September 2016, NHTSA solicited applications to participate in the program, wherein selected states would inform consumers—at no charge—about open recalls using all means that permit consumers to register vehicles within the state (e.g., in person, Internet, and mail).[39]

---

[38] The FAST Act directs NHTSA to implement such a pilot program. Pub. L. No. 114-94, § 24105, 129 Stat. 1312, 1704.

[39] NHTSA, *State Notification to Consumers of Motor Vehicle Recall Status*, RFA No. DTNH2216R00096 (Sept. 28, 2016). Eligibility was limited to the state department or office responsible for motor vehicle registration.

According to NHTSA, only one state applied for the grant. In September 2017, NHTSA awarded the sole applicant $223,000.[40]

Under the program, the grantee needs to collect and report program performance data, including the extent to which open recalls have been identified and repaired. In addition, the grantee must report whether certain notification means were more effective than others and what could be done to improve the program. Upon completion of the pilot program, NHTSA is required to evaluate the extent to which open recalls identified have been remedied. Auto manufacturers we met with were generally supportive of the program. Specifically, representatives from 9 of the 10 manufacturers told us that notifying consumers about open recalls during vehicle registration can raise consumer awareness or improve recall completion rates.

## Proposed Rulemaking

In September 2016, NHTSA issued a Notice of Proposed Rulemaking (NPRM), which proposes to require auto manufacturers to notify consumers about open recalls by electronic means—such as e-mails, phone calls, and text messages, in addition to First-Class Mail.[41] As we described earlier, auto manufacturers are currently required to notify consumers about safety recalls affecting their vehicles via First-Class Mail. According to NHTSA, the NPRM aims to aid in efficiently and effectively improving recall completion rates, by proposing that manufacturers provide notification using electronic means in addition to First-Class Mail.

Consumers in our focus groups as well as auto manufacturers and consumer associations we interviewed generally supported additional notification using electronic means.

- *Consumers in our focus groups*: As we discussed earlier, 69 of the consumers in our focus group discussion sessions reported they would prefer to receive additional notification by at least one type of electronic means. However, only 7 consumers actually received such notifications—suggesting a gap between industry notification practices and notification preferences for these consumers.

[40] NHTSA awarded the grant to the Maryland Department of Transportation Motor Vehicle Administration. See https://www.nhtsa.gov/press-releases/us-dot-and-maryland-mvacollaborate-improve-recall-remedy-rates. When NHTSA published the Request for Application, the Administrator approved $2 million out of the Enforcement Office's budget to fund the pilot program grants. Congress then appropriated funds that were available to be used for this grant program in the Consolidated Appropriations Act of fiscal year 2017, and in the explanatory statement accompanying the Act, Congress directed NHTSA to use $1.5 million for the pilot program grants.

[41] *Update Means of Providing Recall Notification*, 81 Fed. Reg. 60,332 (Sept. 1, 2016). The FAST Act directs NHTSA to issue such a rule. Pub. L. No. 114-94, § 24104(a), 129 Stat. 1312, 1703.

- *Auto manufacturers*: Representatives from 9 of 10 manufacturers we interviewed told us they generally support providing notification using electronic means. Although the NPRM proposes a broad definition of electronic means to give manufacturers flexibility to determine the most effective means, these representatives also shared implementation concerns.[42] For example, representatives from 1 of the 9 manufacturers told us that—although the company collects email addresses from some customers for other purposes—not all customers provide e-mail addresses, and those collected are not always accurate. As we discussed previously, most manufacturers we met with currently use supplemental electronic means notification on a case-by-case basis.
- *Consumer associations*: Similarly, both consumer associations we interviewed told us additional electronic notification can help reach consumers who do not complete repairs after receiving initial mailed notification.

NHTSA's proposal would maintain manufacturer reporting requirements, though it may result in additional reporting.[43] This additional information could help the agency evaluate the effectiveness of various means of consumer notification.[44] We previously found that NHTSA may be able to use manufacturers' data to identify what factors make some recalls more or less successful than others. We recommended that NHTSA use the recall data it collects to analyze particular patterns or trends that may characterize successful recalls and determine whether these factors represent best practices.[45]

If the NPRM is finalized, manufacturers would provide NHTSA with representative copies of the newly required electronic notifications, in addition to mailed notifications, and would specify the electronic means used, such as e-mail or text message. According

---

[42] Specifically, the NPRM defines electronic means to include notification by electronic mail, text messages, radio or television notifications, vehicle infotainment console messages, over-the-air alerts, social media or targeted online campaigns, telephone calls, automated or otherwise, or other real time means.

[43] Manufacturers are required to include in their reports to NHTSA "representative copies of all notices, bulletins, and other communications that relate directly to the defect...and are sent to more than one manufacturer, distributor, dealer or purchaser." 49 C.F.R. § 573.6(c)(10). Because electronic notifications are already encompassed within "notices, bulletins, and other communications," manufacturers voluntarily providing 577-compliant notices via electronic means are already required to provide representative copies of those notices to NHTSA. If the NPRM is finalized, manufacturers would be required to provide electronic notification, in addition to First-Class Mail. Accordingly, manufacturer reporting would likely increase, since manufacturers would have to provide NHTSA with representative copies of all electronic and mailed notifications.

[44] According to NHTSA officials, currently, if a manufacturer is voluntarily providing 577- compliant notices via electronic means, they are providing representative copies of those notifications to NHTSA through the online Recalls Portal. However, the current Recalls Portal does not allow manufacturers to select the means of the notice (e.g., mail, e-mail, text, etc.). If the NPRM is finalized, NHTSA plans to update the online Recalls Portal so manufacturers can select the type of electronic means used for the notification.

[45] GAO-11-603. NHTSA has taken steps to address this recommendation, for example, by analyzing annual recall completion rates by manufacturer, model year, and vehicle component to determine trends and identify risk factors associated with lower recall rates. We are currently reviewing whether NHTSA's analysis is sufficient to close the recommendation as implemented. The report also included three additional recommendations to encourage vehicle owners to comply with safety recalls, provide vehicle owners with specific information about whether their vehicle is involved in a recall, and identify factors that affect recall completion rates, among other things. NHTSA implemented these three recommendations.

to NHTSA officials, this information could allow the agency to track and evaluate the effectiveness of various notification means used by manufacturers by, for example, comparing completion rates across means—a key step in identifying best practices that could encourage consumers to complete repairs. However, it is too early for NHTSA to conduct such an evaluation, because the agency has not issued a final rule. NHTSA officials told us the agency is working with the administration on NHTSA's regulatory portfolio and priorities, including this rulemaking.

## Collaboration with Stakeholders

NHTSA has also taken steps to collaborate with industry stakeholders and explore consumer education best practices. For example, in April 2015 NHTSA hosted a day-long workshop that brought together auto industry stakeholders to examine public education of the recall process. During the workshop, participants identified current barriers to the public's awareness of auto recalls and discussed potential solutions to address them, such as using text messages and social media to communicate with younger consumers and using different delivery methods for recall notices. Similarly, in January 2016 NHTSA and 18 auto manufacturers adopted a set of *Proactive Safety Principles* to explore and employ new ways to increase safety recall participation rates.[46] For example, NHTSA and auto manufacturers agreed to share industry best practices and policies based on lessons learned from ongoing safety recalls.

The Independent Monitor of Takata in conjunction with NHTSA has also issued a set of coordinated communications recommendations based on consumer research, best practices observed during the Takata recall, and discussions with manufacturers.[47] For example, the recommendations encourage manufacturers to:

- pursue a "multi-touch" communications strategy that employs nontraditional means, such as e-mail and text messages;
- convey risk in clear, accurate and urgent terms; and
- include a clear "call to action" designed to facilitate prompt and efficient scheduling of repairs.

According to NHTSA officials, the agency relies on auto manufacturers to evaluate the effectiveness of these efforts.[48] However, agency officials told us NHTSA reviews

---

[46] U.S. Department of Transportation, et al., *Proactive Safety Principles* (Jan. 15, 2016).

[47] John Buretta, Letter to Affected Vehicle Manufacturers, *Independent Monitor of Takata and the Coordinated Remedy Program* (New York, N.Y.: Dec. 23, 2016).

[48] According to NHTSA officials and most manufacturers we met with, NHTSA initially worked with manufacturers on an ad hoc basis to help ensure manufacturers' auto recall websites made information available to the public, as required. In January 2016, NHTSA took steps to formalize this process by

manufacturers communication plans as part of the Takata recall's Coordinated Remedy Program and provides ongoing recommendations on manufacturers' communication language, approach, and strategies.

## CONCLUSION

With the recent steep increase in safety defect vehicle recalls and continued low recall completion rates, it is vital for consumers to be able to easily access and use publicly available auto recall information.

NHTSA has taken important steps to improve its website—which provides safety recall information to consumers—resulting in most consumers in our focus groups finding the website easy to use. However, the difficulties some experienced in attempting to complete essential auto recall tasks demonstrated that NHTSA.gov does not always reflect key website usability practices for website design. Although NHTSA plans to conduct a website usability study with consumers after consolidating its websites, it has not determined a completion date for this effort—an essential step for organizations to effectively guide their information technology efforts. Without such a date, the website usability difficulties may persist and limit the effectiveness of NHTSA.gov in providing consumers with recall information about their vehicles. By addressing these difficulties in the interim, NHTSA can better assure that consumers obtain this information, which can be vital to their safety.

## RECOMMENDATIONS FOR EXECUTIVE ACTION

We are making the following two recommendations to NHTSA:

The Administrator of NHTSA should determine a completion date for the agency's website consolidation effort. (Recommendation 1)

The Administrator of NHTSA should, while the agency continues its website consolidation effort, take interim steps to improve the usability of the auto recall areas of NHTSA.gov by addressing the website usability difficulties we identified. (Recommendation 2)

---

conducting an overarching review of the auto recall websites of manufacturers who, as previously noted, are required to allow consumers to search a vehicle's recall remedy status on their website using the VIN. In January 2017, NHTSA established this process as an annual review.

## Agency Comments

We provided a draft of this chapter to DOT for review and comment. In its written comments, reproduced in appendix VI, DOT stated that it concurred with our recommendations. The department also provided technical comments, which we incorporated as appropriate.

Susan Fleming
Director, Physical Infrastructure Issues

## Appendix I: Objectives, Scope, and Methodology

This chapter examines the use of publicly available auto recall information for safety defects affecting passenger vehicles.[49] The report addresses the following objectives: (1) How do consumers and industry stakeholders use publicly available auto recall information? (2) How easy or difficult to use do consumers find the auto recall areas of NHTSA.gov? (3) What steps, if any, has the National Highway Traffic Safety Administration (NHTSA) taken to raise consumer awareness about auto recalls and how has NHTSA evaluated the effectiveness of these steps?

We define publicly available auto recall information to include information on the auto recall areas of NHTSA.gov, such as examples of notification letters that manufacturers mail to consumers. This chapter focuses on safety defect vehicle recalls affecting passenger vehicles that are initiated when a defect in a vehicle or vehicle equipment creates an unreasonable safety risk, as determined by NHTSA or a manufacturer.[50]

To determine how consumers use publicly available auto recall information, we conducted and analyzed transcripts and questionnaires from 12 consumer focus groups we conducted with used and new vehicle owners who had experienced an auto recall in the last 24 months. Each focus group was split into two sessions: (1) a discussion session to explore participants' thoughts, experiences, and preferences about auto recall information and (2) a website usability testing session. Also, we administered a questionnaire as part of each of these sessions. For the discussion session, we asked consumers about the recall notification process and how they used the recall information, and for the website usability testing session, we asked consumers to fill in a questionnaire

---

[49] Passenger vehicles include cars, pickup trucks, sport utility vehicles, large passenger vans, and minivans, but exclude other vehicles, such as motorcycles, recreational vehicles, and commercial trucks.

[50] NHTSA is responsible for overseeing two types of recalls: compliance and safety defect recalls. We did not examine compliance recalls, nor did we examine car seat, tire, and other equipment (e.g., vehicle accessories and after-market equipment such as lighting, trailer hitches, and bike racks) recalls as these products have different consumer notification requirements. We did not review Technical Service Bulletins.

during the session itself as they assessed the usability of the auto recall areas of NHTSA's website. We conducted the 12 focus groups at six locations across the country, with each group including 7 or 8 consumers for a total of 94 participants. Half of the focus groups were comprised of consumers who had completed the repair and the remaining half included consumers who had not completed the repair.

We selected the six focus group locations to provide population and geographic dispersion. To ensure geographic dispersion, we selected at least one location in each U.S. Census region (see Table 3). To ensure population dispersion, we selected Metropolitan Statistical Areas representing a range of population sizes based on 2015 U.S. Census estimates.[51] To ensure our selection included the perspectives of vehicle owners in geographically distant or isolated communities, we also selected a rural location, which we defined as a city or town that has a population of less than 50,000 inhabitants and is not an urbanized area contiguous and adjacent to a city or town that has a population of greater than 50,000 inhabitants.

Using information provided by the participants, we selected focus group participants based on age, income, gender, education level, race, and ethnicity to ensure we collected a range of perspectives on auto recall information use. However, since we did not select a representative sample of participants, focus group results are not generalizable to all vehicle owners.

**Table 3. Characteristics of Locations We Selected to Conduct Focus Groups with Consumers**

| Location | Census region | Metropolitan Statistical Area (MSA) | Rank of MSA (population)[a] |
|---|---|---|---|
| Bethesda, Maryland | South | Washington-Arlington-Alexandria, DC-VA-MD WV Metro Area | 6th (6,097,684) |
| Chicago, Illinois | Midwest | Chicago-Naperville-Elgin, IL-IN-WI Metro Area | 3rd (9,551,031) |
| East Rutherford, New Jersey | Northeast | New York-Newark-Jersey City, NY-NJ-PA Metro Area | 1st (20,182,305) |
| Fresno, California | West | Fresno, CA, Metro Area | 56th (974,861) |
| Jackson, California | West | —b | —b (4,613) |
| Raleigh, North Carolina | South | Raleigh, NC, Metro Area | 44th (1,273,568) |

Source: GAO. | GAO-18-127.

[a]MSA rank and population estimates based on 2015 Census population estimates as of July 1, 2015.

[b]Jackson, CA, is not part of an MSA.

[51] Metropolitan Statistical Areas are locations that are associated with one or more urbanized areas with at least 50,000 people and include the central county or counties along with the surrounding commuting population.

During focus group discussion sessions, we asked participants to discuss factors they considered when deciding whether to repair their recalled vehicle and then to select the single most influential factor. Each of the 12 focus group sessions was audio recorded and transcriptions were created; transcripts served as the record for each group. We then evaluated those transcripts using systematic content analysis to identify the factors consumers considered when deciding whether to complete repairs and any suggested improvements to the auto recall communication process. The analysis was conducted in three steps. First, two analysts independently developed a code framework and then worked together to resolve any discrepancies. Second, each transcript was coded independently by analysts using the framework and any discrepancies were resolved by both analysts agreeing on the coding of the associated statement by a participant. Third, if needed, another analyst adjudicated any continued disagreement between coders.

Because the transcripts did not include a unique identifier for each focus group participant, we conducted our analysis of focus group session discussions at the group level (i.e., of the 12 focus groups we conducted). We also administered and analyzed a questionnaire as part of each discussion session to quantify responses regarding consumers' use of auto recall information, including how they received and preferred to receive auto recall notifications. Our analysis of the questionnaire responses was conducted at the individual consumer level (i.e., of the 94 consumers who participated).

These focus group sessions were structured, guided by a moderator who used a standardized list of questions to encourage participants to share their thoughts, experiences, and preferences. We also conducted two pretest focus groups at our headquarters and made some revisions to the focus group guide prior to beginning the sessions with consumers. Methodologically, focus groups are not designed to demonstrate the extent of a problem or to generalize results to a larger population or provide statistically representative samples or reliable quantitative estimates. Instead, they are intended to generate in-depth information about the reasons for the focus group participants' thoughts, experiences, and preferences on specific topics.

The projectability of the information produced by our focus group sessions is limited. For example, the information includes only the responses from the vehicle owners from the 12 selected groups and their individual responses to questions we asked. The experiences and preferences expressed may not reflect other vehicle owners' thoughts and preferences. In addition, while the composition of the groups was designed to ensure a range of age and education levels, among the other criteria mentioned previously, the groups were not constructed using a random sampling method.

To determine how industry stakeholders use auto recall information, we interviewed selected auto manufacturers, selected franchised and independent auto dealerships, NHTSA program officials, and other industry stakeholders.

Specifically, we interviewed representatives from the following 10 auto manufacturers, selected based on each manufacturer's sales market share (small, medium, and large), place of ownership (foreign and domestic), and experience with auto recalls (lower to higher based on the average annual number of auto recall campaigns and average market share of each manufacturer from 2010 to 2014) to collect a range of perspectives on how manufacturers use auto recall information:

- General Motors
- Ford Motor Company
- Toyota Motor Corporation
- Fiat Chrysler Automobiles
- Honda Motor Company
- Kia Motors Corporation
- BMW
- Volvo Cars
- Jaguar Land Rover
- Tesla Motors, Inc.

To understand the perspective of auto dealers, we interviewed four franchised dealerships, one in each of the four U.S. Census regions where we conducted focus groups with consumers. We also interviewed three independent auto dealerships in two U.S. Census regions. The results of these interviews are not generalizable to all auto manufacturers and dealerships, but provide insights about how some industry stakeholders use auto recall information.

We conducted interviews with NHTSA program officials to understand NHTSA's role in the auto recall process. In addition, we interviewed other stakeholders, including the Independent Monitor of Takata, which assists NHTSA in overseeing the Takata recall, as well as officials from consumer associations and other industry groups (see Table 4).

**Table 4. List of Industry Stakeholders We Interviewed**

| |
|---|
| Advocates for Highway and Auto Safety |
| Alliance of Automobile Manufacturers |
| Center for Auto Safety |
| National Automobile Dealers Association |
| National Independent Automobile Dealers Association |

Source: GAO. | GAO-18-127.

To evaluate how easy or difficult consumers find the auto recall areas of NHTSA.gov to use, we reviewed various website usability resources to understand federal and industry key website usability practices for making websites easy to use, such as focusing on design and how easily users can find information. In addition, we reviewed federal standards for internal control related to communicating quality information externally.[52] During our usability testing sessions, we asked consumers to attempt to complete auto recall tasks—the primary means NHTSA.gov provides for consumers to access information about auto recalls affecting their vehicles—and discuss their experiences. We then compared consumers' experiences with the usability of the website against these practices.

To identify key website usability practices, we analyzed guidance documents from NHTSA and other federal agencies. For example, we analyzed the General Services Administration's (GSA) and the Department of Health and Human Services' *Research-Based Web Design & Usability Guidelines*, which includes quantified, peer-reviewed guidelines intended to help federal agencies improve the design and usability of their information-based websites.[53] We also analyzed GSA's *Requirements for Federal Websites and Digital Services*, and the U.S. Digital Services Playbook to identify key practices for making websites easy to use. Identified key practices are: (1) design and content— focusing on the layout, headers, and design; (2) navigation—how easily users can find information; (3) clarity—the ability to read and digest content; (4) identity and purpose—whether the site clearly presents its purpose; and (5) accessibility—the ability of people with physical or mental disabilities to use the site.

To analyze the results of focus group website testing sessions, we performed a systematic content analysis of the session transcripts using the same content analysis methods described above and an analysis of the questionnaire we administered to each participant during the website usability sessions. Specifically, we analyzed the transcripts from the website usability testing sessions to account for consumers' experiences, including their initial impressions of the website and any suggested usability improvements. We also analyzed the results of the questionnaire that each participant completed where participants were asked to mark responses regarding their experience including an assessment of the usability of the auto recall areas of NHTSA.gov.

[52] GAO, *Standards for Internal Control in the Federal Government*, GAO-14-704G (Washington, D.C.: September 2014).

[53] GSA and the Department of Health and Human Services, *Research-Based Web Design & Usability Guidelines* (Washington, D.C.: August 2006). GSA also offers website usability evaluation services to federal agencies. The Department of Health and Human Services manages usability.gov, a website where the federal government has published ways to assess a website's usability and, in partnership with GSA, issued guidance and best practices for designing federal websites.

Our analysis of the results from the questionnaire responses was conducted at the individual consumer level (i.e., of the 94 consumers who participated) while our analysis of focus group session discussions was conducted at the group level (i.e., of the 12 focus groups we conducted).

To corroborate the results of usability testing sessions we conducted with the consumers in our focus groups, we requested that five website usability professionals from GSA's Federal User Experience Community conduct an independent evaluation of the auto recall areas of NHTSA.gov against federal and industry key website usability practices (described above).[54] The website usability professionals developed a website usability evaluation form, which they used to individually evaluate the auto recall areas of NHTSA's website. The website usability professionals then met to form a consensus and provided us with one final group evaluation of the website usability of the auto recall areas of NHTSA.gov. Also, although neither our usability testing nor the website usability evaluation conducted by website usability professionals directly addressed accessibility, we interviewed responsible agency officials about how the agency assesses the accessibility of NHTSA.gov.[55]

We also requested and analyzed website data provided by NHTSA to understand how consumers access and use NHTSA.gov. Requested data included the number of subscribers to NHTSA's Recall Notification E-mail System Sign-up; the number of weekly vehicle identification number (VIN) searches performed on NHTSA.gov from August 2014 through May 2017; and NHTSA.gov usage data by device (i.e., usage by mobile devices, tablets, and desktop computers). We assessed the reliability of these data by reviewing any supporting documents provided by the agency and interviewing responsible NHTSA officials, and concluded the data were sufficiently reliable for our reporting purposes.

While we did not independently review the usability of auto manufacturers' auto recall websites, we requested and reviewed the results of any audits that NHTSA performed of these websites, including whether the websites met statutory and regulatory requirements for providing auto recall information to the public. We then corroborated any audit findings by reviewing the auto recall websites of the selected auto manufacturers that we interviewed.

---

[54] GSA's Federal User Experience Community is comprised of federal program managers, subject matter experts, designers, and developers with expertise in website usability.

[55] Section 794d of Title 29 of the U.S. Code requires that federal agency information technology allows members of the public with disabilities to have access to and use of information and data that is comparable to the access to and use of those without disabilities.

To determine any steps NHTSA has taken to raise consumer awareness about auto recalls and how NHTSA evaluates the effectiveness of any steps, we reviewed relevant statutes, regulations, and proposed rules, including the Fixing America's Surface Transportation Act and a Notice of Proposed Rulemaking related to recall notification methods.[56] We also reviewed agency and other documents that describe or evaluate NHTSA's public awareness activities. For example, we analyzed NHTSA's strategic planning documents—such as NHTSA's Strategic Plan 2016–2020—to identify ongoing public awareness activities along with their related goals, objectives, or performance metrics. Similarly, we requested and analyzed any documents NHTSA uses to evaluate the effectiveness of its public awareness activities, including performance reports for NHTSA's ongoing *Safe Cars Save Lives* campaign.

To assess the reliability of data included in these performance reports— such as VIN searches performed—we reviewed agency documentation and interviewed agency officials about the reliability, accuracy, and completeness of the data and determined the data were sufficiently reliable for our reporting purposes. We reviewed performance management practices as provided in the Government Performance and Results Act of 1993 (GPRA), the GPRA Modernization Act of 2010, and standards for internal control in the federal government to identify any opportunities for improvement.[57] We also performed a literature review to identify any related published articles and research studies.

To understand how NHTSA implements and evaluates any public awareness activities, we also interviewed responsible agency officials from NHTSA's Office of Communications and Consumer Information and other offices. In addition, we discussed NHTSA's public awareness efforts during interviews with industry stakeholders, including selected auto manufacturers, selected franchised and independent auto dealerships, and other industry stakeholders. We analyzed the results of these interviews along with the focus group discussions we conducted with consumers (discussed above) to identify perspectives on the effectiveness of NHTSA's public awareness steps.

We conducted this performance audit from October 2016 to December 2017 in accordance with generally accepted government auditing standards. Those standards require that we plan and perform the audit to obtain sufficient, appropriate evidence to provide a reasonable basis for our findings and conclusions based on our audit objectives. We believe that the evidence obtained provides a reasonable basis for our findings and conclusions based on our audit objectives.

---

[56] Pub. L. No. 114-94, 129 Stat. 1312; and *Update Means of Providing Recall Notification*, 81 Fed. Reg. 60,332 (Sept. 1, 2016).

[57] GAO-14-704G.

# Appendix II: Example of an Auto Manufacturer's Recall Notification Letter

TOYOTA

**Toyota Motor Sales, U.S.A., Inc.**
19001 South Western Avenue
P.O. Box 2991
Torrance, CA 90509-2991

**URGENT SAFETY RECALL**
This is an important Safety Recall.
The remedy will be performed at
**NO CHARGE** to you.

**Multiple Models and Model Years**
**Takata Front Passenger Airbag Inflator (Zone A)**
IMPORTANT SAFETY RECALL ***(Remedy Notice)***
This notice applies to your vehicle: VIN ABCDEFGH987654321
**NHTSA RECALL NO. 16V-340 & 17V-006**

Dear Toyota Customer:

This notice is sent to you in accordance with the requirements of the National Traffic and Motor Vehicle Safety Act. Toyota has decided that a defect, which relates to motor vehicle safety, exists in the vehicles described below:

- 2006 – 2011 Yaris Hatchback
- 2007 – 2012 Yaris Sedan
- 2008 – 2012 Scion xB
- 2009 – 2012 Corolla
- 2009 – 2012 Matrix
- 2010 – 2012 4Runner
- 2011 – 2012 Sienna

You received this notice because our records, which are based primarily on state registration and title data, indicate that you are the current owner.

**What is the problem?**

The subject vehicles are equipped with front passenger airbag inflators produced by Takata. The propellant in these inflators may degrade after prolonged exposure to high absolute humidity and fluctuating high temperatures. Degraded propellant can cause inflator rupture during airbag deployment. In the event of an inflator rupture, metal fragments could pass through the airbag cushion material, striking the vehicle occupants, and result in serious injury or death.

**What will Toyota do?**

Any authorized Toyota dealer will replace the airbag inflator or the airbag assembly, depending on the vehicle model, at ***NO CHARGE*** to you.

**What should you do?**

***This is an important Safety Recall.***

**Please contact any authorized Toyota dealer to schedule an appointment to have the remedy performed as soon as possible.**

***Until the remedy is performed, we recommend that you do not operate the vehicle with an occupant in the front passenger seat.*** We sincerely apologize for any inconvenience this will cause, but we are taking this action to ensure your safety.

**The repair will take approximately 1.5 hours. However, depending on the dealer's work schedule, it may be necessary to make your vehicle available for a longer period of time.**

**What if you have other questions?**

- For more information about Takata Recalls please see Toyota's website (www.toyota.com/recall) or the National Highway Traffic Safety Administration (NHTSA) website (www.safercar.gov).
- If you require further assistance, you may contact your local Toyota dealer or the Toyota Customer Experience Center at 1-888-270-9371 Monday through Friday, 7:00 a.m. to 7:00 p.m., Saturday 7:00 a.m. through 4:30 p.m. Central Time.

To visit Toyota.com/recall from your smart phone, scan the QR code to the left. Here you will find the most current Takata recall information and be able to check repair applicability specific to your VIN #.

If you believe that the dealer or Toyota has failed or is unable to remedy the defect within a reasonable time, you may submit a complaint to the Administrator, National Highway Traffic Safety Administration, 1200 New Jersey Avenue S.E., Washington, D.C. 20590, or call the toll free Vehicle Safety Hot Line at 1-888-327-4236 (TTY: 1-800-424-9153), or go to http://www.safercar.gov.

GOP Remedy

Spanish translation on back side
Traducción en español en el lado inverso

If you would like to update your vehicle ownership or contact information, you may do so by registering at www.toyota.com/ownersupdate. You will need your full 17-digit Vehicle Identification Number (VIN) to input the new information.

***If you are a vehicle lessor***, Federal Law requires that any vehicle lessor receiving this recall notice must forward a copy of this notice to the lessee within ten days.

**What if you have previously paid for repairs to your vehicle for this specific condition?**

If you have previously paid for repair to your vehicle for this specific condition prior to receiving this letter, please mail a copy of your repair order, proof-of-payment and ownership information to the following address for reimbursement consideration:

Toyota Customer Experience Center – TSR
Toyota Motor Sales, USA, Inc.
c/o Toyota Motor North America, Inc.
P O Box 259001 – SSC/CSP Reimbursements
Plano, Texas 75025-9001

We have sent this notice in the interest of your continued satisfaction with our products, and we sincerely regret any inconvenience this condition may have caused you.

Thank you for driving a Toyota.

Sincerely,

TOYOTA MOTOR SALES, U.S.A., INC.

TOYOTA

Toyota Motor Sales, U.S.A., Inc.

RETIRO DE SEGURIDAD URGENTE
Este es un retiro de seguridad importante.
La reparación se efectuará
**SIN COSTO** para usted.

**Múltiples modelos y años de los modelos**
**Takata de inflador de la bolsa de aire del pasajero delantero (zona A)**
IMPORTANTE RETIRO DE SEGURIDAD ***(Aviso de Reparación)***
Este aviso aplica a su vehículo: VIN ABCDEFGH987654321
**NO. DE RETIRO DE NHTSA 16V-340 Y 17V-006**

Estimado cliente de Toyota:

Esta notificación se le envía de acuerdo con los requisitos establecidos en el Acta de Tráfico Nacional y de Seguridad de Vehículos Motorizados. Toyota ha decidido que existe un defecto relacionado con la seguridad de los vehículos motorizados descritos a continuación:

- Yaris con portón trasero de años 2006 a 2011
- Yaris sedán de años 2007 a 2012
- Scion xB de años 2008 a 2012
- Corolla de años 2009 a 2012
- Matrix de años 2009 a 2012
- 4Runner de años 2010 a 2012
- Sienna de años 2011 a 2012

Usted recibió este aviso porque nuestros registros, basados principalmente en la información de registro y titularidad estatal, indican que usted es el propietario actual.

**¿Cuál es el problema?**

Los vehículos afectados están equipados con infladores de la bolsa de aire del pasajero delantero fabricados por Takata. El propulsor de estos infladores podría degradarse tras una exposición prolongada a una humedad absoluta elevada y a temperaturas fluctuantes altas. De ser así, podría causar la rotura del inflador cuando se activa la bolsa de aire. En el caso de que se rompiese el inflador, cabría la posibilidad de que los fragmentos metálicos resultantes atravesasen el sistema de amortiguación de la bolsa de aire y golpeasen potencialmente a los ocupantes del vehículo, con lo que podrían causarles heridas o lesiones de gravedad o la muerte.

**¿Qué hará Toyota?**

Cualquier concesionario Toyota autorizado reemplazará el inflador de la bolsa de aire o el conjunto de bolsas de aire, dependiendo del modelo del vehículo, ***SIN CARGO*** para usted.

**¿Qué debe hacer usted?**

*Este es un retiro de seguridad importante.*

**Por favor, póngase en contacto con cualquier concesionario Toyota autorizado para concertar una cita a fin de realizar esta reparación lo antes posible.**

***Hasta que la reparación se lleve a cabo, le recomendamos que no conduzca el vehículo con un ocupante en el asiento del pasajero delantero.*** Lamentamos profundamente cualquier inconveniente que esta situación pueda ocasionarle, pero estas medidas se toman por su seguridad.

**La reparación tomará aproximadamente 1.5 horas. Sin embargo, dependiendo del horario de trabajo del concesionario, es posible que necesiten su vehículo por más tiempo.**

**¿Qué puede hacer si tiene otras preguntas?**

- Para más información sobre retiros de seguridad de Takata, visite el sitio web de Toyota (www.toyota.com/recall) o el de la *National Highway Traffic Safety Administration* (Administración Nacional de Seguridad Vial en Autopistas, NHTSA) (www.safercar.gov).
- Si necesita más asistencia, puede comunicarse con su concesionario Toyota local o con el Centro de Experiencia del Cliente de Toyota, al 1-888-270-9371, de lunes a viernes, de 7:00 a.m. a 7:00 p.m., o los sábados, de 7:00 a.m. a 4:30 p.m., hora central.

Para visitar Toyota.com/recall desde su smartphone, escanee el código QR de la izquierda. Aquí encontrará la información del retiro de seguridad de Takata más reciente y podrá comprobar si la reparación es aplicable a su N.º de VIN específico

GSP Remedy

English version on front side
Versión en inglés en el frente

Si considera que el concesionario o Toyota no han logrado o no pueden solucionar el defecto dentro de un plazo razonable, puede presentar una queja al Administrador, a la *National Highway Traffic Safety Administration* [Administración Nacional de Seguridad Vial en Autopistas], 1200 New Jersey Avenue S.E., Washington, D.C. 20590, o llame sin costo a la línea directa de Seguridad Automotor al 1-888-327-4236 (TTY: 1-800-424-9153), o visite www.safercar.gov.

Si desea actualizar la información de contacto o de propiedad de su vehículo, puede hacerlo registrándose en www.toyota.com/ownersupdate. Necesitará su Número de Identificación del Vehículo (VIN) de 17 dígitos para ingresar la nueva información.

***Si usted es arrendador del vehículo***, la Ley Federal exige que toda persona que arrienda vehículos y reciba este aviso de retiro de seguridad envíe una copia del mismo al arrendatario dentro de los diez días.

**¿Qué sucede si usted ya pagó previamente por reparar su vehículo por esta condición en particular?**

Si ya pagó previamente por la reparación de su vehículo en lo que respecta a esta condición específica, envíe una copia de su orden de reparación, la prueba de pago y los datos de titularidad a la siguiente dirección para que se considere el reembolso:

Toyota Customer Experience Center – TSR
Toyota Motor Sales, USA, Inc.
c/o Toyota Motor North America, Inc.
P O Box 259001 – SSC/CSP Reimbursements
Plano, Texas 75025-9001

Hemos enviado este aviso porque estamos interesados en su constante satisfacción con nuestros productos y lamentamos profundamente cualquier inconveniente que esta situación pudiera haberle ocasionado.

Gracias por conducir un Toyota.

Atentamente,

TOYOTA MOTOR SALES, U.S.A., INC.

# APPENDIX III: ANNUAL RECALL COMPLETION RATES BY VEHICLE COMPONENT AND VEHICLE TYPE

The National Highway Traffic Safety Administration (NHTSA) is required to conduct a biennial analysis of vehicle safety recall completion rates and submit the results of its analysis in a report to certain congressional committees.[58] The report must include, among other things, the annual recall completion rate by vehicle type and vehicle component (such as brakes, fuel systems, and air bags) for each of the 5 years preceding the year the report is submitted. According to NHTSA's May 2017 report, completion rates for all vehicles combined ranged between 63 percent and 67 percent between calendar year 2011 and calendar year 2014 (see Table 5). However, NHTSA reported wider variation when the recall completion rates are broken down by vehicle type. Similarly, the report found that completion rates for most component categories fall within a range of 60 percent to 75 percent (see Table 6).[59]

NHTSA's completion rate formula is:

$$\frac{\text{Count of vehicles remedied}\sim}{(\text{Count of vehicles in recall} - \text{vehicles exported, stolen, scrapped, other})\sim} * 100$$

[58] Pub. L. No. 114-94, § 24104(c), 129 Stat. 1312, 1703-04. NHTSA must conduct an analysis and submit a report not later than 1 year after December 4, 2015, and biennially thereafter for 4 years.

[59] National Highway Traffic Safety Administration, *Report to Congress: "Vehicle Safety Recall Completion Rates Report"* (May 2017), 14.

## Table 5. Auto Recall Annual Completion Rates by Vehicle Type, Calendar Years 2011 through 2014

| | **Annual completion rate**[a] | | | |
|---|---|---|---|---|
| Vehicle type | 2011 | 2012 | 2013 | 2014 |
| Passenger Car | 73% | 76% | 76% | 60% |
| Multipurpose Passenger Vehicle[b] | 74% | 52% | 59% | 67% |
| Light Truck | 46% | 58% | 45% | 93% |
| Mix[c] | 75% | 65% | 62% | 73% |
| Percent remedied by calendar year | 65% | 65% | 63% | 67% |

Source: National Highway Traffic Safety Administration (NHTSA). | GAO-18-127

[a]NHTSA's annual completion rate counts include recalls issued between calendar years 2010 and 2014 in which the manufacturer reported the recall's completion status for at least 5 quarters after the remedy program became available (as of July 1, 2016). The rate is a volume-based, weighted metric, such that the more vehicles affected by the recall, the more weight or influence it has on the computed rate.

[b]Multipurpose passenger vehicles include, for example, sport utility vehicles and mini vans.

[c]The mix category includes recalls that involved a combination of passenger cars, multipurpose vehicles, and light trucks.

## Table 6. Auto Recall Annual Completion Rates by Vehicle Component, Calendar Years 2011 through 2014

| | **Annual completion rate**[a] | | | |
|---|---|---|---|---|
| Component name[b] | 2011 | 2012 | 2013 | 2014 |
| Air Bags | 59% | 51% | 66% | 70% |
| Electrical System | 86% | 61% | 79% | 62% |
| Electronic Stability Control/Traction Control | 92% | —[c] | 79% | 63% |
| Engine and Engine Cooling | 72% | 68% | 83% | 81% |
| Equipment | 84% | 47% | 85% | 67% |
| Fuel System | 49% | 79% | 50% | 73% |
| Latches/Locks/Linkages | —[c] | 80% | 61% | 78% |
| Lighting | 51% | 59% | 60% | 58% |
| Power Train | 76% | 65% | 67% | 76% |
| Seat Belts | 82% | 73% | 58% | 77% |
| Seats | 78% | 89% | 49% | 67% |
| Service/Parking Brakes | 78% | 58% | 68% | 68% |
| Steering | 70% | 72% | 49% | 67% |
| Structure | 46% | 83% | 42% | 66% |
| Suspension | 61% | 67% | 59% | 65% |
| Tires and Wheels | 86% | 38% | 89% | 81% |
| Vehicle Speed Control | 69% | 48% | 65% | 60% |
| Visibility | 83% | 68% | 60% | 62% |

Source: National Highway Traffic Safety Administration (NHTSA). | GAO-18-127

[a]NHTSA's annual completion rate counts include recalls issued between calendar years 2010 and 2014 in which the manufacturer reported the recall's completion status for at least five quarters after the remedy program became available (as of July 1, 2016). Recalls that had not reached this maturation point—including recalls filed in calendar year 2015—were not counted. Completion rates include light vehicles in the following major categories: light trucks, multipurpose passenger vehicles such as sport utility vehicles and mini vans, and passenger cars. The rate is a volume-based, weighted metric, such that the more vehicles affected by the recall, the more weight or influence it has on the computed rate.

[b]When a recall included multiple defective components, that recall was included in each component category. According to NHTSA, while the agency strives to be consistent in its component classification approach, a degree of subjectivity is required in classifying some vehicle components, given the variety of components that can necessitate a recall. Also, inconsistencies across manufacturers can present challenges to utilizing a uniform taxonomy for vehicle components.

[c]NHTSA did not report a completion rate for this component.

The annual completion rate is a volume-based, weighted metric, such that the more vehicles affected by the recall, the more weight or influence it has on the computed rate.[60]

# APPENDIX IV: FOCUS GROUP PARTICIPANTS' RESPONSES TO RECALL NOTIFICATION QUESTIONNAIRE

Focus group participants responded to a questionnaire we administered to collect information on consumers' auto recall notification preferences during our discussion sessions. Table 7 shows participants' responses to the administered questionnaire, by age group. We present these responses by age group, because consumers' notification preferences may vary according to their ages.

**Table 7. Focus Group Participants' Responses to Administered Recall Notification Questionnaire, by Age Group**

| Responses | Number of responses (percentage of age group) | | | |
|---|---|---|---|---|
| | 21-34 years old (21) | 35-54 years old (44) | 55+ years old (29) | Total (94) |
| **Question: Did you receive a notification letter in the mail from the manufacturer informing you about the recall on your specific vehicle? (Select one)** | | | | |
| Yes | 18 (86%) | 43 (98%) | 29 (100%) | **90** |
| No | 3 (14%) | 1 (2%) | 0 (0%) | **4** |
| **Question: In what other ways were you notified or did you become aware of the safety recall on your specific vehicle? (Select all that apply)** | | | | |
| Other mailed correspondence from the manufacturer | 4 (19%) | 11 (25%) | 11 (38%) | **26** |
| Mail from a dealer | 6 (29%) | 13 (30%) | 5 (17%) | **24** |
| Automated phone call | 1 (5%) | 1 (2%) | 1 (3%) | **3** |
| Live/non-automated phone call | 2 (10%) | 0 (0%) | 0 (0%) | **2** |
| Electronic mail (e-mail) message | 2 (10%) | 1 (2%) | 0 (0%) | **3** |
| Text message | 0 (0%) | 0 (0%) | 0 (0%) | **0** |
| In person at a dealership | 3 (14%) | 6 (14%) | 3 (10%) | **12** |
| In person at an auto repair shop (non-dealership) | 0 (0%) | 1 (2%) | 0 (0%) | **1** |
| Other | 4 (19%) | 1 (2%) | 7 (24%) | **12** |
| **Question: How would you prefer to be notified about safety recalls affecting your specific vehicle? (Select all that apply)** | | | | |
| Mail | 19 (90%) | 37 (84%) | 24 (83%) | **80** |
| Automated phone call | 7 (33%) | 7 (16%) | 2 (7%) | **16** |

[60] According to NHTSA, the agency is unable to verify the numbers of remedied vehicles reported by manufacturers with the available data. Likewise, the agency cannot verify the numbers of vehicles reported as exported, stolen, scrapped, or otherwise legitimately deducted from the number of vehicles recalled.

| Responses | Number of responses (percentage of age group) | | | |
|---|---|---|---|---|
| | 21-34 years old (21) | 35-54 years old (44) | 55+ years old (29) | Total (94) |
| Live/non-automated phone call | 6 (29%) | 7 (16%) | 2 (7%) | **15** |
| Electronic mail (e-mail) message | 13 (62%) | 30 (68%) | 13 (45%) | **56** |
| Text message | 5 (24%) | 13 (30%) | 4 (14%) | **22** |
| In person at a dealership | 9 (43%) | 7 (16%) | 3 (10%) | **19** |
| In person at an auto repair shop (non-dealership) | 5 (24%) | 5 (11%) | 1 (3%) | **11** |
| Other | 0 (0%) | 0 (0%) | 0 (0%) | **0** |
| **Question: Have you sought out additional information about the safety recall on your specific vehicle? (Select one)** | | | | |
| Yes | 9 (43%) | 15 (34%) | 10 (34%) | **34** |
| No | 12 (57%) | 29 (66%) | 19 (66%) | **60** |
| **Question: If you sought out additional information, how did you seek out additional information? (Select all that apply)** | | | | |
| Searched the Internet | 7 (33%) | 9 (20%) | 6 (21%) | **22** |
| Contacted the manufacturer | 0 (0%) | 5 (11%) | 0 (0%) | **5** |
| Contacted a dealer | 4 (19%) | 8 (18%) | 6 (21%) | **18** |
| Other | 1 (5%) | 0 (0%) | 0 (0%) | **1** |
| **Question: Have you ever signed up to receive e mail alerts about safety recalls that may affect your vehicle? (Select one)** | | | | |
| Yes | 1 (5%) | 3 (7%) | 0 (0%) | **4** |
| No | 20 (95%) | 41 (93%) | 29 (100%) | **90** |
| **Question: If you signed up, where did you sign up to receive the e-mail alerts? (Select all that apply)[a]** | | | | |
| Manufacturer website | 0 (0%) | 2 (5%) | 0 (0%) | **2** |
| Dealer website | 0 (0%) | 2 (5%) | 0 (0%) | **2** |
| Government website | 1 (5%) | 0 (0%) | 0 (0%) | **1** |
| Other | 0 (0%) | 0 (0%) | 0 (0%) | **0** |
| **Question: Have you ever downloaded a mobile application to view information about safety recalls that may affect your vehicle? (Select one)** | | | | |
| Yes | 0 (0%) | 0 (0%) | 0 (0%) | **0** |
| No | 21 (100%) | 44 (100%) | 29 (100%) | **94** |

Source: GAO. | GAO-18-127.

[a]One participant marked more than one response for this question.

## APPENDIX V: FOCUS GROUP PARTICIPANTS' RESPONSES TO WEBSITE USABILITY QUESTIONNAIRE

Focus group participants responded to a questionnaire we administered to collect information on the usability of NHTSA.gov during our usability testing sessions. Table 8 shows focus group participants' responses to the administered questionnaire, by age group. We present these responses by age group, because consumers' website usability needs or preferences may vary according to their ages.

## Table 8. Focus Group Participants' Responses to Administered Website Usability Questionnaire, by Age Group

| Responses | Number of responses (percentage of age group) | | | |
|---|---|---|---|---|
| | 21-34 years old (21) | 35-54 years old (44) | 55+ years old (29) | Total (94) |
| **1) In the space provided, please write down the website you would have chosen to find information about your vehicle's recall** | | | | |
| NHTSA.gov | 0 (0%) | 1 (2%) | 2 (7%) | 3 |
| Safercar.gov | 2 (10%) | 4 (9%) | 2 (7%) | 8 |
| Manufacturer website | 7 (33%) | 18 (41%) | 13 (45%) | 38 |
| Other | 12 (57%) | 21 (48%) | 12 (41%) | 45 |
| **2a) Try to find out if there are any recalls on your vehicle's Year, Make, and Model. Did you find any recalls for this vehicle? (If so, mark only one response below to indicate how easy it was to find the information)** | | | | |
| Very easy | 16 (76%) | 31 (70%) | 15 (52%) | 62 |
| Somewhat easy | 3 (14%) | 7 (16%) | 6 (21%) | 16 |
| Neither easy nor difficult | 0 (0%) | 1 (2%) | 2 (7%) | 3 |
| Somewhat difficult | 1 (5%) | 5 (11%) | 4 (14%) | 10 |
| Very difficult | 1 (5%) | 0 (0%) | 2 (7%) | 3 |
| **2b) For those of you who found that there were recalls on your vehicle's Year, Make, and Model, try to find more information about these recalls. (Mark only one response below to indicate how easy it was to find the information)[a]** | | | | |
| Very easy | 13 (62%) | 24 (56%) | 13 (46%) | 50 |
| Somewhat easy | 7 (33%) | 8 (19%) | 7 (25%) | 22 |
| Neither easy nor difficult | 0 (0%) | 3 (7%) | 2 (7%) | 5 |
| Somewhat difficult | 1 (5%) | 6 (14%) | 6 (21%) | 13 |
| Very difficult | 0 (0%) | 2 (5%) | 0 (0%) | 2 |
| **3) Using your vehicle identification number, try to determine if there are any recalls affecting your vehicle. (Mark only one response below to indicate how easy it was to find the information)** | | | | |
| Very easy | 11 (52%) | 42 (95%) | 23 (79%) | 76 |
| Somewhat easy | 7 (33%) | 2 (5%) | 3 (10%) | 12 |
| Neither easy nor difficult | 2 (10%) | 0 (0%) | 1 (3%) | 3 |
| Somewhat difficult | 0 (0%) | 0 (0%) | 1 (3%) | 1 |
| Very difficult | 1 (5%) | 0 (0%) | 1 (3%) | 2 |
| **4) You just bought a new vehicle. Try to find out if there is a way to sign up for e-mail recall alerts. (Mark only one response below to indicate how easy it was to find the information)** | | | | |
| Very easy | 4 (19%) | 20 (45%) | 10 (34%) | 34 |
| Somewhat easy | 6 (29%) | 15 (34%) | 11 (38%) | 32 |
| Neither easy nor difficult | 8 (38%) | 3 (7%) | 4 (14%) | 15 |
| Somewhat difficult | 3 (14%) | 3 (7%) | 2 (7%) | 8 |
| Very difficult | 0 (0%) | 3 (7%) | 2 (7%) | 5 |
| **5) Having performed these tasks, what are your overall impressions of how easy it is to use the auto recall areas of NHTSA.gov? (Mark only one response below to indicate how easy it was to perform all of these tasks)** | | | | |
| Very easy | 4 (19%) | 20 (45%) | 5 (17%) | 29 |
| Somewhat easy | 15 (71%) | 17 (39%) | 17 (59%) | 49 |
| Neither easy nor difficult | 1 (5%) | 2 (5%) | 5 (17%) | 8 |
| Somewhat difficult | 1 (5%) | 5 (11%) | 2 (7%) | 8 |
| Very difficult | 0 (0%) | 0 (0%) | 0 (0%) | 0 |

Source: GAO. | GAO-18-127.

[a]Only the 92 respondents who completed the vehicle year, make, and model search in 2a and found recalls for their vehicles responded to 2b.

Note: Some percentages do not add up to 100 percent due to rounding.

# APPENDIX VI: COMMENTS FROM THE DEPARTMENT OF TRANSPORTATION

U.S. Department of Transportation
Office of the Secretary of Transportation

Assistant Secretary for Administration

1200 New Jersey Avenue, SE
Washington, DC 20590

Susan A. Fleming
Director, Physical Infrastructure Issues
U.S. Government Accountability Office (GAO)
441 G Street NW
Washington, DC 20548

NOV 17 2017

Dear Ms. Fleming:

The National Highway Traffic Safety Administration's (NHTSA) mission is to save lives, prevent injuries, and reduce economic costs due to motor vehicle crashes. One of the key elements of achieving this mission is ensuring that consumers are aware of safety-related recalls. In support of this critical responsibility, NHTSA.gov launched in December 2016 as a consumer-facing site, written in plain language and organized to reflect the way consumers think about safety. Using the latest Web technology, best practices in user experience, and responsive design, NHTSA.gov puts information at the fingertips of any user, whether via smartphone, tablet, or computer. The final phase of the website redesign is expected to be completed by December 31, 2018.

In addition to a complete website redesign, NHTSA has also taken the following actions to further improve the usability of its website and to enhance the consumer experience:

- NHTSA prominently placed a simple-to-use tool on the homepage that enables consumers to enter a vehicle identification number (VIN) that immediately lets them know if their vehicle has any open safety recalls initiated in the last 15 years.
- To provide ongoing support, NHTSA implemented a suite of website performance measurement dashboards that monitor performance of the website's pages as well as the VIN lookup tool. These dashboards are continuously reviewed, allowing for the detection and immediate repair of any performance issues related to both the VIN lookup tool and other web content.
- The NHTSA.gov redesign project began with extensive user testing, usability testing, stakeholder interviews, and public focus groups. Usability testing continues to be a critical element of NHTSA's ongoing performance measurement and continual website adjustment.

Upon review of the GAO's draft report, we concur with the two recommendations to determine a completion date for NHTSA's website consolidation effort and to take interim steps to improve the usability of auto recall areas of NHTSA.gov as identified by GAO. We will provide a detailed response to each recommendation within 60 days of the final report's issuance.

Sincerely,

Keith Nelson
Assistant Secretary for Administration

In: Consumer Protection
Editor: Ralf Schaefer
ISBN: 978-1-53615-876-2


*Chapter 2*

# EVENT TICKET SALES: MARKET CHARACTERISTICS AND CONSUMER PROTECTION ISSUES*

***United States Government Accountability Office***

## ABBREVIATIONS

| | |
|---|---|
| BOTS Act | Better Online Ticket Sales Act of 2016 |
| DOJ | Department of Justice |
| FTC | Federal Trade Commission |
| IP | Internet protocol |

## WHY GAO DID THIS STUDY

Tickets for concerts, theater, and sporting events can be purchased— typically online—from the original seller (primary market) or a reseller (secondary market). Some state and federal officials and others have raised issues about ticketing fees, the effect of the secondary market on ticket prices, and the transparency and business practices of some industry participants. Event ticketing is not federally regulated. However, federal legislation enacted in 2016 restricts bots (ticket-buying software). Also, the Federal Trade Commission (FTC) has taken two enforcement actions related to deceptive marketing by ticket sellers under its broad FTC Act authority.

* This is an edited, reformatted and augmented version of United States Government Accountability Office; Report to Congressional Requesters, Publication No. GAO-18-347, dated April 2018.

GAO was asked to review issues around online ticket sales. This chapter examines (1) what is known about online ticket sales, (2) consumer protection issues related to such sales, and (3) potential advantages and disadvantages of selected approaches to address these issues.

GAO focused on concert, theater, and major league sporting events for which there is a resale market. GAO analyzed data on fees, ticket volume, and resale prices from a variety of sources; reviewed the largest ticket sellers' websites and purchase processes; and reviewed federal and state laws and relevant academic literature. GAO also interviewed and reviewed documentation from government agencies; consumer organizations; ticket sellers; venue operators; promoters and managers; sports leagues; and academics (selected for their experience and to provide a range of perspectives).

## What GAO Found

Ticket pricing, resale activity, and fees for events vary. Tickets to popular events sold on the primary market sometimes are priced below the market price, partly because performers want to make tickets affordable and maintain fans' goodwill, according to industry representatives. Tickets are often resold on the secondary market at prices above face value. In a nongeneralizable sample of events GAO reviewed, primary and secondary market ticketing companies charged total fees averaging 27 percent and 31 percent, respectively, of the ticket's price.

Consumer protection issues include difficulty buying tickets at face value and the fees and marketing practices of some market participants.

- Professional resellers, or brokers, have a competitive advantage over consumers in buying tickets as soon as they are released. Brokers can use numerous staff and software ("bots") to rapidly buy many tickets. As a result, many consumers can buy tickets only on the resale market at a substantial markup.
- Some ticket websites GAO reviewed did not clearly display fees or disclosed them only after users entered payment information.
- "White-label" resale sites, which often appear as paid results of Internet searches for venues and events, often charged higher fees than other ticket websites—sometimes in excess of 40 percent of the ticket price—and used marketing that might mislead users to think they were buying tickets from the venue.

Selected approaches GAO reviewed, such as ticket resale restrictions and disclosure requirements, would have varying effects on consumers and businesses.

- Nontransferable tickets. At least three states restrict nontransferable tickets—that is, tickets whose terms do not allow resale. Nontransferable tickets allow more consumers to access tickets at a face-value price. However, they also limit consumers' ability to sell tickets they cannot use, can create inconvenience by requiring identification at the venue, and according to economists, prevent efficient allocation of tickets.
- Price caps. Several states cap the price at which tickets can be resold. But according to some state government studies, the caps generally are not effective because they are difficult to enforce.
- Disclosure requirements. Stakeholders and government research GAO consulted generally supported measures to ensure clearer and earlier disclosure of ticket fees, although views varied on the best approach (for example, to include fees in an "all-in" price or disclose them separately).

Some market-based approaches are being used or explored that seek to address concerns about secondary market activity. These approaches include technological tools and ticket-buyer verification to better combat bots. In addition, a major search engine recently required enhanced disclosures from ticket resellers using its advertising platform. The disclosures are intended to protect consumers from scams and prevent potential confusion about who is selling the tickets.

April 12, 2018

The Honorable Greg Walden
Chairman

The Honorable Frank Pallone, Jr.
Ranking Member
Committee on Energy and Commerce
House of Representatives

The Honorable Bill Pascrell, Jr.
House of Representatives

The Honorable Fred Upton
House of Representatives

In recent years, consumers and others have raised issues about the online ticket marketplace for concerts, commercial theater, and sporting events.[1] For example, some consumers have complained about difficulty obtaining face-value tickets for popular events at the primary, or initial, sale to the general public—only to find the tickets immediately available at high markups on the secondary, or resale, market. In response, event organizers and legislators have targeted ticket bots—automated software that ticket brokers can use to buy large volumes of tickets. The Better Online Ticket Sales Act of 2016 (BOTS Act) restricted the use of bots and gave the Federal Trade Commission (FTC) and state attorneys general the authority to pursue violators with civil actions.[2] Other issues that have been raised include the amount of ticket fees and restrictions on transferring some tickets.

You asked us to review the marketplace and consumer protection issues related to online ticket sales. This chapter examines (1) what is known about primary and secondary online ticket sales, (2) the consumer protection concerns that exist related to online ticket sales, and (3) potential advantages and disadvantages of selected approaches to address these concerns.

To address the first objective, we obtained and analyzed data on ticket volume and resale prices obtained from ticket sellers' websites for a nonprobability sample of 22 events, which were selected to represent a variety of event types and popularity levels. We collected data from October 16 through December 20, 2017. We also reviewed trade industry data on ticket prices and sales.

To address the second objective, we reviewed the websites of 6 primary market ticket sellers, 11 secondary ticket exchanges, and 8 ticket sellers using "white-label" websites.[3] For a sample of 31 events, chosen to reflect a mix of event types and venue sizes (e.g., arenas, theaters), we reviewed the process of purchasing tickets online and documented when and how clearly fees and restrictions were disclosed. In addition, we assessed the accuracy of information that customer service departments of three large secondary ticket exchanges provided. We also reviewed relevant enforcement activity by federal and state agencies and obtained and analyzed summary complaint data from FTC's Consumer Sentinel Network database.

To address the third objective, we reviewed federal and selected state laws and examined the experiences of three U.S. states (Connecticut, Georgia, and New York) with relevant event ticketing laws. We also reviewed foreign government reports to obtain information on relevant ticketing restrictions in two foreign countries (Canada and the United Kingdom) with similar consumer protection issues reviewed in this chapter.

---

[1] For purposes of this chapter, we use "online" to refer to activity that occurs on a website or through a mobile application. Although this chapter focuses on online ticketing, in some cases the issues discussed could also apply to tickets purchased via telephone or at a physical location.

[2] Better Online Ticket Sales Act of 2016, Pub. L. No. 114-274, 130 Stat. 1401 (2016) (BOTS Act).

[3] A white-label website is a sales website built by one company that allows affiliates to use the software to build their own, uniquely branded websites.

For all three objectives, we reviewed documentary evidence (such as academic studies, trade reports and databases, and industry literature) and interviewed staff from FTC, Department of Justice (DOJ), and three state offices of attorney general; consumer organizations; primary and secondary ticket sellers; venue operators, event promoters, and artists' managers and agents; major sports leagues; and academics who have studied the ticket marketplace—all of whom were selected for their experience and to provide a range of perspectives. For more information on our scope and methodology, see appendix I.

We conducted this performance audit from November 2016 to April 2018, in accordance with generally accepted government auditing standards. Those standards require that we plan and perform the audit to obtain sufficient, appropriate evidence to provide a reasonable basis for our findings and conclusions based on our audit objectives. We believe that the evidence obtained provides a reasonable basis for our findings and conclusions based on our audit objectives. We conducted our related investigative work in accordance with investigative standards prescribed by the Council of the Inspectors General on Integrity and Efficiency.

## BACKGROUND

### The Ticketing Marketplace

The marketplace for primary and secondary ticketing services consists of several types of participants, including primary market ticketing companies, professional ticket brokers, secondary market ticket exchanges, and ticket aggregators (see Table 1). Other parties that play a role in event ticketing, as discussed later in this chapter, include artists and their managers, booking agents, sports teams, producers, promoters, and operators of event venues (such as clubs, theaters, arenas, or stadiums).[4]

The private research firm IBISWorld estimated that online ticketing services (including ticketing for concerts, sporting events, live theater, fairs, and festivals) represented a $9 billion market in 2017, which included both the primary and secondary markets.[5]

---

[4] Although the terms vary with use, "promoter" generally refers to a person or company that contracts with artists or their representatives to arrange events. Promoters also secure venues in which events will occur, arrange for production services, and market events to the public. "Producer" generally refers to a person or company that oversees all aspects of a theater production, including hiring creative staff (such as writers, directors, composers, choreographers, and performers), securing financing and a venue, and promoting the event. For this chapter, we use "event organizers" to refer to a combination of artists, managers, booking agents, promoters or producers, and venue operators.

[5] IBISWorld, *Online Event Ticket Sales in the US.: Market Research Report*, (December 2017).

Another private research firm, Statista, estimated that U.S. online ticketing revenues for sports and music events totaled about $7.1 billion in 2017.[6] Estimates of the total number of professional ticket sellers vary. IBISWorld estimated that the U.S. market for online event ticket sales included 2,571 businesses in 2017. The Census Bureau lists more than 1,500 ticket services companies as of 2015 based on the business classification code for ticket services. However, this does not provide a reliable count of companies in the event ticketing industry because it includes companies selling tickets for services such as bus, airline, and cruise ship travel, among other services.

**Table 1. Key Participants in the Primary and Secondary Markets for Event Tickets**

| Participant | Description |
|---|---|
| Primary market ticketing companies | Companies that provide initial-sale ticketing services for events |
| Professional ticket brokers | Companies or individuals who buy tickets, usually on the primary market, with the intention of reselling at a profit |
| Secondary market ticket exchanges | Online resale platforms that facilitate transactions between third parties (brokers or consumers), but generally do not maintain their own ticket inventory |
| Ticket aggregators | Websites that aggregate in one place the resale listings from multiple secondary ticket exchanges |

Source: GAO. | GAO-18-347.

However, a small number of companies conducts the majority of event ticket sales. In the primary ticket market—where tickets originate and are available at initial sale—Ticketmaster is the largest ticketing company. DOJ estimated that Ticketmaster (whose parent company is now Live Nation Entertainment) held more than 80 percent of market share in 2008, and it was still the market leader as of 2017.[7] Less than a dozen other companies control most of the rest of the primary market, by our estimates. In the secondary market—where resale occurs—more companies are active, but StubHub estimated it held roughly 50 percent of market share as of 2017. According to Moody's Investors Service, Ticketmaster, which in addition to its primary market ticketing has a U.S. resale subsidiary, held the second-largest market share as of 2016.

The majority of ticket sales occur online, through a website or mobile application. Ticketmaster's parent company reported that 93 percent of its primary tickets were sold online in 2017.[8] The industry research group LiveAnalytics reported that in 2014, 68

[6] Statista, "Event Tickets," accessed January 17, 2018, https://www.statista.com/outlook/264/109/event-tickets/united-states.

[7] Competitive Impact Statement, United States of America v. Ticketmaster Entertainment, Inc., No. 1:10-cv-00139 (D. D.C. Jan. 25, 2010); Live Nation Entertainment, Inc., Annual Report (Form 10-K) (Feb. 27, 2018). DOJ based its market share estimate on the number of major concert venues Ticketmaster served at the time.

[8] Live Nation Entertainment, Inc. 2017 10-K.

percent, 50 percent, and 49 percent of people attending concerts, sporting events, and live theater or arts events, respectively, had recently purchased a ticket online.[9]

## Regulation

The event ticketing industry is not federally regulated. However, the Federal Trade Commission Act prohibits unfair or deceptive acts or practices in or affecting commerce, and FTC can enforce the act for issues related to event ticketing and ticketing companies.[10] One federal statute specifically addresses ticketing issues—the BOTS Act, which prohibits, among other things, circumventing security measures or other systems intended to enforce ticket purchasing limits or order rules.[11] The act also makes it illegal to sell or offer to sell any event ticket obtained through these illegal methods and granted enforcement authority to FTC and state attorneys general.[12]

The Department of Justice's Antitrust Division plays a role in monitoring competition in the event ticketing industry. In 2010, Live Nation and Ticketmaster—respectively, the largest concert promoter and primary ticket seller in the United States—merged to form Live Nation Entertainment, Inc. DOJ approved the merger after requiring Ticketmaster to license its primary ticketing software to a competitor, sell off one ticketing unit, and agree to be barred from certain forms of retaliation against venue owners who use a competing ticket service. DOJ may also inspect Live Nation's records and interview its employees to determine or secure compliance with the terms of the final judgment clearing the merger.[13]

State government agencies generally invoke state laws on unfair and deceptive acts and practices to address ticketing violations, according to representatives of two state attorney general offices. In addition, several states have laws that directly apply to event ticketing. For example, some states restrict the use of bots, several other states impose price caps (or upper limits) on ticket resale prices, and states including Connecticut, New York, and Virginia restrict the use of nontransferable tickets (tickets with terms that do not allow resale). Several states require brokers to be licensed and adhere to certain professional standards, such as maintaining a physical place of business and a toll-free telephone number, and offering a standard refund policy.[14]

---

[9] LiveAnalytics, *U.S. Live Event Attendance Study*, June 2014. These included ticket purchases from both primary and secondary market sources.

[10] *See* 15 U.S.C. § 45(a)(1) (2017); 15 U.S.C. § 45c (2017).

[11] BOTS Act, *supra*.

[12] BOTS Act, §2(a)-(c).

[13] *United States of America v. Ticketmaster Entertainment, Inc.*, No. 1:10-cv-00139 (D.D.C. July 30, 2010).

[14] In addition to certain state requirements, at least 200 brokers belong to the National Association of Ticket Brokers, which requires its members to adhere to a code of ethics that includes a variety of customer service and consumer protection provisions.

# Ticketing Practices, Prices, Fees, and Resale Vary by Industry and Event

The concert, sports, and theater industries vary in how they price and distribute tickets. Many tickets are resold on the secondary market, typically at a higher price. Among a nongeneralizable sample of events we reviewed, we observed that primary and secondary market ticketing companies charged total fees averaging 27 percent and 31 percent, respectively, of the ticket's price.

## On the Primary Market, Ticketing Practices Vary by Industry and Popular Events Are Sometimes Priced below Market

### *Concerts*

Ticketing practices for major concerts include presales and pricing that varies based on factors like location and the popularity of the performer. Tickets to popular concerts are often first sold through presales, which allow certain customers to purchase tickets before the general on-sale. Common presales include those for holders of certain credit cards or members of the artist's fan club, although promoters, venues, or other groups also may offer presales. Credit card companies might provide free marketing for events or other compensation in exchange for exclusive early access to tickets for their cardholders. In addition, the artist usually has the option to sell a portion of tickets to its fan club. The venue's ticketing company might want to limit the number of tickets allocated to fan clubs because the artist and manager can sell them through a separate ticketing platform, according to three event organizers we interviewed.

There are no comprehensive data on the proportion of tickets sold through presales because this information is usually confidential. Industry representatives told us that 10 percent to 30 percent of tickets for major concerts typically are offered through presales, although it can be as many as about 65 percent of tickets for major artists performing at large venues. In addition, fan club presales usually represent 8 percent of tickets, although it may be more if the fan club presale uses the venue's ticketing company, according to two event organizers. A large ticketing company told us that 10 percent of tickets may be available for fan club presales. A 2016 study by the New York State Office of the Attorney General found that an average of 38 percent of tickets were allotted to presales for the 74 highest-grossing concerts at selected New York State venues in 2012–2015.[15]

[15] New York State Office of the Attorney General, *Obstructed View: What's Blocking New Yorkers from Getting Tickets* (New York, N.Y.: 2016). This figure included both fan club and credit card presales. Some of the concerts included multiple shows or tour stops by the same artist.

Additionally, venues, promoters, agents, and artists commonly hold back a small portion of tickets from public sale. "Holds" may be given or sold to media outlets, high-profile guests, or friends and family of the artist. They also may be used to provide flexibility when the seating configuration is not yet final. Promoters typically will release unused holds before the event, offering the tickets to the public at face value.

As with presales, little comprehensive data exist on the proportion of tickets reserved for holds. Industry representatives told us holds typically represent a relatively small number of tickets—a few hundred for major events or perhaps a thousand for a stadium concert. The New York Attorney General report's review of a sample of high-grossing New York State concerts found that approximately 16 percent of tickets, on average, were allocated for holds. Of those holds, many went to venue operators— for example, one arena with around 21,000 seats usually received more than 900 holds per concert held there.

The average face-value ticket price in 2017 among the top 100 grossing concert tours in North America was $78.93, according to Pollstar.[16] Concert ticket prices vary by city or day of the week, based on anticipated demand. The main parties involved in price setting are the artist and her or his management team, promoter, and booking agent. Venues sometimes provide input based on their knowledge of prevailing prices in the local market. Ticketing companies sometimes offer tools or support to help event organizers price tickets based on their analysis of sales trends.

Concert ticket prices are generally set to maximize profits, according to event organizers. In terms of production costs, the artist's guarantee—the amount the artist is paid for each performance—is usually the largest expense. The most popular artists can command the highest guarantees and their concerts also tend to have the highest production costs.

However, for some high-demand events, tickets might be "underpriced"— that is, knowingly set below the market clearing price that would provide the greatest revenue.[17] Artists may underprice their tickets for a variety of reasons, according to industry stakeholders and our literature review:

- Reputation risk. Artists may avoid very high prices because they do not want to be perceived as gouging fans. Similarly, event organizers told us some artists have a certain brand or image—such as working-class appeal—that could be harmed by charging very high ticket prices.

---

[16] Pollstar, *2017 Year End Business Analysis* (Fresno, Calif.: Pollstar, 2018). Pollstar is a trade publication covering the worldwide concert industry.

[17] For the purposes of this chapter, we consider high-demand events to be those for which tickets sell out early in the on-sale and prices are higher on the resale market. The market clearing price refers to the price at which the number of tickets available for sale equals the number of tickets customers are willing to buy, resulting in neither a surplus nor a shortage.

- Affordability. Some event organizers told us that artists want to price tickets below market to provide access to fans at all income levels.
- Sold-out show. Event organizers may price tickets lower to ensure a sold-out show, which can improve the artist and event organizers' reputations and might help future sales.
- Audience mix. Some artists prefer to have the most enthusiastic fans at their shows, rather than just those able to pay the most, especially in the front rows, where tickets are generally the most expensive.
- Ancillary revenue. Better attendance through lower ticket prices can increase merchandise and concession sales, which can be a substantial source of revenue.

In addition, event organizers may unintentionally underprice concert tickets because of imperfect information about what consumers are willing to pay. Tickets are also priced based on the prices and sales of the artist's (or similar artists') past tours, but demand can be hard to predict. Three event organizers told us that they have started using data from the ticket resale market to help set prices because that is a good gauge of the true market price.

### *Sporting Events*

For major league professional sports, most decisions about ticket pricing and ticket distribution are made by the individual teams rather than by the league.[18] According to the three major sports leagues we interviewed, their teams generally sell most of their tickets through season packages, with the remainder sold for individual games. Teams favor packages because they guarantee a certain level of revenue for the season. Representatives of two major sports leagues told us that their teams sold an average of 85 percent and 55 percent, respectively, of their tickets through season packages. One league told us that some of its teams increasingly offer not only full-season packages, but also partial-season packages. Another league said that in some cases, its teams might need to reserve a certain number of single game-day tickets—for example, as part of an agreement when public funds helped build a new stadium.

Representatives of the three sports leagues we interviewed told us that their teams do not use presales and holds to the same extent as the concert industry. Although teams do not sell a significant number of tickets through presales, they might offer first choice of seats to season ticket holders or individuals who purchased tickets in the past. In terms of holds, one league told us it requires its teams to hold a small number of tickets for the visiting team and teams might also hold a few tickets for sponsors and performers.

[18] In this chapter, sporting events refer to games played by teams of the four largest professional sports leagues in the United States, which are Major League Baseball, the National Football League, the National Basketball Association, and the National Hockey League.

Another league told us it does not have league-wide requirements on holds, but its teams sometimes hold a small number of seats for media.

Sports teams generally set their ticket prices to maximize revenue, based on supply and anticipated demand, according to the leagues we interviewed. Ticket prices typically vary year-to-year, based on factors such as the team's performance the previous season and playing in a new stadium.[19] Teams in many leagues use "dynamic pricing" for individual game tickets. They adjust prices as the game approaches based on changing demand factors, such as team performance and the weather forecast. The sports leagues with whom we spoke said teams' pricing considerations are based in part on a desire to have affordable tickets for fans of different income levels. In addition, one league told us its teams rely heavily on revenues other than ticket sales, such as from television deals and sponsorships.

### *Theater*

Tickets for Broadway and national touring shows are distributed through direct online sales as well as several additional channels, including day-of-show discount booths, group packages, and call centers.[20] Industry representatives told us that these shows use presales and holds, but not as extensively as the concert industry. At our request, a company provided us with data for five Broadway shows from June 2016 to September 2017.[21] Approximately 13 percent of tickets in this sample were sold through presales, almost all of which were group sales (offered to particular groups prior to the general on-sale). Less than 1 percent of tickets in this sample were sold through presales offered to specific credit cardholders. Two shows in high demand held back an average of about 6 percent of tickets, while the other three shows held back about 1 percent.

Producers and venue operators generally set prices, which are influenced by factors like venue capacity and the length of run needed to recoup expenses, according to industry representatives. According to the Broadway League, from May 22, 2017, to February 11, 2018, the average face-value price of a Broadway show was $123—an average of $127 for musicals and $81 for plays. Industry representatives told us they sell about 10 percent of tickets through day-of-show discount booths. Even the most popular shows typically offer steep discounts for a small number of tickets through lotteries or other means.

---

[19] Patrick Rishe and Michael Mondello, "Ticket Price Determination in Professional Sports: An Empirical Analysis of the NBA, NFL, NHL, and Major League Baseball," *Sport Marketing Quarterly*, vol. 13, no. 2 (2004), 111.

[20] In this chapter, theater refers to Broadway and national tours, which are generally commercial productions. We are excluding community and most nonprofit theater.

[21] We asked a company that collects data on Broadway ticketing to provide us with summary statistics on holds and presales for a small sample of shows that played in June 2016 through September 2017, and to separate the results for high-demand shows (defined as selling 90 percent or more of available seats). The company selected and provided data on five shows, two of which were high-demand shows.

Tickets for some of the most popular Broadway shows have sometimes been underpriced, according to Broadway theater representatives, who told us they feel obligated to maintain relatively reasonable prices and to allow consumers of varying financial resources to attend their shows. Additionally, some shows are underpriced because their popularity was not anticipated. At the same time, in recent years, producers have started charging much higher prices (sometimes exceeding $500) for premium seats or for shows in very high demand, which allows productions to capture proceeds that would otherwise be lost to the secondary market.

### *Relationships between Event Organizers and Brokers*

Sometimes event organizers work directly with brokers to distribute tickets on the secondary market. For high-demand events, event organizers may seek to capture a share of higher secondary market prices without the reputation risk of raising an event's ticket prices directly. For lower-demand events, selling tickets directly to brokers can guarantee a certain level of revenue and increase exposure (by using multiple resale platforms rather than a single ticketing site).

- In major league sports, teams sell up to 30 percent of seats directly to brokers, according to a large primary ticket seller.
- For Broadway theater, one company told us it regularly distributes about 8 percent to 10 percent of its tickets to a few authorized secondary market brokers.
- In the concert industry, it is unclear how often artists and event organizers sell tickets directly through the secondary market. Any formal agreements would be in business-confidential contracts, according to industry representatives, and artists may be concerned about disclosing them for fear of appearing to profit from high resale prices.

All the artists' representatives with whom we spoke denied that their clients sold tickets directly to secondary market companies. However, a Vice President of the National Consumers League has cited evidence of cases in which ticket holds reserved for an artist were listed on the secondary market.[22] A representative of one secondary market company told us of two cases in which representatives of popular artists approached his company about selling blocks of tickets for upcoming tours.

---

[22] *Legislative Hearing on 17 FTC Bills, House of Representatives, Energy and Commerce Committee, Subcommittee on Commerce, Manufacturing, and Trade*, 114th Cong. 187- 198 (May 24, 2016) (statement of John Breyault, Vice President, Public Policy, Telecommunications, and Fraud; National Consumers League).

## Tickets to Popular Events Are Often Resold on the Secondary Market at Prices above Face Value

Ticket resale prices can be significantly higher than primary market prices and brokers account for most sales on major ticket exchanges. When tickets on the primary market are priced below market value—that is, priced less than what consumers are willing to pay—it creates greater opportunities for profit on the secondary market. Resale transactions typically occur on secondary ticket exchanges—websites where multiple sellers can list their tickets for resale and connect with potential buyers. Primary ticketing companies have also entered the resale market. For example, Ticketmaster allows buyers to resell tickets through its TM+ program, which lists resale inventory next to primary market inventory, and it owns the secondary ticket exchange TicketsNow.com.

Generally speaking, the secondary market serves two types of sellers: (1) those who buy or otherwise obtain tickets with the intent of reselling them at a profit (typically, professional brokers), and (2) individuals trying to recoup their money for an event they cannot attend (or sports season ticket holders who do not want to attend all games or use resale to finance part of their season package). Representatives from the four secondary ticket exchanges with whom we spoke each said that professional brokers represent either the majority or overwhelming majority of ticket sales on their sites.

Sellers set their own prices on secondary ticket exchanges, but some exchanges offer pricing recommendations. The exchanges allow adjustment of prices over time, and sellers can lower prices if tickets are not selling, or raise prices if demand warrants. Software tools exist that assist sellers in setting prices and in automatically adjusting prices for multiple ticket listings.

However, resale prices are not always higher than the original price, and thus brokers assume some risk. In some cases, the market price declines below the ticket's face value—for example, for a poorly performing sports team. The leading ticket exchange network has publicly stated that it estimates that 50 percent of tickets resold on its site sell for less than face value. However, we were unable to obtain data that corroborated this statement.

Relatively few studies have looked at the ticket resale market for major concert, sporting, or theatrical events. Our review of relevant economic literature identified six studies that looked at ticket resale prices, one of which also looked at the extent of resale (see Table 2). In general, the studies found a wide range of resale prices, perhaps reflecting the different methodologies and samples used or the limited amount of information on ticket resale. Additionally, the data reported are several years old and will not fully reflect the current market.

## Table 2. Selected Research on Ticket Resale Prices and the Extent of Resale

| Study title | Author and source | Study description | Findings | |
|---|---|---|---|---|
| | | | Ticket prices | Extent of resale |
| "Resale and Rent-Seeking: An Application to Ticket Markets" | Phillip Leslie and Alan Sorenson, *The Review of Economic Studies*, vol. 81, no. 1 (2013) | Using a sample of 56 concerts for popular artists in 2004, the study compared the number of tickets and resale prices from a major secondary ticket exchange and an online auction site to the number of tickets sold and prices in the primary market. | Seventy-four percent of tickets were resold above face value and 26 percent of tickets were resold below face value. The average resale price overall was 41 percent higher than the face-value price. | On average, about 5 percent of tickets were resold, with a range among concerts of 3–17 percent. |
| "Obstructed View: What's Blocking New Yorkers from Getting Tickets" | New York State Office of the Attorney General (2016) | Reviewed data from six brokers on 90,000 sales transactions made from 2010–2014 that showed the prices at which the brokers purchased and resold the tickets. | On average, the resale price was 49 percent higher than the face-value price. By broker, the average markup ranged from 15 percent to 112 percent. | Not addressed (n/a). |
| "Primary-Market Auctions for Event Tickets: Eliminating the Rents of 'Bob the Broker'?" | Aditya Bhave and Eric Budish, NBER Working Paper No. 23770 (National Bureau of Economic Research, Cambridge, Mass., 2017) | Reviewed face-value and resale prices of tickets to 576 concerts in 2007 and 2008. Looking at the best seats sold using auctions, the study compared the tickets' original face-value prices to initial-sale (by auction) prices and secondary market prices. | Secondary market prices, which were close to the auction prices, were about double the tickets' face-value prices. | n/a |
| "An Examination of Dynamic Ticket Pricing and Secondary Market Price Determinants in Major League Baseball" | Stephen L. Shapiro and Joris Drayer, *Sport Management Review*, vol. 17, no. 2 (2014) | Looking at 12 games in a Major League Baseball team's 2010 season, the study compared the tickets' face-value prices and season ticket holder prices to listed prices on a major secondary ticket exchange. | The average listed resale price was 103 percent higher than the average price paid by season ticket holders and about 45 percent higher than the average single game-day price.[a] | n/a |
| "An Examination of Underlying Consumer Demand and Sport Pricing Using Secondary Market Data" | Joris Drayer, Daniel A. Rascher, and Chad D. McEvoy, *Sport Management Review*, 15 (2012). | The study compared the secondary market sale price to the primary market price for all 32 NFL teams in the 2007– 2008 season. | The average secondary market price was 143 percent higher than the average primary market price. | n/a |
| "Pricing Behavior in Perishable Goods Markets: Evidence from Secondary Markets for Major League Baseball Tickets" | Andrew Sweeting, *Journal of Political Economy*, 120, no. 6 (2012). | The study compared 2007 ticket prices for the home games of 29 Major League Baseball teams to listed prices on a major resale exchange and online auction site. | The average listed resale price was about twice the corresponding face-value price, although prices declined as game-day approached.[a] | n/a |

Source: GAO-selected research. | GAO-18-347.

[a]"Listed" resale price refers to the price listed and not necessarily to the price at which the ticket actually sold.

For illustrative purposes, we reviewed secondary market ticket availability and prices for a nongeneralizable sample of 22 events.[23] Among our selected events, the proportion of seats that were listed for resale ranged from 3 percent to 38 percent. In general, among the 22 events we reviewed, listed resale prices tended to be higher than primary market prices. For example, tickets for one sold-out rock concert had been about $50 to $100 on the primary market but ranged from about $90 to $790 in secondary market listings.

For 7 of the 22 events, we observed instances in which tickets were listed on the resale market even when tickets were still available from primary sellers at a lower face-value price.[24] For example, one theater event had secondary market tickets listed at prices ranging from $248 to $1,080 (average of $763), while a substantial number of tickets for comparable seats were still available on the primary market at $198 to $398.[25] We did not have data to determine whether the resale tickets actually sold at their listed price. However, as discussed later, it is possible that some consumers buy on the secondary market, at a higher price, because they are not aware that they are purchasing from a resale site rather than the primary seller.

## Total Ticket Fees Averaged 27 Percent on the Primary Market and 31 Percent on the Secondary Market for Events We Reviewed

Ticket fees vary in amount and type among the primary and secondary markets, and among different ticketing companies and events.

### *Primary Market Fees*

Companies that provide ticketing services on the primary market typically charge fees to the buyer that are added to the ticket's list price and can vary considerably. A single ticket can have multiple fees, commonly including a "service fee," a per-order "processing fee," and a "facility fee" charged by the venue. Most primary ticketing companies offer free delivery options, such as print-at-home or mobile tickets, but charge additional fees for delivery of physical tickets.

---

[23] We reviewed data from two ticket resale sites for a sample of 22 events, 17 of which we categorized as high-demand. We also reviewed data from the primary ticket market for each event. We defined high-demand events as those that were likely to sell out, which we assessed by reviewing past attendance at other events for the same artist, sports team, or theatrical event. We focused on high-demand events because they have been the focus of interest in issues regarding resale activity. For each event, we determined (1) the proportion of tickets listed on the secondary market, and (2) how listed resale prices compared to face-value prices. Events were selected to represent concert, sporting, and theater events at different demand levels (popular versus other events). We collected data between October 16 and December 20, 2017.

[24] We did not have information on how many tickets were available at various price points and it is possible that the differences in pricing could have been due to the number or quality of seats on the primary market.

[25] To combine data from the two resellers, we computed median weekly ticket prices for each event from each vendor, and then computed an average weighted by the number of available tickets on each website. The primary and secondary market prices do not include fees.

Venues usually have an exclusive contract with a single ticketing company and typically negotiate fees for all events at the venue, though in some cases they do so by category of event. Ticketing companies and venues usually share fee revenue and in some cases, the venue receives the majority of the fee revenue, according to primary ticketing companies.[26] In addition, event organizers told us that promoters occasionally negotiate with the venue to add ticket fees or receive fee revenue.

Ticketing companies told us that they do not have a set fee schedule and amounts and types of fees vary among venues. Fees can be set as a fixed amount, a fixed amount that varies with the ticket's face value (for example, $5 for tickets below $50 and $10 for tickets above $50), a percentage of face value, or other variations.

While ticketing fees vary considerably, the 2016 New York Attorney General report found average ticket fees of 21 percent based on its review of ticket information for more than 800 tickets at 150 New York State venues.[27] (In other words, a ticketing company would add $21 in fees to a $100 ticket, for a total price to the buyer of $121.) The 21 percent figure encompassed all additional fees, including service fees and flat fees, like delivery or order processing fees.

We conducted our own review of ticketing fees for a nongeneralizable sample of a total of 31 concert, theater, and sporting events across five primary ticket sellers' websites:[28]

- In total, the combined fees averaged 27 percent of the ticket's face value, and we observed values ranging from 13 percent to 58 percent.[29]
- Service fees were, on average, 22 percent of the ticket's face value, and we observed values ranging from 8 percent to 37 percent.
- Fourteen of the events we reviewed had an additional order processing fee, ranging from $1.00 to $8.20.
- Five of the events we reviewed had an additional facility fee, ranging from $2.00 to $5.10.

---

[26] Ticketing companies earn revenue from tickets they sell through their website, mobile application, call center, or physical outlets. However, they typically do not earn any fee revenue from season tickets or tickets sold through the venue box office, or through the artists' fan clubs when the fan club tickets are sold on a third-party ticketing company's platform.

[27] New York State Office of the Attorney General, 29, 41. The report collected fee information and ticket prices for 150 New York venues listed on three primary ticketing websites. For each venue, fee information was collected for up to three randomly selected events and, for each event, information was collected for every seating category (e.g., orchestra, balcony).

[28] A GAO investigator and a GAO analyst collected data between June 19, 2017, and January 16, 2018 on the ticket fees charged for online purchase by five primary ticketing companies. From one to three concert, theater, and sporting events were reviewed for each company, covering 12 events and 10 venues in total. Ticket fees were also reviewed for an additional 20 events sold by the largest ticketing company.

[29] These totals encompassed both fees that were charged as a percentage of face value (such as "service" fees) and fixed-dollar fees (such as "order processing" fees).

Table 3 shows the ticketing fees observed for events sold through three of the largest ticket companies we reviewed.

**Table 3. Observed Fees Charged by Three of the Largest Primary Ticketing Companies**

| Company | Service fee charged to buyer (as a percent of the face value) | Facility fee | Order processing fee |
|---|---|---|---|
| Ticket company A | 23–27% | None observed | $1.00 |
| Ticket company B | 19–27% | $2.00 | None observed |
| Ticket company C | 8–37% | $2.85–$5.10 | $3.92–$8.20 |

Source: GAO analysis of primary ticket sellers' websites. | GAO-18-347.

Notes: Not every ticket we observed had a facility fee or an order processing fee. In total, we observed 28 events from these three companies.

A sixth ticketing company that focuses on theater uses a different fee structure. It simply charges two flat service fees across all of its events ($7 for tickets below $50 and $11 for tickets above $50), plus a base per-order handling charge of $3. Additionally, we noted that the 6 sporting events we observed tended to have lower fees than the 16 concerts and 9 theater events we observed. Specifically, sporting events had total fees averaging roughly 20 percent, compared to about 30 percent for concerts and theater.

### *Secondary Market Fees*

Fees charged by secondary ticket exchanges we reviewed were higher than those charged by primary market ticket companies.[30] Secondary ticket exchanges often charge service and delivery fees to ticket buyers on top of the ticket's listed price. For 7 of the 11 secondary ticket exchanges we reviewed, the service fee was a set percentage of the ticket's list price. Three of the remaining exchanges charged fees that varied across events, and the fourth did not charge service fees. Among the 10 exchanges that charged fees:

- In total, the combined fees averaged 31 percent of the ticket's listed price, and we observed values ranging from 20 percent to 56 percent.
- Service fees, on average, were 22 percent of the ticket's listed price, and we observed values ranging from 15 percent to 29 percent.
- In addition to the service fee, 8 of the 10 exchanges charged a delivery fee for mobile or print-at-home tickets, ranging from $2.50 to $7.95.

---

[30] A GAO investigator and a GAO analyst gathered information on fees charged for seven events on the websites of 11 secondary market ticketing companies, which included nine ticket exchanges and two aggregators of ticket resale websites. For each website, from three to five events were reviewed, which included at least one concert, theater, and sporting event per site.

- Eight of the exchanges also charged a fee to the seller (in addition to the buyer), which was typically 10 percent of the ticket's sale price. (For example, if a ticket sells for $100, the seller would receive $90 and the exchange $10.)

Table 4 provides additional information about the fees charged by three of the largest ticket resale exchanges.

**Table 4. Fees Charged by Three of the Largest Ticket Resale Exchanges**

| Exchange | Service fee charged to buyer (as a percent of ticket price) | Delivery fee charged to buyer | Fee charged to seller (as a percent of ticket price) |
|---|---|---|---|
| Resale exchange A | 10–25% | Download: $2.50 or $7.95 Mail: $14.95 | 0–10% |
| Resale exchange B | 21–24% | None | 10% |
| Resale exchange C | 29–30% | Download: $7.95 Mail: $15.00 | 0–10% |

Source: GAO review of secondary ticket exchange websites. | GAO-18-347.

Note: We observed three events per resale exchange. For resale exchanges A and C, data were obtained both from our observations and from communication with company officials.

## Consumer Protection Concerns Include the Ability to Access Face-Value Tickets and the Fees and Clarity of Some Resale Websites

The technology and other resources of professional brokers give them a competitive advantage over individual consumers in purchasing tickets at their face-value price. Views vary on the extent to which the use of holds and presales also affect consumers. Many ticketing websites we reviewed did not clearly display their fees up front, and a subset of websites— referred to as white-label—used marketing practices that might confuse consumers. Other consumer protection concerns that have been raised involve the amount charged for ticketing fees, speculative and fraudulent tickets, and designated resale exchanges (resale platforms linked to the primary ticket seller).

### For Tickets to Popular Events, Consumers Often Must Pay More Than Face Value

Tickets to popular events often are not available to consumers at their face-value price, frequently because seats sell out in the primary market almost as soon as the venue puts them on sale.

### *Brokers' Competitive Advantage*

Brokers whose business is to purchase and resell tickets have a competitive advantage over individual consumers because they have the technology and resources to purchase large numbers of tickets as soon as they go on sale. Some consumer advocates, state officials, and event organizers believe that brokers unfairly use this advantage to obtain tickets from the primary market, which restricts ordinary consumers from buying tickets at face value. As a result, consumers may pay higher prices than they would if tickets were available on the primary market. In addition, some event organizers and primary ticket sellers have expressed frustration that the profits from the higher resale price accrue to brokers who have not played a role in creating or producing the event.

Some professional brokers use software programs known as bots to purchase large numbers of tickets very quickly. When tickets first go on sale, bots can complete multiple simultaneous searches of the primary ticket seller's website and reserve or purchase hundreds of tickets, according to the 2016 report by the New York State Office of the Attorney General.[31] Seats reserved by a bot—even if ultimately not purchased— appear online to a consumer as unavailable. This, in turn, can make inventory appear artificially low during the first minutes of the sale and lead consumers to the secondary market to seek available seats, according to event organizers we interviewed.[32] Bots can also automate the ticket-buying process, as well as identify when additional tickets are released and available for purchase. During its investigation of the ticketing industry, the New York State Office of the Attorney General identified an instance in which a bot bought more than 1,000 tickets to a single event in 1 minute.[33]

In addition, bots can be used to bypass security measures that are designed to enforce ticket purchase limits. For example, bots can use advanced character recognition to "read" the characters in a test designed to ensure that the buyer is human.[34] Although the BOTS Act of 2016 restricts the use of bots, as discussed later, it is not yet clear the extent to which the act has reduced their use.

---

[31] New York State Office of the Attorney General, 15. We did not identify comprehensive information on the prevalence of the use of bots in purchasing event tickets. Representatives from one primary ticketing company told us it believes bots accounted for 21 percent of online ticket inquiries (i.e., attempts to access the system and not necessarily actual purchases) for two high-demand shows over a 3 month period (which it identified based on certain characteristics associated with bot use). Other ticket sellers with whom we spoke said they believe bots are still widely used, especially for the most popular events. However, one said it did not have a reliable estimate on the use of bots, noting that they do not have any way of being certain whether or not a bot was used to purchase a ticket.

[32] Primary ticket sellers typically limit the amount of time buyers have to complete a purchase—for example, 10 minutes from selecting tickets to completing payment. During this time, the selected tickets are removed from the inventory and appear to other buyers to be unavailable.

[33] New York State Office of the Attorney General, 18.

[34] A common security measure is the Completely Automated Public Turing test to tell Computers and Humans Apart, commonly known as CAPTCHA, which asks users to prove they are human by identifying characters in distorted text or by selecting images that meet certain requirements ("Identify all photos with a car"). In some cases, bots are programmed to bypass this test. In other cases, the bot submits images of the tests to human workers who complete it, according to the report of the New York State Office of the Attorney General.

Brokers have other advantages over consumers in the ticket buying process, according to the New York State Attorney General's report and industry stakeholders we interviewed. For example, some brokers employ multiple staff, who purchase tickets as soon as an event goes on sale. In addition, brokers can bypass sellers' limits on the number of tickets allowed to be purchased by using multiple names, addresses, credit card numbers, or IP (Internet protocol) addresses.[35] Finally, to access tickets during a presale, some brokers join artists' fan clubs or hold multiple credit cards from the company sponsoring the presale.

### *Role of Holds and Presales*

Holds and presales may limit the number of tickets available to consumers at face value, according to some consumer groups, secondary market companies, and other parties. For example, the National Consumers League testified that events with many holds and presales sell out more quickly during the general on-sale because fewer seats are available.[36] Consumers may not be aware that many seats are no longer available by the time of the general on-sale. In addition, the National Consumers League and New York State Office of the Attorney General said they believe the use of holds and presales raise concerns about equity and fairness. They noted that most holds go to industry insiders who have a connection to the promoter or venue, while credit card presales are available only to cardholders, who typically are higher-income. The New York State Attorney General's office and seven event organizers with whom we spoke expressed concerns that presales benefit brokers, who take special measures to access tickets during presales.

However, other industry representatives told us that holds and presales do not adversely affect consumers. They noted that for most events, the number of tickets sold through presales is not very high and few tickets are held back. Additionally, two event organizers and representatives from a primary ticketing company noted that most presales are accessible to a broad range of consumers—such as tens of millions of cardholders. As a result, the distinction between what constitutes a presale and a general on-sale can be slim. Furthermore, some fan clubs may try to limit brokers' use of presales. For example, one manager said his artist's fan club gives priority for presales to long-time fan club members.

In addition, some industry representatives noted that holds and presales serve important functions that can benefit consumers. For example, credit card presales can reduce event prices by funding certain marketing costs, and fan club presales can offer better access to tickets to artists' most enthusiastic fans, according to event organizers

---

[35] Ticketing companies often limit the number of tickets a consumer can purchase during a single transaction. An Internet protocol (IP) address is a unique string of numbers that identifies each computer using the Internet to communicate over a network.

[36] Breyault, 2, 5. The National Consumers League is a nonprofit consumer advocacy organization.

with whom we spoke. And as noted earlier, holds serve various functions, such as providing flexibility for seating configuration.

## Some Ticketing Websites We Reviewed Were Not Fully Transparent about Ticket Fees and Relevant Disclosures

Among the largest primary and several secondary market ticketing companies, we identified instances in which fee information was not fully transparent. We reviewed the ticket purchasing process for a selection of primary and secondary ticketing companies' websites, including a subset of secondary market websites known as "white-label" websites. We reviewed the extent to which the companies' websites clearly and conspicuously presented their fees and other relevant information and also recorded the point at which fees were disclosed in the purchase process.[37] While FTC staff guidance states that there is no set formula for a clear and conspicuous disclosure, it states that among several key factors are whether the disclosure is legible, in clear wording, and proximate to the relevant information.[38] In recent reports, the National Economic Council (which advises the President on economic policy) and FTC staff have expressed concern about businesses that use "drip pricing," the practice of advertising only part of a product's price up front and revealing additional charges later as consumers go through the buying process.[39]

### *Primary Market Ticketing Companies*

For the 23 events we reviewed, the largest ticketing company—believed to have the majority of the U.S. market share—frequently did not display its fees prominently or early in the purchase process.[40]

- For 14 of 23 events we reviewed, fees could be learned only by (1) selecting a seat; (2) clicking through one or two additional screens; (3) creating a user name and password (or logging in); and (4) clicking an icon labeled "Order Details," which displayed the face-value price and the fees.

---

[37] We did not, however, conduct a legal compliance review for these disclosures and we do not offer an opinion as to whether any of our findings about selected websites would meet the relevant FTC standard for unfair or deceptive practices.

[38] Federal Trade Commission, *.com Disclosures: How to Make Effective Disclosures in Digital Advertising* (March 2013) (staff guidance).

[39] White House National Economic Council, *The Competition Initiative and Hidden Fees* (Washington, D.C.: December 2016); and Mary W. Sullivan, *Economic Analysis of Hotel Resort Fees* (Washington, D.C.: January 2017), Federal Trade Commission Bureau of Economics Staff Report.

[40] We reviewed the purchase process on the company's website for 23 events, which included events at 13 different venues of varying sizes, including arenas and theaters. We collected data between June 20, 2017, and January 16, 2018.

- For 5 of the 23 events, the customer did not have to log in to see the fees, but the fees were visible only by clicking the "Order Details" icon.
- For 4 of the 23 events, fees were displayed before log-in and without the need to take additional steps.
- Additionally, for 21 of the 23 events, ticket fees were displayed in a significantly smaller font size than the ticket price.

For the five other primary market ticketing companies whose ticketing process we reviewed, fees were displayed earlier in the purchase process and more conspicuously.[41] All five companies displayed fees before asking users to log in, including one that displayed fees during the initial seat selection process. Four of the five companies displayed fees in a font size similar to that of other price information and in locations on the page that were generally proximate to relevant information. However, for all companies we reviewed, fees and total ticket prices were not displayed during the process of browsing for different events.

We found that two primary ticket sellers that sometimes offer nontransferable tickets (that is, tickets whose terms and conditions prohibit transfer) had prominently and clearly disclosed the special terms of those tickets—for example, that the buyer's credit card had to be presented at the venue and the entire party had to enter at the same time.[42] One company's website displayed these conditions on a separate screen for 10 seconds before allowing the buyer to proceed. The other company's website similarly displayed information about the tickets' nontransferability on a separate page in clear language in a font size similar to the pricing information.

### *Secondary Ticket Exchanges*

We also reviewed disclosure of fees and other relevant information on the websites of 11 secondary ticket exchanges and resale aggregators.[43] Two of the 11 websites displayed their fees conspicuously and early in the purchase process, and a third site did not charge ticketing fees. However, we found that ticket resale exchanges sometimes lacked transparency about their fees:

- Fees often were revealed only near the end. Seven of the 11 websites disclosed ticket fees only near the end of the purchase process, after the consumer entered an e-mail or logged in. Three of those seven websites displayed fee information only after the credit card number or other payment information was submitted.

---

[41] For each of these five ticketing companies, a GAO investigator and a GAO analyst reviewed the purchase process for between one and three events. We believe these ticketing companies are among the largest in the U.S.

[42] According to industry stakeholders, nontransferable tickets are rarely used. Due to their rarity, we could only identify one event using nontransferable tickets from each of two ticket sellers at the time of our analysis.

[43] The 11 companies included 9 secondary ticket exchanges and 2 ticket resale aggregators, which aggregate listings from multiple exchanges. For each, we reviewed the purchase process for between three and five events.

- Fees sometimes were not conspicuously located. On 2 of the 11 websites, some fees were not displayed alongside the ticket price, but instead were only visible by clicking a specific button.
- Font sizes were small in two cases. On 2 of the 11 websites, fees were displayed in a font size significantly smaller than other text.

In contrast to primary market sellers, secondary market sellers' websites sometimes did not clearly disclose when a ticket was nontransferable.[44] Disclosures on secondary market ticket exchanges varied, in part because individual sellers are permitted to enter their own descriptions about ticket characteristics. In some cases, the seller identified nontransferable tickets only by labeling them "gc," indicating that a gift card would be mailed to the buyer to present for entry to the venue.[45]

To further review nontransferable ticket listings, we contacted the customer service representatives of three large secondary ticket exchanges to ask about a nontransferable ticket listing.[46] We asked if we would have difficulty using the ticket because the venue's or ticket seller's website stated that only the original buyer could use the ticket, with one website noting that picture identification might be required for entry. Customer service representatives of all three exchanges told us that despite the purported restrictions, we would be able to use the ticket to gain entry to the venue. To confirm these statements, we contacted officials of these venues, who acknowledged that picture identification had not been required for entry at these events.

Consumers may not always be aware they are purchasing tickets from a secondary market site at a marked-up price. In a 2010 enforcement action, FTC settled a complaint against Ticketmaster after alleging, among other things, that the company steered consumers to its resale site, TicketsNow, without clear disclosures that the consumer was being directed to a resale website. The settlement requires Ticketmaster, TicketsNow, and any other Ticketmaster resale websites to clearly and conspicuously disclose when a consumer is on a resale site and that prices may exceed face value, and to include "reseller price" or "resale price" with ticket listings. In addition, in January 2018, the National Advertising Division, a self-regulatory organization, asked FTC to investigate the fee disclosure practices of StubHub, a large secondary ticket exchange, alleging the

---

[44] According to some industry stakeholders, nontransferable tickets are sometimes resold, although the tickets' terms and conditions prohibit it.

[45] Because nontransferable tickets often require the buyer's credit card or other identification be presented at the venue, brokers will sometimes purchase tickets using a prepaid card that is mailed to the buyer.

[46] For two of the companies, a GAO investigator and a GAO analyst sent eight e-mails to each customer service department. For the third company, five "live chats" were conducted with customer service representatives. Each e-mail or live chat inquired about one of two events using nontransferable tickets. We did not identify ourselves as representing GAO during these contacts.

company did not clearly and conspicuously disclose its service fees when it provides ticket prices.[47]

### *White-Label Websites for Ticket Resale*

A subset of ticket resale websites, known as "white label," used marketing practices that might confuse consumers. A company providing white-label support allows affiliates to connect its software to their own, uniquely branded website.[48] This is sometimes also described as a "private label" service in the industry. For event ticketing, a ticket exchange offering white-label support provides the affiliate company with access to its ticket inventory and services, such as order processing and customer service. However, the affiliate uses its own URL (website address), sets the ticket prices and fees, and conducts its own marketing and advertising. Two secondary ticket exchanges operate white-label affiliate programs, under which affiliates create unique white-label websites for ticket resale.

While we did not identify data on the number of white-label websites for event ticketing, they commonly appear in the search results for all types of venues, including smaller venues like clubs and theaters. White-label websites often market themselves through paid advertising on Internet search engines, appearing at the top of search results for venues. Thus, they are often the first search results consumers see when searching for event tickets.[49] Figure 1 provides a hypothetical example of a white-label advertisement on a search engine, as well as the typical appearance of a white-label website.

In 2014, FTC and the State of Connecticut announced settlements with TicketNetwork—one of the exchanges operating a white-label program— and two of its affiliates after charges of deceptively marketing resale tickets.[50] The complaint alleged that these companies' advertisements and websites misled consumers into thinking they were buying tickets from the original venue at face value when they were actually purchasing resale tickets at prices often above face value. According to the complaint, the

---

[47] The National Advertising Division is an investigative unit of the Council of Better Business Bureaus' Advertising Self-Regulatory Council. According to an Advertising Self-Regulatory Council press release, StubHub declined to comply with the division's previous recommendations, stating that its fee disclosure practices were in line with industry practice and that consumers generally understand that fees will be added at the end of the purchase process. See Advertising Self-Regulatory Council, "NAD Refers StubHub Pricing Claims to FTC for Further Review After Advertiser Declines to Comply with NAD Decision on Disclosures" news release, January 16, 2018, http://www.asrcreviews.org/nad-refers-stubhub-pricing-claims-to-ftc-for-further-review-after-advertiser-declines-to-comply-with-nad-decision-on-disclosures/.

[48] White-label programs are used in many industries, not just event ticketing. For example, there are white-label software search engines for booking airlines and hotels.

[49] Two of the largest search engines offer advertising services that allow companies to appear in the search results related to selected products or services. Advertisers identify keywords relevant to their products and when users search for those keywords, their advertisements will appear on top of or next to the relevant search results. These advertised search results are usually identified in some manner to separate them from other search results. Use of paid search results for event ticketing is not limited to white-label websites and is a common marketing practice of many primary and secondary market ticket sellers.

[50] *See* Federal Trade Commission v. TicketNetwork, Inc., No. 3:14-cv-1046 (D. Conn. Aug. 12, 2014); Federal Trade Commission v. SecureBoxOffice, LLC, No. 3:14-cv-1046 (D. Conn. Aug. 12, 2014); Federal Trade Commission v. Ryadd, Inc., No. 3:14-cv-1046 (D. Conn. Aug. 12, 2014).

affiliate websites frequently used URLs that included the venue's name and displayed the venue's name prominently on their websites in ways that could lead consumers to believe they were on the venue's website. The settlements prohibited the company and its affiliates from misrepresenting that they are a venue website or that they are offering face-value tickets, and from using the word "official" on the websites, advertisements, and URLs unless the word is part of the event, performer, or venue name. They also required that the websites disclose that they are resale marketplaces, that ticket prices may exceed the ticket's face value, and that the website is not owned by the venue or other event organizers.

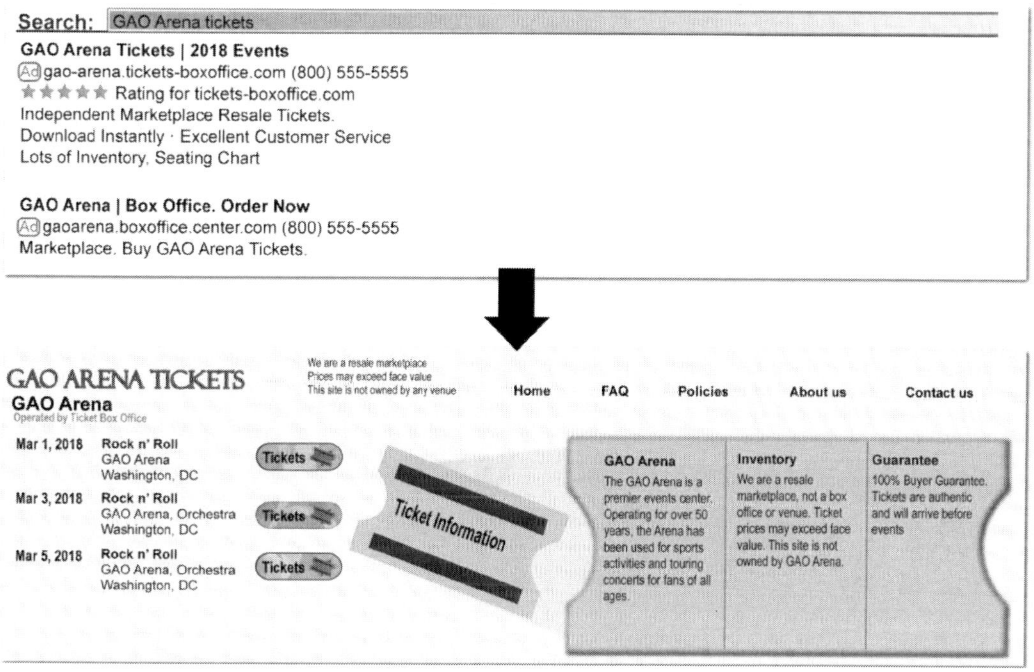


Source: GAO. | GAO-18-347.

Note: "GAO Arena" is a fictitious venue used for illustrative purposes.

Figure 1. Hypothetical Example of White-Label Search Results and Website.

FTC staff with whom we spoke told us that they were aware that similar practices have continued among other white-label companies. Staff told us they have continued to monitor white-label websites and related consumer complaints. Additionally, a wide range of stakeholders with whom we spoke—including government officials, event organizers, and other secondary ticket sellers—expressed concerns about these websites. In particular, they were concerned that consumers confused white-label websites for the venue's website.

We reviewed 17 websites belonging to eight companies that were affiliates of the two secondary ticket exchanges offering white-label programs.[51] We identified the sites by conducting online searches for nine venues (including stadiums, clubs, and theaters) on two of the largest search engines. All nine of the venues had at least one white-label site appear in the paid advertising above the search results. We observed the following:

- Sites could be confused with that of the official venue. Fourteen of the 17 white-label websites we reviewed used the venue's name in the search engine's display URL, in a manner that could lead a consumer to believe it was the venue's official website. In addition, 5 of the 17 webpages used photographs of the venue and 11 provided descriptions of the venue (such as its history) that could imply an association with the venue.
- Fees were higher than on other resale sites. Total ticketing fees (such as "service charges") for the white-label sites ranged from 32 percent to 46 percent of the ticket's list price, with an average of 38 percent. These fees were generally higher than those of other ticket resellers—for example, the secondary ticket exchanges that we reviewed charged average fees of 31 percent.
- Fees were revealed only near the end. All 17 of the white-label sites we reviewed disclosed their fees late in the purchase process. Ticketing fees and total prices were provided only after the consumer had entered either an e-mail address or credit card information.
- Other key disclosures were present but varied in their conspicuousness. All 17 of the white label webpages we reviewed disclosed on their landing page and check-out page that they were not associated with the venue and were resale sites whose prices may be above face value. However, this information was presented in a small font or in an inconspicuous location (not near the top of the page) for the landing page of 7 of these webpages, as well as for the check-out page of 12 of the 17 webpages.
- Ticket prices were higher than other resale sites. The ticket price charged for the events we reviewed on the white-label sites had an average markup of about 180 percent over the primary market price.[52] By comparison, other ticket resale websites we reviewed had an average markup of 74 percent.

---

[51] Companies that use white-label ticketing sites typically have multiple websites displaying different URLs in online search results. We reviewed the purchase process for between one and four events per site. For each event, we recorded the prices and fees charged, and how and when the site disclosed its fees and that it was a resale site.

[52] The primary market price includes the face value and any additional fees, which we obtained from the primary ticket sellers' websites. We compared the primary market price to the total price on the white-label site (including fees).

In some cases, we observed white-label websites selling event tickets when comparable tickets were still available from the primary seller at a lower price. For example, two white-label sites were offering tickets to an event for $90 and $111, respectively, whereas the venue's official ticketing website was offering comparable seats for $34. (All figures include applicable fees). Given the significantly higher cost for the same product, some consumers may be purchasing tickets from a white-label site only because they mistakenly believe it to be the official venue's site. As we discuss in greater detail later in this chapter, in February 2018, Google implemented requirements for resellers using its AdWords service that are intended, among other things, to prevent consumer confusion related to white-label sites.

## Other Consumer Protection Issues Have Been Identified

Ticket fees, the use of speculative tickets, ticket fraud, and designated resale exchanges have raised consumer protection concerns among government agencies, industry stakeholders, and consumer advocates.

### *Amount Charged for Ticket Fees*

Consumer protection advocates, event organizers, and some government entities have expressed concerns about high ticket fees.[53] For example, the New York State Attorney General's report expressed concern about what it deemed high ticketing fees charged for unclear purposes. The report found that among online platforms, vendors of event tickets appeared to charge fees to consumers higher than most other online vendors.[54] Concerns about high ticket fees also were frequently cited in 2009 congressional hearings on the proposed merger of Live Nation and Ticketmaster.[55] In addition, some managers and agents we interviewed said their clients were dissatisfied with high ticket fees. Data we received from FTC's Consumer Sentinel Network indicated 67 complaints related specifically to event ticket fees from 2014 through 2016.[56]

---

[53] As previously noted, we found that the primary and secondary markets had average fees of 27 percent and 31 percent, respectively, of face value or listed price.

[54] New York State Office of the Attorney General, 31.

[55] *Hearing on Competition in the Ticketing and Promotion Industry, Judiciary Committee of the United States House of Representatives, Subcommittee on Courts and Competition Policy,* 111th Cong. 1 (Feb. 26, 2009) and *The Ticketmaster/Live Nation Merger: What Does It Mean for Consumers and the Future of the Concert Business?*, Committee on the Judiciary of the United States Senate, Subcommittee on Antitrust, Competition Policy and Consumer Rights of the Committee, 111th Cong. 1 (Feb. 24, 2009). (For example, see testimony of Edmund Mierzwinski, Consumer Program Director, U.S. Public Interest Research Group).

[56] FTC's Consumer Sentinel Network is a database of consumer complaints received by FTC, as well as those filed with certain other federal and state agencies and nongovernmental organizations, including the Consumer Financial Protection Bureau and the Better Business Bureaus. For our review, we asked FTC staff to search the database from 2014 through 2016 using the terms "ticket," types of events (e.g., concert, sport, theater, game, show), and "fee" or "charge." We asked FTC to limit the search to complaints received against 6 primary ticketing companies and 11 secondary ticket resale exchanges or aggregators.

A 2010 analysis by the Department of Justice said that the dominance of one company, Ticketmaster, in the primary ticketing market allowed the company to maintain high ticket fees.[57] The report noted high barriers to entry for competitors, among which were high startup costs, Ticketmaster's reputation for providing quality service to venues, and long-term exclusive contracts that large venues typically sign with one ticketing company. In addition, with the merger, Live Nation Entertainment owns both the largest primary ticket seller (Ticketmaster) and largest promoter (Live Nation), and owns many large venues and an artist management company. When the ticketing company is owned by a major promoter, the combined firm's ability to bundle ticketing services and access to artists would require competitors to offer similar services in order to compete effectively, according to the Department of Justice analysis. In an attempt to mitigate these potential effects, the Department of Justice final judgment on the merger prohibited certain forms of retaliation against venues that contract with other ticketing companies. In the United Kingdom, where the venue and promoter typically contract with multiple ticket sellers, ticket fees are lower than in the United States— around 10 percent to 15 percent of the ticket's face value, according to a recent study.[58]

Industry experts generally consider the secondary market for event ticketing to be more competitive than the primary market because of the large number of brokers participating in the industry.[59] According to a report by the National Economic Council, fees in this market may be higher than expected because of the lack of transparency described earlier—consumers may be more willing to accept high fees and less likely to comparison shop when fees are disclosed at the end of a multistep purchase process. An FTC staff report made a similar point regarding hotel resort fees, noting that fees disclosed only at the end of the shopping process could harm consumers by making it more difficult to comparison shop for hotels.[60] In addition, consumers who are led to believe that white-label ticketing sites are the official venue site may accept high fees because they think they are buying tickets from the primary ticketing provider, according to two industry representatives with whom we spoke.

The level of fees in the secondary market might also be affected by partnerships between the primary and secondary ticket seller. Primary ticketing companies sometimes offer resale options or use of designated resale exchanges (discussed below). The American Antitrust Institute has expressed the view that these relationships can reduce

---

[57] Competitive Impact Statement, United States of America v. Ticketmaster Entertainment, Inc., No. 1:10-cv-00139 (D. D.C. Jan. 25, 2010).

[58] Michael Waterson, *Independent Review of Consumer Protection Measures Concerning Online Secondary Ticketing Facilities*, a report prepared at the request of the United Kingdom Department for Business, Innovation and Skills and Department for Culture, Media and Sport (London: May 2016), 30-31.

[59] For example, see Daniel A. Rascher and Andrew D. Schwarz, "The Antitrust Implications of 'Paperless Ticketing' on Secondary Markets," *Journal of Competition Law and Economics* 9, no. 3 (May 2013), 659.

[60] Sullivan, 27.

inventory for rival secondary sellers and in turn, can result in higher fees, as the primary ticket seller essentially has a monopoly over both markets.[61]

### *Speculative Tickets*

A speculative ticket refers to a ticket put up for sale by a broker when the broker does not yet have the ticket in hand, perhaps because the event has not yet gone on sale. Brokers may sell speculative tickets because they anticipate they will be able to secure the tickets (whether on the primary or secondary market) and sell them for a profit. The terms of use of most secondary sites we reviewed did not allow speculative ticket listings. However, while we were unable to identify comprehensive data on the extent of speculative tickets, numerous industry representatives told us that these sites commonly do not enforce this prohibition and listing of speculative tickets was widespread. One common form of speculative ticketing occurs when brokers offer tickets after a popular artist has announced a concert schedule but not yet begun ticket sales, according to industry representatives.

Several concerns exist around the use of speculative ticketing:

- The buyer may never get the ticket. Speculative ticket listings can result in canceled orders if the broker cannot obtain the ticket, or cannot obtain it at a price that would result in a profit. For example, it was reported that many fans who thought they purchased tickets to the 2015 Super Bowl actually purchased speculative tickets that were subsequently canceled when the supply of tickets was less than expected.[62] According to industry stakeholders, consumers can typically obtain a refund on a canceled order from the broker or secondary ticket exchange, but may still face disappointment, inconvenience, or costs associated with nonrefundable travel to the planned event.
- The seat location is not guaranteed. Brokers selling speculative tickets typically do not specify the seat number but rather promise a certain section of the venue, according to two event organizers we interviewed. However, because the broker does not have the ticket in hand, consumers can receive seats that are worse or different than advertised.

---

[61] James D. Hurwitz, *Restrictive Paperless Tickets: A White Paper by the American Antitrust Institute* (Washington, D.C.: 2012), 36-37, 41-42. The American Antitrust Institute is an independent, nonprofit organization dedicated to promoting competition through its research, education, and advocacy.

[62] For example, see Geoff Baker, "Super Bowl dream becomes nightmare for Seahawks fans after shortage of tickets," *Seattle Times*, January 31, 2015, accessed on February 8, 2018. https://www.seattletimes.com/sports/seahawks/super-bowl-dream-becomesnightmare-for-seahawks-fans-after-shortage-of-tickets/.

- Speculative ticketing can cause consumer confusion. One large ticket resale exchange told us it only allows trusted brokers to sell speculative tickets under certain circumstances and requires sellers to use a special label for these listings. However, we observed other exchanges that are less transparent and do not make clear to the buyer that the ticket is speculative. Consumers may not be aware that tickets have not officially gone on sale yet and eventually may be available on the primary market at a lower price.

In its 2010 enforcement action against Ticketmaster and its resale exchange, TicketsNow.com, FTC alleged that the companies failed to tell buyers that many of the resale tickets advertised were being sold speculatively.[63] The settlement required Ticketmaster and its affiliates to disclose if a ticket was being sold speculatively and to otherwise refrain from misrepresenting the status of tickets. FTC staff also sent warning letters to other resale companies that may have been at risk of violating the FTC Act with regard to their speculative ticketing practices. More recently, in 2015 a request by the New York State Attorney General resulted in three major ticket exchanges removing speculative ticket listings for an upcoming tour. Representatives from one of the secondary ticket exchanges told us that while it is difficult to determine if a listing is truly speculative, they have removed listings when they have information from event organizers to indicate that no one could have obtained the tickets.

Posing as a consumer, a GAO investigator made 11 inquiries to customer service representatives of two of the largest secondary ticket exchanges about two events listing tickets that appeared to be speculative.[64] The customer service representatives generally acknowledged that the sellers did not yet have the tickets in hand but assured the investigator that the tickets would be provided.

### *Fraudulent Tickets*

Event tickets are sometimes fraudulent—for example, a fraudster may create and sell a counterfeit ticket or multiple copies of the same print-at-home ticket, according to industry representatives. We did not identify comprehensive data on the extent of ticket fraud. Event organizers with whom we spoke said that they typically only see a handful of fraudulent tickets at popular events, and do not consider fraudulent ticketing to be a widespread problem. A limited search of FTC's Consumer Sentinel Network data identified relatively few complaints—an estimated 19 related to fraudulent tickets from

---

[63] Complaint at 8-9, Federal Trade Commission v. Ticketmaster L.L.C., No. 1:10-cv-01093 (D. Ill. Feb. 18, 2010).

[64] We identified ticket listings that appeared to be speculative by searching for events that had been announced but for which tickets had not yet been released through a general on-sale or presale. Acting in an undercover capacity, the investigator contacted one company's customer service through eight e-mail inquiries (each sent from a different email address) and the other company through three separate "live chats."

2014 through 2016.[65] Industry representatives told us fraudulent tickets are most common for the most popular events and were often purchased on the street outside the venue or through an online classified advertisement.

According to industry representatives, fraudulent ticketing is rare on secondary market exchanges, in part because the exchanges can take action against sellers of fraudulent tickets, such as fining them or banning them from future sales. The National Association of Ticket Brokers requires its members to have a policy to reimburse consumers for fraudulent tickets.[66] Two secondary market participants told us the most common fraudulent activity they must address is credit card fraud by buyers rather than invalid tickets posted by sellers.

### *Designated Resale Exchanges*

Designated resale exchanges are resale platforms that are linked to the primary ticket seller. They are most commonly used in major league sports. The four major sports leagues have agreements with one of two ticketing companies that allow consumers to buy and sell tickets through an official "fan-to-fan" resale marketplace. In addition, some individual teams and venues have an agreement with a third company to use its resale platform, which uses paperless tickets and can facilitate ticket transfers from one consumer to another or restrict transfers altogether (such as with nontransferable tickets).

On these exchanges, when a consumer lists a ticket for resale, the exchange electronically confirms the seller's identity, then cancels the original ticket information (such as a barcode) and reissues the ticket with the new buyer's name.[67] According to the three sports leagues we interviewed, designated resale exchanges are generally optional—for example, the sports leagues allow brokers and consumers to use other secondary market exchanges as well.

A representative of one of the major sports leagues told us the exchanges provide added revenue to teams because the teams receive some of the fee revenues from sales on the exchanges. The exchanges provide data on event attendees, which is valuable for marketing and security purposes, according to another sports league and a primary ticket seller. In addition, the exchanges can reduce resale fraud because the primary seller verifies the legitimacy of the ticket being resold, according to representatives of the three leagues we interviewed.

---

[65] Our estimate of the number of complaints from 2014 through 2016 related to ticket fraud was derived by having FTC staff search the Consumer Sentinel Network for complaints including the term "ticket" and at least one term signifying fraud (e.g., "fake," "invalid"). The search included only complaints against six primary ticketing companies and 11 secondary ticket resale exchanges or aggregators that we identified.

[66] The National Association of Ticket Brokers is a trade association that represents ticket sellers in the secondary market and is comprised of over 200 broker members.

[67] League officials we interviewed explained that although they have league-wide resale partnerships with certain companies, individual teams or clubs sometimes have their own partnerships with other companies.

However, some academics and secondary market participants we interviewed have argued that designated resale exchanges work to the detriment of consumers. For example, one academic study stated that a primary ticket seller's dominance in the secondary market can substantially reduce inventory for rival secondary sellers, thus impeding competition in the resale market.[68] The study stated that reduced secondary market competition, in turn, can result in higher fees.

In 2015, a U.S. district court dismissed StubHub's antitrust complaint against the Golden State Warriors basketball team and Ticketmaster, LLC. StubHub claimed that the Warriors' and Ticketmaster's exclusive resale agreement restricted secondary market competition for professional basketball tickets in the Bay Area, but the court disagreed.[69]

Some designated resale exchanges use price floors, below which consumers may not sell their tickets. One sports league's exchange has a price floor of $6, while the exchanges of two other sports leagues do not have league-wide price floors, according to league representatives. In addition, we identified instances of individual teams using price floors on their designated resale exchanges.[70] One purpose of price floors is to protect brand reputation, according to league representatives, because too low a ticket price can lessen an event's perceived value. Price floors also can prevent the secondary market from undercutting a team's own (primary market) price. However, some consumer organizations and secondary ticket sellers said price floors were unfriendly to consumers. Season ticket holders might be unable to sell tickets for low-demand games for which market prices were lower than the floors. In addition, the New York State Attorney General's office noted that consumers might not always be aware that price floors were in effect and thus pay more than they would on another exchange.[71]

## EFFECTS OF TICKET RESALE RESTRICTIONS AND DISCLOSURES ON CONSUMERS AND BUSINESS WOULD VARY

Policymakers, consumer organizations, and industry participants have proposed or implemented a number of ticket resale restrictions and disclosure requirements, each of which have or would have advantages and disadvantages for consumers or industry participants (see Table 5). Event ticketing is not federally regulated and some industry participants are using or exploring technology and other market-based approaches to address concerns related to secondary market activity.

---

[68] Rascher and Schwarz, 693.

[69] Order Granting Defendants Motion to Dismiss, *StubHub, Inc. v. Golden State Warriors, LLC*, No. C 15-1436 MMC, 2015 U.S. Dist. LEXIS 151188, at *4 (N.D. Cal. Nov. 5, 2015).

[70] For example, we identified one basketball team with a $20 price floor for tickets sold on its designated resale exchange, and a baseball team's deal with a major ticket resale exchange that set a price floor of 50 percent of the ticket's original season ticket price.

[71] New York State Office of the Attorney General, 32.

**Table 5. Potential Advantages and Disadvantages of Selected Legislative or Regulatory Actions Related to Ticket Resale**

| Action | Description | Key advantages | Key disadvantages |
|---|---|---|---|
| Prohibiting nontransferable tickets | Prohibiting tickets that do not allow transfer from one person to another and therefore restrict resale | Ensures ticketholders can recoup costs on tickets they cannot use<br>Efficient allocation because tickets go to those willing to pay the most | Reduced opportunity for consumers to access tickets at lower face-value price |
| Price caps | Capping the price at which tickets can be resold (i.e., limits the markup) | Keeps prices down for consumers by restricting markups<br>Still preserves consumers' ability to resell and recoup costs | Challenging to enforce<br>Could send resale activity underground, where there are fewer protections<br>Inefficient allocation because tickets do not go to those willing to pay the most |
| Requiring up-front disclosure of ticket fees or requiring all-in pricing | Legislative or regulatory requirement to provide up-front disclosure of fees during ticketing process or to wrap fees into the listed price | Increased transparency that allows better consumer decision making and facilitates comparison shopping | Would restrict companies' flexibility in choosing how to disclose fees<br>Compliance challenges |
| Requiring disclosure of ticket's face value on resale sites | Legislative or regulatory requirement that resellers show a ticket's face value alongside the list price | Makes the markup transparent and helps ensure consumers know they are buying from a resale site<br>Can help consumers assess quality of seat | Could impose challenges for businesses in identifying face value<br>Challenging to enforce |
| Requiring disclosure of ticket availability | Legislative or regulatory requirement that venue or event organizers disclose how many tickets are available when event goes on sale | Transparency for consumers on how many tickets are actually available for sale | Unclear how useful this information is for consumers<br>Compliance challenges<br>May require businesses to disclose proprietary information |

Source: GAO | GAO-18-347.

Note: None of these requirements are in effect at the federal level, but some have been implemented or considered at the state level, as described elsewhere in this chapter.

## Nontransferable Tickets Can Reduce the Price Some Consumers Pay but Also Limit Flexibility

Some event organizers make tickets to their events nontransferable—that is, the terms and conditions of the ticket prohibit its transfer from one person (in whose name the ticket is issued) to another. The prohibition can be enforced by requiring consumers to bring to the venue the credit or debit card used for purchase and matching photo identification. The consumer then receives a seat locator slip—akin to a consumer swiping a credit card at the airport to retrieve a boarding pass.

At least three states—Connecticut, New York, and Virginia—have laws that restrict ticket issuers' ability to sell nontransferable tickets.[72] Similar legislation has been introduced in several other states in recent years.[73]

The use of nontransferable tickets, even in states where they are legal, is relatively uncommon. For example, an artist advocacy group told us that some events that use them make only the first several rows of seats nontransferable. One large primary ticketing company told us it estimated that less than 5 percent of its events used nontransferable tickets, while another told us nontransferable tickets represented less than 1 percent of its tickets in total. Almost all nontransferable tickets are for concerts; the practice is rare for sporting events and theater, according to industry stakeholders with whom we spoke.

### *Advantages of Nontransferable Tickets*

Advantages to consumers of nontransferable tickets stem from the goal of preventing ticket resale—allowing consumers to pay face value rather than a higher price on the secondary market. As described earlier, markups on the secondary market can be substantial. Proponents of nontransferable tickets, which include a large primary ticket seller and some event organizers and well-known artists, have argued they are an important tool that makes it harder for brokers to resell tickets for profit.

We identified one empirical study on the effects of nontransferable tickets on resale activity. A 2013 study in the *Journal of Competition Law and Economics* compared two events using nontransferable tickets to comparable events using transferable tickets at the same venues. It found that nontransferable tickets significantly reduced resale and that prices were significantly higher for the relatively small portion of nontransferable tickets that were resold.[74]

In addition, there is anecdotal evidence that nontransferable tickets reduce the rate of resale and allow more consumers to access tickets at face-value prices. Many stakeholders told us that making tickets nontransferable reduces secondary market activity, with some stakeholders citing specific examples.[75] For instance, the manager of a large concert venue that primarily uses nontransferable tickets told us that resale is much less common for the venue's events than for comparable events at similar venues. Similarly, the manager of a major musical artist told us that using nontransferable tickets for a subset of seats on a recent arena tour resulted in minimal listings for those seats on

---

[72] See N.Y. ARTS & CULT. AFF. LAW § 25.30(1)(c) (Consol. 2018); 2017 CONN. ACTS 17-28 (Reg. Sess.); VA. CODE ANN. § 59.1-466.5 - 59.1-466.7 (2017). New York's law has been in place since 2010, while Connecticut's and Virginia's laws were passed in 2017.

[73] For example, legislation was introduced in Alabama, Maryland, and Missouri that would restrict nontransferable tickets.

[74] Rascher and Schwarz, 655-708. In this study, a theoretical model was developed and an empirical analysis was performed to demonstrate the potential impact of "paperless ticketing," a form of nontransferable tickets, on the quantity and price of resale tickets relative to conventional ticketing.

[75] Industry stakeholders expressing this view included two primary ticket sellers; two booking agents; two venue managers; Broadway representatives; an artists' advocate group; a manager; a promoter; a secondary ticket seller; and the New York State Office of the Attorney General.

the secondary market. The New York State Attorney General's report stated that nontransferable paperless tickets "appear to be one of the few measures to have any clear effect in reducing the excessive prices charged on the secondary markets and increasing the odds of fans buying tickets at face value."[76] But, while we identified evidence that nontransferable tickets limit resale, they may not eliminate resale because sellers may not follow the restriction.

### *Disadvantages of Nontransferable Tickets*

However, other parties—including primary and secondary market participants, consumer advocacy groups, academics, and government agencies—have noted that nontransferable tickets can have the following disadvantages to consumers and adverse effects on markets:

#### Financial Loss

With nontransferable tickets, ticket buyers who cannot attend an event can lose the ability to recoup their money through resale.

#### Inconvenience

Nontransferable tickets can be inconvenient because the buyer may need to present identification, a debit or credit card, or both, to gain entry to the venue, which can create delays. Nontransferable tickets also can create challenges for consumers buying tickets for others (including as a gift) because the ticket terms may require the buyer and original purchase card be present to gain entry. However, a primary ticket seller and a promoter told us these obstacles can be overcome—for example, through mechanisms allowing buyers to transfer tickets upon request, and by using processes to speed venue entry (such as automated kiosks).

#### Economic Inefficiency

When nontransferable tickets are priced below the prevailing market price in the primary market, this creates excess demand, and tickets are sold without regard to consumers' willingness to pay.[77] Traditional economics maintains that an efficient market would result in tickets going to those willing to pay the highest price, which nontransferability inhibits by restricting a secondary market.[78] In addition, some academics have noted that consumers may be less willing to buy nontransferable tickets because they do not offer the "insurance" that comes with the ability to resell them.[79]

---

[76] New York State Office of the Attorney General, 36. The report recommended repealing the state's prohibition on nontransferable tickets.

[77] Rascher and Schwarz, 682.

[78] Hurwitz, 43; Rascher and Schwarz, 667.

[79] See, for example, Pascal Courty, *Pricing Challenges in the Live Events Industry: A Tale of Two Industries* (January 2015), 7; Hurwitz, 38; and Rascher and Schwarz, 667. Staff we interviewed from the Department of

### Potential Impingement on Property Rights

Some consumer groups and secondary market participants have argued that nontransferable ticket policies impinge on consumers' property rights. These parties argue that once consumers buy a ticket, they should be able to do whatever they like with it.[80]

### Effect on Competition

The New York State Attorney General's office and some economics literature have cautioned that use of nontransferable tickets by primary ticketing companies can impede competition in the secondary market by making these companies' own resale exchanges the only way to transfer tickets.[81]

## Caps on Resale Prices Can Have Advantages and Disadvantages

Several states have caps on the price at which tickets can be resold, while others have repealed caps and some studies have questioned their enforceability. For example, Kentucky generally prohibits the resale of event tickets for more than either face value or the amount charged by the venue, and Massachusetts prohibits resale by brokers of most tickets for more than $2 above face value, with the exception of relevant service charges.[82] New Jersey allows a maximum markup of 20 percent or $3 (whichever is greater) for nonbrokers and a maximum markup of 50 percent for registered brokers, but does not limit resale prices for nonbrokers for sales over the Internet.[83] A number of other states— including Minnesota, Missouri, New York, and Connecticut—repealed their price cap laws in the 2000s. However, the New York State Attorney General's 2016 report recommended bringing back a price cap, through a "reasonable limit" on resale markups.[84]

Price caps are generally intended to protect consumers from high markups and increase the fairness of ticket distribution so that the wealthiest consumers do not have disproportionate access to tickets. In theory, price caps offer consumers the advantages of nontransferable tickets without the disadvantages: they limit high secondary-market

---

Justice's Antitrust Division also mentioned that the inability to resell nontransferable tickets could be a deterrent for potential buyers.

[80] Some courts have treated tickets as revocable licenses. For example, in a 2014 civil case regarding a National Football League (NFL) team's ticket sales practices, the U.S. District Court of the Western District of Washington stated that tickets to an NFL game are not tangible goods, but instead revocable licenses. *See e.g.*, Williams v. NFL, No. C14- 1089 MJP, 2014 U.S. Dist. LEXIS 155488, at *9 (D. Wash. Oct. 31, 2014); James T. Reese and Mark A. Dodds, "Let's Hear It for the Home Team: *Williams v. National Football League* Upholds Geographic Ticket Sales Ban," *Sport Marketing Quarterly*, vol. 24, no. 2 (2015).

[81] New York State Office of the Attorney General, 37; Hurwitz, 36-37; Rascher and Schwarz, 693-694.

[82] See KY. REV. STAT. ANN. § 518.070 (LexisNexis 2017); MASS. GEN. LAWS ch. 140, § 185D (2017).

[83] N.J. STAT. § 56:8-33 (2017).

[84] New York State Office of the Attorney General, 37.

prices but still allow consumers to transfer tickets to others or resell tickets they cannot use.

However, three government studies we reviewed stated that price caps are difficult to enforce and are rarely complied with. A 1999 report by the New York Attorney General noted that ticket resellers "almost universally disregarded" a cap in place at the time.[85] Representatives from the office told us enforcement of such a cap might be easier now because the secondary market is largely on the Internet, which offers greater price transparency. A 2016 study of the United Kingdom's ticket market noted that enforcement of a price cap was complicated by the fact that ticket resellers were not a well-defined group and sales could occur on various platforms and across jurisdictions.[86] Similarly, the New York State Department of State noted in 2010 that enforcement of price caps can be challenging.[87]

In addition, critics of price caps have said that caps might force resale activity underground, which would reduce transparency and protections (such as refund guarantees) that legitimate secondary market exchanges provide. Both the largest ticket exchange and the largest primary market ticket company have opposed price caps, with the ticket exchange arguing that they would result in street-corner transactions, where the risk of counterfeit and fraud would be significant.[88] On formal exchanges, transactions can be monitored and regulated. As with nontransferable tickets, price caps also can create economic inefficiencies because tickets are not necessarily allocated to those willing to pay the highest price.[89]

A 2010 study by the New York State Department of State compared publicly available secondary market listings for high-demand concerts in New York to the same artists' concerts in nearby states with price caps. It found no definitive evidence that price caps resulted in greater or lesser availability on the secondary market or in lower resale prices.[90] The study noted that online resale prices routinely exceeded the price caps. However, the authors of the study acknowledged that their findings were limited by their inability to obtain data on ticket sales and availability from secondary sellers.

---

[85] New York State Office of the Attorney General, *Why Can't I Get Tickets?: Report on Ticket Distribution Practices* May 1999, 21. New York repealed its price cap in 2007.

[86] Michael Waterson, *Independent Review of Consumer Protection Measures Concerning Online Secondary Ticketing Facilities*, a report prepared at the request of the United Kingdom Department for Business, Innovation and Skills and Department for Culture, Media and Sport (London: May 2016), 22-23, 150-151.

[87] New York State Department of State, *Report on Ticket Reselling and Article 25 of the Arts and Cultural Affairs Law* (Albany, N.Y.: Feb. 1, 2010), 33.

[88] StubHub, "StubHub Open Letter to Fans Following Passage of the Ontario Ticket Sales Act," December 13, 2017, accessed December 14, 2017, https://www.newswire.ca/news-releases/stubhub-open-letter-to-fans-following-passage-ofthe-ontario-ticket-sales-act-663928593.html.

[89] See, for example, Hurwitz, 35.

[90] New York State Department of State, 26.

## Stakeholder Views Vary on Effects of Additional Disclosure Requirements

Legislative or regulatory actions to improve disclosure and transparency of ticket fees, resale markups, and ticket availability have advantages and disadvantages.

### *Up-Front Fee Disclosure*

Some government stakeholders have suggested improving fee transparency through a legal requirement to disclose ticket fees earlier in the purchase process. As discussed earlier, ticketing companies in the primary and secondary markets vary on when and how they disclose their fees, and some disclose fees only upon checkout. No federal law expressly addresses fee disclosure in event ticketing. However, at least one state requires disclosure of fees at the beginning of the purchase process.[91]

On the primary market, up-front fee disclosure helps decision making by informing consumers of the total ticket price early in the process. It also helps consumers decide whether to buy from the ticketer's website or at the box office, where there typically are no fees. On the secondary market, up-front fee disclosure aids comparison shopping by helping consumers identify the resale exchange with the best total price. Sellers that do not provide enough or full information on prices through hidden fees could have competitive advantage because they would be perceived as offering lower prices over their competitors who do provide full information showing the price. For products and services in general, FTC staff guidance advocates that fees be disclosed up front, particularly before the point at which the consumer has decided to make a purchase.[92]

Figure 2 provides examples of different approaches to displaying prices and fees.

Currently, FTC relies on the Federal Trade Commission Act—which prohibits unfair or deceptive acts or practices—to address problems related to fee disclosures. But FTC staff said it is challenging and resource-intensive to use the act to address inadequate fee disclosures industry-wide because it requires proving violations on a case-by-case basis.[93] FTC staff told us that, depending on the circumstances, a legislative disclosure requirement that specified requirements for fees could facilitate enforcement activity and create a more level playing field for consumers and sellers. Eleven industry stakeholders and three consumer advocacy groups with whom we spoke similarly expressed support

---

[91] Connecticut requires any advertisement for an in-state event to include the total price and the portion of that price (in dollars) that represents a service charge. CONN. GEN. STAT. § 53-289a (2017).

[92] For example, see Federal Trade Commission, *.com Disclosures: How to Make Effective Disclosures in Digital Advertising*, March 2013, 14. Similarly, Canada's Competition Bureau, an independent Canadian law enforcement agency, has stated that not disclosing fees up front can be misleading to consumers because the advertised price is not attainable. See Competition Bureau Canada, "Calling All Ticket Vendors: Be Upfront about the True Cost of Tickets," July 4, 2017, accessed March 12, 2018, https://www.canada.ca/en/competition-bureau/news/2017/06/calling_all_ticketvendorsbeupfrontaboutthe truecostoftickets.html.

[93] Industry stakeholders expressing this view included two managers, one agent, one promoter, two artist advocacy groups, four secondary market ticket exchanges, and the National Association of Ticket Brokers.

for a requirement that ticketing fees be disclosed up front. Many noted that fees should be fully transparent to consumers.

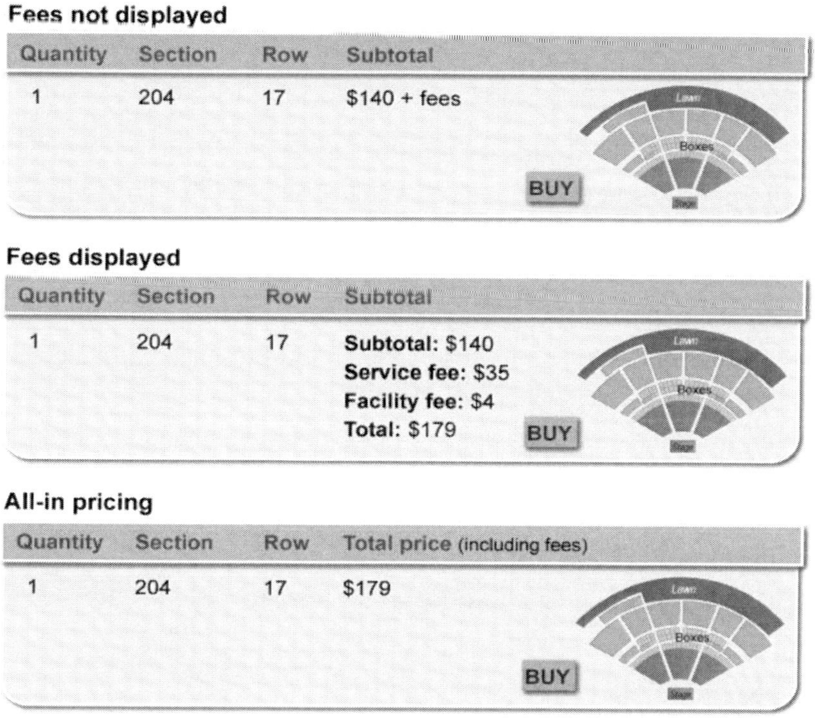


Source: GAO. | GAO-18-347.

Note: These examples are illustrative and are not based on actual tickets or events.

Figure 2. Hypothetical Examples of How a Ticket Price and Fees Can Initially Be Displayed.

However, a primary ticket seller, two venue managers, and a secondary ticket seller we interviewed questioned the need for an up-front fee disclosure requirement. For example, a primary ticket seller stated that knowing fees up front would not affect a consumer's decision of whether or not to buy a ticket. The two venue managers believed that the timing of the fee disclosure was not important, as long as fees are disclosed before consumers complete the purchase. Representatives of one secondary ticket exchange said that up-front disclosure of fees could be challenging because a ticket's fee is not stable—for example, the fee can change based on price fluctuations, different delivery methods, and the use of promotion codes.

The National Economic Council has stated that "all-in pricing," a form of up-front pricing, may be preferable to other methods of fee disclosure.[94] All-in pricing incorporates the ticket's face value and all mandatory fees and taxes, as illustrated in Figure 2 above. According to the National Economic Council, all-in pricing eases comparison across vendors. The FTC staff report analyzing hotel resort fees supported

[94] White House National Economic Council, 16.

all-in pricing for that industry because it said that breaking out fees, instead of providing a single total price, hindered consumer decision making and often resulted in consumers underestimating the total price.[95] Officials from two state attorney general offices told us that all-in pricing could be advantageous, noting that fee disclosures represent their most significant enforcement issue related to the ticketing industry.

Three secondary ticket sellers told us they might support a requirement to provide all-in pricing, but only if it was required of all ticket sellers. In 2014, the largest secondary market ticketing company began using all-in pricing, with its listings displaying a single total price that incorporated fees. However, the company soon discontinued all-in pricing as the default because, it told us, it put the company at a competitive disadvantage with other secondary market providers whose fees were not included in the initial ticket price displayed to consumers.[96] A requirement that all ticket sellers provide up-front fee disclosure would mitigate or resolve that issue.

One argument against a requirement for all-in pricing is that such regulation would restrict ticket companies' flexibility in choosing how to disclose fees. In addition, a manager, a promoter, and two artist advocacy groups said all-in pricing could give fans the incorrect impression that the artist was charging the full ticket price and receiving its revenues, because the portion of the price going toward ticketing fees would not be transparent.

### *Disclosing Face Value on Resale Sites*

Some federal and state policymakers have proposed requirements for resellers to disclose a ticket's face value on secondary ticket websites. Georgia and New York State have enacted similar requirements, with statutes requiring resellers to disclose both the face value of tickets and their list price.[97]

Requiring that ticket resellers disclose the ticket's face value can have several advantages. First, it makes the reseller's markup transparent. Second, it can help consumers assess the quality of the seat location and compare similar seats across resale listings. Third, it might reduce the possibility that consumers mistake a reseller's website for a venue website, as described earlier. This, in turn, could encourage consumers to recognize they are viewing a secondary market exchange and comparison shop for a better price elsewhere.

---

[95] Sullivan, 27.

[96] The company still provides the customer the option of displaying all-in pricing at the listing page, as do some other secondary market providers.

[97] Georgia's ticketing law requires brokers to disclose to the purchaser, in writing, the difference between a ticket's face value and the price being charged. GA. CODE ANN. § 43- 4B-28(a)(3) (2017). New York requires licensed resellers to post a price list showing the established (face value) price charged by the operator of the place of entertainment for which the ticket is being resold. N.Y. ARTS & CULT. AFF. LAW §25.23 (Consol. 2018). At least two foreign jurisdictions—the United Kingdom and Ontario, Canada—have similar laws, according to a United Kingdom government study of the country's ticket resale market and a Canadian government press release.

However, a requirement that resellers disclose a ticket's face value can present challenges because the definition of "face value" may not always be clear, according to three ticket resellers and FTC Bureau of Consumer Protection staff. If the face value does not incorporate fees and taxes charged on the primary market, it would not reflect the full amount paid by the original buyer. Similarly, some tickets are sold through VIP packages that do not itemize the price of the ticket and other components, such as backstage access or parking. In addition, with dynamic pricing, a ticket's face value can change frequently. Furthermore, season tickets may display a higher face value than the season ticket holder paid because teams usually sell the packages at a discount.

A requirement to disclose a ticket's face value also could create compliance costs for secondary ticket exchanges, and could be difficult to enforce, according to some stakeholders. Three secondary ticket exchanges told us they do not currently collect information on a ticket's face value and would have difficulty verifying the value provided by the listing broker—in part because of the challenges in defining face value, as described above. The New York State Office of the Attorney General stated in its 2016 report that most resellers cannot comply with the state's disclosure requirement because most secondary ticket exchanges do not offer the option to show the ticket's face value alongside its list price, despite having the capability to add such functionality.[98] In addition, an official from Georgia's Athletic and Entertainment Commission told us that resellers largely disregarded the state's requirement to disclose face value.

### *Disclosing Ticket Availability*

Another proposal, advocated by secondary market stakeholders, among others, would require primary ticket sellers to disclose how many tickets are available when an event first goes on sale to the general public. For instance, a venue or ticket seller might be required to provide the venue capacity and number of tickets available for sale after accounting for presales and holds. A 2017 law in Ontario, Canada, requires primary ticket sellers to provide certain information about venue capacity and presales, according to testimony by the Ontario Attorney General.[99]

Such a disclosure would provide consumers a clearer picture of ticket availability and help them manage expectations and make informed decisions, according to three consumer advocacy groups and two academics with whom we spoke. In addition, the National Association of Ticket Brokers and a secondary ticket exchange stated that disclosing ticket availability would shed light on what some consider excessive holds and presales by the primary market. They said that brokers often are blamed when events quickly sell out on the primary market, whereas there may have been relatively few tickets available for sale in the first place. The New York State Office of the Attorney

[98] New York State Office of the Attorney General, 34.

[99] *Official Report of Debates (Hansard) No. 136*, Legislative Assembly of Ontario, 2nd Session, 41st Parliament (Dec. 13, 2017).

General stated that the lack of transparency about the manner in which tickets are distributed creates a level of mistrust among consumers.

However, many primary market stakeholders with whom we spoke— including promoters, managers, venue operators, and primary ticket sellers—said such a disclosure would have little-to-no benefit. First, some of them noted that ticket inventory can change as event production details evolve and holds are released, making it difficult to provide an accurate number of tickets available at any one time. Second, some said this disclosure would be confusing or meaningless for consumers, with one promoter noting that for high-demand events, a consumer's odds of getting a ticket are low regardless of whether he or she knows the number of available tickets. Another promoter noted that the seat maps used to select seats when purchasing tickets already provide information on ticket availability. Many stakeholders also told us such a disclosure would only help brokers by giving them information useful in buying tickets and setting resale prices. In addition, a venue manager noted that information on ticket sales is considered proprietary and artists and event organizers should not be required to disclose confidential business information.[100]

## Event Ticketing Is Not Federally Regulated and Some Stakeholders Cite Market-Based Approaches to Address Concerns about Secondary Market Activity

Federal agencies face constraints in addressing ticketing issues. Some industry players are implementing technological and market-based approaches that seek to address concerns about secondary market activity.

### *Federal Regulatory Environment*

As noted earlier, the event ticketing industry is not federally regulated. In contrast, in the airline industry, the Department of Transportation can issue regulations regarding the disclosure of airline fees.[101] Staff from FTC's Bureau of Consumer Protection told us that—in addition to the enforcement activity noted earlier—they monitor consumer complaints related to the event ticket industry. However, they said they have resource and

---

[100] When initially introduced in October 2017, the Ticket Sales Act enacted by Ontario, Canada, included a provision requiring advance disclosure of the number of tickets to be sold to the general public, according to a statement by the Attorney General of Ontario. He stated that this provision was dropped after opposition from artists and venue operators, who claimed, among other things, that it would provide useful market information advantageous to ticket brokers.

[101] For example, since 2010, the Department of Transportation has taken or has proposed a range of actions to improve the transparency of airlines' fees for optional services, such as requiring certain airlines to disclose optional service fees on their websites. See GAO, *Commercial Aviation: Information on Airline Fees for Optional Services*, GAO-17-756 (Washington, D.C. Sept. 20, 2017).

other constraints that make it difficult to conduct industrywide investigations related to ticketing practices.

Issues around the level and transparency of fees are not unique to the event ticketing industry. For example, as noted earlier, FTC staff have raised concerns about mandatory "resort fees" charged by many hotels but not immediately disclosed (such as in online price search results).[102] In addition, according to the National Economic Council, sellers of other goods and services—such as car dealers and telecommunications companies—sometimes offer low prices up front that rise substantially with the addition of mandatory fees revealed later in the purchase process.[103] As such, options for regulating the transparency of fees can have applicability broader than that of event ticketing.

As noted earlier, the BOTS Act, which prohibits circumventing security measures or other systems intended to enforce ticket purchasing limits or order rules, went into effect in December 2016. However, a variety of industry, consumer, academic, and government stakeholders have expressed doubt that the BOTS Act would have much of an effect on prohibited bot use. Several of these stakeholders told us that bot users can easily evade detection and that enforcement of the act would be extremely difficult, in part because a lot of bot use occurs—or could shift—outside the United States. As of February 2018, FTC had not taken any enforcement action related to the act, but FTC staff told us they were monitoring the situation.

The degree to which legislation combatting bots is effective may depend in part on the extent to which state attorneys general pursue enforcement actions. As of February 2018, we identified two states that had taken enforcement actions related to bot use. In May 2017, the New York State Office of the Attorney General announced settlements totaling $4.11 million with five ticket brokers which, among other offenses, violated New York State law by using bots to purchase and resell tickets.[104] In April 2016, the office announced settlements totaling $2.7 million with six ticket brokers for similar violations.[105] In February 2018, the Washington State Office of the Attorney General announced settlements totaling $60,000 with two ticket companies that used bots in violation of the state's ticketing law.[106]

### *Market-Based Approaches*

Industry players, including ticket companies and event organizers, are using or exploring technology and market-based approaches that seek to address concerns about

---

102 Sullivan, 1.

103 White House National Economic Council, 9-15.

104 New York State Office of the Attorney General, *A.G. Schneiderman Announces $4.19 Million In Settlements with Six Companies That Illegally Purchased and Resold Hundreds of Thousands of Tickets to Concerts and Other NY Events* (May 11, 2017).

105 New York State Office of the Attorney General, *A.G. Schneiderman Announces $2.7 Million In Settlements With Six Ticket Brokers That Illegally Bought And Resold Tickets In Bulk* (Apr. 27, 2016).

106 Washington State Office of the Attorney General, *Ticket Sales Company to Pay $60k for Use of Ticket Bots* (Feb. 8, 2018).

secondary market activity. Examples of these approaches and their potential effects include the following:

- Delivery delays. Ticket sellers sometimes use delivery delays, meaning they do not provide the ticket immediately upon purchase. Instead, buyers receive their tickets (in paper or print-at-home form) closer to the day of the event. Delivery delays can inhibit resale activity because they give brokers less time to buy and resell tickets, and allow primary ticket sellers to review whether brokers and bots made bulk purchases, according to some promoters and primary ticket sellers. However, secondary market sellers we interviewed generally argued against delivery delays, with two sellers saying it can be inconvenient and stressful for consumers to receive a ticket just a few days before an event.[107]
- Dynamic pricing. The use of dynamic pricing—which adjusts prices over time based on demand—can reduce secondary market activity by pricing tickets closer to their market clearing price. Raising primary market ticket prices, such as through dynamic pricing, does not necessarily benefit consumers but can help ensure that more ticket revenue accrues to the artist or team rather than ticket resellers.
- Verified fan program. At least one major ticket company has a program to sell tickets to pre-approved "verified fans," to help ensure that more consumers and fewer brokers can access tickets on the primary market.
- New technology. Two stakeholders noted the potential for distributed ledger technology in ticketing.[108] The technology associates a unique identification code with the ticket and its owner, which can help restrict transfer of the ticket and ensure its authenticity.
- Adding concerts. Artists can seek to make their ticket prices accessible by increasing the supply of seats—for example, one major artist has added concert dates with the express purpose of matching ticket supply to demand to prevent higher resale prices.
- Face-value resale exchanges. Resale exchanges used by some artists only allow resale at face value (plus a limited amount to account for primary market fees). This allows consumers to recoup their ticket costs if their plans change, while preventing resale markups.

---

[107] In addition, the National Association of Ticket Brokers and one ticket reseller told us they view delivery delays as an attempt to force ticketholders to use the primary sellers' own secondary marketplaces. They said this was demonstrated by tickets that otherwise have delivery delays being available for instant resale on the resale sites of some primary sellers.

[108] Distributed ledger technology allows participants in a peer-to-peer network to share and retain identical secured records through a decentralized database.

Market-based approaches also may augment regulatory and enforcement action with regard to problems discussed earlier around transparency. In February 2018, Google's AdWords service—which offers paid advertising alongside search results—implemented new certification requirements for businesses that resell event tickets. First, resellers using AdWords must clearly disclose on their website or mobile application that they are a secondary market company and not the primary provider of the tickets.

They cannot imply they are the primary provider by using words such as "official" or by including the artist or venue name in their website's URL— practices we noted earlier that were being used by some white-label websites. Second, resellers must prominently disclose when their ticket prices are higher than face value and disclose a price breakdown, including any fees, before the customer provides payment information. Google said in a statement that these measures were intended to protect customers from scams and prevent potential confusion. However, due to the recency of this change, it is too early to determine how it will affect the marketplace.

In addition, the advertising industry's self-regulatory organization has taken steps to address potentially misleading pricing practices in the ticket industry. The Advertising Self-Regulatory Council sets standards for truth and accuracy for national advertisers, monitors the marketplace, and holds advertisers responsible for their claims.[109] As noted earlier, the organization recently referred a major ticket company to FTC for not following its recommendations to conspicuously disclose its fees.[110] Although the council can play a role in monitoring deceptive advertising related to ticketing, it also faces constraints—for example, it addresses practices case-by-case and its recommendations depend on voluntary compliance by the advertiser.

No matter what efforts are made to address concerns about the ticket marketplace, some of the consumer dissatisfaction with event ticketing stems from an intractable issue: demand for tickets to highly popular events exceeds supply. As such, no activity, outside of expanding the supply, is likely to effectively address one key source of consumer dissatisfaction: that tickets are not available to popular sold-out events.

## AGENCY COMMENTS

We provided a draft of this chapter to DOJ and FTC for review and comment. We received technical comments from FTC, which we incorporated as appropriate. We also provided relevant excerpts of the draft for technical review to selected private parties cited in our report, and included their technical comments as appropriate.

---

[109] Advertising Self-Regulatory Council, "ASRC Snapshot," accessed February 2, 2018, http://www.asrcreviews.org/about-us/.

[110] Advertising Self-Regulatory Council, "NAD Refers StubHub Pricing Claims to FTC for Further Review After Advertiser Declines to Comply with NAD Decision on Disclosures," (New York, NY: Jan. 16, 2018).

As agreed with your offices, unless you publicly announce the contents of this chapter earlier, we plan no further distribution until 30 days from the report date. At that time, we will send copies to DOJ, FTC, the appropriate congressional committees and members, and others.

Michael Clements
Director, Financial Markets and Community Investment

## APPENDIX I: OBJECTIVES, SCOPE, AND METHODOLOGY

The objectives of this chapter were to examine (1) what is known about primary and secondary online ticket sales, (2) the consumer protection concerns that exist related to online ticket sales, and (3) potential advantages and disadvantages of selected approaches to address these concerns. The scope of our work generally focused on ticketing for large concert, theater, and sporting events for which there is a resale market.

To develop background information on the U.S. ticketing industry, we analyzed business classification codes from the North American Industry Classification System, which assigns a 6-digit code to each industry based on its primary activity that generates the most revenue. The code we selected, "All Other Travel Arrangement and Reservation Services," includes theatrical and sports ticket agencies, as well as automobile club road and travel services and ticket offices for airline, bus, and cruise ship travel. Because the Census data do not distinguish event ticketing from other services in particular, we determined the data do not provide a reliable count of companies in the event ticketing industry. In addition, we obtained publicly available data from private research firms and reviewed the largest publicly held ticketing companies' annual public filings with the Securities and Exchange Commission (Form 10-K). We also collected information from firms that collect data related to the ticketing industry, such as IBISWorld and LiveAnalytics.

To examine what is known about primary and secondary online ticket sales, we reviewed data related to ticket prices and sales published by Pollstar, a concert industry trade publication, and the Broadway League, a trade organization representing commercial theater. In addition, we obtained and analyzed data on ticket volume and resale prices for a nongeneralizable sample of 22 events. These events were selected because they (1) occurred in relatively large venues (more than 500 seats) that typically experience ticket resale activity; (2) represented a mix of event types (13 concerts, 3 commercial theater productions, and 6 sporting events); and (3) represented a mix of popularity, including 17 events that would be expected to be in high demand. We defined high-demand events as those that were likely to sell out, which we assessed by reviewing past attendance at other events for the same artist or theatrical event. For sports, we assessed demand by reviewing team performance and rankings. We collected data from October 16 through December 20, 2017. For each event, we analyzed:

- resale prices and volume, through data obtained from publicly available listings on the websites of two secondary ticket exchanges;
- primary market prices and availability, through data obtained from the websites of primary market ticket sellers; and
- event capacity, through data obtained from Billboard or Pollstar (trade publications) for concerts, the Broadway League for theater, and ESPN.com (a media company) for sporting events.

To examine consumer protection concerns, we reviewed the websites of 6 primary market ticket sellers, 11 secondary ticket exchanges, and 8 "white-label" ticket websites.[111] We collected data from June 19, 2017, through January 16, 2018.

- For the primary market ticket seller that represents the majority of market share, we observed the online ticket purchase process for 23 events. Three events were selected using the process described below and the remaining 20 were chosen to reflect 2 events at each of 10 venues, selected because they were among the 200 top-selling arenas or 200 top-selling theaters in the United States in 2017, according to Pollstar.
- For each of the 5 other primary market ticket sellers and the 11 secondary ticket exchanges, we observed the online ticket purchase process for 1–5 events. For each primary ticket seller, we selected one event per category (concert, theater, and sports). For consistency and comparability across companies, we also limited events to the same state (which did not extensively limit ticket resale) and time period. We also selected 2 events in another state because they used nontransferable tickets. For the secondary ticket exchanges, we used 3–5 events from our review of primary ticket sellers' websites. If the event was no longer available, we selected an alternative event at the same venue.
- For each of the 8 white-label ticket sellers, we reviewed 1–4 events from the events described above. In some cases, the same event was not available so we selected an alternative event at the same venue.

For these events—31 events in total—we documented (1) the ticket fees charged, (2) at what point in the purchase process the fees were disclosed, and (3) any restrictions to

[111] A white-label website is a sales website built by one company that allows affiliates to use the software to build their own, uniquely branded websites, which often appear as paid results of Internet searches for venues and events. We identified these websites by conducting searches on two of the largest search engines for the venues of the events we selected for review.

the ticket. In addition, we assessed the clarity, placement, and font size of the fees, restriction information, and—for white-label websites—disclaimers that the website was a ticket resale website. We worked with a GAO investigator to review the websites that required users to provide an e-mail address or credit card information before viewing fees. Analysts followed a protocol to help ensure consistency of observations and completed a data collection instrument for each website. A second analyst independently reviewed each website to verify the accuracy of information collected by the first analyst. Any discrepancies between the two analysts were identified, discussed, and resolved by referring to the source websites.

A GAO investigator acting in an undercover capacity contacted the customer service departments of three large secondary ticket exchanges to inquire about two events for which tickets were nontransferable (not allowed to be resold) and two events for which listed tickets were speculative (not yet in-hand by the seller). The nontransferable tickets were identified through press releases and articles about popular touring artists and the speculative tickets were identified by searching for events that had been announced but were not yet for sale on the primary market. The investigator contacted customer service through 16 e-mails to one company and 8 online "live chats" with another company. For the third company, the investigator sent 8 e-mails about nontransferable tickets and did not inquire about speculative tickets because this company labeled such tickets. We also contacted the venues hosting these events to help assess the accuracy of the information provided by the ticket companies' customer service departments.

In addition, we reviewed enforcement activity by federal and state agencies related to ticketing and ticket companies. We also collected information on the number of consumer complaints by requesting the Federal Trade Commission (FTC) conduct a search of its Consumer Sentinel Network database, which includes complaints submitted to FTC, the Consumer Financial Protection Bureau, the Better Business Bureaus, and other sources. The search results covered calendar years 2014– 2016 and used the term "ticket" with terms related to events (e.g., "concert," "sport," "theater"), sold-out events (e.g., "sold-out"); fees; fraudulent tickets (e.g., "fake"); delayed delivery (e.g., "late,"); or nontransferable tickets (e.g., "paperless"). We selected our initial search terms by reviewing terms used in similar complaints on the Better Business Bureau website. We made modifications to our search string based on suggestions from FTC staff who reviewed the results of a preliminary search. To help ensure that results were related to event ticket sellers, we limited the search to complaints against the 6 primary ticket sellers and 11 secondary ticket exchanges in our scope. We assessed the reliability of the complaint data by interviewing agency officials. In addition, we have assessed the reliability of Consumer Sentinel Network data as part of previous studies related to consumer protection and found the data to be reliable for the purposes of gauging the extent of consumer complaints about event ticketing. However, in general, consumer complaint data have limitations as an indicator of the extent of problems. For example, not all consumers who experience problems may file a complaint, and not all complaints are necessarily legitimate or categorized appropriately. In addition, a consumer could submit a complaint more than once, or to more than one entity, potentially resulting in duplicate complaints.

To examine the potential advantages and disadvantages of selected approaches to address consumer protection concerns, we reviewed federal and selected state laws related to event ticket sales. At the federal level, these included the Better Online Ticket Sales Act of 2016 and relevant provisions of the Federal Trade Commission Act. To determine which states had laws related to ticket resale or disclosure, we reviewed compilations of state ticketing laws from the National Association of Ticket Brokers, a secondary ticket seller's website, and a law firm publication, and we conducted independent research and verification. We reviewed ticketing-related legislation—selected for its relevance to the approaches covered in our review—in Connecticut, New York, and Georgia. We reviewed state government reports and interviewed state officials to get information on the states' experiences with these laws. We also consulted foreign government reports to obtain information on relevant laws or regulations in Canada and the United Kingdom, which have reported similar consumer protection issues as we reviewed in our report.

To address all of our objectives, we conducted searches of various databases, such as ProQuest, Academic OneFile, Nexis, Scopus, and the National Bureau of Economic Research, to identify sources such as peer-reviewed academic studies; law review articles; news and trade journal articles; government reports; and hearings and transcripts related to ticketing issues. We examined summary-level information about each piece of literature, and from this review, identified articles that were germane to our report. We generally focused on articles from 2009 and later. We identified additional articles and reports through citations in literature we reviewed and from expert recommendations.

For the articles we used to cite empirical findings or to support arguments on advantages and disadvantages of selected resale restrictions or disclosure requirements, we conducted a methodology and soundness review. We eliminated one study on pricing and one study on price caps because we believed the methods were not sufficiently rigorous.

In addition, we identified and reviewed relevant congressional testimony on proposed ticketing legislation. We reviewed the Department of Justice's competitive impact statement and testimonies with regard to the 2010 merger of Ticketmaster and Live Nation. We interviewed staff from the FTC's Bureau of Consumer Protection and Bureau of Economics, the Department of Justice's Antitrust Division, and the New York State Office of the Attorney General, and we conducted a group interview, coordinated by the National Association of Attorneys General, with staff from the offices of the attorney general of Pennsylvania and Texas. We also interviewed representatives of three consumer organizations: Consumer Action, the National Association of Consumer

Advocates, and the National Consumers League; four trade associations: the Broadway League, Future of Music Coalition, National Association of Ticket Brokers, and the Recording Academy; as well as four primary ticket sellers, five secondary ticket exchanges and aggregators, one broker, five venue operators, three event promoters (who also operate venues), five artists' managers and booking agents, three major sports leagues, and three academics who have studied the ticket marketplace. These organizations and individuals were selected based on their experience and prominence in the marketplace and to provide a range of perspectives.

We conducted this performance audit from November 2016 to April 2018 in accordance with generally accepted government auditing standards. Those standards require that we plan and perform the audit to obtain sufficient, appropriate evidence to provide a reasonable basis for our findings and conclusions based on our audit objectives. We believe that the evidence obtained provides a reasonable basis for our findings and conclusions based on our audit objectives. Our investigative staff agent conducted all related investigative work in accordance with investigative standards prescribed by the Council of the Inspectors General on Integrity and Efficiency.

- all mobile numbers.

Robocalls to business landlines are not covered by the TCPA.

Robocalls are popular with many industry groups, such as real estate, telemarketing, and direct sales companies. The majority of companies who use robocalling are legitimate businesses, but some are not. Those illegitimate businesses may not just be annoying consumers—they may also be trying to defraud them.

The Federal Trade Commission (FTC) and Federal Communications Commission (FCC) regularly cite "unwanted and illegal robocalls" as their number-one complaint category. These complaints, as well as complaints to congressional offices, have spurred Congress to take action in an effort to protect consumers. Congress has held hearings to investigate efforts to develop technical solutions to stop illegal robocalls and ways to update the TCPA to better protect consumers, especially seniors and other vulnerable groups (e.g., immigrants without a good understanding of English). Six bills have been introduced in the 115th Congress to address this issue. Legislative efforts have included proposals to expand the definition of "spoofing"[3] to include text messages and calls made from outside the United States, as well as to protect seniors from fraud perpetrated through robocalls.

### The Do Not Call Registry

In addition to regulating robocalls, the TCPA authorized the National Do Not Call (DNC) Registry. The registry, which was created in 2003, allows consumers to "opt out" of receiving telemarketing calls on their landline and mobile phones, regardless of whether they are robocalls or not. As of September 30, 2017, the registry had nearly 230 million active registrations,[4] up from about 226 million[5] at the same time in 2016.

## Classification of Telemarketing Calls

The TCPA does not prohibit all robocalls, that is, not all robocalls are illegal. Legal robocalls are used by legitimate call originators for political, public service, and emergency messages, which are legal. Illegal robocalls are usually associated with fraudulent telemarketing campaigns, although an illegal robocall under the TCPA does

[3] "Spoofing" is the act of falsifying caller ID information to present a false name and number, thereby making fraud easier to commit.

[4] Federal Trade Commission, *FY2017 National Do Not Call Registry Data Book*, December 2017, https://www.ftc.gov/ sites/default/files/filefield_paths/dnc_data_book_fy2017.pdf. Hereinafter, "*FY2017 Data Book*."

[5] *FY2017 Data Book*.

not necessarily mean that the robocall is fraudulent. For example, it is illegal to make a marketing robocall to a cellphone without written consent. That call would not necessarily be intended to defraud the consumer. The TCPA also treats calls to mobile phones differently than calls to landlines and treats calls to consumers differently than calls to businesses. This chapter addresses robocalls that are both illegal under the TCPA and intended to defraud, not robocalls that are defined *only* as illegal.

## Calls to Landlines

Robocalls to consumer landlines are illegal under the TCPA without prior written consent. An autodialer legally may be used to call a consumer landline, but only if the call does not use a prerecorded or artificial voice. The exceptions to the landline robocall prohibition are

- calls for emergency purposes,
- purely informational calls (e.g., school closings, flight delays),
- calls made for a noncommercial purpose (e.g., charities, political parties), and
- calls made by a business that do not include an advertisement or constitute telemarketing (e.g., product recall notices).

Unlike the case for consumer landlines, nearly all sales calls to a business landline—including for a product or service from a telemarketer—are generally exempt from the DNC and robocall rules of the FTC. The two exceptions are if the caller is trying to make a

- sale to an employee at work that does not relate to work,[6] in which case the caller must comply with the DNC and robocall rules for a consumer landline; and
- sale of "nondurable office or cleaning supplies" (e.g., printer ink), in which case the caller must comply with the robocall rules.

## Calls to Mobile Phones

Robocalls to both consumer and business mobile phones without written consent are generally illegal under the TCPA. Exceptions to this rule are public service and

---

[6] For example, a call made to a farm employee about farming supplies is legal, but a call made to that same employee regarding a magazine subscription would be illegal.

emergency messages, but political robocalls to mobile phones are illegal without prior consent.

Consent for some other non-telemarketing calls does not need to be in writing, but even if a consumer has previously given consent, that consent may be revoked at any time. Subsequent calls would then be illegal.

## THE GROWTH OF ROBOCALLS—AND COMPLAINTS

Despite the existence of the DNC Registry and the fact that most robocalls are illegal, the number of robocalls continues to grow in the United States. In 2016, YouMail[7] reported an average of 2.4 billion robocalls being made each month. In May 2018, that figure rose to an all-time high of 4.1 billion robocalls, up sharply from the previous high of 2.9 billion robocalls in August 2017 (see *Figure 1*).

YouMail states that this latest figure equals about 12 to 13 calls per person each month in the United States, up from just under 8 calls in January 2018.[8]

Consumer complaints continue to grow as well (see *Table 1*). The FTC received over 7.1 million complaints about robocalls in FY2017, up from 5.3 million complaints in FY2016.[9]

## CIVIL JURISDICTION OVER ROBOCALLS

Both the FTC and the FCC, as well as individual states, have jurisdiction over robocalls and fraudulent calls; they can impose civil fines on those who break the law. In addition, in some instances, other federal agencies, such as the Department of Homeland Security, the Department of the Treasury, and the Internal Revenue Service (IRS), may prosecute robocall-related cases under criminal law.

---

[7] The YouMail Robocall Index is cited by both the FCC and FTC. It is considered the most accurate estimate of monthly robocall statistics. In addition to compiling the National Robocall Index, YouMail is a developer of visual voicemail and robocall blocking software.

[8] According to an August 25, 2017, email to CRS from YouMail CEO Alex Quilici, YouMail's base is predominantly mobile numbers, but also includes some voice-over-Internet-protocol lines. The Robocall Index calculations are made with certain assumptions: YouMail users are representative; mobile and VoIP lines have the same robocall behavior; missed call traffic to YouMail represents the vast majority of robocalls that users get; the estimate of people who get phone calls is correct; etc. The company states that these assumptions are true of its samples, but admits they may not be true overall. YouMail then extrapolates a final figure based on the number of people using YouMail and the number of people with phone numbers in the United States, assuming that YouMail is representative of total call traffic. That is, for each active YouMail account in a given month, the company knows how many robocalls are made to its subscribers. There are roughly 250 million mobile, VoIP, and traditional phone lines in the United States.

[9] *FY2017 Data Book.*

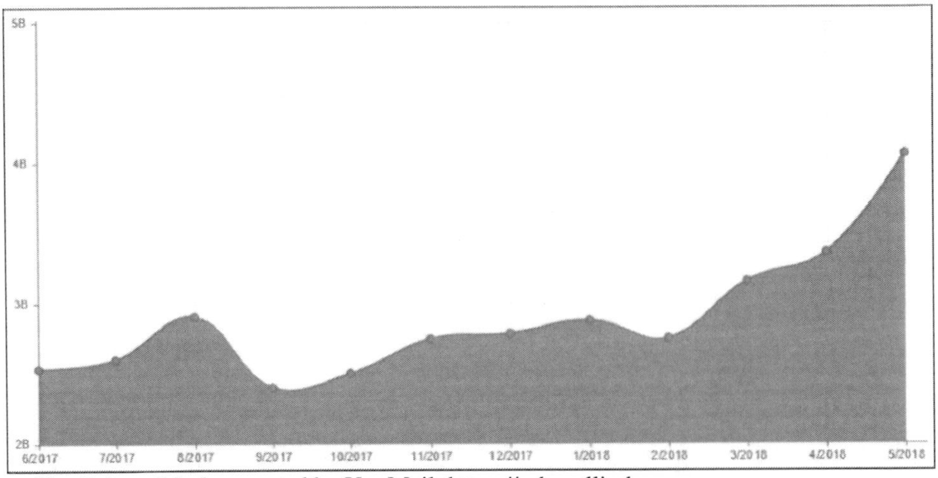


Source: The Robocall Index created by YouMail, https://robocallindex.com.

Figure 1. Monthly Volume of U.S. Robocalls, June 2017-May 2018.

**Table 1. Annual Active Registration and Complaint Figures (June 27, 2003 through September 30, 2017)**

| Fiscal Year | Active Registrations | Increase in Active Registrations | Complaints per Year | Cumulative Complaints |
|---|---|---|---|---|
| 2003 | 50,267,097 | 50,267,097 | 0 | 0 |
| 2004 | 61,741,124 | 11,474,027 | 579,838 | 579,838 |
| 2005 | 103,193,927 | 41,452,803 | 669,474 | 1,249,312 |
| 2006 | 126,981,844 | 23,787,917 | 1,149,818 | 2,399,130 |
| 2007 | 145,756,274 | 18,774,430 | 1,297,865 | 3,696,995 |
| 2008 | 166,582,471 | 20,826,197 | 1,767,798 | 5,464,793 |
| 2009 | 183,505,798 | 16,923,327 | 1,808,351 | 7,273,144 |
| 2010 | 192,917,741 | 9,411,943 | 1,633,813 | 8,906,957 |
| 2011 | 200,520,793 | 7,603,052 | 2,273,516 | 11,180,473 |
| 2012 | 207,938,719 | 7,417,926 | 3,840,556 | 15,021,029 |
| 2013 | 213,400,640 | 5,461,921 | 3,748,646 | 18,769,675 |
| 2014 | 217,855,659 | 4,455,019 | 3,241,086 | 22,010,761 |
| 2015 | 222,841,484 | 4,985,825 | 3,578,711 | 25,589,481 |
| 2016 | 226,001,288 | 3,159,804 | 5,340,234 | 30,929,715 |
| 2017 | 229,816,164 | 3,814,876 | 7,157,370 | 38,087,085 |

Source: Federal Trade Commission, FY2017 National Do Not Call Registry Data Book, December 2017, https://www.ftc.gov/sites/default/files/filefield_paths/dnc_data_book_fy2017.pdf.

Note: Active registration and complaint figures reflect the total number of phone numbers registered and the total number of National Do Not Call Registry complaints submitted to the FTC as of September 30, 2017.

## Federal Trade Commission

The FTC regulates trade, including all telemarketing practices, regardless of how a call is initiated. The FTC's focus is on protecting consumers from scams and enforcing the rules associated with the DNC Registry. The FTC's primary concerns are the content of the call, whether that call was fraudulent, and whether the call was made to a number on the DNC Registry.

The Telemarketing and Consumer Fraud and Abuse Prevention Act,[10] which became law in 1994, authorized the FTC to regulate telemarketing calls. As required by the law, the FTC promulgated the Telemarketing Sales Rule (TSR),[11] which

- requires telemarketers to disclose certain information;
- prohibits misrepresentations by telemarketers;
- sets limits on the times of day that telemarketers may call consumers;
- prohibits calls to a consumer who has asked not to be called again; and
- sets payment restrictions for the sale of certain goods and services.

The FTC rules apply only to interstate calls (calls that originate in one state and end in another), not intrastate calls (calls that originate and end in the same state), as the FTC does not have jurisdiction over intrastate trade activities. The FTC provides exemptions similar to those of the FCC, but the FTC specifically excludes any exemption for telemarketers calling on behalf of exempt entities. For example, a politician running for office cannot hire a contractor to make robocalls on behalf of the campaign.

## FEDERAL COMMUNICATIONS COMMISSION

The FCC regulates communications, including all telemarketing calls, regardless of whether they are fraudulent or not. Its focus is on the call itself, rather than the content of the call. The FCC's authority to regulate robocalls comes from the TCPA and its rules apply to both interstate and intrastate calls (with exemptions for certain entities and certain types of calls, as noted previously).

### States

States have their own laws covering intrastate telemarketing calls. Many of the laws have exemptions, like those of the FCC and FTC. Plus, many states claim authority to apply their statutes to calls originating outside the state.

---

[10] 15 U.S.C. 6101-6108, as amended.

[11] 16 C.F.R. Part 310. Available at https://www.law.cornell.edu/cfr/text/16/part-310.

## RECENT FTC ACTION RELATED TO ROBOCALLS

The FTC has undertaken vigorous law enforcement efforts against those making illegal calls. The FTC has brought 131 law enforcement actions against more than 750 companies and individuals that the agency alleged were responsible for placing billions of fraudulent telemarketing calls to consumers in violation of the Telemarketing Sales Rule.[12] The FTC has obtained more than $1.5 billion in judgments against these violators and banned many of them from making robocalls in the future. (See *Appendix D* for a summary of the cases and fines imposed by the FTC on individuals and companies for conducting fraudulent robocall campaigns.)

In addition to enforcement actions against individuals responsible for making robocalls intended to defraud, the FTC is pursuing technical solutions to block robocalls, including its Robocall Challenge program. (Details of the individual challenges and the winners are included in *Appendix B*.)

### Sharing Consumer Complaint Data with Telecommunications Service Providers

As of August 1, 2017, when consumers report DNC or robocall violations to the FTC, the robocaller phone numbers provided are released each day to telecommunications carriers and other industry partners that are implementing technical call-blocking solutions.[13]

The consumer complaint data are critical to achieving the goal of this initiative, as many existing call-blocking solutions rely on "blacklists." These blacklists are databases of telephone numbers that have received a significant number of consumer complaints. The data being provided include the date and time an unwanted call was received, the general subject matter of the call (such as debt reduction, energy, warranties, home security, etc.), and whether the call was a robocall. Using this information, carriers can better determine which calls should be blocked or flagged before they reach consumers' phones. To ensure the most complete databases can be compiled, the FTC has made it as easy as possible for consumers to report unwanted calls. This information is particularly helpful to law enforcement and industry. The data are posted to the FTC website every weekday (with Monday postings including weekend data) on the "Do Not Call Reported Calls Data" web page.[14]

---

[12] A listing of recent actions the FTC has taken against violators, including those sending out illegal robocalls can be found at https://www.ftc.gov/news-events/media-resources/do-not-call-registry/enforcement and at https://www.ftc.gov/news-events/media-resources/do-not-call-registry/robocalls.

[13] Federal Trade Commission, "FTC Escalates the Fight Against Illegal Robocalls Using Consumer Complaints to Aid Industry Call-Blocking Solutions," press release, August 1, 2017, https://www.ftc.gov/news-events/press-releases/ 2017/08/ftc-escalates-fight-against-illegal-robocalls-using-consumer.

[14] This information is available at https://www.ftc.gov/site-information/open-government/data-sets/do-not-call-data.

## RECENT FCC ACTION RELATED TO ROBOCALLS

Since 2016, the FCC has taken various actions to address the problem of illegal, fraudulent, and unwanted robocalls. The agency's most recent actions include convening a Robocall Strike Force and promulgating new rules that will empower telecommunications providers with new tools to stop robocalls. For a summary of the cases and fines imposed by the FCC on individuals and companies for conducting fraudulent robocall campaigns, see *Appendix E*.

### Robocall Strike Force

On July 26, 2016, then-Chairman of the FCC Tom Wheeler asked the telecommunications industry to "develop an action plan for providing consumers with robust robocall-blocking solutions."[15] On August 19, 2016, a 60-day "Strike Force" convened[16] and created four work groups: Authentication; Empowering Consumer Choice; Detection, Assessment, Traceback, and Mitigation; and Regulatory Support/Root Cause Removal. These work groups subsequently developed both short- and long-term plans to address the FCC Chairman's request. Highlights of their work are described below.

#### *Robocall Strike Force Report*

Each work group contributed to the Strike Force report issued on October 16, 2016.[17] Topics included the development of technical standards and consumer education plans and goals. Additionally, the Detection Work Group developed, implemented, and tested a Do Not Originate (DNO) Registry to stop unwanted calls from reaching customers.

#### *The Do Not Originate Registry Trial*

The intent of the DNO Registry is to block numbers that should never originate any call: invalid numbers, valid numbers that are not allocated to a voice service provider, and valid numbers that are allocated but not assigned to a subscriber.[18] With the FCC's

---

[15] Federal Communications Commission, Statement of Chairman Wheeler on Progress Toward Offering Consumer Robocall Blocking Choices, July 25, 2016, https://apps.fcc.gov/edocs_public/attachmatch/DOC-340458A1.docx.

[16] Members of the Robocall Strike Force were AT&T, Apple, Bandwidth.com, Birch, Blackberry, British Telecom, CenturyLink, Charter, Cincinnati Bell, Comcast, Cox, Ericsson, FairPoint, Frontier, GENBAND, Google, Inteliquent, Level 3, LG, Microsoft, Nokia, Qualcomm, Rogers, Samsung, SilverStar, Sirius/XM, Sprint, Syniverse, T-Mobile, US Cellular, Verizon, West, and Windstream.

[17] Federal Communications Commission, *FCC-Industry Robocall Strike Force Report*, October 26, 2016, https://transition.fcc.gov/cgb/Robocall-Strike-Force-Final-Report.pdf.

[18] Federal Communications Commission, "In the Matter of Advanced Methods to Target and Eliminate Unlawful Robocalls," CG Docket No. 17-59, Notice of Proposed Rulemaking and Notice of Inquiry, March 23, 2017, https://apps.fcc.gov/edocs_public/attachmatch/FCC-17-24A1.pdf.

permission, the Strike Force performed a trial of this concept. The trial was considered a success by the Strike Force and the FCC,[19] playing a significant role in reducing IRS scam calls by about 90% from September 2016 to February 2017.[20]

## Public Notice on Blocking Unwanted Robocalls

During the time that the Robocall Strike Force was convened, the FCC released a Public Notice[21] clarifying one aspect of its robocall rules. Specifically, the FCC clarified that if a subscriber to a telephone number requests call blocking to prevent that telephone number from being spoofed, a voice service provider (regardless of the type of service: traditional landline, VoIP, or mobile) may block such calls so they do not reach the intended recipient consumer. The clarification was intended to encourage initiatives such as the DNO database.

## Twitter Town Hall on Robocalls

On November 4, 2016, the FCC held a "Twitter Town Hall" on robocalls. During the town hall, the FCC policy staff talked to the public about robocall policies, consumer tips, and concerning trends. A transcript of the event is available online using the hashtag #RobocallChat.[22]

## Ringless Voicemail: "All About the Message" Petition for Declaratory Ruling

On March 31, 2017, a company called "All About the Message" (AATM) filed a petition[23] for a declaratory ruling requesting that the FCC declare the delivery of a voice message directly to a voicemail box does not constitute a call that is subject to the prohibitions on the use of an automatic telephone dialing system or an artificial or

---

[19] Federal Communications Commission, "FCC Acts to Confront 'IRS Debt' Scam Robocalls and Malicious Caller ID Spoofing," March 23, 2017, https://apps.fcc.gov/edocs_public/attachmatch/DOC-344034A1.pdf.

[20] According to a September 6, 2017, email to CRS from YouMail CEO Alex Quilici, the reduction in IRS scam calls from September 2016 to February 2017 was attributable to the DNO Registry Trial and successful law enforcement actions; similarly, the drop in robocalls from May to June 2017 was attributed to a large-scale arrest of robocallers in India.

[21] Federal Communications Commission, "Clarification on Blocking Unwanted Robocalls," September 30, 2016, https://apps.fcc.gov/edocs_public/attachmatch/DA-16-1121A1.pdf.

[22] See https://twitter.com/search?f=tweets&q=%23RobocallChat&src=typd.

[23] All About the Message, "In the Matter of Rules and Regulations Implementing the Telephone Consumer Protection Act of 1991," Petition for Declaratory Ruling, CG Docket No. 02-278, March 31, 2017, https://ecfsapi.fcc.gov/file/104010829816078/Petition%20for%20Declaratory%20Ruling%20of%20All%20About%20the%20Message%20LLC.pdf. Hereinafter, "All About the Message Petition."

prerecorded voice under the TCPA. In short, AATM requested that a robocall that goes directly to a consumer's voicemail not be categorized as an illegal robocall.

Although there was some support for such a ruling, including from the Republican National Committee[24] and the U.S. Chamber of Commerce,[25] in the end, the company withdrew the petition.[26] It may have done so because of the overwhelming amount of negative press coverage and comments filed in opposition to the petition.[27] However, since the petition was withdrawn, the company is entitled to file it again.

## Notice of Proposed Rulemaking and Notice of Inquiry

Stemming from the work of the Regulatory Support/Root Cause Removal Work Group, on March 23, 2017, the FCC released "Advanced Methods to Target and Eliminate Unlawful Robocalls," a Notice of Proposed Rulemaking (NPRM) and Notice of Inquiry (NOI).[28]

### *Notice of Proposed Rulemaking*

The NPRM sought comment on FCC-proposed rules regarding the DNO Registry and clarified guidance contained in the 2016 Public Notice. The FCC sought comment on a proposal that would authorize providers to block calls from three categories of numbers: invalid numbers, valid numbers that are not allocated to a voice service provider, and valid numbers that are allocated but not assigned to a subscriber. These are the same criteria used in the DNO Registry trial.

### *Notice of Inquiry*

In the Notice of Inquiry, the FCC sought input on

---

24 All About the Message Petition, Comments of the Republican National Committee, May 18, 2017, https://ecfsapi.fcc.gov/file/1051800793918/RNC%20Comments%20on%20AATM%20Petition.pdf.

25 All About the Message Petition, Comments of the U.S. Chamber of Commerce, May 18, 2017, https://consumermediallc.files.wordpress.com/2017/05/chambercomments.pdf.

26 All About the Message Petition, Hackleman, Olive & Judd (Attorneys for All About the Message), "Re: Petition for Declaratory Ruling of All About the Message, LLC," June 20, 2017, https://ecfsapi.fcc.gov/file/1062101171891/2017- 06-20%20Letter%20to%20Ms.%20Dortch.pdf.

27 See, for example, Eversheds Sutherland, LLP, "All Dressed Up and Nowhere to Go: Ringless Voicemail FCC Petition Withdrawn," June 28 2017, https://us.eversheds-sutherland.com/NewsCommentary/Legal-Alerts/201496/Legal-AlertAll-Dressed-Up-and-Nowhere-to-Go-Ringless-Voicemail-FCC-Petition-Withdrawn.

28 Federal Communications Commission, "In the Matter of Advanced Methods to Target and Eliminate Unlawful Robocalls," CG Docket No. 17-59, Notice of Proposed Rulemaking and Notice of Inquiry, March 23, 2017, https://apps.fcc.gov/edocs_public/attachmatch/FCC-17-24A1.pdf. This was published in the *Federal Register* on May 17, 2017, setting July 3, 2017, as the deadline for submitting comments and July 31, 2017, as the deadline for submitting reply comments. https://www.federalregister.gov/documents/2017/05/17/2017-09463/advanced-methods-totarget-and-eliminate-unlawful-robocalls. Hereinafter, "Robocall NPRM."

- possible standards that could be used to indicate to a reasonably high degree of certainty that a call is illegal, and
- whether to adopt a safe harbor provision to protect carriers in case they inadvertently violate the FCC's call completion requirements in blocking a suspected robocaller.

The agency also asked for comments regarding ways that callers who make legitimate calls can guard against being blocked and to ensure that legitimate callers whose calls are blocked by mistake can prevent further blocking.

### *NPRM/NOI Comments and Reply Comments*

The vast majority of participants[29] in this proceeding supported the FCC's plans as laid out in the NPRM, specifically, to permit carriers to block outgoing calls at the request of a subscriber, as well as calls originating from invalid numbers, unallocated numbers, and allocated but unassigned numbers. They also supported enacting a broad safe harbor to protect carriers engaged in call blocking.

The FTC also proposed expanding the coverage of the DNO Registry beyond robocalls to certain live calls. One of the largest categories of complaints to the DNC is about impostor calls, in which the caller pretends to be someone else, like an IRS agent. In about one-third of those cases, consumers have indicated the call was not a robocall. So, while 60% of monthly DNC complaints to the FTC are about robocalls, "live" calls also generate hundreds of thousands of complaints each month.[30] The FTC believes that provider-based blocking would not be complete without the ability to block illegal "live" calls that target numbers registered on the DNC Registry.

Commenters also broadly agreed that the FCC should avoid imposing burdensome processes or creating any complex new infrastructure, such as a "white list" (a set of numbers that may be called) or any centralized database or administrator.

## Report and Order and Further Notice of Proposed Rulemaking[31]

In November 2017, the FCC promulgated rules on the creation and use of the DNO Registry.[32] The new rules explicitly allow service providers to block calls from two

[29] All filings in this proceeding can be found at https://www.fcc.gov/ecfs/search/filings?proceedings_name=17-59&q=Advanced%20Methods%20to%20Target%20and%20Eliminate%20Unlawful%20Robocalls&sort=date_disseminated,DESC.

[30] Federal Trade Commission, Comments to the Robocall NPRM, July 3, 2017, https://www.ftc.gov/system/files/documents/advocacy_documents/ftc-staff-comment-federal-communications-commission-supporting-fccs-proposedexpansion-provider/ftc_comment_to_fcc_re_nprm_noi_call_blocking_07032017.pdf.

[31] Certain aspects of this rule dealing with reassigned numbers and the definition of "autodialer" were successfully challenged in court. Those issues are addressed in detail in CRS Legal Sidebar LSB10139, *(Robo)Call Me Maybe: Robocalls to Wireless Phones Under the Telephone Consumer Protection Act*, by Kathleen Ann Ruane.

categories of number: (1) numbers that the subscriber has asked to be blocked, such as "in-bound only" numbers (numbers that should not ever originate a call); and (2) unassigned numbers, as the use of such a number indicates that the calling party is intending to defraud a consumer.

The FCC also established safeguards to mitigate the possibility of blocking desired calls. The commission is also seeking further comment on additional mitigation techniques and comment on two issues related to the new rules. Additionally, the order contains a requirement that the Consumer and Governmental Affairs Bureau, in consultation with the Federal Trade Commission's Bureau of Consumer Protection, to prepare a report on the state of robocalling in the United States and to submit it to the commission within a year from publication of the order in the *Federal Register*.

### *Report and Order*

The new rules give voice service providers the option of blocking illegal robocalls in certain, well-defined circumstances, providing the telecommunications industry the flexibility to block illegal calls. The record showed broad support among consumer groups, telecommunications service providers, government, and callers for blocking DNO calls. The FCC did not accept the assertion of some commenters that any gains from blocking DNO numbers would be temporary, because those making illegal robocalls will simply choose other numbers to spoof when their calls are blocked.

### *Blocking at the Request of the Subscriber to the Originating Number*

The FCC provided clarification that telecommunications providers may block calls when they receive a request from the subscriber to which the originating number is assigned. For example, "in-bound only" numbers to government agencies such as the IRS should not be originating calls. The commission found that where the subscriber did not consent to the number being used, the call was very likely made to annoy and defraud.

### *Calls Purporting to Originate from Unassigned Numbers*

The new order explicitly allows providers to block calls purporting to originate from a number that is unassigned, as use of such a number provides a strong indication that the calling party is spoofing the Caller ID to potentially defraud and harm a consumer. The commission identified three categories of unassigned numbers

- numbers that are invalid under the North American Numbering Plan (NANP);
- numbers that have not been allocated by the North American Numbering Plan Administrator (NANPA) or the Pooling Administrator (PA) to any provider; and

[32] Federal Communications Commission, "In the Matter of Advanced Methods to Target and Eliminate Unlawful Robocalls," CG Docket No. 17-59, Report and Order and Further Notice of Proposed Rulemaking, November 16, 2017, https://apps.fcc.gov/edocs_public/attachmatch/FCC-17-24A1.pdf.

- numbers that NANPA or PA has allocated to a provider, but are not currently used.

Providers are now allowed to block calls purporting to be from numbers that fall into any of these categories.

***Further Notice of Proposed Rulemaking***

In the Further Notice of Proposed Rulemaking (FNPRM), the FCC is seeking comment on potential mechanisms to

- ensure that erroneously blocked calls can be unblocked as quickly as possible and without undue harm to callers and consumers; and
- measure the effectiveness of the commission's robocall rules and the industry's technical efforts to block robocalls.

***Mechanisms to Ensure Erroneously Blocked Calls Can Be Unblocked***

In the Report and Order, the FCC encourages providers who block calls under approved criteria to identify and quickly rectify erroneous blocking. In the FNPRM, the commission is seeking comments on whether it should require providers who block calls to establish a formal challenge mechanism or appeals process. Some of the questions posed were[33]

- Should we require blocking providers to establish a challenge mechanism by which callers can inform them of erroneous blocking and such blocking can quickly be fixed?
- What is the quickest way for callers to be informed of blocking, e.g., should providers send an intercept message to callers to notify them of the block with contact information by which a caller can report and rectify the situation?
- Should challenge mechanisms be different based on the scale of the blocking provider?
- What challenge mechanisms are blocking providers considering adopting, even absent a requirement? Is such a requirement necessary? Does our informal complaint process provide a mechanism to surface erroneous blocking to providers and correct it?
- Are there ways we could modify our informal complaint process to address the time-sensitive nature of erroneous call blocking?
- Are there other Commission processes that would provide an appropriate mechanism for rectifying erroneous blocking?

---

[33] Ibid.

***Measuring the Effectiveness of FCC and Industry Anti-Robocall Efforts***

The commission also asked, if it were to adopt a reporting obligation on all service providers, what information should be collected? Some of the questions posed were[34]

- Should providers be required to report the quantity of false positives? Should this be a quarterly requirement or an annual requirement?
- In what ways could the information collected help the commission evaluate the effectiveness of our efforts as well as those of industry and/or support additional measures to combat illegal robocalls?
- What consumer benefits would come from requiring all voice service providers to publicly report the number of illegal robocalls blocked each day/month/year?
- What are the costs of requiring voice service providers to report this information? Should we consider different requirements for smaller providers? Alternatively, should the commission use data from the FCC's Consumer Complaint Data Center as a benchmark for determining the effectiveness of FCC and industry efforts?
- Are there other Commission or third-party data sources that the commission could use to assess the effectiveness of its efforts as well as industry's at targeting illegal robocalls?

***Robocall Report***

The FCC directed that the report should encompass both the progress made by industry, government, and consumers in combatting illegal robocalls, as well as the remaining challenges to continuing these efforts. It asked for a focus on quantitative data, including calling trends and consumer complaints. The intent of the report is to provide insight into the current state of the robocalling problem and how to target additional measures to help consumers.

## THE DO NOT ORIGINATE REGISTRY: STAKEHOLDER POSITIONS

The DNO Registry, to be established through the FCC's November 2017 Order, has broad support from telecommunications service providers and consumer groups, but only conditional support for limited intervention from groups representing telemarketers and other legal call originators.

---

[34] Ibid.

## Telecommunications Industry

Telecommunications service providers generally support the registry, but have expressed concern about the expected high cost to fully implement it and how those costs would be covered. The costs would likely vary based on the architecture and size of the network, as well as the solutions a company selects. Further, the registry would likely require continual upgrades to keep up with new methods developed by the robocallers. Telecommunications service providers ideally want a funding mechanism that could be used for onetime costs, short-term initiatives, and longer-term initiatives related to the registry. Part of a three-pronged[35] solution proposed by the telecommunications industry is to ask Congress to appropriate funds for this purpose.[36]

The telecommunications industry has also recommended that Congress amend 47 C.F.R. Section 64.2105 to state that calls blocked to protect consumers from receiving illegal robocalls will not be considered when evaluating the long-distance call completion rates. Other changes to existing law could place more robocall scams under criminal jurisdiction rather than civil jurisdiction. Escalating the manner in which robocallers are punished by adding prison time to the fines imposed might have more effect than the fines alone seem to have—especially since most fines are suspended because the individual is unable to pay.

## Consumer Groups

Consumer groups have been unequivocal in their support for additional restrictions on robocalls and implementation of the DNO Registry. Together, the Consumers Union, Consumer Action, Consumer Federation of America, National Association of Consumer Advocates, National Consumer Law Center, Public Citizen, and Public Knowledge submitted joint comments to the FCC's robocall proceeding, "Advanced Methods to Target and Eliminate Unlawful Robocalls." These groups support the FCC's proposals, but also asked the FCC to

- explicitly permit and encourage the providers, where it can be done reliably and with the consumer's consent, to use additional tools, such as advanced analytics, to identify and block clearly illegal robocalls;

---

[35] The other two elements of this strategy are a subscription service and surcharges/fees levied across the customer base. The subscription service element would give customers the option to subscribe to a basic service or a premium service. A basic service could include standard call blocking, call logging, and illegal call reporting features. A premium service could include optional robocall protection features such as a fraudulent call threat score and call treatment options. The surcharge/fee element would apply a small surcharge or fee to the customer's monthly bill for the entire customer base. Such a fee could be collected as a separate "Robocall Mitigation Fee" or could be added to existing fee categories, such as the "Cost Recovery Charge."

[36] Robocall NPRM.

- clarify that providers should make available to consumers the option to block calls that fail to authenticate their Caller ID information (i.e., ensure the person calling is who they say they are);
- continue to press providers to offer effective, optional, comprehensive, and free call-blocking tools to all of their customers to help block legal but unwanted robocalls, which they already have permission to do; and
- revise the definition of "illegal robocall" for the purposes of these rules so that it is clear that it includes autodialed or prerecorded text messages and voicemails.[37]

## Telemarketing Industry and Other Legal Call Originators

The U.S. Chamber of Commerce has long expressed a concern over congressional action related to telemarketing calls.[38] In September 2016, the chamber wrote to the chairman of the House Committee on Energy and Commerce asking that the committee not make any legislation overly broad. For example, it asked that companies not be penalized for contacting customers for informational calls regarding prescription reminders, low bank account balance alerts, etc.[39]

The Professional Association for Customer Engagement (PACE)[40] is another industry group that has expressed concern specifically about the establishment of the DNO Registry and the potential harm to its members if their calls are misidentified. In response to this concern, PACE created the Communication Protection Coalition (CPC), a cross-industry group of stakeholders interested in mitigating the harm caused by blocking and mislabeling of legal calls. The CPC web page states

> As a result of the FCC's Robocall Strike Force initiatives, the carriers and their associated analytics companies are making decisions about your calls. These unregulated analytics companies apply their own algorithms to determine if a call should be blocked from ringing your customer's phone or replace your Caller ID with a label such as "Scam Likely", "Robocaller", "Fraud Call", "Telemarketer" or "Debt Collector."
>
> The issue that is very concerning to PACE and our members is that the algorithms do not take into account legal entities delivering legal calls for which consent has been

---

[37] Consumers Union, et al., "Comments in the Matter of Advanced Methods to Target and Eliminate Unlawful Robocalls," CG Docket No. 17-59, Notice of Proposed Rulemaking and Notice of Inquiry, June 30, 2017, https://www.citizen.org/system/files/case_documents/robocalls-nprm-and-noi-final.pdf.

[38] The chamber has been active on this issue since 2011. See U.S. Chamber of Commerce, "Telephone Consumer Protection Act (TCPA)," web page, https://www.uschamber.com/issue-brief/telephone-consumer-protection-act-tcpa.

[39] U.S. Chamber of Commerce, letter to Congressman Fred Upton, September 15, 2016, https://www.us chamber.com/ sites/default/files/documents/files/160915_tcpa_hearing_upton.pdf.

[40] Professional Association for Customer Engagement website, http://www.paceassociation.org/.

provided. The analytics companies are merely applying their algorithm without knowing all the facts regarding the call.[41]

On September 20, 2017, PACE held the first CPC meeting. It was attended by carriers, analytics companies, PACE members, industry associations, and federal regulators, including two industry members of the Robocall Strike Force. The initial meeting ended with consensus on the need for cooperation from all parties to develop best practices and a proposal to consider inviting consumer groups to participate in future meetings. The next meeting was scheduled for January 2018.[42]

## CONGRESSIONAL ACTION, 115TH CONGRESS

In the 115th Congress, 12 bills aimed at curtailing robocalls and protecting consumers have been introduced (*Table 2*). Most of these bills are focused on the larger issue of spoofing, as well as curtailing robocalls for debt collection and politically oriented messages; two bills are aimed at protecting seniors from predatory robocalls intended to defraud them.

Three hearings have been held on robocalls in the 115th Congress

- "Do Not Call: Combating Robocalls and Caller ID Spoofing" House Committee on Energy and Commerce Subcommittee on Digital Commerce and Consumer Protection April 27, 2018.
  Information about this hearing, including video and testimony, can be found online at https://energycommerce.house.gov/hearings/do-not-call-combating-robocalls-and-caller-id-spoofing.
- "Abusive Robocalls and How We Can Stop Them"
  Senate Committee on Commerce, Science, and Transportation April 18, 2018.
  Information about this hearing, including video and testimony, can be found online at https://www.commerce.senate.gov/public/index.cfm/hearings?ID=E0EB17D2-A895-40B4-B385-F94EA2716957.
- "Still Ringing Off the Hook: An Update on Efforts to Combat Robocalls" Senate Special Committee on Aging October 4, 2017.[43]
  Information about this hearing, including video and testimony, can be found online at https://www.aging.senate.gov/hearings/still-ringing-off-the-hook-an-update-on-efforts-to-combat-robocalls.

---

[41] Communication Protection Coalition web page, http://www.paceassociation.org/coalition.

[42] PACE, Minutes of the September 20, 2017, Communications Protection Coalition meeting, http://www.paceassociation.org/files/CPC%20Meeting%20Minutes%20Sept%202017.pdf.

[43] The hearing page is available at https://www.aging.senate.gov/hearings/still-ringing-off-the-hook-an-update-on-efforts-to-combat-robocalls.

## Table 2. Proposed Legislation, 115th Congress[44]

| |
|---|
| *Seniors Fraud Prevention Act of 2017 (S. 81, H.R. 444)*<br>S. 81 was introduced by Senator Amy Klobuchar on January 10, 2017; it was passed on August 2, 2017. The bill was reported[45] by the Senate Committee on Commerce, Science, and Transportation on August 11, 2017, and referred to the House Committee on Energy and Commerce Subcommittee on Digital Commerce and Consumer Protection.<br>H.R. 444 was introduced by Representative Theodore Deutch on January 11, 2017. It was referred to the House Committee on Energy and Commerce Subcommittee on Digital Commerce and Consumer Protection on January 25, 2017.<br>*Summary:* These bills would direct the FTC to establish an office within the Bureau of Consumer Protection to advise the FTC on the prevention of fraud targeting seniors and to assist the FTC in monitoring the market for mail, television, internet, telemarketing, and recorded message telephone call (robocall) fraud targeting seniors. |
| *Spoofing Prevention Act of 2017[46] (S. 134, H.R. 423)*<br>*S. 134 was introduced by Senator Bill Nelson on January 12, 2017; it was passed on August 3, 2017. The bill was received in the House and held at the desk on August 4, 2017.*<br>*H.R. 423 was introduced by Representative Grace Meng on January 10, 2017; it was passed on January 23, 2017. The bill was referred to the House Committee on Energy and Commerce on January 24, 2017.*<br>*Summary: These bills would amend the Communications Act of 1934 to expand the prohibition against knowingly transmitting misleading or inaccurate caller identification information to apply to (1) persons outside the United States if the recipient of the call is within the United States, and (2) text messages.* |
| *Robo Calls Off Phones ("Robo COP") Act (H.R. 740)*<br>H.R. 740 was introduced by Representative Virginia Foxx on January 30, 2017. It was referred to the House Committee on Energy and Commerce Subcommittee on Digital Commerce and Consumer Protection on February 3, 2017.<br>There is no Senate companion bill.<br>*Summary:* This bill would direct the FTC to revise the DNC registry provisions of the TSR to prohibit politically oriented recorded message telephone calls to telephone numbers listed on that registry. |
| *Help Americans Never Get Unwanted Phone Calls ("HANGUP") Act (S. 564, H.R. 5633)*<br>S. 564 was introduced by Senator Edward Markey on March 8, 2017, and referred to the Senate Committee on Commerce, Science, and Transportation the same day.<br>H.R. 5633 was introduced by Representative Anna Eshoo on March 8, 2017, and referred to the Committee on Commerce, Science, and Transportation.<br>*Summary:* These bills would amend the Communications Act of 1934 and the Bipartisan Budget Act of 2015 to repeal provisions that authorize the use of robocall equipment to call mobile telephones or residential telephone lines to collect debts owed to the U.S. government. The bill would also extend the TCPA to restrict government contractors and other legal entities from using robocall equipment without the prior consent of the called party. (Currently, government contractors are exempt from TCPA restrictions under an FCC declaratory ruling released on July 5, 2016.) |
| *Consolidated Appropriations Act, 2018 (H.R. 1625)*<br>H.R. 1625 became P.L. 115-141 on March 23, 2018. The law contains a provision that expanded and clarified the existing prohibition on misleading or inaccurate caller identification information. |
| *Repeated Objectionable Bothering of Consumers on Phones (ROBOCOP) Act (H.R. 5573)*<br>H.R. 5573 was introduced by Representative Jackie Speier on April 18, 2018, and referred to the House Committee on Energy and Commerce. |

[44] Additionally, Representative Debbie Dingell has circulated the CEASE Robocalls Act, which would lift the communications common carrier exemption in the FTC Act to permit the FTC to bring enforcement actions against telecommunications carriers and VoIP providers when they engage in unfair and deceptive practices with respect to illegal robocalls. It has not been introduced.

[45] The House report is available at https://www.congress.gov/bill/115th-congress/senate-bill/81; the Senate report is available at https://www.congress.gov/congressional-report/115th-congress/senate-report/141/.

[46] https://www.congress.gov/congressional-report/115th-congress/senate-report/91/1.

**Table 2. (Continued)**

| |
|---|
| *Robocall Enforcement Enhancement Act (S. 2694)*<br>S. 2694 was introduced by Senator Brian Schatz on April 18, 2018, and referred to the Senate Committee on Commerce, Science, and Transportation.<br>Summary: This bill would amend the Communications Act of 1934 to lengthen the statute of limitations from two years to three years for spoofing violations, lengthen the statute of limitations from one year to three years for robocall violations, and amend how the FCC imposes penalties for illegal use of automated telephone equipment. |
| *Stopping Bad Robocalls Act (S. 3078, H.R. 6026)*<br>S. 3078 was introduced by Senator Edward Markey on June 7, 2018, and referred to the House Committee on Energy and Commerce.<br>H.R. 6026 was introduced by Representative Frank Pallone on June 18, 2018, and referred to the Senate Committee on Commerce, Science, and Transportation.<br>*Summary:* These bills clarify the prohibitions on making robocalls, require the FCC to establish a nationwide database of reassigned telephone numbers, and require the FCC, in consultation with the FTC, to submit to Congress a report regarding enforcement of robocall regulations. Specifically, these bills were introduced in response to the May 2018 U.S. Court of Appeals for the D.C. Circuit case striking down the FCC's definition of an automatic telephone dialing system. |
| *Deter Obnoxious, Nefarious, and Outrageous Telephone Calls (DO NOT Call) Act (S. 3149)*<br>S. 3149 was introduced by Senator Catherine Cortez Masto on June 27, 2018, and referred to the Senate Committee on Commerce, Science, and Transportation.<br>*Summary:* This bill would provide for criminal penalties, including fines and imprisonment, for robocall violations detailed in the legislation. |
| *Telephone Robocall Abuse Criminal Enforcement and Deterrence (TRACED) Act (S. 3655)*<br>S. 3655 was introduced by Senators John Thune and Ed Markey on Novermber 16, 2018, and referred to the Senate Committee on Commerce, Science, and *Transportation.*<br>*Summary:* S. 3655 gives regulators more time to find violators, increases civil forfeiture penalties for perpetrators, promotes call authentication and blocking adoption, and brings relevant federal agencies and state attorneys general together to address impediments to criminal prosecution of robocallers who intentionally break the law. |

## OUTLOOK

Based on their long history, scammers appear determined to continue their attempts to defraud consumers. Robocalls make these efforts easier. The FTC asserts that law enforcement on its own cannot completely solve the problem of robocalls. Technological solutions, including robust call-blocking technology, likely will also be required. The DNO Registry, a technology solution that has been proven to significantly decrease robocalls, is supported by most stakeholders, but concerns remain with legitimate telemarketers who fear it may negatively impact them. The FCC intended to address these concerns in 2018. The impacts of the FTC initiatives on fraudulent robocalls, and the resulting impacts in the telemarketing industry, may continue to be oversight issues for Congress.

# Appendix A. Options for Responding to Unwanted Robocalls

Because robocalls to consumers and businesses are not treated the same under existing laws and regulations, consumers and businesses have different options for responding to robocalls. Both the FTC and FCC have published consumer guidance for how to deal with unwanted calls

- *Stop Unwanted Calls and Texts*, Federal Communications Commission;[47] and
- *Blocking Unwanted Calls*, Federal Trade Commission.[48]

Cutting down on unwanted robocalls most likely will reduce consumer exposure to fraudulent ones, along with every other type of unwanted robocall.

## Reporting a Violation (Consumers)

Consumers can file a complaint with both the FCC and FTC. The agencies choose which robocallers to pursue for legal or regulatory enforcement based partly on these complaints.

- Complaints can be filed with the FCC at https://consumercomplaints.fcc.gov/hc/en-us/requests/new?ticket_form_id=39744 (Under "Phone Issues," select "Unwanted Calls.")
- Complaints can be filed with the FTC at https://complaints.donotcall.gov/complaint/complaintcheck.aspx.
- Prior to filing a complaint, consumers should confirm that their number is in the DNC Registry. This can be done at https://donotcall.gov/confirm/conf.aspx.

## Reporting a Violation (Businesses)

Businesses have limited legal recourse against robocallers, but they can still take steps to curtail them. If a business receives a call that falls into one of the two exceptions above—sale to an employee at work that does not relate to work or sale of "nondurable

---

[47] Federal Communications Commission, "Stop Unwanted Calls, Texts, and Faxes," web page, https://www.fcc.gov/unwanted-calls.

[48] Federal Trade Commission, "Blocking Unwanted Calls," web page, https://www.consumer.ftc.gov/articles/0548-blocking-unwanted-calls.

office or cleaning supplies"—the business can report it to the FTC using the same website listed above for consumers.

## Blocking Robocalls (Consumers and Businesses)

Both consumers and business can take advantage of a number of technical options for blocking robocalls.

### *Third-Party Blocking Services for Landlines*

Blocking services provided by commercial firms can be used by individual consumers, small businesses, and large businesses. For VoIP services, some of these options may be "cloud-based," meaning they are managed from a remote location rather than on-site.

Consumers and businesses with a small number of lines may employ a third-party blocking service. One such example is Nomorobo, a winner of the 2013 Robocall Challenge[49] hosted by the FTC. (See *Appendix B* for information about the Robocall Challenge.) Nomorobo is a cloud-based solution that uses "simultaneous ringing," which routes incoming calls to a second telephone line managed by Nomorobo. In the Nomorobo solution, this second line would identify and hang up on the illegal robocall before it can ring through to the user. Nomorobo uses a database of known robocallers compiled with the help of the FTC, user reports, and its own "honeypots."[50] If a call gets a match in the Nomorobo database, the call is not allowed to reach the intended recipient. If there is not a match, the call is allowed to go through.

One example of an enterprise-wide service for large businesses is Pindrop,[51] which provides robocall solutions to secure phone communications. The company developed and deploys patented "Phoneprinting" technology that can identify, locate, and authenticate phone devices just from the call audio, thereby detecting fraudulent calls as well as verifying legitimate callers. The service is used globally by banks, insurers, brokerages, and retailers. The company states that its service succeeds in detecting over 80% of fraud—even against first-time callers.

### *Third-Party Mobile Phone Applications*[52]

Both consumers and businesses can download software applications ("apps"), often free, to their mobile phones to filter out calls from unidentified callers and/or numbers not in the person's contact list. One app is YouMail. While YouMail is primarily used for

---

[49] Federal Trade Commission, 2013 Robocall Challenge, April 2013, https://robocall.devpost.com.

[50] A "honeypot" is a set of thousands of telephone lines that answers and traps incoming calls by capturing caller IDs and voice recordings. The FTC also employs honeypots in its fight against robocallers.

[51] https://www.pindrop.com.

[52] Additionally, some mobile phones come equipped with call-blocking features.

voicemail transcriptions, it also provides protection against robocalls. The data the company collects through the app is used to calculate the Robocall Index. Another app requires a caller to enter the first two letters of the recipient's last name for the call to go through. Users of Apple's iPhone can download and use the Nomorobo app[53] for a monthly fee. An Android-compatible Nomorobo app is expected to be available soon. CTIA,[54] the wireless industry association, has a web page that lists existing Android apps.[55]

### *Telecommunications Carrier Services*

Traditional landline, internet-based (i.e., VoIP), and mobile telephone carriers provide customers with various options for blocking robocalls. *Table A-1, Table A-2,* and Table A-3 contain details of the offerings of each type of provider, as reported by Consumer Reports.[56] An October 2016 Consumer Reports examination[57] found that the quality of these services varied greatly among carriers. Overall, this examination found that consumers using internet-based phone services have the best call-blocking options and that most phone companies are not providing strong protection to their traditional landline and wireless customers.

**Table A-1. Landline Robocall Blocking Services**

| Provider | Price | Uses Nationwide Database to Block Calls | Offers Personal Blacklist | Rejects Anonymous Calls | Offers Do Not Disturb | Offers Personal Whitelist |
|---|---|---|---|---|---|---|
| Sonic | | Free | | • | | |
| CenturyLink | | $$ | • | • | • | • |
| Windstream | | $ | • | • | • | • |
| Frontier | | $ | • | • | | |
| Fairpoint | | $$ | | • | | |
| Verizon | | $$ | • | • | | |
| AT&T | | $$ | • | • | | |

Source: Carla Fried, "New Study Finds Some Phone Companies Offer Better Robocall Protections Than Others," Consumer Reports, October 26, 2016, https://www.consumerreports.org/consumer-protection/the-bestservice-providers-for-blocking-robocalls/.

Note: $ means $5 or less, and $$ means $6 or more per month.

[53] Nomorobo, http://www.nomorobo.com/ios/.

[54] CTIA is a trade association representing the wireless communications industry in the United States. When the organization was established in 1984, it was known as the "Cellular Telecommunications Industry Association. Later, that name was changed to the "Cellular Telecommunications and Internet Association," and then "CTIA—The Wireless Association." Since 2015, the organization is known as "CTIA."

[55] CTIA, "Android Robocall Blocking," https://www.ctia.org/consumer-tips/robocalls/android-robocall-blocking.

[56] *Consumer Reports* is a magazine published by Consumers Union, a nonprofit organization focused on product testing, consumer-oriented research, public education, and advocacy.

[57] Carla Fried, "New Study Finds Some Phone Companies Offer Better Robocall Protections Than Others," *Consumer Reports*, October 26, 2016, http://www.consumerreports.org/consumer-protection/the-best-service-providers-forblocking-robocalls/.

**Table A-2. VoIP Robocall Blocking Services**

| Provider | Price | Uses Nationwide Database to Block Calls | Offers Personal Blacklist | Rejects Anonymous Calls | Offers Do Not Disturb | Offers Personal Whitelist |
|---|---|---|---|---|---|---|
| Time Warner Cable | Free | • | • | • | • | • |
| CenturyLink | Free | | • | • | • | • |
| Verizon FiOS | Free | | • | • | • | • |
| AT&T U-verse | Free | | • | • | • | • |
| Ooma | $$ | • | • | • | • | |
| Comcast | Free | | • | • | | |
| Frontier | Free | | • | • | | |

Source: Carla Fried, "New Study Finds Some Phone Companies Offer Better Robocall Protections Than Others," Consumer Reports, October 26, 2016, https://www.consumerreports.org/consumer-protection/the-bestservice-providers-for-blocking-robocalls/.

Note: $ means $5 or less, and $$ means $6 or more per month.

**Table A-3. Mobile Robocall Blocking Services**

| Provider | Price | Uses Nationwide Database to Block Calls | Offers Personal Blacklist | Rejects Anonymous Calls | Offers Do Not Disturb | Offers Personal Whitelist |
|---|---|---|---|---|---|---|
| RingPlus | Free | • | • | • | • | |
| Boost | $ | • | • | • | | |
| T-Mobile | $ | | • | | • | • |
| Sprint | Free | | • | | • | |
| AT&T Wireless | $ | | • | | | |
| Verizon Wireless | $ | | • | • | • | |
| U.S. Cellular | $ | | • | | | |

Source: Carla Fried, "New Study Finds Some Phone Companies Offer Better Robocall Protections Than Others," Consumer Reports, October 26, 2016, https://www.consumerreports.org/consumer-protection/the-bestservice-providers-for-blocking-robocalls/.

Note: $ means $5 or less, and $$ means $6 or more per month.

### *Call-Blocking Devices*

Businesses and consumers can install devices to stop robocalls. These devices work with traditional and VoIP landlines with Caller ID. There are at least four such devices available. These devices generally use a "blacklist" or a "whitelist." The former blocks all calls in the list (all others are allowed), while the latter only allows calls that are on the list (all others are blocked). Some devices use both types of lists.[58]

---

[58] All the devices tested are reviewed in the article "Consumers Put Robocall-Blocking Devices to the Test," *Consumerist*, July 28, 2015, https://consumerist.com/2015/07/28/consumers-put-robocall-blocking-devices-to-the-test/.

One example of a device that uses both a blacklist and a whitelist is the Digitone Call Block Plus (see *Figure A-1*). This device, like the others, is installed between the telephone wall jack and the telephone.

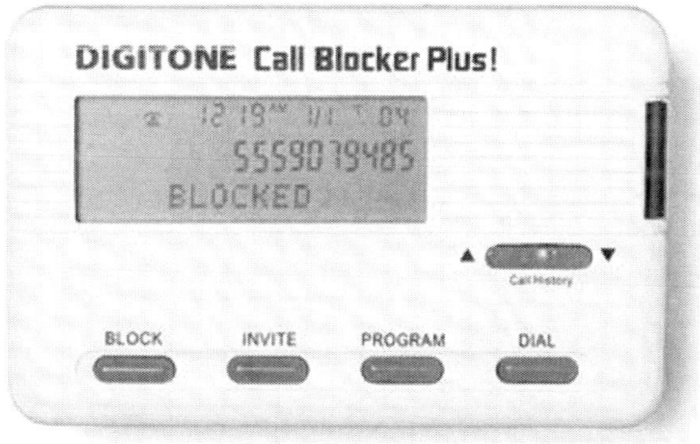


Source: "Consumers Put Robocall-Blocking Devices to the Test," *Consumerist*, July 28, 2015, https://consumerist.com/2015/07/28/consumers-put-robocall-blocking-devices-to-the-test/.

Figure A-1. Digitone Call Blocker Plus. (An Example of a Blocking Device)

## APPENDIX B. RECENT LAW ENFORCEMENT ACTIONS AGAINST ROBOCALLERS

One of the most enduring and harmful methods used in an attempt to defraud people is the "IRS Scam." It has been perpetrated by numerous entities since about 2013. This scam involves callers who claim to be employees of the IRS, using fake names and bogus identification. The callers may even know details about their targets and they usually use spoofed telephone numbers. Potential victims are told they owe money to the IRS and are threatened with arrest. They are also told that the amount owed must be paid immediately using gift cards or a wire transfer. Potential victims may not even be safe if they do not answer the phone: if the phone isn't answered, the scammers often leave an "urgent" message demanding a return call. Some scammers have even used video relay services to try to scam deaf and hard of hearing individuals. In another variation of the scam, recent immigrants with limited knowledge of English are approached in their native language. In these cases, victims are threatened with deportation. Phone scams of this kind have been on the IRS's "Dirty Dozen" list of scams since 2014. The IRS believes that the scam is responsible for over $54 million in losses to victims.

# Appendix C. The FTC's Robocall Challenge Program

In response to the significant growth in complaints about robocalls from consumers, the FTC held four Robocall Challenges, discussed below.

## The Original Robocall Challenge

The original FTC challenge, held in 2013, asked participants to develop a solution to block illegal robocalls on landlines and mobile phones. There were two winners: Aaron Foss for Nomorobo[59] and Serdar Danis for "Robocall Filtering System and Device with Autonomous Blacklisting, Whitelisting, Graylisting and Caller ID Spoof Detection."[60]

Both winning entries work by intercepting and filtering out robocalls using technology to blacklist robocaller phone numbers and whitelist numbers associated with acceptable incoming calls. Both proposals also filter out unapproved robocallers by employing a CAPTCHA-style[61] test to prevent illegal calls from ringing through to a user.

## Zapping Rachel

The second challenge, held in 2014, was called Zapping Rachel. In this challenge, security experts were asked to build tools that investigators could use to track and minimize illegal robocalls. The challenge had three phases:

- The Creator Phase challenged contestants to build a honeypot[62] that identifies inaccurate information in incoming calls, such as spoofed caller IDs, or determines which calls are likely robocalls. The winning entry used a combination of an audio CAPTCHA filter,[63] call detail analysis, and recording and transcription analysis to determine the likelihood that an incoming call was a robocall.[64]

---

[59] Nomorobo, https://nomorobo.com.

[60] Serdar Danis and Aaron Foss each received $25,000 for their solutions.

[61] A CAPTCHA is a program that protects websites against computer programs logging into them by generating and grading tests that humans can pass, but current computer programs cannot. "CAPTCHA" stands for "Completely Automated Public Turing Test to Tell Computers and Humans Apart."

[62] As defined earlier in this chapter, a "honeypot" is a set of thousands of telephone lines that answers and traps incoming calls by capturing caller IDs and voice recordings. The FTC employs honeypots in its fight against robocallers.

[63] An audio CAPTCHA allows visitors to request a pronunciation of the CAPTCHA code.

[64] Jon Olawski received $3,133.70 for his winning honeypot.

- The Attacker Phase challenged contestants to circumvent an existing honeypot and prevent it from collecting information on incoming calls. The winning entry, "Droid Rachel," circumvented the honeypot by employing a four-step targeting process that screened out phone numbers potentially connected to a honeypot, and optimized Droid Rachel's ability to send robocalls using unsuspecting consumers' Android phones.[65]
- The Detective Phase challenged contestants to analyze call data from an existing honeypot and develop algorithms to predict which calls were likely robocalls. The winning solution focused on metrics such as the number of calls made, whether the number called was a toll-free number, and the time of the call to identify likely robocalls.[66]

## Robocalls: Humanity Strikes Back

The third challenge, Robocalls: Humanity Strikes Back, was held in 2015. Contestants were asked to create tools people could use to block and forward robocalls automatically to a honeypot. The winner of this contest was RoboKiller,[67] created by Ethan Garr and Bryan Moyles.

## DetectaRobo

As part of the National Day of Civic Hacking in June 2015, the FTC challenged the public with DetectaRobo,[68] the agency's fourth contest. Participants were asked to analyze call data and create algorithms that could predict which calls were likely robocalls. Three of the 19 teams that registered were selected as demonstrating superior functionality, accuracy, innovation, and creativity.

- The winning team in this challenge was "Team HaV" (Ved Deshpande and M. Henry Linder).
- The two runners-up were—
    - "Team Milibo" (Sridhar Ramakrishnan and Shuping Liu) and
    - "Team RDAC" (Charles Julian Knight, Taylor Kelley, Ian Moraes, Rohan Smith, Will Mavis, John Cowhig, Sean Browning, James Albert Snow, and Pablo River).

---

[65] Jan Volzke received $3,133.70 for his solution.

[66] The winning team of Yang Yang and Jens Fischer shared $3,133.70. The judges also selected two honorable mentions, Sean Beck and DarkTyphoon, who each received $1,337.

[67] Robokiller, http://www.robokiller.com.

[68] DetectaRobo, https://www.ftc.gov/news-events/contests/detectarobo.

## Appendix D. Fines Imposed on Robocallers by the FTC, 2017

The Federal Trade Commission has successfully concluded four cases against fraudulent robocallers, summarized below.

### Justin Ramsey

On April 13, 2017, the FTC obtained a settlement order with Justin Ramsey, the ringleader of telemarketing operations that bombarded consumers with illegal robocalls and called phone numbers listed on the National DNC Registry. The order banned Ramsey and his company, Prime Marketing LLC, from, among other things, placing robocalls to individuals to sell goods or services and initiating sales calls to numbers listed on the DNC Registry. Ramsey and Prime Marketing were also fined a $2.2 million civil penalty, to be suspended upon payment of $65,000.

According to the FTC's January 2017 complaint, in 2012 and 2013 Ramsey and several codefendants made millions of robocalls to consumers and also placed millions of calls to phone numbers listed on the DNC Registry. In just one week in July 2012, the complaint states, the defendants made more than 1.3 million illegal robocalls to consumers nationwide, 80% of which were to numbers listed on the DNC Registry. From 2014 through 2016, Ramsey continued his unlawful telemarketing through his new company, Prime Marketing. During April and May of 2016, Ramsey and Prime Marketing initiated at least 800,000 calls to numbers in the DNC Registry. The other defendants in the case, except Ramsey and Prime Marketing, settled the commission's charges at the same time the agency filed its complaint.[69]

### Aaron Michael Jones and Steven Stansbury[70]

On June 2, 2017, a federal district court judge in California approved default judgments proposed in January 2017 by the FTC against Aaron Michael Jones, Steven Stansbury, and nine associated companies for making billions of illegal telemarketing robocalls to consumers. The FTC estimated that more than 100 million illegal robocalls per year were made to numbers listed on the DNC Registry.

---

[69] Federal Trade Commission, "Recidivist Robocaller Settles FTC Telemarketing Complaint," press release, April 13, 2017, https://www.ftc.gov/news-events/press-releases/2017/04/recidivist-robocaller-settles-ftc-telemarketingcomplaint.

[70] Federal Trade Commission, "FTC Obtains Court Judgments Against California-based Robocallers Who Placed Billions of Illegal Calls, Federal Trade Commission," press release, June 2, 2017, https://www.ftc.gov/news-events/press-releases/2017/06/ftc-obtains-court-judgments-against-california-based-robocallers.

In addition to permanently banning Jones, Stansbury, and their companies from all telemarketing activities, including initiating robocalls, the order imposed a $2.7 million penalty against each of them, payable to the FTC. Seven of the nine individual defendants, and corporate defendant Local Lighthouse Corp., agreed to court orders that settled the FTC's charges in January.

## All Us Marketing LLC

There were numerous defendants in this case, together doing business as All Us Marketing LLC (previously known as Payless Solutions). These individuals were responsible for thousands of calls to consumers nationwide making false claims about bogus debt relief services. After convincing consumers to provide their credit card information, the defendants charged them between $300 and $4,999 up front, but provided nothing in return. In some cases, the defendants used consumers' personal information to apply for new credit cards. The complaint also charged the defendants with making many calls to consumers whose phone numbers were on the DNC Registry, along with several other violations of the TSR and Florida's Telemarketing and Consumer Fraud and Abuse Act.

This large case, involving 15 defendants, was settled on June 5, 2017, with eight orders entered by a federal district court against Orlando-based individuals and companies. The order imposed financial judgments on 12 of the defendants that totaled $4,890,797. The orders also permanently ban most of the defendants from robocalling, telemarketing, or providing so-called "debt relief" services. The orders against three other defendants were for lesser amounts: two were fined $389,915 and one was fined $640,747.

## Caribbean Cruise Lines[71]

In February 2017, the FTC, along with nine states and the Tennessee Valley Authority[72] settled with the remaining defendants who assisted Caribbean Cruise Lines, Inc. (CCL), a Florida-based cruise line company, in running an illegal telemarketing campaign that made billions of robocalls. Most defendants had settled their charges in 2015. In settling the final charges, CCL's owner Fred Accuardi was barred from

[71] Federal Trade Commission, "Caribbean Cruise Lines Robocall Operation in Permanent Dry Dock," press release, February 21, 2017, https://www.ftc.gov/news-events/press-releases/2017/02/ftc-states-put-remaining-defendantsmassive-caribbean-cruise.

[72] The nine states and one federally owned corporation were: Colorado, Florida, Indiana, Kansas, Mississippi, Missouri, North Carolina, Ohio, Washington, and the Tennessee Regulatory Authority. The attorneys general of these states helped the FTC in bringing this case.

robocalling and illegal telemarketing, as well as helping anyone else make such calls. The settlement order also includes a judgment of $1.35 million, which is to be suspended after the defendants pay $2,500.

The CCL robocall campaign ran from October 2011 through July 2012 and averaged approximately 12 million to 15 million illegal sales calls a day. Consumers who answered these calls typically heard a prerecorded message telling them they had been selected to participate in a 30-second research survey, after which they would receive a "free" two-day cruise to the Bahamas. In reality, the calls were designed to market CCL's cruises and various up-sell packages. The illegal robocalls generated millions of dollars for CCL.

# APPENDIX E. FINES IMPOSED ON ROBOCALLERS BY THE FCC, 2017

Changes in technology have made it easier and cheaper for robocallers to manipulate caller ID information. To address this problem, the Federal Communications Commission has focused both on enforcement actions and on pursuing policies to help consumers and their service providers block malicious robocalls.

## Adrian Abramovich

In June 2017, the FCC took its first enforcement action under the 2009 Truth in Caller ID Act. It proposed[73] a $120 million fine—its largest ever—on a Florida-based robocaller, Adrian Abramovich.[74] Abramovich is believed to have been responsible for 96 million spoofed robocalls over the final three months of 2016. Of those calls, about 90% were made to mobile phones and 10% to landline phones. The calls used "neighborhood spoofing" technology that uses the local area code and the first three digits of the recipient's own phone number to encourage people to answer the calls. If the call was answered, recipients would hear a recorded message asking them to press one to

[73] Before a case can be settled, a case requires that after a fine has been proposed, the company must have an opportunity to make its case and fully respond to the notice served. At the FCC, the Enforcement Bureau reviews the case, conducts any additional investigation necessary, and makes any adjustments to the case as appropriate, including reducing or even cancelling a fine if warranted. After this review, the case is either closed with a mutually agreeable settlement or, if not settled, the FCC may vote to assess a fine through a forfeiture order. Even after the Forfeiture Order, a company may continue to challenge an enforcement action before the commission. Once it has exhausted its right to challenge an enforcement action before the commission, however, a company is required to pay the fine imposed in the Forfeiture Order. If the company does not do so within the required time, the fine is considered a debt to the United States and is referred to the U.S. Department of Justice for a collection action.

[74] Federal Communications Commission, "In the Matter of Adrian Abramovich, Marketing Strategy Leaders, Inc., and Marketing Leaders, Inc.," File No. EB-TCD-15-00020488, Citation and Order, Prerecorded Message Violations and Wire Fraud, June 22, 2017, https://apps.fcc.gov/edocs_public/attachmatch/FCC-17-80A1.pdf.

hear about vacation deals from travel companies such as Marriott, Expedia, Hilton, and TripAdvisor. Callers would then be transferred to call centers in Mexico, where live operators would try to sell them vacation packages at Mexican timeshare facilities not affiliated with the companies in the recorded messages.

### Philip Roesel

The FCC proposed a fine of $82 million on robocaller Philip Roesel in August 2017.[75] This robocaller, doing business as Wilmington Insurance Quotes, reportedly made more than 21 million spoofed robocalls in violation of the Truth in Caller ID Act. Based on subpoenaed records, the FCC verified that 82,106 health insurance telemarketing calls were made from October 2016 through January 2017 using falsified caller ID information. The fine was based on these verified calls, which were found to target vulnerable consumers, including the elderly, the infirm, and low-income families.

## APPENDIX F. PROPOSED LEGISLATION, 109TH-114TH CONGRESSES

Both the House and the Senate introduced legislation during this timeframe aimed at protecting consumers from fraudulent robocalls.

### House of Representatives

One bill related to robocalls has passed the House since 2005 (H.R. 5175, the "Democracy is Strengthened by Casting Light on Spending in Elections" (DISCLOSE) Act, in the 111th Congress). The DISCLOSE Act contained one relatively narrow provision related to public safety, prohibiting robocalls to public service access points (911 call centers). Other legislation proposed in the House of Representatives during this timeframe would have

- expanded the ability of the FCC to impose forfeiture penalties;
- expanded the statute of limitations and increased the maximum penalty for certain violations;

---

[75] Federal Communications Commission, "In the Matter of Best Insurance Contracts, Inc., and Philip Roesel, dba Wilmington Insurance Quotes," File No. EB-TCD-16-00023195, Citation and Order, Prerecorded Message Violations and Wire Fraud, August 4, 2017, https://apps.fcc.gov/edocs_public/attachmatch/FCC-17-107A1.pdf.

- expanded prohibitions on providing inaccurate caller ID data to apply to persons outside the United States if the recipient of the call is within the United States;
- directed providers of spoofing services to take such steps as the FCC may prescribe to verify that users do not engage in caller ID information violations;
- expanded the definition of "caller identification information" to include text messages;
- amended the federal criminal code to make it a crime to knowingly initiate a commercial robocall from within the United States or to a recipient within the United States;[76]
- directed the FTC to establish an office within the Bureau of Consumer Protection to advise the FTC on the prevention of fraud targeting seniors; and
- directed the FTC to revise the DNC Registry provisions of the TSR to prohibit politically oriented recorded message telephone calls to telephone numbers listed on that registry.[77]

## Senate

Legislation proposed during this timeframe would have:

- directed the FTC to establish an office within the Bureau of Consumer Protection to advise on the prevention of fraud targeting seniors;
- authorized the FCC to impose forfeiture penalties, without first sending a citation regarding the charged violation, against persons not licensed by the FCC who violate prohibitions on the use of robocall equipment; and
- amended the federal criminal code to make it a crime to knowingly initiate most commercial robocalls, without the prior written consent of the recipient, from within the United States or to a recipient within the United States.

The Senate has not passed any bills related to robocalls since 2005.

---

[76] Without the prior written consent of the recipient.

[77] A "politically oriented recorded message telephone call" is defined as an outbound telephone call that plays a recorded message that promotes, advertises, campaigns, or solicits donations for or against a political candidate or regarding a political issue; or uses a political candidate's name.

In: Consumer Protection
Editor: Ralf Schaefer

ISBN: 978-1-53615-876-2


*Chapter 4*

# INTERNET PRIVACY AND DATA SECURITY: ADDITIONAL FEDERAL AUTHORITY COULD ENHANCE CONSUMER PROTECTION AND PROVIDE FLEXIBILITY*

*Alicia Puente Cackley*

Chairman Portman, Ranking Member Carper, and Members of the Subcommittee:

Thank you for the opportunity to testify today about Internet privacy and data security issues. The United States does not have a comprehensive data privacy law at the federal level and instead relies in part on a sectoral approach with industry-specific laws enforced by various agencies governing areas such as healthcare and financial services. In addition, the Federal Trade Commission (FTC) currently has the lead in overseeing Internet privacy across all industries, with some exceptions. Specifically, FTC addresses consumer concerns about Internet privacy using its broad authority to protect consumers from unfair and deceptive trade practices. FTC has jurisdiction over a broad range of entities and activities that are part of the Internet economy, including websites, applications (apps), advertising networks, data brokers, device manufacturers, and others.

My testimony today addresses (1) FTC's role and authorities for overseeing Internet privacy, (2) stakeholders' views on potential actions to enhance federal oversight of consumers' Internet privacy, and (3) breaches of personally identifiable information.

---

* This is an edited, reformatted and augmented accessible version of the United States Government Accountability Office Testimony Before the Permanent Subcommittee on Investigations, Committee on Homeland Security and Governmental Affairs, U.S. Senate, Publication No. GAO-19-427T, dated March 7, 2019.

This statement is primarily based on our January 2019 report on Internet privacy.[1] This work included evaluating FTC's Internet privacy enforcement actions and authorities and interviewing various stakeholders, including representatives from industry, consumer advocacy groups, and academia, as well as FTC staff and former FTC and Federal Communications Commission (FCC) commissioners. We also interviewed officials from other federal oversight agencies—such as the Consumer Financial Protection Bureau (CFPB), Food and Drug Administration (FDA), and the Equal Employment Opportunity Commission (EEOC)— about the strengths and limitations of their regulatory and enforcement authorities and approaches. A complete description of our scope and methodology can be found in our January 2019 report. This statement also includes some additional information on data breaches from our August 2018 report on Equifax.[2]

We conducted the performance audit on which this statement is primarily based from October 2017 through January 2019 in accordance with generally accepted government auditing standards. Those standards require that we plan and perform the audit to obtain sufficient, appropriate evidence to provide a reasonable basis for our findings and conclusions based on our audit objectives. We believe that the evidence obtained provides a reasonable basis for our findings and conclusions based on our audit objectives.

## BACKGROUND

In April 2018, Facebook disclosed that a Cambridge University researcher may have improperly shared the data of up to 87 million of Facebook's users with a political consulting firm. This followed other incidents in recent years involving the misuse of consumers' personal information from the Internet, which about three-quarters of Americans use. These types of incidents have raised public concern because Internet-based services and products, which are essential for everyday social and economic purposes, often collect and use various forms of personal information that could cause users harm if released.

The federal privacy framework for private-sector companies is comprised of a set of tailored laws that govern the use and protection of personal information for specific purposes, in certain situations, or by certain sectors or types of entities. Such laws protect

---

[1] GAO, *Internet Privacy: Additional Federal Authority Could Enhance Consumer Protection and Provide Flexibility*, GAO-19-52 (Washington, D.C.: Jan. 15, 2019).

[2] GAO, *Data Protection: Actions Taken by Equifax and Federal Agencies in Response to the 2017 Breach*, GAO-18-559 (Washington, D.C.: Aug. 30, 2018).

consumers' personal information related to their eligibility for credit, financial transactions, and personal health, among other areas.[3]

We reported in 2013 that no overarching federal privacy law governs the collection and sale of personal information among private-sector companies, including information resellers—companies that collect and resell information on individuals.[4] We found that gaps exist in the federal privacy framework, which does not fully address changes in technology and the marketplace. We recommended that Congress consider legislation to strengthen the consumer privacy framework to reflect the effects of changes in technology and the marketplace. Such legislation has not been enacted.

## FTC's Role and Authorities for Overseeing Internet Privacy

As we reported in January 2019, FTC is primarily a law enforcement agency with authority to, among other things, address consumer concerns about Internet privacy, both for Internet service providers and content providers. It does so using its general authority under section 5 of the FTC Act, which prohibits "unfair or deceptive acts or practices in or affecting commerce."[5]

Even though the FTC Act does not speak in explicit terms about protecting consumer privacy, the Act authorizes such protection to the extent it involves practices FTC defines as unfair or deceptive. According to FTC, an act or practice is "unfair" if it causes, or is likely to cause, substantial injury not reasonably avoidable by consumers and not outweighed by countervailing benefits to consumers or competition as a result of the practice. FTC has used this "unfairness" authority to address situations where a company has allegedly failed to properly protect consumers' data, for example. According to FTC, a representation or omission is "deceptive" if it is material and is likely to mislead consumers acting reasonably under the circumstances. FTC has applied this "deceptiveness" authority to address deceptions related to violations of written privacy policies and representations concerning data security, for example.

FTC staff investigate Internet privacy complaints from various sources and also initiate investigations on their own. If FTC staff have reason to believe that an entity is engaging in an unfair or deceptive practice, they may forward an enforcement recommendation to the commission. The commission then determines whether to pursue

---

[3] These laws include the Fair Credit Reporting Act, the Gramm-Leach-Bliley Act, and the Health Insurance Portability and Accountability Act.

[4] GAO, *Information Resellers: Consumer Privacy Framework Needs to Reflect Changes in Technology and the Marketplace,* GAO-13-663 (Washington, D.C.: Sept. 25, 2013).

[5] 15 U.S.C. § 45(a)(1).

an enforcement action.[6] With certain exceptions, FTC generally cannot directly impose civil monetary penalties for Internet privacy cases. Instead, FTC typically addresses Internet privacy cases by entering into settlement agreements requiring companies to take actions such as implementing reasonable privacy and security programs. If a company then violates its settlement agreement with FTC, the agency can request civil monetary penalties in court for the violations. In addition, FTC can seek to impose civil monetary penalties directly for violations of certain statutes and their implementing regulations, such as the statute pertaining to the Internet privacy of children and its corresponding regulations.

FTC has not promulgated rules under section 5 specific to Internet privacy. According to FTC staff, the process the agency must use to issue such rules—known as the Magnuson-Moss procedures—includes steps that add time and complexity to the rulemaking process. FTC has not promulgated any regulations using the Magnuson-Moss procedures since 1980. Although FTC has not implemented its section 5 authority by issuing regulations regarding internet privacy, it has issued regulations when directed and authorized by Congress to implement other statutory authorities using a different set of rulemaking procedures. These procedures, spelled out in section 553 of the Administrative Procedures Act (APA),[7] are those that most federal agencies typically use to develop and issue regulations.

APA section 553 establishes procedures and requirements for what is known as "informal" rulemaking, also known as notice-and-comment rulemaking. Among other things, section 553 generally requires agencies to publish a notice of proposed rulemaking in the Federal Register. After giving interested persons an opportunity to comment on the proposal by providing "data, views, or arguments," the statute then requires the agency to publish the final rule in the Federal Register.

In contrast, the rulemaking procedures that FTC generally must follow to issue rules under the FTC Act are the Magnuson-Moss procedures noted above. These are required by the Magnuson-Moss Warranty Act amendments to the FTC Act and impose additional rulemaking steps beyond APA section 553. These steps include providing the public and certain congressional committees with an advance notice of proposed rulemaking (in addition to the notice of proposed rulemaking). FTC's rulemaking under Magnuson-Moss also calls for, among other things, oral hearings, if requested, presided over by an independent hearing officer and preparation of a staff report after the conclusion of public hearings, giving the public the opportunity to comment on the report.

FTC has promulgated regulations using the APA section 553 notice-andcomment rulemaking procedures when authorized or directed by specific statutes. For example, the

[6] FTC staff operate separately from the FTC commission itself, which is the set of five commissioners, including the chair, who ultimately have responsibility for deciding upon courses of action, including enforcement actions.

[7] 5 U.S.C. § 553.

1998 Children's Online Privacy Protection Act (COPPA) required FTC to issue regulations concerning children's online privacy; promulgate these regulations using the APA section 553 process; and, in determining how to treat a violation of the rules, to treat it as an unfair or deceptive act or practice in most cases. COPPA governs the online collection of personal information from children under the age of 13 by operators of websites or online services, including mobile applications. COPPA contained a number of specific requirements that FTC was directed to implement by regulation, such as requiring websites to post a complete privacy policy, to notify parents directly about their information collection practices, and to obtain verifiable parental consent before collecting personal information from their children or sharing it with others.

Laws and regulations may be enforced in various ways, for example, by seeking civil monetary penalties for non-compliance. As mentioned, FTC has authority to seek civil monetary penalties when a company violates a settlement agreement or certain statutes or regulations. For example, in March 2018, FTC announced that it is investigating whether Facebook's current privacy practices violate a settlement agreement that the company entered into with FTC. In the case that resulted in the 2012 settlement, FTC had charged Facebook with deceiving consumers by telling them they could keep their information private, but then allowing it to be shared and made public. FTC also has authority to seek civil monetary penalties for violations of the COPPA statute as well as FTC's COPPA regulations.

In our January 2019 Internet privacy report, we found that during the last decade, FTC filed 101 Internet privacy enforcement actions to address practices that the agency alleged were unfair, deceptive, a violation of COPPA, a violation of a settlement agreement, or a combination of those reasons. Most of these actions pertained to first-time violations of the FTC Act for which FTC does not have authority to levy civil monetary penalties. In nearly all 101 cases, companies settled with FTC, which required the companies to make changes in their policies or practices as part of the settlement.

## Stakeholders and FTC Identified Potential Actions to Enhance Federal Oversight of Consumers' Internet Privacy

Various stakeholders we interviewed for our January 2019 Internet privacy report said that opportunities exist for enhancing Internet privacy oversight. Most industry stakeholders said they favored FTC's current approach—direct enforcement of its unfair and deceptive practices statutory authority, rather than promulgating and enforcing regulations implementing that authority. These stakeholders said that the current approach allows for flexibility; that regulations could hinder innovation, create loopholes, and become obsolete; and that rulemakings can be lengthy. Other stakeholders, including consumer advocates and most former FTC and FCC commissioners we interviewed, favored having FTC issue and enforce regulations. Stakeholders said that regulations can provide clarity, flexibility, and act as a deterrent, and may also promote fairness by giving companies notice of what actions are prohibited.

Those stakeholders who believe that FTC's current authority and enforcement approach is unduly limited identified three main actions that could better protect Internet privacy: (1) enactment of an overarching federal privacy statute to establish general requirements governing Internet privacy practices of all sectors, (2) APA section 553 notice-and-comment rulemaking authority, and (3) civil penalty authority for any violation of a statutory or regulatory requirement, rather than allowing penalties only for violations of settlement agreements or consent decrees that themselves seek redress for a previous statutory or regulatory violation.

## Privacy Statute

Stakeholders from a variety of perspectives—including academia, industry, consumer advocacy groups, and former FTC and FCC commissioners—told us that a statute could enhance Internet privacy oversight by, for example, clearly articulating to consumers, industry, and privacy enforcers what behaviors are prohibited. Some stakeholders suggested that such a framework could either designate an existing agency (such as FTC) as responsible for privacy oversight or create a new agency. For example, in Canada, the Office of the Privacy Commissioner, an independent body that reports directly to the Parliament, was established to protect and promote individuals' privacy rights.

Some stakeholders also stated that the absence of a comprehensive Internet privacy statute affects FTC's enforcement. For example, a former federal enforcement official from another oversight agency said that FTC is limited in how it can use its authority to take action against companies' unfair and deceptive trade practices for problematic Internet privacy practices. Similarly, another former federal enforcement official from another agency said that FTC is limited in how and against whom it can use its unfair and deceptive practices authority noting, for example, that it cannot pursue Internet privacy enforcement against exempted industries.[8]

In addition, some stakeholders said FTC's section 5 unfair and deceptive practices authority may not enable it to fully protect consumers' Internet privacy because it can be difficult for FTC to establish that Internet privacy practices are legally unfair. Because of this difficulty, some stakeholders said that FTC relies more heavily on its authority to

---

[8] The FTC Act prohibits FTC from taking action against companies such as telecommunications carriers, airlines and railroads under certain circumstances. FTC also does not have jurisdiction over banks, credit unions, or savings and loans institutions.

take enforcement action against deceptive trade practices compared with the agency's unfair trade practices authority. This is consistent with the results of our analysis of FTC cases, which showed that in a majority of the actions FTC settled, FTC alleged that companies engaged in practices that were deceptive. Furthermore, a recently decided federal appeals court case illustrates potential limits on FTC's enforcement remedies. The court found that FTC could not direct the company, which was accused of unfair practices, to create and implement comprehensive data security measures for the personal information the company stored on its computer networks as a remedy for the practices alleged. Instead, the court ruled that FTC's authority was limited to prohibiting specific illegal practices.[9]

## APA Notice-and-Comment Rulemaking

Various stakeholders said that there are advantages to overseeing Internet privacy with a statute that provides APA section 553 notice-and-comment rulemaking authority. Officials from other consumer and worker protection agencies we interviewed described their enforcement authorities and approaches. For example, officials from CFPB and FDA, both of which use APA section 553 notice-and-comment rulemaking, said that their rulemaking authority assists in their oversight approaches and supports their enforcement actions. EEOC officials said that regulations are used to guide investigations that establish whether enforcement action is appropriate.

## Ability to Levy Civil Penalties for Initial Violations

Some stakeholders suggested that FTC's ability to levy civil penalties could also be enhanced. As noted, FTC can levy civil penalties against companies for violating certain regulations, such as COPPA regulations, or for violating the terms of a settlement agreement already in place. According to most former FTC commissioners and some other stakeholders we interviewed, FTC should be able to levy fines for initial violations of section 5 of the FTC Act. An academic told us that the power of an agency to levy a fine is a tangible way to hold industries accountable.

---

[9] In this case, FTC filed a complaint against LabMD, a medical laboratory, under section 5 of the FTC Act for allegedly committing an unfair act or practice by failing to provide reasonable and appropriate security for personal information on its computer networks. On appeal, the Eleventh Circuit ruled that FTC's cease and desist order exceeded its authority because it did not prohibit a specific act or practice but instead, mandated a complete overhaul of the company's data-security program. *LabMD, Inc. v. FTC*, 891 F.3d 1286 (11th Cir. 2018).

## BREACHES INVOLVING PERSONALLY IDENTIFIABLE INFORMATION HIGHLIGHT THE IMPORTANCE OF SECURITY AND PRIVACY

Recent data breaches at federal agencies, retailers, hospitals, insurance companies, consumer reporting agencies, and other large organizations highlight the importance of ensuring the security and privacy of personally identifiable information collected and maintained by those entities. Such breaches have resulted in the potential compromise of millions of Americans' personally identifiable information, which could lead to identity theft and other serious consequences. For example, the breach of an Equifax online dispute portal from May to July 2017 resulted in the compromise of records containing the personally identifiable information of at least 145.5 million consumers in the United States and nearly 1 million consumers outside the United States. We reported in August 2018 that Equifax's investigation of the breach identified four major factors—identification, detection, segmenting of access to databases, and data governance—that allowed the attacker to gain access to its network and extract information from databases containing personally identifiable information.[10] In September 2017, FTC and CFPB, which both have regulatory and enforcement authority over consumer reporting agencies such as Equifax, initiated an investigation into the breach and Equifax's response. Their investigation is ongoing.

According to a 2017 National Telecommunications and Information Administration (NTIA) survey conducted by the U.S. Census Bureau, 24 percent of American households surveyed avoided making financial transactions on the Internet due to privacy or security concerns.[11] NTIA's survey results show that privacy concerns may lead to lower levels of economic productivity if people decline to make financial transactions on the Internet. Consumers who were surveyed indicated that their specific concerns were identity theft, credit card or banking fraud, data collection by online services, loss of control over personal information, data collection by government, and threats to personal safety.

Recent data breaches and developments regarding Internet privacy suggest that this is an appropriate time for Congress to consider what additional actions are needed to protect consumer privacy, including comprehensive Internet privacy legislation. Although FTC has been addressing Internet privacy through its unfair and deceptive practices authority and FTC and other agencies have been addressing this issue using statutes that target specific industries or consumer segments, the lack of a comprehensive federal privacy statute leaves consumers' privacy at risk. Comprehensive legislation addressing Internet privacy that establishes specific standards and includes APA notice-and-comment rulemaking and first-time violation civil penalty authorities could enhance the federal

---

[10] GAO-18-559.

[11] NTIA, *Most Americans Continue to Have Privacy and Security Concerns, NTIA Survey Finds* (Washington, D.C.: Aug. 20, 2018) *available at* https://www.ntia.doc.gov/blog/2018/most-americans-continue-have-privacy-and-securityconcerns-ntia-survey-finds (last visited Mar. 5, 2019).

government's ability to protect consumer privacy, provide more certainty in the marketplace as companies innovate and develop new products using consumer data, and provide better assurance to consumers that their privacy will be protected. In our January 2019 report, we recommended that Congress consider developing comprehensive legislation on Internet privacy that would enhance consumer protections and provide flexibility to address a rapidly evolving Internet environment. Issues that should be considered include:

- which agency or agencies should oversee Internet privacy;
- what authorities an agency or agencies should have to oversee Internet privacy, including notice-and-comment rulemaking authority and first-time violation civil penalty authority; and
- how to balance consumers' need for Internet privacy with industry's ability to provide services and innovate.

Chairman Portman, Ranking Member Carper, and Members of the Subcommittee, this concludes my prepared statement. I would be pleased to respond to any questions you may have at this time.

In: Consumer Protection
Editor: Ralf Schaefer

ISBN: 978-1-53615-876-2


*Chapter 5*

# WELLS FARGO—A TIMELINE OF RECENT CONSUMER PROTECTION AND CORPORATE GOVERNANCE SCANDALS*

***Cheryl RL Cooper and Raj Gnanarajah***

Wells Fargo Bank, N.A., is a large federally chartered depository bank. It is a subsidiary of Wells Fargo and Company, a bank holding company (hereafter, Wells Fargo or the Bank). Wells Fargo is the fourth largest bank in the United States with $1.9 trillion in assets at the end of 2018. In 2016, a scandal involving Wells Fargo creating fake accounts—which may have harmed more than 2 million consumers—increased scrutiny of the bank by Congress, financial regulators, and the public. Since the scandal was revealed to the public, certain of Wells Fargo's business practices have continued to raise concerns relating to consumer protection and corporate governance, leading to additional congressional oversight and interest.

This In Focus provides a brief overview of federal regulation of Wells Fargo and a timeline of key events involving the company since the scandal's disclosure. It then discusses a few relevant policy issues, including consumer protection and corporate governance, and highlights recent instances of congressional oversight of the bank.

* This is an edited, reformatted and augmented version of Congressional Research Service Publication No. IF11129, dated March 8, 2019.

## Overview of Regulation

Similar to other large banks, several federal financial regulators have overlapping oversight authority of Wells Fargo. Although the Office of the Comptroller of the Currency (OCC), Federal Reserve, and Federal Deposit Insurance Corporation (FDIC) each have safety and soundness authority, the OCC is the primary prudential regulator of Wells Fargo's bank subsidiary. The OCC regulates Wells Fargo's internal controls, its management of operational and reputational risks, and the phases of its deposit and lending activities. The Federal Reserve has authority over the bank holding company. The Bureau of Consumer Financial Protection (CFPB) regulates and supervises Wells Fargo for consumer protection compliance.

## Key Events

The following provides a timeline of selected events involving Wells Fargo since the reveal of the fake accounts scandal. Most of the consumer protection issues discussed below came to light as a result of consumer complaints or lawsuits that were eventually disclosed by the bank.

### 2016

- September 2016: Wells Fargo pays $185 million in fines to the CFPB, OCC, and the City and County of Los Angeles for creating about 1.5 million unauthorized deposits and 623,000 credit card accounts in customers' names without their knowledge. Wells Fargo also discloses that it previously fired 5,300 employees for their involvement in creating these fake accounts.

In coordination with the Department of Justice (DOJ), the OCC assesses $20 million in civil money penalties against Wells Fargo for violating the Servicemembers Civil Relief Act (SCRA; P.L. 108-189). The OCC also orders the bank to make restitution to servicemembers who were harmed. Violations include failure to accurately disclose servicemembers' active duty status to the court prior to evicting those servicemembers and failure to obtain court orders prior to repossessing 413 servicemembers' automobiles. In November 2017, Wells Fargo admitted it had illegally repossessed another 450 servicemembers' cars.

- *October 2016*: Wells Fargo's CEO John Stumpf retires. Between forfeiture and eventual clawbacks, he surrenders $69 million in compensation. Another key executive, Carrie Tolstedt, surrenders $67 million in compensation.

December 2016: As a consequence of deficiencies in Wells Fargo's "living will," regulators restrict Wells Fargo's ability to grow its business. P.L. 111-203 (often called the Dodd-Frank Act) requires certain companies to submit a living will to regulators to show how large banks would unwind themselves in the event of a large financial loss.

## 2017

- *March 2017:* The OCC downgrades Wells Fargo's Community Reinvestment Act (CRA) rating to "needs to improve," from "Outstanding" due to Wells Fargo's discriminatory and illegal credit practices, including the fake accounts scandal.
- April 2017: The *Sales Practices Investigation Report* (SPIR) issued by Wells Fargo reveals that the bank's board of directors and bank executives knew of many of the issues underlying the fake accounts scandal as far back as 2002 but did not take corrective action and did not fully disclose the issues until September 2016.
- *July 2017:* Wells Fargo admits that it charged about 570,000 customers for auto insurance on car loans without verifying whether these customers already had existing insurance. As a consequence, up to 20,000 customers may have defaulted on their car loans.
- *October 2017:* Wells Fargo admits it wrongly fined 110,000 mortgage clients for missing a deadline, even though the delays were the bank's fault.

## 2018

*February 2018:* The Federal Reserve restricts Wells Fargo's growth until it improves its governance and controls. Wells Fargo announces it will replace four members of its board by the end of the year.

- *April 2018:* Wells Fargo, CFPB, and OCC reach a $1 billion settlement of issues related to Wells Fargo's auto-loan insurance and mortgage practices.

- *July 2018:* Reportedly, Wells Fargo refunded millions of dollars for charges related to add-on services, such as pet insurance and legal services, it added onto customers' accounts without the customers' full knowledge.
- *August 2018:* Wells Fargo pays a $2.1 billion fine to DOJ for misrepresenting the type of mortgages it sold to investors between 2005 and 2007.

Wells Fargo discloses that it incorrectly denied loan modifications for 625 people; 400 of whom had their homes foreclosed.

**2019**

- January 2019: Wells Fargo releases its annual financial results for 2018. The bank earned as profits $22.4 billion in 2018 and $22.2 billion in 2017. It recorded $86.4 billion in revenue in 2018 as compared with $88.4 billion in 2017. The bank spent $25.8 billion on share repurchases and dividend payments in 2018.

## Consumer Protection

As a result of the various issues described above, federal financial regulators entered into multiple consent orders with the bank to address the harm to consumers and to strengthen Wells Fargo's consumer compliance risk management structures.

These consent orders required Wells Fargo to set aside funds to compensate harmed consumers. Some forms of financial harm caused by Wells Fargo may be relatively straightforward to identify, such as fees that individuals paid on unauthorized accounts. Other forms of harm, however, may be more difficult to identify and measure, like effects on a consumer's credit score.

As part of these consent orders, Wells Fargo has also agreed to take actions to improve the bank's consumer compliance risk management. In 2016, the bank agreed to undergo an independent consultant's review of its consumer compliance practices, including its sales practices, and develop a plan to improve its consumer compliance management. In 2018, as additional consumer protection concerns were revealed, the consent order required Wells Fargo to develop a robust enterprise-wide compliance risk management plan and perform an internal audit of its practices.

## CORPORATE GOVERNANCE

Wells Fargo is a publically traded firm, which means that it must comply with securities laws and corporate governance rules from the Securities and Exchange Commission. A major component of corporate governance is the business environment created by the board of directors and senior management.

As a result of the events described above, some have raised issues with how Wells Fargo's senior leadership's emphasized cross-selling products and meeting specific sales goals. According to the SPIR, employees felt pressure to sell unwanted or unneeded products to customers and open unauthorized accounts due to an aggressive sales culture and performance management that focused on cross-selling. The report suggests Wells Fargo's decentralized corporate structure might have obscured the scale and nature of the underlying problems. According to the SIPR, this structure allowed parts of the bank to operate without oversight, impeding corporate risk management functions.

A second area of concern is how late Wells Fargo disclosed to investors the potential damage to the bank from these events. Such disclosures are governed by securities laws. Wells Fargo argues that it was not required to disclose these issues earlier, because the related fines were small and not material compared with its earnings. Others argue that the reputational risk to Wells Fargo made these issues material and thus they should have been disclosed earlier.

The bank has made efforts to address concerns with its corporate governance. In October 2016, Wells Fargo's board named the Chief Operating Officer, Timothy Sloan, as the new CEO. Also, the board separated the role of the chairman and CEO and fired other key executives related to the fake accounts scandal. In addition to the new CEO, seven of the thirteen board members have been replaced since 2016, including the chair of the board.

## CONGRESSIONAL OVERSIGHT

The various Wells Fargo developments highlight a number of issues for potential congressional oversight relating to the performance of federal financial regulators and banks that are considered "too big to fail." On the one hand, several regulators, such as the OCC and the CFPB, had supervisory authority over Wells Fargo, yet did not detect widespread fraudulent practices that occurred over an extended period of time. On the other hand, since 2016, the OCC, the CFPB, and the Federal Reserve have issued consent orders limiting the bank's growth and requiring it to make changes in its consumer protection and corporate governance practices. Critics continue to assert that regulatory enforcement measures against Wells Fargo have been too focused on assessing fines rather than on other measures, including breaking up the bank. During this time, regulators also have increased their scrutiny of financial institutions' culture and compliance management practices for all examined institutions.

Congress has continued to express interest in issues surrounding Wells Fargo. Between 2016 and 2018, both the previous CEO, John Stumpf, and the current CEO, Timothy Sloan, have testified before Congress. The House Financial Services Committee has scheduled a hearing with Timothy Sloan for March 12, 2019.

In: Consumer Protection
Editor: Ralf Schaefer
ISBN: 978-1-53615-876-2


*Chapter 6*

# CONSUMER DATA PROTECTION: ACTION NEEDED TO STRENGTHEN OVERSIGHT OF CONSUMER REPORTING AGENCIES*

*Michael Clements*

## WHY GAO DID THIS STUDY

CRAs collect, maintain, and sell to third parties large amounts of sensitive data about consumers, including Social Security numbers and credit card numbers. Businesses and other entities commonly use these data to determine eligibility for credit, employment, and insurance. In 2017, Equifax, one of the largest CRAs, experienced a breach that compromised the records of at least 145.5 million consumers.

This statement is based on GAO's February 2019 report on the CRA oversight roles of FTC and CFPB. This statement summarizes (1) measures FTC has taken to enforce CRA compliance with requirements to protect consumer information, (2) measures CFPB has taken to ensure CRA protection of consumer information, and (3) actions consumers can take after a breach.

* This is an edited, reformatted and augmented accessible version of the United States Government Accountability Office Testimony Before the Subcommittee on Economic and Consumer Policy, Committee on Oversight and Reform, House of Representatives, Publication No. GAO-19-469T, dated March 26, 2019.

## WHAT GAO RECOMMENDS

In its February 2019 report, GAO recommended that Congress consider giving FTC civil penalty authority to enforce GLBA's safeguarding provisions. GAO also recommended that CFPB (1) identify additional sources of information on larger CRAs, and (2) reassess its prioritization of examinations to address CRA data security. CFPB neither agreed nor disagreed with GAO's recommendations.

## WHAT GAO FOUND

In its February 2019 report, GAO found that since 2008, the Federal Trade Commission (FTC) has settled 34 enforcement actions against various entities related to consumer reporting violations of the Fair Credit Reporting Act (FCRA), including 17 actions against consumer reporting agencies (CRA). Some of these settlements included civil penalties—fines for wrongdoing that do not require proof of harm—for FCRA violations or violations of consent orders. However, FTC does not have civil penalty authority for violations of requirements under the Gramm-Leach-Bliley Act (GLBA), which, unlike FCRA, includes a provision directing federal regulators and FTC to establish standards for financial institutions to protect against any anticipated threats or hazards to the security of customer records. To obtain monetary redress for these violations, FTC must identify affected consumers and any monetary harm they may have experienced. However, harm resulting from privacy and security violations can be difficult to measure and can occur years in the future, making it difficult to trace a particular harm to a specific breach. As a result, FTC lacks a practical enforcement tool for imposing civil money penalties that could help to deter companies, including CRAs, from violating data security provisions of GLBA and its implementing regulations.

Since 2015, the Consumer Financial Protection Bureau (CFPB) has had five public settlements with CRAs. Four of these settlements included alleged violations of FCRA; and three included alleged violations of unfair, deceptive, or abusive practices provisions. CFPB is also responsible for supervising larger CRAs (those with more than $7 million in annual receipts from consumer reporting) but lacks the data needed to ensure identification of all CRAs that meet this threshold. Identifying additional sources of information on these CRAs, such as by requiring them to register with the agency through a rulemaking or leveraging state registration information, could help CFPB ensure that it can comprehensively carry out its supervisory responsibilities. After the Equifax breach, CFPB used its existing supervisory authority to examine the data security of certain CRAs. CFPB's process for prioritizing which CRAs to examine does not routinely include an assessment of companies' data security risks, but doing so could help

CFPB better detect such risks and prevent the further exposure or compromise of consumer information.

Consumers can take actions to mitigate the risk of identity theft—such as implementing a fraud alert or credit freeze—and can file a complaint with FTC or CFPB. However, consumers are limited in the direct actions they can take against CRAs. Consumers generally cannot exercise choice in the consumer reporting market—such as by choosing which CRAs maintain their information— if they are dissatisfied with a CRA's privacy or security practices. In addition, according to CFPB, consumers cannot remove themselves from the consumer reporting market entirely.

Chairman Krishnamoorthi, Ranking Member Cloud, and Members of the Subcommittee:

I am pleased to be here today to discuss our recent work on the oversight of consumer reporting agencies' (CRA) data protection. As you know, CRAs collect, maintain, and sell to third parties large amounts of sensitive data about consumers, including Social Security numbers and credit card numbers. The 2017 data breach of Equifax highlighted the data security risks associated with CRAs and underscored the importance of appropriate federal oversight in this market where consumers have limited control over whether or which CRAs possess their information.

This statement is based on our February 2019 report.[1] For this work, we focused on the CRA oversight roles of the Federal Trade Commission (FTC) and the Consumer Financial Protection Bureau (CFPB). FTC and CFPB have taken steps to enforce CRA compliance with requirements to protect consumer information. However, this statement and our report identified specific actions that could strengthen the oversight of these companies and better protect consumers from the compromise of their personal information.

This statement discusses (1) measures FTC has taken to enforce CRA compliance with requirements to protect consumer information, (2) measures CFPB has taken to ensure CRA protection of consumer information, and (3) actions consumers can take after a breach. For this work, we reviewed the types of enforcement actions available to FTC and CFPB for violations of relevant laws, as well as specific enforcement actions these agencies have brought against CRAs. We also reviewed CFPB examination guidance for supervising these CRAs, including CFPB's internal guidelines for conducting data security examinations. In addition, we reviewed documents related to CFPB's process for prioritizing which institutions and which product lines should receive supervisory examination. We interviewed officials from FTC and CFPB on their oversight activities. We conducted the work on which this statement is based in

---

[1] GAO, Consumer Data Protection: Actions Needed to Strengthen Oversight of Consumer Reporting Agencies, GAO-19-196 (Washington, D.C.: Feb. 21, 2019).

accordance with generally accepted government auditing standards. More details on our methodology can be found in our February 2019 report.

# BACKGROUND

## Oversight Agencies

FTC and, most recently, CFPB, are the federal agencies primarily responsible for overseeing CRAs. FTC has authority to investigate most organizations that maintain consumer data and to bring enforcement actions for violations of statutes and regulations that concern the security of data and consumer information.[2] CFPB, created in 2010 by the Dodd-Frank Wall Street Reform and Consumer Protection Act (Dodd-Frank Act), has enforcement authority over all CRAs for violations of certain consumer financial protection laws.[3] In general, it also has the authority to issue regulations and guidance for those laws. CFPB has supervisory authority over larger market participants in the consumer reporting market. In 2012, CFPB defined larger market participant CRAs as those with more than $7 million in annual receipts from consumer reporting.[4] CFPB's supervision of these companies includes monitoring, inspecting, and examining them for compliance with the requirements of certain federal consumer financial laws and regulations. As discussed below, these laws include most provisions of the Fair Credit Reporting Act (FCRA); several provisions of the Gramm-Leach-Bliley Act (GLBA); and provisions of the Dodd-Frank Act concerning unfair, deceptive, or abusive acts or practices.[5]

## Data Breaches and the Equifax Breach

Although there is no commonly agreed-upon definition of "data breach," the term generally refers to an unauthorized or unintentional exposure, disclosure, or loss of sensitive information. This information can include personally identifiable information

[2] *See* 15 U.S.C. §§ 6801-6809; 16 C.F.R. § 314.1(a) and § 314.3(b)(2)-(3).
[3] Pub. L. No. 111-203, tit. X, 124 Stat. 1376, 1955 (2010).
[4] *See* Defining Larger Participants of the Consumer Reporting Market, 77 Fed. Reg. 42874 (July 20, 2012).
[5] The rulemaking authority for GLBA's safeguards provision and FCRA's red flags and records disposal provisions are statutorily excluded from CFPB's authority. *See* 12 U.S.C. § 5481(12)(F),(J). According to CFPB staff, CFPB can examine the data security practices of larger market participant CRAs for compliance with the provisions of the Dodd-Frank Act, including the prohibition of unfair, deceptive, or abusive acts or practices; and can obtain information about CRAs' compliance management systems, including those for data security. *See* 12 U.S.C. § 5514(b)(1). However, CFPB staff said they cannot examine for compliance with or enforce the data security standards in these provisions of GLBA and FCRA or the FTC's implementing rules, even at larger market participant CRAs.

such as Social Security numbers, or financial information such as credit card numbers. A data breach can be inadvertent, such as from the loss of an electronic device; or deliberate, such as the theft of a device or a cyber-based attack by individuals or groups, including an organization's own employees, foreign nationals, or terrorists.[6] Data breaches have occurred at all types of organizations, including private, nonprofit, and federal and state entities.

In the Equifax data breach, Equifax system administrators discovered on July 29, 2017, that intruders had gained unauthorized access via the Internet to a server housing the company's online dispute portal.[7] The breach compromised the personally identifiable information of at least 145.5 million individuals, and included names, addresses, and birth dates; and credit card, driver's license, and Social Security numbers.[8] Equifax's investigation of the breach identified the following factors that led to the breach: software vulnerabilities, failure to detect malicious traffic, failure to isolate databases from each other, and inadequately limiting access to sensitive information such as usernames and passwords. Equifax's public filings after the breach noted that the company took steps to improve security and notify individuals about the breach. Our August 2018 report provides more information on the breach and Equifax's response.[9]

## FTC Has Taken Enforcement Measures against CRAs but Lacks Civil Penalty Authority for GLBA Data Protection Provisions

FTC enforces compliance with consumer protection laws under authorities provided in FCRA, GLBA, and the FTC Act. As we reported in February 2019, according to FTC, in the last 10 years, it has brought 34 enforcement actions for FCRA violations, including 17 against CRAs. In addition, FTC said that it has taken 66 actions against companies (not just in the last 10 years), including CRAs, that allegedly engaged in unfair or deceptive practices relating to data protection.

---

[6] For more information on types of cyberattacks, see GAO, Cybersecurity: Bank and Other Depository Regulators Need Better Data Analytics and Depository Institutions Want More Usable Threat Information, GAO-15-509 (Washington, D.C.: July 2, 2015).

[7] Equifax's online dispute portal is a web-based application that allows an individual to upload documents to research and dispute an inaccuracy in their Equifax credit report.

[8] On October 2, 2017, Equifax revised the number of affected individuals from 143 million to 145.5 million after it had incorrectly concluded that one of the attackers' queries had not returned any data. On March 1, 2018, Equifax stated that it had identified approximately 2.4 million U.S. consumers whose names and partial driver's license information were stolen, but as of August 2018, Equifax had not determined how many of these individuals were included in the estimate of 145.5 million affected individuals.

[9] See GAO, Data Protection: Actions Taken by Equifax and Federal Agencies in Response to the 2017 Breach, GAO-18-559 (Washington, D.C.: Aug. 30, 2018).

In some circumstances, FTC enforcement authority can include civil money penalties—monetary fines imposed for a violation of a statute or regulation.[10] However, FTC's civil penalty authority does not extend to initial violations of GLBA's privacy and safeguarding provisions. These provisions require administrative, physical, and technical safeguards with an emphasis on protection against anticipated threats and unauthorized access to customer records. For violations of GLBA provisions, FTC may seek an injunction to stop a company from violating these provisions and may seek redress (damages to compensate consumers for losses) or disgorgement (requirement for wrongdoers to give up profits or other gains illegally obtained).

Determining the appropriate amount of consumer compensation requires FTC to identify the consumers affected and the amount of monetary harm they suffered. In cases involving security or privacy violations resulting from data breaches, assessing monetary harm can be difficult. In addition, consumers may not be aware that their identities have been stolen as a result of a breach and or identity theft, and related harm may occur years in the future. It can also be difficult to trace instances of identity theft to specific data breaches. According to FTC staff, these factors can make it difficult for the agency to identify which individuals were victimized as a result of a particular breach and to what extent they were harmed and then obtain related restitution or disgorgement. Having civil penalty authority for GLBA provisions would allow FTC to fine a company for a violation such as a data breach without needing to prove the monetary harm to individual consumers. FTC staff noted that in the case of a data breach, each consumer record exposed could constitute a violation; as a result, a data breach that involved a large number of consumer records could result in substantial fines.

In 2006, we suggested that Congress consider providing FTC with civil penalty authority for its enforcement of GLBA's privacy and safeguarding provisions.[11] We noted that this authority would give FTC a practical tool to more effectively enforce provisions related to security of data and consumer information. Following the 2008 financial crisis, Congress introduced several bills related to data protection and identity theft, which included giving FTC civil penalty authority for its enforcement of GLBA. However, in the final adoption of these laws, Congress did not provide FTC with this authority. Since that time, data breaches at Equifax and other large organizations have highlighted the need to better protect sensitive personal information. Accordingly, we continue to believe FTC and consumers would benefit if FTC had such authority, and we recommended in our February 2019 report that Congress consider providing FTC with civil penalty authority for the privacy and safeguarding provisions of GLBA to help ensure that the agency has the tools it needs to most effectively act against data privacy and security violations.

---

[10] *See* 15 U.S.C § 45(l). Generally, a civil money penalty is one of several forms of monetary sanctions that an agency can impose on a violator as a punitive measure.

[11] GAO-06-674.

## CFPB Enforces and Examines CRAs for Compliance with Consumer Protection Laws but Does Not Fully Consider Data Security in Prioritizing Examinations

CFPB enforces compliance with most provisions of FCRA; several provisions of GLBA; and the prohibition of unfair, deceptive, or abusive acts or practices under the Dodd-Frank Act.[12] In our February 2019 report, we noted that since 2015, CFPB has had five public settlements with CRAs. Four of these settlements included alleged violations of FCRA, and three included alleged violations of provisions related to unfair, deceptive, or abusive practices. CFPB also has an ongoing investigation of Equifax's data breach.

Under its existing authority, CFPB has examined several larger market participant CRAs, but may not be identifying all CRAs that meet the $7 million threshold. CFPB staff told us that as of October 2018, they were tracking between 10 and 15 CRAs that might qualify as larger market participants. CFPB staff told us that they believe the CRA market is highly concentrated and there were not likely to be many larger market participants beyond the 10 to 15 they are tracking. However, CFPB staff said that the 10 to 15 CRAs may not comprise the entirety of larger market participants, because CRAs' receipts form consumer reporting may vary from year to year, and CFPB has limited data to determine whether CRAs meet the threshold.

Our January 2009 report on reforming the U.S. financial regulatory structure noted that regulators should be able to identify institutions and products that pose risks to the financial system, and monitor similar institutions consistently.[13] CFPB could identify CRAs that meet the larger market participant threshold by requiring such businesses to register with it, subject to a rulemaking process and cost-benefit analysis of the burden it could impose on the industry. Another method CFPB could use to identify CRAs subject to its oversight would be to leverage information collected by states. We recommended in February 2019 that CFPB identify additional sources of information, such as through registering CRAs or leveraging state information, that would help ensure the agency is

---

[12] CFPB has authority under FCRA, except for the provisions governing the disposal of information and the "red flags" of identity theft. Those provisions were carved out of the CFPB's authority by section 1002(12)(F) of the Dodd-Frank Act. See 12 U.S.C. § 5481(12)(F). The red flags rule requires financial institutions and creditors (as defined by statute) to implement a written identity theft prevention program designed to detect the red flags of identity theft in their day-to-day operations, among other things. The disposal provision requires any person who maintains or otherwise possesses consumer information for a business purpose to dispose of such information properly by taking reasonable measures to protect against unauthorized access to or use of the information in connection with its disposal. See 15 U.S.C. §§ 1681m(e), 1681s(a)(1) and 1681w(a)(1) and 16 C.F.R. pts. 681 and 682. Those provisions remain under FTC's authority and apply to entities, including CRAs as applicable, subject to the agency's jurisdiction. In addition, CFPB has authority over title V, subtitle A of GLBA, except for the data safeguards in section 501(b) of GLBA, 15 U.S.C. 6801(b). The data safeguards provision was carved out of the CFPB's authority by section 1002(12)(J) of the Dodd-Frank Act. See 12 U.S.C. § 5481(12)(J). That provision remains under FTC's jurisdiction with respect to CRAs and certain other entities. See 15 U.S.C. §§ 6801, 6804, 6805, and 16 C.F.R. pt. 314.

[13] GAO-09-216.

tracking all CRAs subject to its authority. CFPB neither agreed nor disagreed with our recommendation.

Each year CFPB determines the institutions (for example, banks, credit unions, non-bank mortgage servicers, and CRAs) and the consumer product lines that pose the greatest risk to consumers, and prioritizes these for examinations. CFPB segments the consumer product market into institution product lines, or specific institutions' offerings of consumer product lines. CFPB then assesses each institution product line's risk to consumers at the market level and institutional level. To assess risk at the market level, CFPB considers market size and other factors that contribute to market risk. To assess risk at the institution level, CFPB considers an institution's market share within a product line, as well as field and market intelligence. Field and market intelligence includes quantitative and qualitative information on an institution's operations for a given product line, including the strength of its compliance management systems, the number of regulatory actions directed at the institution, findings from prior CFPB examinations, and the number and severity of consumer complaints CFPB has received about the institution.

CFPB then determines specific areas of compliance to assess by considering sources such as consumer complaints, public filings and reports, and past examination findings related to the same or similar products or institutions. Most recently, CFPB examinations of CRA's consumer reporting have focused on issues such as data accuracy, dispute processes, compliance management, and permissible purposes.

Although CFPB's examination prioritization incorporates several important factors and sources, the process does not routinely include assessments of data security risk, such as how institutions detect and respond to cyber threats. CFPB staff said the bureau cannot examine for or enforce compliance with the data security standards in provisions of GLBA and FCRA or FTC's implementing rules, even at larger participant CRAs. After the Equifax breach, however, CFPB used its existing supervisory authority to develop internal guidelines for examining data security, and conducted some CRA data security examinations.[14] CFPB staff said that they do not routinely consider data security risks during their examination prioritization process and have not reassessed the process to determine how to incorporate such risks going forward.

Statute requires CFPB to consider risks posed to consumers in the relevant product and geographic markets in its risk-based supervision program. In addition, federal internal control standards state that agencies should identify, analyze, and respond to risks related to achieving defined objectives. This can entail considering all significant

[14] CFPB's general supervisory authority includes (1) assessing compliance with the requirements of federal consumer financial law, including the Dodd-Frank Act's prohibition of unfair, deceptive, and abusive acts or practices; (2) obtaining information about the activities and compliance systems of the examined institution; and (3) detecting and assessing risks of consumer financial products and services to consumers and markets. See 12 U.S.C. § 5514(b)(1). CFPB staff noted that unless the bureau finds that the institution has violated the Dodd-Frank Act's prohibition on unfair, deceptive, or abusive acts or practices, or another provision of federal consumer financial law over which CFPB has authority, the bureau cannot take enforcement action, and can only make supervisory recommendations.

internal and external factors to identify risks and their significance, including magnitude of impact, likelihood of occurrence, nature of the risk, and appropriate response.[15] In light of the Equifax breach, as well as CFPB's acknowledgment of the CRA market as a higher-risk market for consumers, it is important for CFPB to routinely consider factors that could inform the extent of CRA data security risk such as the number of consumers that could be affected by a data security incident and the nature of potential harm resulting from the loss or exposure of information. In our February 2019 report, we recommended that CFPB assess whether its process for prioritizing CRA examinations sufficiently incorporates the data security risks CRAs pose to consumers, and take any needed steps identified by the assessment to more sufficiently incorporate these risks. CFPB neither agreed nor disagreed with our recommendation.

## Regulators Inform Consumers about Protections Available and Consumers Can Take Some Actions after a CRA Data Breach

In our February 2019 report, we noted that FTC and CFPB provide educational information for consumers on ways to mitigate the risk of identity theft. In addition, after a breach, FTC and CFPB publish information specific to that breach. For example, shortly after Equifax's announcement of the breach, FTC published information on when the breach occurred, the types of data compromised, and links to additional information on Equifax's website. Similarly, CFPB released three blog posts and several social media posts that included information on ways that consumers could protect themselves in the wake of the breach and special protections and actions for service members.[16]

At any time, consumers can take actions to help mitigate the risk of identity theft. For example, consumers can implement a credit freeze free of charge, which can help prevent new-account fraud by restricting potential creditors from accessing the consumer's credit report.[17] Similarly, implementing a free fraud alert with a credit bureau can help prevent fraud because it requires a business to verify a consumer's identity before issuing credit.[18]

---

[15] GAO, *Standards for Internal Control in the Federal Government*, GAO-14-704G (Washington, D.C.: Sept. 10, 2014)

[16] CFPB placed all of the information related to the Equifax breach, including information about known or potential scams, at www.consumerfinance.gov/equifaxbreach.

[17] A credit freeze generally allows consumers to request a freeze on their credit reports by contacting each of the nationwide CRAs. Consumers are given a unique personal identification number or password that they use to temporarily lift or remove the freeze (for example, when they are applying for credit or employment). In May 2018, Congress passed the Economic Growth, Regulatory Relief, and Consumer Protection Act, which requires that, free of charge, CRAs place credit freezes no later than 1 business day after and lift credit freezes no later than 1 hour after receiving a direct request from a consumer via telephone or secure electronic means. Pub. L. No. 115-174, § 301(a), 132 Stat. 1296, 1326 (2018) (codified at 15 U.S.C. § 1681c–1(i)).

[18] Consumers who suspect that they have been or are about to become victims of fraud can request an initial fraud alert at no cost with any one of the three nationwide consumer reporting agencies, which automatically notify

However, consumers are limited in the direct actions they can take against a CRA in the event of a data breach, for two primary reasons. First, consumers generally cannot determine the source of the data used to commit identity theft. As a result, it can be difficult to link a breach by a CRA (or any other entity) to the harm a consumer suffers from a particular incidence of identity theft, which makes it challenging to prevail in a legal action. Second, unlike with many other products and services, consumers generally cannot exercise choice if they are dissatisfied with a CRA's privacy or security practices. Specifically, consumers cannot choose which CRAs maintain information on them. In addition, consumers do not have a legal right to delete their records with CRAs, according to CFPB staff, and therefore cannot choose to remove themselves entirely from the CRA market.

FTC and CFPB have noted that the level of consumer protection required can depend on the consumer's ability to exercise choice in a marketplace. For example, when determining whether a practice constitutes an unfair practice, FTC considers whether the practice is one that consumers could choose to avoid. Similarly, according to CFPB staff, the consumer reporting market may pose higher risk to consumers because consumers cannot choose whether or which CRAs possess and sell their information.

Chairman Krishnamoorthi, Ranking Member Cloud, and Members of the Subcommittee, this concludes my prepared remarks. I would be happy to answer any questions that you may have.

the other two. See 15 U.S.C. § 1681c-1(a)(1). An initial fraud alert stays on the victim's credit file for not less than one year. Consumers with identify theft reports may request an extended fraud alert, which lasts for seven years. See 15 U.S.C. § 1681c-1(b)(1). Active duty alerts, which last for not less than one year, are available to deployed service members. See 15 U.S.C. § 1681c-1(c).

In: Consumer Protection
Editor: Ralf Schaefer
ISBN: 978-1-53615-876-2


*Chapter 7*

# CONSUMER DATA PROTECTION: ACTIONS NEEDED TO STRENGTHEN OVERSIGHT OF CONSUMER REPORTING AGENCIES*

***United States Government Accountability Office***

## ABBREVIATIONS

| | |
|---|---|
| CFPB | Consumer Financial Protection Bureau |
| CRA | Consumer Reporting Agency |
| Dodd-Frank Act | Dodd-Frank Wall Street Reform and Consumer Protection Act |
| FCRA | Fair Credit Reporting Act |
| FTC | Federal Trade Commission |
| FTC Act | Federal Trade Commission Act |
| GLBA | Gramm-Leach-Bliley Act |

## WHY GAO DID THIS STUDY

CRAs collect, maintain, and sell to third parties large amounts of sensitive data about consumers, including Social Security numbers and credit card numbers. Businesses and other entities commonly use these data to determine eligibility for credit, employment,

* This is an edited, reformatted and augmented version of the United States Government Accountability Office Report to Congressional Requesters, Publication No. GAO-19-196, dated February 2019.

and insurance. In 2017, Equifax, one of the largest CRAs, experienced a breach that compromised the records of at least 145.5 million consumers.

GAO was asked to examine issues related to federal oversight of CRAs. Among other things, this chapter discusses (1) measures FTC has taken to enforce CRA compliance with requirements to protect consumer information, (2) measures CFPB has taken to ensure CRA protection of consumer information, and (3) actions consumers can take after a breach. GAO reviewed relevant laws, documentation related to CRA examinations, and policies and practices of selected CRAs; and interviewed representatives of regulatory agencies, CRAs, consumer and industry groups, and Attorneys General from four states with consumer reporting requirements.

## What GAO Recommends

GAO recommends that Congress consider giving FTC civil penalty authority to enforce GLBA's safeguarding provisions. GAO also recommends that CFPB (1) identify additional sources of information on larger CRAs, and (2) reassess its prioritization of examinations to address CRA data security. CFPB neither agreed nor disagreed with GAO's recommendations.

## What GAO Found

Since 2008, the Federal Trade Commission (FTC) has settled 34 enforcement actions against various entities related to consumer reporting violations of the Fair Credit Reporting Act (FCRA), including 17 actions against consumer reporting agencies (CRA). Some of these settlements included civil penalties— fines for wrongdoing that do not require proof of harm—for FCRA violations or violations of consent orders. However, FTC does not have civil penalty authority for violations of requirements under the Gramm-Leach-Bliley Act (GLBA), which, unlike FCRA, includes a provision directing federal regulators and FTC to establish standards for financial institutions to protect against any anticipated threats or hazards to the security of customer records. To obtain monetary redress for these violations, FTC must identify affected consumers and any monetary harm they may have experienced. However, harm resulting from privacy and security violations can be difficult to measure and can occur years in the future, making it difficult to trace a particular harm to a specific breach. As a result, FTC lacks a practical enforcement tool for imposing civil money penalties that could help to deter companies, including CRAs, from violating data security provisions of GLBA and its implementing regulations.

Since 2015, the Consumer Financial Protection Bureau (CFPB) has had five public settlements with CRAs. Four of these settlements included alleged violations of FCRA; and three included alleged violations of unfair, deceptive, or abusive practices provisions. CFPB is also responsible for supervising larger CRAs (those with more than $7 million in annual receipts from consumer reporting) but lacks the data needed to ensure identification of all CRAs that meet this threshold. Identifying additional sources of information on these CRAs, such as by requiring them to register with the agency through a rulemaking or leveraging state registration information, could help CFPB ensure that it can comprehensively carry out its supervisory responsibilities. According to CFPB staff, the bureau does not have authority to examine for or enforce the GLBA's safeguards provisions. After the Equifax breach, however, CFPB used its existing supervisory authority to examine the data security of certain CRAs. CFPB's process for prioritizing which CRAs to examine does not routinely include an assessment of companies' data security risks, but doing so could help CFPB better detect such risks and prevent the further exposure or compromise of consumer information.

If a CRA experiences a data breach, affected consumers can take actions to mitigate the risk of identity theft—such as implementing a fraud alert or credit freeze—and can file a complaint with FTC or CFPB. However, consumers are limited in the direct actions they can take against the CRA. Consumers generally cannot exercise choice in the consumer reporting market—such as by choosing which CRAs maintain their information—if they are dissatisfied with a CRA's privacy or security practices. In addition, according to CFPB, consumers cannot remove themselves from the consumer reporting market entirely because they do not have a legal right to delete their records with CRAs. This limited control by consumers, coupled with the large amount and sensitive nature of the information CRAs possess, underscores the importance of appropriate federal oversight of CRAs' data security.

February 21, 2019

The Honorable Ron Wyden
Ranking Member
Committee on Finance
United States Senate

The Honorable Elizabeth Warren
Ranking Member
Subcommittee for Financial Institutions and Consumer Protection
Committee on Banking, Housing, and Urban Affairs
United States Senate

The Honorable Maxine Waters
Chairwoman
Committee on Financial Services
House of Representatives

The Honorable Elijah Cummings
Chairman
Committee on Oversight and Reform
House of Representatives

In 2017, the consumer reporting agency (CRA) Equifax, Inc., disclosed that it had experienced a data breach and that unknown individuals had extracted from its databases sensitive consumer information—such as names, addresses, birth dates, and credit card, driver's license, and Social Security numbers—of at least 145.5 million consumers in the U.S. Such unauthorized access to personally identifiable information could lead to identity theft, raising concerns among policymakers about how CRAs in general are collecting, using, and protecting sensitive consumer information. We have addressed issues related to data breaches and identity theft in our prior work, including our recent analysis of the Equifax data breach.[1]

According to the Consumer Financial Protection Bureau (CFPB), the consumer reporting market comprises more than 400 companies, and the Consumer Data Industry Association reports that these companies issue three billion reports and make more than 36 billion updates to consumer files each year. These companies collect vast amounts of sensitive consumer information, package it into consumer reports, and sell the reports to third parties.[2] Banks, employers, and others use these reports to make credit, employment, insurance, and other decisions. According to a 2018 Department of the Treasury report, the three nationwide CRAs— Equifax, Experian, and TransUnion— maintain credit files on nearly 210 million Americans.[3]

You asked us to examine issues related to the causes of the Equifax breach, Equifax's response to the breach, federal oversight of CRAs, and the role of CRAs in federal agencies' implementation of government programs.[4] This chapter, one in a series of our reports that addresses these issues, examines the oversight of CRAs, specifically (1) the

---

[1] See GAO, Data Protection: Actions Taken by Equifax and Federal Agencies in Response to the 2017 Breach, GAO-18-559 (Washington, D.C.: Aug. 30, 2018).

[2] A consumer report is a CRA's communication of information bearing on a consumer's credit worthiness, credit standing, credit capacity, character, general reputation, personal characteristics, or mode of living that is used or expected to be used or collected for the purpose of serving as a factor in establishing the consumer's eligibility for credit, insurance, employment, or other authorized purposes. 15 U.S.C. § 1681a(d)(1).

[3] Department of the Treasury, A Financial System That Creates Economic Opportunities: Nonbank Financials, Fintech, and Innovation (Washington, D.C.: July 2018).

[4] GAO-18-559 addresses questions related to the causes and impacts of the Equifax breach and Equifax's response to the breach, and a forthcoming report will address the role of CRAs in federal agencies' implementation of government programs.

federal laws and regulations governing CRAs' collection, use, and protection of consumer information; (2) measures the Federal Trade Commission (FTC) has taken to enforce CRA compliance with requirements to protect consumer information; (3) measures CFPB has taken to ensure that CRAs protect consumer information; and (4) FTC's and CFPB's roles in assisting consumers following a data breach and actions consumers can take following a data breach of a CRA.

To examine the laws governing CRAs, we identified relevant laws and reviewed them for their application to CRAs. We interviewed and reviewed documentation from the three nationwide CRAs and interviewed three additional CRAs that produce or compile consumer reporting information.[5] We selected these CRAs because they are not sector-specific and hold information on a broad segment of the population. We conducted a site visit to Equifax's Alpharetta, Georgia data center to learn more about steps the company takes to comply with relevant consumer protection laws. In addition, we interviewed staff from CFPB and FTC, and the Office of the Attorney General of four states with existing or proposed information protection laws or regulations that vary from federal requirements (California, Illinois, Massachusetts, and New York). We also interviewed associations representing companies that furnish consumer information to and use consumer reports from CRAs—the American Bankers Association, the Property Casualty Insurance Association of America, and the National Retail Federation—about their roles in the collection, use, and protection of consumer data, and steps they take to comply with relevant laws. To assess FTC and CFPB measures to enforce information protection provisions and to ensure CRAs' proper collection, use, and protection of consumer information, we reviewed documents from FTC and CFPB. We reviewed the types of enforcement actions available to FTC and CFPB for violations of relevant laws, as well as specific enforcement actions these agencies have brought against CRAs. We also reviewed documentation on the scope of CFPB examinations of larger market participant CRAs since 2015, as well as findings from recent CRA examinations.[6] In addition, we reviewed CFPB examination guidance for supervising these CRAs, including CFPB's internal guidelines for conducting data security examinations. We also reviewed documents related to CFPB's process for prioritizing which institutions and which product lines should receive supervisory examination, and we interviewed CFPB staff about this process. We interviewed officials from FTC and CFPB on their oversight activities, and we interviewed representatives of industry, consumer, and privacy groups on their views about supervision and oversight of CRAs.

---

[5] We use "nationwide CRA" to refer to what the Fair Credit Reporting Act (FCRA) defines as a "consumer reporting agency that compiles and maintains files on consumers on a nationwide basis." FCRA defines this phrase as a consumer reporting agency that regularly engages in the practice of assembling or evaluating, and maintaining public record information and credit account information regarding consumers residing nationwide for the purpose of furnishing consumer reports to third parties bearing on a consumer's credit worthiness, credit standing, or credit capacity. 15 U.S.C. § 1681a(p).

[6] CFPB defines larger market participant CRAs as those with more than $7 million in annual receipts from consumer reporting. *See* 12 C.F.R. § 1090.104(b).

To assess FTC's and CFPB's roles in assisting consumers, as well as actions consumers can take following a data breach of a CRA, we reviewed the two agencies' websites and other publicly available consumer educational materials. We also interviewed staff from these agencies about their roles in assisting consumers following a breach. To identify actions consumers can take following a data breach, we reviewed our prior related reports and spoke with the industry and consumer representatives noted above.[7] See app. I for a more detailed discussion of our scope and methodology for this chapter.

We conducted this performance audit from November 2017 to February 2019 in accordance with generally accepted government auditing standards. Those standards require that we plan and perform the audit to obtain sufficient, appropriate evidence to provide a reasonable basis for our findings and conclusions based on our audit objectives. We believe that the evidence obtained provides a reasonable basis for our findings and conclusions based on our audit objectives.

## BACKGROUND

### The Consumer Reporting Process

Information on consumers is exchanged through a consumer reporting process that includes consumers, CRAs, furnishers, and users of that information (see fig.1).

- *Consumers* are individuals whose information is collected and shared to make eligibility decisions, such as for credit, insurance, or employment.[8]
- *CRAs* are companies that assemble or evaluate consumer information for the purpose of furnishing consumer reports to third parties who use the reports to determine consumer eligibility for employment, or products and services such as credit and insurance.
- *Furnishers* are entities such as banks or credit card companies that provide CRAs with consumer information, such as account openings, bill payments, or delinquency information. CRAs use this information, along with other

[7] Prior GAO reports included GAO, Identity Theft Services: Services Offer Some Benefits but Are Limited in Preventing Fraud, GAO-17-254 (Washington, D.C: Mar. 30, 2017) and GAO, Personal Information: Key Federal Privacy Laws Do Not Require Information Resellers to Safeguard All Sensitive Data, GAO-06-674 (Washington, D.C.: June 26, 2006).

[8] Under the Gramm Leach Bliley Act (GLBA), Pub. L. No. 106-102, 113 Stat. 1338 (1999), a "consumer" is an individual who obtains, from a financial institution, financial products or services which are to be used primarily for personal, family, or household purposes. 15 U.S.C. § 6809(9). Under FCRA, Pub. L. No. 91-508, tit. VI, §§ 601-622, 84 Stat. 1114, 1127-1136 (1970), a "consumer" is an individual. 15 U.S.C. § 1681a(c). For purposes of this chapter, we use "consumer" to refer to any individual about whom a CRA has consumer report information, such as payment history, regardless of whether the individual engaged the services of the CRA.

information, including from public records such as bankruptcies, to compile consumer reports.

- *Users* are banks, credit card companies, employers, or other entities that use consumer reports to make eligibility decisions for individual consumers. Users vary in the specific information they request from CRAs and how they interpret the data. Some institutions, such as banks, may act as both furnishers and users.

During the consumer reporting process, a consumer would not necessarily interact with the CRA; however, if the consumer discovered inaccurate information on their credit report as a result of, for example, being denied credit, the consumer could file a dispute with the CRA or the furnisher. Consumers may also request copies of their consumer reports from CRAs directly, and CRAs may provide consumers with disclosures about how their information is being shared.

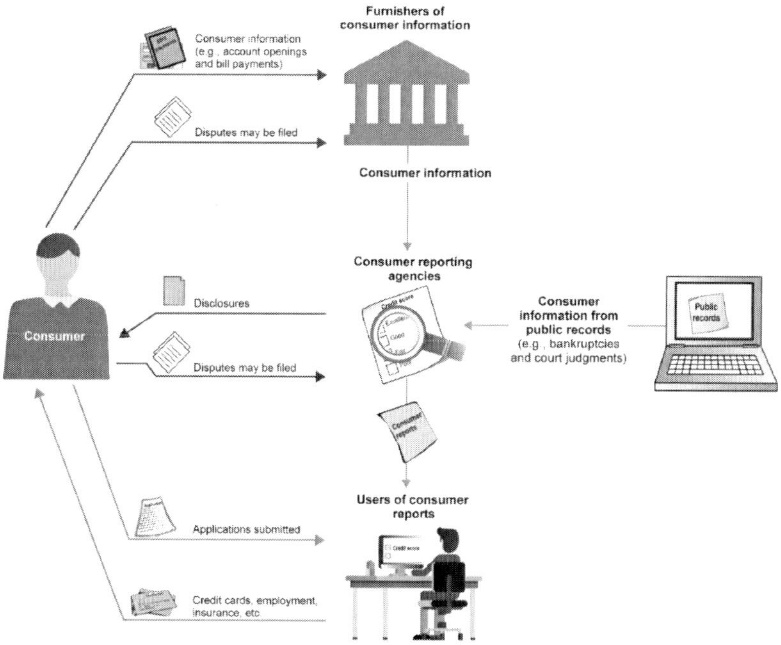


Source: GAO analysis of consumer reporting information. | GAO-19-196.

Figure 1. The Consumer Reporting Process.

## Oversight Agencies

FTC and, most recently, CFPB, are the federal agencies primarily responsible for overseeing CRAs. FTC has authority to investigate most organizations that maintain consumer data and to bring enforcement actions for violations of statutes and regulations that concern the security of data and consumer information.[9] CFPB, created in 2010 by the Dodd-Frank Wall Street Reform and Consumer Protection Act (Dodd-Frank Act), has enforcement authority over all CRAs for violations of certain consumer financial protection laws.[10] In general, it also has the authority to issue regulations and guidance for those laws. CFPB has supervisory authority over larger market participants in the consumer reporting market. In 2012, CFPB defined larger market participant CRAs as those with more than $7 million in annual receipts from consumer reporting.[11] CFPB's supervision of these companies includes monitoring, inspecting, and examining them for compliance with the requirements of certain federal consumer financial laws and regulations. As discussed below, these laws include most provisions of the Fair Credit Reporting Act (FCRA); several provisions of the Gramm-Leach-Bliley Act (GLBA); and provisions of the Dodd-Frank Act concerning unfair, deceptive, or abusive acts or practices.[12]

## Data Breaches and the Equifax Breach

Although there is no commonly agreed-upon definition of "data breach," the term generally refers to an unauthorized or unintentional exposure, disclosure, or loss of sensitive information. This information can include personally identifiable information such as Social Security numbers, or financial information such as credit card numbers. A data breach can be inadvertent, such as from the loss of an electronic device; or deliberate, such as from the theft of a device. A breach can also occur as a result of a cyber-based attack by individuals or groups, including organizations' own employees, foreign nationals, or terrorists.[13] Data breaches have occurred at all types of organizations, including private, nonprofit, and federal and state entities.

In the Equifax data breach, Equifax system administrators discovered on July 29, 2017, that intruders had gained unauthorized access via the Internet to a server housing the

---

[9] *See* 15 U.S.C. §§ 6801-6809); 16 C.F.R. § 314.1(a) and § 314.3(b)(2)-(3).

[10] Pub. L. No. 111-203, tit. X, 124 Stat. 1376, 1955 (2010).

[11] *See* Defining Larger Participants of the Consumer Reporting Market, 77 Fed. Reg. 42874 (July 20, 2012).

[12] The rulemaking authority for GLBA's safeguards provision and FCRA's red flags and records disposal provisions are statutorily excluded from CFPB's authority. *See* 12 U.S.C. § 5481(12)(F),(J). According to CFPB staff, CFPB can examine the data security practices of larger market participant CRAs for compliance with the provisions of the Dodd-Frank Act, including the prohibition of unfair, deceptive, or abusive acts or practices, and can obtain information about CRAs' compliance management systems, including those for data security. *See* 12 U.S.C. § 5514(b)(1). However, CFPB staff said they cannot examine for compliance with or enforce the data security standards in these provisions of GLBA and FCRA or the FTC's implementing rules, even at larger market participant CRAs.

[13] For more information on types of cyberattacks, see GAO, Cybersecurity: Bank and Other Depository Regulators Need Better Data Analytics and Depository Institutions Want More Usable Threat Information, GAO-15-509 (Washington, D.C.: July 2, 2015).

company's online dispute portal.[14] The breach compromised the personally identifiable information of at least 145.5 million individuals, and included names, addresses, and birth dates; and credit card, driver's license, and Social Security numbers.[15] Equifax's investigation of the breach identified factors that led to the breach: software vulnerabilities, failure to detect malicious traffic, failure to isolate databases from each other, and inadequately limiting access to sensitive information such as usernames and passwords. Equifax's public filings after the breach noted that the company took steps to improve security and notify individuals about the breach. Our August 2018 report provides more information on the breach and Equifax's response.[16]

While data breaches do not always result in measurable harm, intruders may retain or resell stolen information to commit identity theft, which can include existing-account fraud and new-account fraud. In existing-account fraud, identity thieves use financial account identifiers, such as credit card or debit card numbers, to take over an individual's existing accounts to make unauthorized charges or withdraw money. In new-account fraud, identity thieves use an individual's identifying data, such as Social Security and driver's license numbers, to open new financial accounts and incur charges and obtain credit in an individual's name without that person's knowledge. In addition, identity thieves may commit synthetic identity fraud, where they combine real and/or fictitious information to create identities with which they may defraud financial institutions, government agencies, or individuals.[17]

## Several Federal Laws Govern the Collection, Use, and Protection of Consumer Information

### FCRA Governs the Accuracy, Use, and Sharing of Consumer Information, and CRAs Reported Taking Actions to Comply

FCRA, enacted in 1970, is one of the primary federal laws governing the personal information that CRAs hold.[18] It governs the accuracy of this information and gives

---

[14] Equifax's online dispute portal is a web-based application that allows an individual to upload documents to research and dispute an inaccuracy in their Equifax credit report.

[15] On October 2, 2017, Equifax revised the number of affected individuals from 143 million to 145.5 million after it had incorrectly concluded that one of the attackers' queries had not returned any data. On March 1, 2018, Equifax stated that it had identified approximately 2.4 million U.S. consumers whose names and partial driver's license information were stolen, but as of August 2018, Equifax had not determined how many of these individuals were included in the estimate of 145.5 million affected individuals.

[16] GAO-18-559.

[17] See GAO, *Highlights of a Forum: Combating Synthetic Identity Fraud,* GAO-17-708SP (Washington, D.C.: July 2017) for more information on synthetic identity fraud.

[18] Pub. L. No. 91-508, tit. VI, §§ 601-622, 84 Stat. 1114, 1127-1136 (1970) (codified as amended at 15 U.S.C. §§ 1681-1681x). In this section, we focus on the primary laws that govern CRAs' collection, use, and protection

consumers rights to view, correct, or opt out of the sharing or use of certain aspects of their personal information among affiliates. FCRA also applies to how CRAs can use and share the information.

### *Accuracy of Collected Information*

FCRA requires that when preparing a consumer report, CRAs follow reasonable procedures to assure "maximum possible accuracy" of the information concerning the individual about whom the report relates.[19] Companies that furnish information to CRAs also must take steps regarding the accuracy of information they report, as required by FCRA and its implementing regulation, Regulation V.[20] A 2012 CFPB report cited steps that nationwide CRAs take to help ensure that information they collect from furnishers is legitimate and accurate.[21] The report notes that initial screening of furnishers generally includes an inspection of the companies' physical headquarters, phone numbers, websites, business licenses, and company records such as annual reports. In addition, these CRAs may hire third-party investigation services to screen for illegal or unethical business practices. They may also conduct additional inspections in response to consumer complaints, variations in data reporting, or changes in a furnisher's ownership. To conduct quality checks on data submitted by furnishers, CFPB reported that the nationwide CRAs check for blank fields or logical inconsistencies. Representatives of CRAs we spoke with provided examples of the quality assurance steps they take. For example, one representative told us that they look for violations of logical patterns, such as a loan going from 30 days past due to 90 days past due over the course of one month. CFPB reported that when inaccuracies are identified, the CRAs can reject the information. These steps may improve the quality of the information received from furnishers, but they cannot ensure the accuracy of such data.

### *Use and Sharing of Information*

FCRA permits CRAs to provide users with consumer reports only if the user has a "permissible purpose," such as to process a credit application, screen a job applicant, or underwrite an insurance policy, subject to limitations where the credit or insurance

---

of consumer information generally. Additional laws may apply to certain specialty CRAs, such as those that collect health-related information.

[19] 15 U.S.C. § 1681e(b).

[20] *See* 15 U.S.C. § 1681s-2(a) and 12 C.F.R. § 1022.42(a). Those who furnish information to CRAs regularly and in the ordinary course of business have a duty to provide accurate information about their transactions or experiences with consumers; if a furnisher determines that information it provided to a CRA is not complete or accurate, the furnisher must promptly notify the CRA about the error and provide any corrections. See 15 U.S.C. § 1681s-2(a)(2). We will discuss requirements related to the accuracy of data collected and used by CRAs in a forthcoming report.

[21] Consumer Financial Protection Bureau, Key Dimensions and Processes in the U.S. Credit Reporting System: A Review of How the Nation's Largest Credit Bureaus Manage Consumer Data (Washington, D.C.: December 2012).

transaction is not initiated by the consumer.[22] FCRA also prohibits the use of a consumer report for any purpose other than that specified to the CRA when the user obtained the report.[23] It also requires that CRAs take steps to validate the legitimacy of users and their requests for consumer report information and apply FCRA requirements to the sharing of information within their companies.[24]

### *Validating the Legitimacy of Users and Their Requests for Consumer Report Information*[25]

Representatives of CRAs told us they take several steps to validate the legitimacy of users and their requests, including verifying credit transactions, periodically evaluating user agreements, and validating users' identities. For example, representatives of one CRA said they sometimes conduct on-site visits to verify the existence of an entity and the business it conducts. In addition, they said they randomly select 6,000 to 8,000 consumer files each year and ask users associated with those files to show proof that the consumers engaged in the credit transactions contained in those files. However, several CRAs told us that these steps cannot guarantee that the users and requests are valid. For example, representatives of one CRA noted that once a user has the information, a CRA would find it difficult to prevent that user from retaining and reusing it for purposes other than the original permissible purpose.

### *Applying FCRA Requirements to Sharing Information Internally*

As amended by the Fair and Accurate Credit Transactions Act of 2003, FCRA limits the ability of affiliated companies to market products or services to consumers using shared consumer data. Affiliates may use consumer report information for product or service marketing only if they clearly and conspicuously disclose to the consumer that the information may be shared for such solicitations, the consumer is provided a simple method to opt out of such solicitations, and the consumer does not opt out.[26] Representatives of CRAs told us that they apply the same FCRA protections when they share consumer reporting data among their departments or subsidiaries, which may use the data for other purposes. For example, one nationwide CRA said that one of its internal groups seeks to ensure that the company implements appropriate legal protections when it shares data for other uses within the company.

Staff from state Attorneys General offices we spoke with told us that their states also have laws pertaining to consumer reporting, which have similar requirements to those in

---

[22] *See* 15 U.S.C. § 1681b.

[23] *See* 15 U.S.C. § 1681b(f).

[24] *See* 15 U.S.C. § 1681e and § 1681s-3(a).

[25] Under FCRA, CRAs must make a reasonable effort to verify the identity of a new prospective user prior to furnishing such user a consumer report. If a CRA has reasonable grounds for believing that a consumer report will not be used for a permissible purpose, the CRA may not furnish the consumer report. 15 U.S.C. § 1681e(a).

[26] See 15 U.S.C. § 1681s-3(a) (as amended by Pub. L. 108–159, tit. II, § 214(a)(2), 117 Stat. 1952, 1980).

FCRA.[27] In addition, they noted that while there is no federal data breach notification law, all 50 states have laws requiring companies to notify consumers in the event of a data breach. According to the National Conference of State Legislatures, those laws have varying requirements, such as the timing or method of notification, and who must be notified.

## GLBA and Other Laws Govern the Protection of Consumer Information

Congress enacted GLBA in part to protect the privacy and security of nonpublic personal information that individuals provide to financial institutions.[28] According to FTC staff, CRAs may be considered financial institutions under GLBA if they collect, maintain, and report on consumer information.[29] As with FCRA, GLBA restricts financial institutions from sharing consumers' private information, but GLBA restricts sharing with nonaffiliated third parties specifically, and those parties face similar restrictions in how they may further share or use the information.[30]

In addition, unlike FCRA, GLBA includes a provision directing FTC and certain federal regulators (not including CFPB) to establish standards specifically with respect to protection against any anticipated threats or hazards to the security of customer records. Specifically, under GLBA, these federal regulators are directed to establish appropriate standards for financial institutions under their jurisdiction to ensure the security and confidentiality of customer records and information; protect against any anticipated threats or hazards to the security or integrity of such records; and protect against unauthorized access to or use of such records or information that could result in substantial harm or inconvenience to any customer.[31] To implement these standards for

---

[27] If a state consumer reporting or protection law conflicts with FCRA, FCRA requirements preempt the state requirements; but if a state consumer reporting law has additional requirements that are consistent with FCRA, the state requirements may apply.

[28] *See* Pub. L. No. 106-102, tit. V, §§ 501-509, 113 Stat. 1338, 1436 (1999) (codified as amended at 15 U.S.C. §§ 6801-6809). Subtitle A of title V of the act contains the privacy, security, and confidentiality provisions relating to nonpublic personal information. 15 U.S.C. §§ 6801-6809.

[29] As applicable to consumer reporting agencies, GLBA privacy provisions (but not its data safeguards provision) are implemented in CFPB's Regulation P, 12 C.F.R. pt. 1016. Under GLBA, "financial institution" is defined as any institution the business of which is engaging in financial activities as described in section 4(k) of the Bank Holding Company Act of 1956 (12 U.S.C. § 1843(k)), among other things. *See* 15 U.S.C. § 6809(3)(A). Activities that are financial in nature includes any activity that the Board of Governors of the Federal Reserve System has determined to be so closely related to banking or managing or controlling banks as to be a proper incident thereto. 12 U.S.C. § 1843(k)(4)(F). Maintaining information related to the credit history of consumers and providing the information to a credit grantor who is considering a borrower's application for credit or who has extended credit to the borrower is considered an activity that is financial in nature. *See* 12 C.F.R. § 225.28(b)(2)(v).

[30] *See* 15 U.S.C. § 6802(c).

[31] *See* 15 U.S.C. § 6801(b). Banking agencies have implemented GLBA's safeguards requirements through the Interagency Guidelines on Information Security. *See* Interagency Guidelines Establishing Standards for Safeguarding Customer Information and Rescission of Year 2000 Standards for Safety and Soundness, 66 Fed. Reg. 8616 (Feb. 1, 2001). Authority to write, supervise for compliance with, and enforce these standards was

CRAs, and other entities that fall under its jurisdiction, FTC adopted its Safeguards Rule, which requires, among other things, that financial institutions have a written information security program, assess the risks to customer information, and evaluate and adjust the information security program in light of foreseeable risks.[32] FTC staff told us that because GLBA applies to information about a consumer with a customer relationship with a financial institution, the Safeguards Rule may not apply in all cases where a CRA holds personal information on individuals.[33] For example, they said that GLBA would more clearly apply if the consumer had purchased credit monitoring or other products or services directly from the CRA, or if the CRA obtained customer information from another financial institution, such as a bank. Representatives of the three nationwide CRAs told us that for purposes of protecting information, they do not distinguish between consumers with whom they have a direct customer relationship and those with whom they do not.

CRAs we spoke with provided examples of how they protect consumer information and meet GLBA requirements to maintain administrative, technical, and physical safeguards. For example, with respect to administrative safeguards, representatives of one CRA said they enforce contractual requirements for data access and data security. Representatives of another CRA said that the technical safeguards they use include firewalls, anti-virus software, and malware protection. Examples of physical safeguards from another CRA included monitoring data centers by video and restricting access to secure data rooms. To address data protection more generally, representatives of CRAs we spoke with told us they routinely conduct internal audits of their data security systems, and that the financial institutions they work with frequently conduct audits of their risk management practices, including CRAs' data security controls.[34]

Provisions related to unfair or deceptive acts or practices also may apply to CRAs' protection of consumer data. Specifically, under FTC's authority, section 5 of the Federal Trade Commission Act (FTC Act) prohibits "unfair or deceptive acts or practices" in or affecting commerce.[35] In the context of privacy and security, these provisions require companies to truthfully represent practices to consumers. For example, FTC has found

carved out of CFPB's authority by section 1002(12)(J) of the Dodd-Frank Act. *See* 12 U.S.C. § 5481(12)(J); *see also* 15 U.S.C. § 6801(b).

[32] *See* 16 C.F.R. § 314.3-4. The Safeguards Rule implements GLBA's requirements for entities that fall under FTC jurisdiction, including CRAs, check-cashing businesses, payday lenders, mortgage brokers, and other entities.

[33] Under GLBA, "consumer" means an individual who obtains from a financial institution financial products or services that are to be used primarily for personal, family, or household purposes, or that individual's legal representative. 15 U.S.C. § 6809(9). Under GLBA's implementing Regulation P, a "customer" is a consumer who has a continuing relationship with a financial institution that provides one or more financial products or services to the consumer primarily for personal, family, or household purposes. *See* 12 C.F.R. § 1016.3(i)-(j).

[34] Federal banking regulators expect supervised financial institutions to exercise due diligence when selecting third parties with which they enter into business relationships and to maintain effective risk management practices with such third parties, which, according to regulators we spoke with, can include CRAs. *See, e.g.*, OCC Bulletin 2013-29, Third-Party Relationships (Oct. 30, 2013).CRAs we spoke with said that because of this expectation, they are subject to frequent data security reviews by their financial institution clients. For example, one nationwide CRA told us it receives roughly 30 to 50 requests for such reviews a month.

[35] *See* 15 U.S.C. § 45.

companies that alleged that they were following certain security protections, but did not in fact have such security features, to have engaged in unfair or deceptive practices. Similarly, the Dodd-Frank Act prohibits providers of consumer financial products or services from engaging in "unfair, deceptive, or abusive acts or practices," and CFPB has authority to enforce and supervise for compliance with this provision.[36] CFPB has alleged that claims to consumers that transactions are safe and secure while simultaneously lacking basic security practices can constitute unfair, deceptive, or abusive acts or practices. FTC and CFPB officials said that in the case of data breaches, they would examine each case individually to determine whether the institution violated these provisions in connection with the breach.

Some states also have laws that protect consumer information, including laws that generally govern data security. For example, staff from the Massachusetts Attorney General's office told us that their state has a data security law similar to FTC's Safeguards Rule but with more specific requirements, including those for malware detection and firewalls. According to the National Consumer Law Center, all 50 states have consumer protection laws that prohibit unfair or deceptive practices. Staff from state Attorneys General offices told us that they can prosecute entities for potential violations of these provisions, including data breaches. They told us that following the Equifax breach, several states' Attorneys General launched a joint investigation into whether Equifax violated state laws, including prohibitions of unfair or deceptive practices. According to staff from one state Attorney General office, as of February 2019, this investigation was ongoing. In addition, Equifax reported that individual states have also filed legal action or have ongoing investigations. For example, Massachusetts and West Virginia have filed civil enforcement actions against Equifax that seek various remedies, including civil penalties.

## FTC Has Taken Enforcement Measures against CRAs but Lacks Civil Penalty Authority for GLBA Data Protection Provisions

### FTC Enforces CRA Compliance with Consumer Protection Laws

FTC enforces compliance with consumer protection laws under authorities provided in FCRA, GLBA, and the FTC Act. FCRA authorizes FTC to enforce compliance for nearly all companies not supervised by either a federal banking regulator or certain other

[36] *See* Pub. L. No. 111-203, §§ 1031, 1036, 124 Stat. 1376, 2005, 2010 (2010) (codified at 12 U.S.C. §§ 5531, 5536).

federal agencies.[37] GLBA authorizes FTC to issue certain rules and enforce compliance for all nonbank financial institutions and other entities not under the jurisdiction of a federal banking regulator, the National Credit Union Administration, Securities and Exchange Commission, or state insurance regulators.[38] The FTC Act authorizes FTC to investigate and take administrative and civil enforcement actions against companies under its jurisdiction that engage in unfair or deceptive acts or practices in or affecting commerce.[39] According to FTC, in the last 10 years, it has brought 34 enforcement actions for FCRA violations, including 17 against CRAs. In addition, FTC said that it had taken a total of 66 actions against companies (not just in the last 10 years), including CRAs, that allegedly engaged in unfair or deceptive practices relating to data protection.

If FTC has reason to believe that a company has violated laws under its jurisdiction, it may initiate an investigation to determine whether to take enforcement action. FTC staff said that in determining whether to take on a case related to privacy and data security matters, they consider factors such as the company's size and the sensitivity of the data in the company's network. For example, FTC may choose not to investigate a data breach of a small company that affects few people; however, it may investigate a potential data security violation of a large company, even without evidence of a breach. Under its statutory authority, FTC can ask or compel companies to produce documents, testimony, and other materials to assist in its investigations.[40] In June 2018, FTC notified Equifax that it was considering legal action against the company as a result of its 2017 data breach, including seeking civil penalties.

If FTC finds that a company violated consumer law, the agency may take several different actions depending on its legal authority and what it considers to be the most appropriate response. For example, FTC may, in administrative proceedings, issue cease-and-desist orders for unfair or deceptive acts or practices. Further, FTC generally may seek a range of remedies from the U.S. district courts, including injunctions, damages to compensate consumers for their actual losses, and disgorgement of ill-gotten funds.[41] In limited circumstances, FTC also may seek civil money penalties, which are monetary fines imposed for a violation of a statute or regulation.[42]

Examples of FTC enforcement actions related to consumer reporting include:

---

[37] *See* 15 U.S.C. § 1681s(a)(1).Other agencies with FCRA enforcement authority include, but are not limited to, the Federal Deposit Insurance Corporation, Office of the Comptroller of the Currency, Board of Governors of the Federal Reserve System, National Credit Union Administration, Securities and Exchange Commission, and Department of Transportation. *See* 15 U.S.C. § 1681s(b)(1).

[38] *See* 15 U.S.C. § 6805(a)(7).

[39] *See* 15 U.S.C. § 45.

[40] *See* 15 U.S.C. § 49.

[41] Injunctions are judicial orders commanding a party to take an action or prohibiting a party from doing or continuing to do a certain activity. Disgorgement requires wrongdoers to give up profits or other gains illegally obtained.

[42] *See* 15 U.S.C § 45(l).Generally, a civil money penalty is one of several forms of monetary sanctions that an agency can impose on a violator as a punitive measure.

- In May 2016, FTC settled with a furnisher that allegedly violated FCRA requirements to have adequate policies and procedures for reporting accurate credit information to CRAs.[43] FTC alleged that a debt collector acting as a furnisher did not have a written policy regarding the accuracy and integrity of information it furnished, and in numerous instances failed to inform consumers about these outcomes.
- In 2011, FTC brought enforcement actions against three CRAs that merge, and then sell, information from the three nationwide CRAs. FTC alleged that these companies did not meet GLBA standards and violated unfair or deceptive practices prohibitions by not providing reasonable and appropriate security for consumers' personal information. These violations included not developing and disseminating information security policies, and not addressing risks by, for example, evaluating the security of end users' computer networks.[44]
- In 2006, FTC settled with ChoicePoint—a CRA—and imposed a $10 million civil penalty for violations of FCRA stemming from a 2005 data breach. In 2009, FTC obtained an additional $275,000 in equitable monetary relief due to ChoicePoint's violation of the order after an additional data breach occurred in 2008.[45]

## FTC's Lack of Civil Penalty Authority for GLBA May Hinder Its Effectiveness in Enforcing Data Security Provisions

As previously discussed, in some circumstances, FTC enforcement authority can include civil money penalties. This includes cases of knowing violations of FCRA.[46] For example, in a 2014 settlement, FTC levied $525,000 in civil penalties against a CRA after alleging that the company did not comply with FCRA provisions to ensure the accurate and permissible use of its reports. FTC does not have civil penalty authority for initial violations of the FTC Act but may obtain civil penalties from companies for violations of FTC Act orders.

FTC's civil penalty authority does not extend to initial violations of GLBA's privacy and safeguarding provisions, which require administrative, physical, and technical safeguards with an emphasis on protection against anticipated threats and unauthorized access to customer records. For violations of GLBA provisions, which are enforced

---

[43] *U.S. v. Credit Protection Assoc. LP*, Case No. 3:16-cv-01255-D (N.D. Tex. May 9, 2016)(stipulated final order for permanent injunction and civil penalty judgment).

[44] In the Matter of ACRA net, Inc.; Settlement One Credit Corp.; and Fajilan and Associates, Inc. d/b/a Statewide Credit Services, 76 Fed. Reg. 7213 (Feb. 9, 2011).

[45] *U.S. v. ChoicePoint, Inc.*, Case No. 1:06-cv-198-JTC (N.D. Ga. Oct. 19, 2009) (supplemental stipulated judgment and order for permanent injunction and monetary relief).

[46] See 15 U.S.C. § 1681s(a)(2)(A). Liability under this provision may be up to $2,500 per violation.

pursuant to FTC Act authority, FTC may seek an injunction to stop a company from violating these provisions and may seek redress (damages to compensate consumers for losses) or disgorgement. However, determining the appropriate amount of consumer compensation requires FTC to identify the consumers affected and the amount of monetary harm they suffered. In cases involving security or privacy violations resulting from data breaches, assessing monetary harm can be difficult. Consumers may not be aware that their identities have been stolen as a result of a breach and or identity theft, and related harm may occur years in the future. In addition, it can be difficult to trace instances of identity theft to specific data breaches. According to FTC staff, these factors can make it difficult for the agency to identify which individuals were victimized as a result of a particular breach and to what extent they were harmed and then obtain related redress or disgorgement. Having civil penalty authority for GLBA provisions would allow FTC to fine a company for a violation such as a data breach without needing to prove the monetary harm to individual consumers.

FTC staff told us and testified before Congress that civil penalties are often the most appropriate remedy for a data breach, and that such penalties serve as an effective deterrent in cases involving weak data privacy and security policies and practices.[47] FTC staff noted that in the case of a data breach, each consumer record exposed could constitute a violation; as a result, a data breach that involved a large number of consumer records could result in substantial fines. Unlike FTC, other regulators have civil penalty authority to punish entities that violate provisions of GLBA. For example, the Office of the Comptroller of the Currency has said that it can enforce GLBA privacy and safeguard provisions with civil money penalties against any insured depository institution or institution-affiliated party subject to its supervision.[48]

In our 2009 report on modernizing the financial regulatory framework, we stated that financial regulators should have the authority to carry out and enforce their statutory missions.[49] In the case of FTC, this includes having the tools necessary to meet its mission of protecting consumers from harm, including the harm caused by misuse of personal information, by having the range of authorities to punish entities for violations of the statutes and regulations the agency enforces.

In 2006, we suggested that Congress consider providing FTC with civil penalty authority for its enforcement of GLBA's privacy and safeguarding provisions.[50] We noted that providing this authority would give FTC a practical enforcement tool to more

---

[47] In December 2018, FTC also held a hearing on data security. This hearing included discussions on several issues, including whether Congress should provide FTC with civil penalty authority for data security enforcement. The full hearing can be accessed at https://www.ftc.gov/news-events/events-calendar/ftc-hearing-competition-consumerprotection-21st-century-december-2018.

[48] Under the Federal Deposit Insurance Act, the federal banking regulators have broad civil money penalty authority. *See* 12 U.S.C. § 1818(i)(2).

[49] GAO, *Financial Regulation: A Framework for Crafting and Assessing Proposals to Modernize the Outdated U.S. Financial Regulatory System,* GAO-09-216 (Washington, D.C: Jan. 8, 2009).

[50] GAO-06-674.

effectively enforce provisions related to security of data and consumer information. Following the 2008 financial crisis, Congress introduced several bills related to data protection and identity theft, which included giving FTC civil penalty authority for its enforcement of GLBA. However, in the final adoption of these laws, Congress did not provide FTC with this authority. Since that time, data breaches at Equifax and other large organizations have highlighted the need to better protect sensitive personal information. Accordingly, we continue to believe FTC and consumers would benefit if FTC had such authority.

# CFPB Enforces and Examines CRAs for Compliance with Consumer Protection Laws but Does Not Fully Consider Data Security in Prioritizing Examinations

## CFPB Enforces and Examines CRA Compliance with Consumer Protection Laws

CFPB enforces compliance with most provisions of FCRA; several provisions of GLBA; and the prohibition of unfair, deceptive, or abusive acts or practices under the Dodd-Frank Act.[51] According to CFPB staff, CFPB cannot enforce data security standards under these statutory provisions or the FTC's implementing rules because CFPB does not have authority to supervise for or enforce compliance with the GLBA's safeguards provision or FCRA's red flags or records disposal provisions.[52]

Since 2015, CFPB has had five public settlements with CRAs. Four of these settlements included alleged violations of FCRA and three included alleged violations of unfair, deceptive, or abusive practices provisions. For example, in March 2017, CFPB settled with Experian for $3 million in civil penalties for an alleged violation of FCRA

[51] CFPB has authority under FCRA, except for the provisions governing the disposal of information and the red flags of identity theft. Those provisions were carved out of the CFPB's authority by section 1002(12)(F) of the Dodd-Frank Act. *See* 12 U.S.C. § 5481(12)(F). The red flags rule requires financial institutions and creditors (as defined by statute) to implement a written identity theft prevention program designed to detect the "red flags" of identity theft in their day-to-day operations, among other things, while the disposal provision requires any person who maintains or otherwise possesses consumer information for a business purpose to dispose of such information properly by taking reasonable measures to protect against unauthorized access to or use of the information in connection with its disposal. *See* 15 U.S.C. §§ 1681m(e), 1681s(a)(1) and 1681w(a)(1) and 16 C.F.R. pts. 681 and 682. Those provisions remain under FTC's authority and apply to entities, including CRAs as applicable, subject to the agency's jurisdiction. In addition, CFPB has authority over title V, subtitle A of GLBA, except for the data safeguards in section 501(b) of GLBA, 15 U.S.C. § 6801(b). The data safeguards provision was carved out of the CFPB's authority by section 1002(12)(J) of the Dodd-Frank Act. *See* 12 U.S.C. § 5481(12)(J). That provision remains under FTC's jurisdiction with respect to CRAs and certain other entities. *See* 15 U.S.C. §§ 6801, 6804, 6805, and 16 C.F.R. pt. 314.

[52] Under GLBA, CFPB has enforcement authority over any financial institution and other covered persons or service providers that are subject to the the agency's jurisdiction and the act, with the exception of the safeguards rule issued under section 501 of GLBA. *See* 15 U.S.C. § 6805(a)(8).

and alleged deceptive acts or practices.[53] Experian marketed to consumers an "educational credit score" that the company claimed lenders used to make credit decisions.[54] CFPB alleged that lenders did not use these "educational credit scores" for this purpose, and that Experian violated FCRA's implementing regulation by requiring consumers to view Experian advertisements before obtaining a free credit report. In December 2015, CFPB levied a fine of $8 million against another CRA—Clarity Services, Inc.—for obtaining consumer reports without a permissible purpose in violation of FCRA and failing to investigate consumer disputes.[55] CFPB is also continuing its investigation of Equifax's data breach.

CFPB supervises the larger market participant CRAs (those with more than $7 million in annual receipts from consumer reporting, as defined by CFPB) and has the authority to examine these CRAs for compliance with federal consumer financial protection laws. From 2015 through 2017, CFPB examined several CRAs. Some of these examinations resulted in findings of deficiencies related to data accuracy and dispute processes, and follow-up examinations were conducted as necessary.[56] As part of its supervisory role, CFPB also periodically monitors the nationwide CRAs by requesting information on their activities and identifying any changes in risk to consumers and the market. CFPB uses this information to learn of changes to a CRA's compliance, personnel, issues raised by the CRA's internal audits, or other developments that might affect CFPB's strategy for supervising the CRA.

## CFPB May Not Be Identifying All CRAs under Its Supervisory Authority

CFPB has examined several larger market participant CRAs, but may not be identifying all CRAs that meet the $7 million threshold. CFPB staff told us that as of October 2018, they were tracking between 10 and 15 CRAs that might qualify as larger market participants (as defined by CFPB). CFPB staff told us that they believe the CRA market is highly concentrated and there were not likely to be many larger market participants beyond the 10 to 15 they are tracking. However, CFPB staff said that the 10 to 15 CRAs may not comprise the entirety of larger market participants because whether CRAs meet the threshold may vary from year to year and CFPB has limited data to determine whether CRAs meet the threshold. Specifically, CFPB staff said that identifying additional larger market participant CRAs can be challenging. For example, the Securities and Exchange Commission does not require nonpublicly traded CRAs to

[53] *In the Matter of Experian Holdings, Inc., et al*, File No. 2017-CFPB-0012 (Mar. 23, 2017) (consent order).

[54] CFPB reported that in addition to the credit scores that are used by lenders, several companies had developed "educational credit scores," which lenders rarely, if ever, used. These scores were intended to inform consumers, but were not used for credit decisions.

[55] *In the Matter of Clarity Services, Inc., et al*, File No. 2015-CFPB-0030 (Dec. 3, 2015) (consent order).

[56] *See, e.g.*, CFPB, *Supervisory Highlights Consumer Reporting Special Edition,* March 2017.

file financial and other information that CFPB could otherwise use to identify these CRAs, which are generally not widely known to the public. In addition, CFPB staff said they do not ask CRAs to provide their annual receipts, with the exception of the specific CRAs being considered for examination in a given year, because CFPB staff said calculating these receipts could create an additional cost to the companies.

Our January 2009 report on reforming the U.S. financial regulatory structure noted that regulators should be able to identify institutions and products that pose risks to the financial system, and monitor similar institutions consistently.[57] One method for identifying institutions for oversight, particularly where data are limited, is to require companies to register with the relevant regulator. For example, among other requirements, insured depository institutions must obtain a charter to operate, and money services businesses generally must register with the Financial Crimes Enforcement Network. Similarly, CFPB could identify CRAs that meet the larger market participant threshold by requiring such businesses to register with them, subject to a rulemaking process and cost-benefit analysis of the burden it could impose on the industry. Another method CFPB could use to identify CRAs and inform its oversight activities would be to leverage information collected by states. Stakeholders we spoke with cited New York and Maine as examples where CRAs are required to register with the state.[58] Implementing strategies such as registration or leveraging existing information could be a cost-effective way for CFPB to identify all CRAs under its authority. Identifying additional sources of information on the population of larger market participant CRAs—including those that are lesser-known, possibly unknown to CFPB, and possibly in possession of large amounts of sensitive consumer information—could help ensure that CFPB has more comprehensive information for carrying out its supervisory responsibilities.[59]

## CFPB's Prioritization of CRA Examinations Does Not Specifically Account for Data Security Risk

To determine which product lines, institutions, and compliance issues to examine, CFPB determines the institutions (for example, banks, credit unions, non-bank mortgage servicers, and CRAs) and the consumer product lines that pose the greatest risk to

---

[57] GAO-09-216.

[58] In June 2018, the New York Department of Financial Services adopted a regulation requiring registration of consumer credit reporting agencies that have assembled, evaluated, or maintained a consumer credit report on one thousand or more New York consumers in the previous 12 months. Similarly, any credit reporting agency that is used by creditors in Maine must register with the Maine Department of Professional and Financial Regulation.

[59] In a prior report, we similarly found that CFPB lacked comprehensive data on all nonbank mortgage servicers. We recommended that CFPB collect more comprehensive data on the identity and number of nonbank mortgage servicers in the market, and CFPB implemented our recommendation. See GAO, *Nonbank Mortgage Servicers: Existing Regulatory Oversight Could Be Strengthened.* GAO-16-278 (Washington, D.C.: March 10, 2016).

consumers, and prioritizes these for examinations annually (see fig.2). CFPB segments the consumer product market into institution product lines, or specific institutions' offerings of consumer product lines. CFPB then assesses each institution product line's risk to consumers at the market level and institutional level. To assess risk at the market level, CFPB considers market size and other factors that contribute to market risk. Market size includes a consideration of a product's market size relative to other consumer finance product markets. Other market risk factors include the potential risk to consumers from new or existing products offered in the market as well as emerging risks and trends in consumer financial products. For example, CFPB noted that a market may be considered higher risk if consumers cannot choose the provider of a financial product or service in that market, or if the transactions occur between two businesses rather than between a business and consumers. Because they do not face the same risk of losing customers as companies in other markets, companies in higher-risk markets may not have the same financial incentives to protect the interests of consumers.

To assess risk at the institution level, CFPB considers an institution's market share within a product line, as well as field and market intelligence. An institution's market share correlates with the number of consumers who could be affected by that institution's practices; therefore, CFPB generally places a higher priority on larger providers of products. Field and market intelligence includes quantitative and qualitative information on an institution's operations for a given product line, including the strength of its compliance management systems, the number of regulatory actions directed at the institution, findings from prior CFPB examinations, information obtained from CFPB's quarterly monitoring of institutions, public reports, and the number and severity of consumer complaints CFPB has received about the institution. Field and market intelligence can also include information about an institution's fair lending practices and its ability to provide fair, equitable, and nondiscriminatory access to credit.

Taking market and institutional considerations together, CFPB places institution product lines into tiers based on its determination of their relative risk to consumers. These risk tiers range from 1 to 5, with 1 being the lowest risk and 5 being the highest risk. Risk tiers then feed into CFPB's development of its supervision strategy, which includes other information, including information from subject matter experts and recent legal and policy decisions that could affect examinations, and consultations with internal stakeholders. CFPB uses both the risk tiers and information from its supervision strategy to identify potential institutions for examination. Following this process, CFPB has regularly determined CRAs' consumer reporting to be a high priority for examination since it began supervising them in 2012.

After identifying institution product lines to examine, CFPB determines specific areas of compliance to assess. These determinations are made by considering sources such as consumer complaints, public filings and reports, and past examination findings related to the same or similar products or institutions. Most recently, CFPB examinations of CRA's consumer reporting have focused on issues such as data accuracy, dispute processes, compliance management, and permissible purposes.

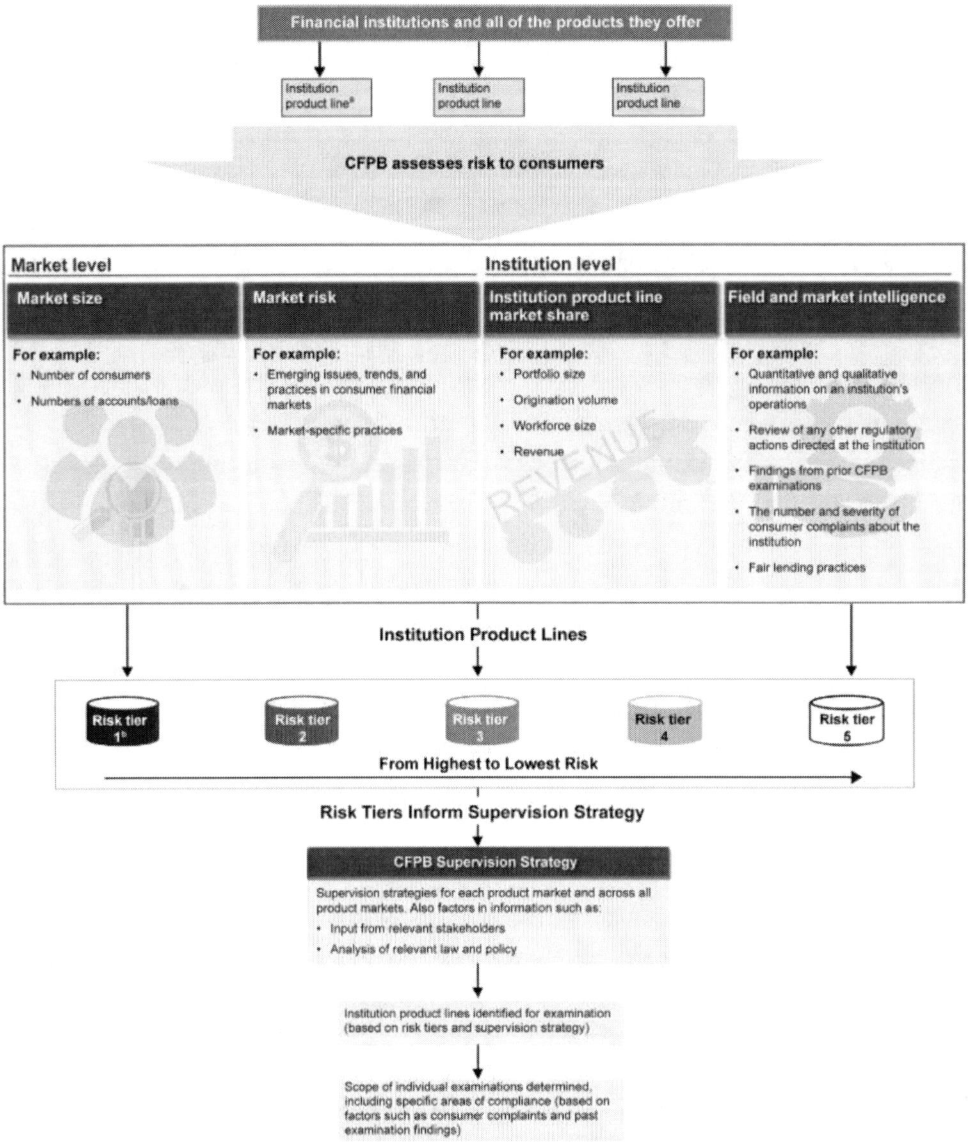


Source: GAO analysis of Consumer Financial Production Bureau (CFPB) information. | GAO-19-196.

[a] Institution product lines are specific products offered by a particular financial institution.

[b] Risk tiers represent CFPB's sorting of institution product lines by the relative risk posed to consumers.

Figure 2. Consumer Financial Protection Bureau (CFPB) Supervision Prioritization Framework.

Although CFPB's examination prioritization incorporates several important factors and sources, the process does not routinely include assessments of data security risk, such as how institutions detect and respond to cyber threats. According to CFPB staff, the agency's process for determining risk tiers incorporates the risk factors specifically cited in the

Dodd-Frank Act, including those related to the size of a product market.[60] The Act also states that CFPB should consider other factors it determines to be relevant; as such, CFPB staff noted that certain elements of data protection have been included in the scope of some of its past CRA examinations. For example, CFPB staff said that in assessing compliance with FCRA's permissible purposes provision, the examination scope would include ensuring that data are not improperly shared. CFPB staff noted that the bureau cannot examine for compliance with or enforce the data security standards in provisions of GLBA and FCRA or FTC's implementing rules, even at larger participant CRAs. After the Equifax breach, however, CFPB used its existing supervisory authority to develop internal guidelines for examining data security, and conduct some CRA data security examinations.[61] CFPB staff said that they do not routinely consider data security risks during their examination prioritization process and have not reassessed the process to determine how to incorporate such risks going forward.

The Dodd-Frank Act requires CFPB, when implementing its risk-based supervision program, to consider risks posed to consumers in the relevant product and geographic markets. In addition, federal internal control standards state that agencies should identify, analyze, and respond to risks related to achieving defined objectives. This can entail considering all significant internal and external factors to identify risks and their significance, including magnitude of impact, likelihood of occurrence, nature of the risk, and appropriate response.[62] In light of the Equifax breach, as well as CFPB's acknowledgment of the CRA market as a higher-risk market for consumers, it is important for CFPB to routinely consider factors that could inform the extent of CRA data security risk such as the number of consumers that could be affected by a data security incident and the nature of potential harm resulting from the loss or exposure of information.

CFPB's reliance primarily on consumer complaints, information from public filings, and information and findings from past examination for prioritizing examinations may not fully detect data security risks that CRAs pose. Data accuracy and dispute resolution feature prominently in consumer complaints, according to CFPB staff, because

---

[60] The Dodd-Frank Act states that CFPB's risk-based supervision program should take into consideration risks posed to consumers in the relevant product markets and geographic markets, including the asset size of the covered person; the volume of transactions involving consumer financial products or services in which the covered person engages; the risks to consumers created by the provision of such consumer financial products or services; the extent to which such institutions are subject to oversight by state authorities for consumer protection; and any other factors that CFPB determines to be relevant to a class of covered persons. *See* Pub. L. No. 111-203, § 1024(b)(2), 124 Stat. 1376, 1987 (2010)(codified at 12 U.S.C. § 5514(b)(2)).

[61] CFPB's general supervisory authority includes (1) assessing compliance with the requirements of federal consumer financial law, including the Dodd-Frank Act's prohibition of unfair, deceptive, and abusive acts or practices; (2) obtaining information about the activities and compliance systems of the examined institution; and (3) detecting and assessing risks of consumer financial products and services to consumers and markets. *See* 12 U.S.C. § 5514(b)(1). CFPB staff noted that unless the bureau finds that the institution has violated the Dodd-Frank Act's prohibition on unfair, deceptive, or abusive acts or practices, or another provision of federal consumer financial law over which CFPB has authority, the bureau is limited to supervisory recommendations.

[62] GAO, *Standards for Internal Control in the Federal Government,* GAO-14-704G (Washington, D.C.: Sept. 10, 2014).

consumers mostly interact with CRAs in these contexts. But consumers likely did not know, for example, about Equifax's data security challenges prior to its breach, so that vulnerability was not a focus of complaints. While the three nationwide CRAs acknowledged the risk of data breaches in recent public filings, other larger participant CRAs may not be publicly traded and therefore may not have public filings. Further, if CFPB's past examinations have not addressed data security, the agency cannot use those past examination findings to target current risks.

The Equifax breach demonstrated the vulnerability that CRAs may face with regard to data security. We have noted that advancements in technology, combined with the increasing sophistication of hackers and others with malicious intent, have increased the risk of sensitive personal information being exposed and compromised.[63] We have also reported that rapid developments in new technologies will continue to pose new threats to security, privacy, and safety.[64] In recent years, insured depository institutions—which, like CRAs, maintain large amounts of sensitive consumer data—have been subject to regular information technology examinations, which, according to one regulator, may include a cybersecurity component. Banking regulators have noted that unauthorized access to the information and systems that support these institutions can affect operations, pose risk to consumers through exposure of private information, and undermine consumer confidence.

The risks may be similar for CRAs—companies that by definition also maintain extensive amounts of sensitive consumer information. By including routine consideration of data security risks into its process for prioritizing CRA examinations, CFPB can better ensure that its supervision of CRAs proactively detects such risks and helps prevent the further exposure or compromise of consumer information.

## Regulators Inform Consumers about Protections Available and Consumers Can Take Some Actions after a CRA Data Breach

### FTC and CFPB Provide Consumers with Information on How to Address Identity Theft Risk

FTC and CFPB provide educational information for consumers on ways to mitigate the risk of identity theft. For example, FTC has a dedicated website (IdentityTheft.gov)

[63] GAO, *High Risk Series: Urgent Actions are Needed to Address Cybersecurity Challenges Facing the* Nation, GAO-18-645T (Washington, D.C.: Jul. 25, 2018).

[64] GAO, *High Risk Series: Progress on Many High Risk Areas, While Substantial Efforts Needed on Others,* GAO-17-317 (Washington, D.C.: Feb.15, 2017.

that allows consumers to report suspected identity theft to FTC and develop and implement a recovery plan. In addition, FTC offers businesses guidance on steps to take in the event of a data breach, including notification of relevant parties and a model notification letter. CFPB's website offers consumers tips on how to protect their information and spot identity theft.[65] CFPB also publishes a consumer guide that lists CRAs and their websites, and ways to obtain free credit reports.

After a breach, FTC and CFPB publish information specific to that breach. For example, shortly after Equifax's announcement of the breach, FTC published information on when the breach occurred, the types of data compromised, and links to additional information on Equifax's website. Similarly, CFPB released three blog posts and several social media posts shortly after Equifax's public announcement of the breach. These included information on ways that consumers could protect themselves in the wake of the breach and special protections and actions for service members.[66]

## Consumers Have Options to Mitigate Identity Theft Risk and Respond to Breaches

At any time, consumers can take actions to help mitigate identity theft risk. For example, consumers can implement a credit freeze free of charge, which can help prevent new-account fraud by restricting potential creditors from accessing the consumer's credit report.[67] Similarly, implementing a free fraud alert with a credit bureau can help prevent fraud because it requires a business to verify a consumer's identity before issuing credit.[68] Consumers also can monitor their credit report for suspicious activity, either through self-review or by using a free or paid credit monitoring service.[69] FTC and others recommend

[65] For example, see https://www.consumerfinance.gov/ask-cfpb/how-can-i-spot-identitytheft-en-1359/.

[66] CFPB placed all of the information related to the Equifax breach, including information about known or potential scams, at www.consumerfinance.gov/equifaxbreach.

[67] A credit freeze generally allows consumers to request a freeze on their credit reports by contacting each of the nationwide CRAs. Consumers are given a unique personal identification number or password that they use to temporarily lift or remove the freeze (for example, when they are applying for credit or employment). In May 2018, Congress passed the Economic Growth, Regulatory Relief, and Consumer Protection Act, which requires that, free of charge, CRAs place credit freezes no later than 1 business day after and lift credit freezes no later than 1 hour after receiving a direct request from a consumer via telephone or secure electronic means. Pub. L. No. 115-174, § 301(a), 132 Stat. 1296, 1326 (2018) (codified at 15 U.S.C. § 1681c–1(i)).

[68] Consumers who suspect that they have been or are about to become victims of fraud can request an initial fraud alert at no cost with any one of the three nationwide consumer reporting agencies, which automatically notify the other two. *See* 15 U.S.C. § 1681c-1(a)(1). An initial fraud alert stays on the victim's credit file for not less than one year. Consumers with identify theft reports may request an extended fraud alert, which lasts for seven years. *See* 15 U.S.C. § 1681c-1(b)(1). Active duty alerts, which last for not less than one year, are available to deployed service members. *See* 15 U.S.C. § 1681c-1(c).

[69] Federal law requires each nationwide consumer reporting agency to provide one free credit report to consumers, upon request, each year. *See* 15 U.S.C. § 1681j(a); 12 C.F.R. § 1022.136. The authorized website for ordering these free credit reports is AnnualCreditReport.com.

that consumers regularly review their credit card and bank statements to detect fraudulent charges.[70]

Consumers whose data have been compromised in any data breach can file a complaint with FTC or CFPB.[71] FTC has an online "complaint assistant," and FTC staff told us they use consumer complaints to help inform their investigatory and enforcement activity. CFPB staff told us that they use consumer complaints to help prioritize examinations and inform enforcement activity. In the 6 months following Equifax's announcement of its data breach, CFPB received more than 20,000 consumer complaints about the impact of the breach or Equifax's response.

However, consumers are limited in the direct actions they can take against a CRA in the event of a data breach, for two primary reasons. First, consumers generally cannot trace the source of the data used to commit identity theft to a particular breached entity. As a result, it can be difficult to link a breach by a CRA (or any other entity) to the harm a consumer suffers from a particular incidence of identity theft, which may make it challenging to prevail in a legal action. Second, unlike with many other products and services, consumers generally cannot exercise choice if they are dissatisfied with a CRA's privacy or security practices. Specifically, consumers cannot choose which CRAs maintain information about them. In addition, consumers do not have a legal right to delete their records with CRAs, according to CFPB staff, and therefore cannot choose to remove themselves entirely from the CRA market.

FTC and CFPB have noted that the level of consumer protection required can depend on the consumer's ability to exercise choice in a marketplace. For example, when determining whether a practice constitutes an unfair practice, FTC considers whether the practice is one that consumers could choose to avoid. Similarly, according to CFPB staff, the consumer reporting market may pose higher risk to consumers because consumers cannot choose whether or which CRAs possess and sell their information.

## CONCLUSION

The 2017 data breach of Equifax highlighted the data security risks associated with CRAs. While companies in many industries have experienced data breaches, CRAs may present heightened risks because of the scope of sensitive information they possess and because consumers have very limited control over what information CRAs hold and how they protect it. These challenges underscore the importance of appropriate federal oversight of CRAs' data security.

---

[70] See GAO-17-254 for additional information about options consumers have to address identity theft, including paid identity theft services.

[71] Consumers can also file complaints with other entities, such as state Attorneys General offices or consumer protection agencies.

While FTC has taken significant enforcement actions against CRAs that have violated federal privacy or data security laws, it is important that the agency have all of the appropriate enforcement options to fulfill its mission of protecting consumers. However, GLBA, one of the key laws governing the security of consumer information, does not provide FTC with civil penalty authority. The remedies that FTC does have available under GLBA—such as disgorgement and consumer redress—may be less practical enforcement tools for violations involving breaches of mass consumer data. Accordingly, providing FTC with civil penalty authority can enable it to more effectively or efficiently enforce GLBA's privacy and safeguarding provisions.

Although CFPB is responsible for overseeing larger market participant CRAs, it lacks the data to identify with certainty all the CRAs under its supervision, in part because the sources it is using, such as public filings, are not comprehensive. Using additional methods to obtain information, such as requiring larger market participant CRAs to register with the agency or leveraging state registration information, would help CFPB ensure it is tracking all CRAs under its supervision and is providing appropriate oversight.

CFPB considers a number of market and institutional factors in prioritizing which CRAs to examine, but data security has not routinely been among these factors. Given the nature and amount of consumer information CRAs hold, as well as increasing threats from hackers and others with malicious intent, vulnerabilities in these companies' data security can pose significant risk to a vast number of consumers. By ensuring that its process for determining the scope of CRA examinations routinely includes factors that would detect data security risks, CFPB can better ensure the effectiveness of its supervision and help prevent further exposure or compromise of consumer information.

## Matter for Congressional Consideration

Congress should consider providing the Federal Trade Commission with civil penalty authority for the privacy and safeguarding provisions of the Gramm-Leach-Bliley Act to help ensure that the agency has the tools it needs to most effectively act against data privacy and security violations. (Matter for Consideration 1)

## Recommendations for Executive Action

We are making two recommendations to CFPB:

The Director of CFPB should identify additional sources of information, such as through registering CRAs or leveraging state information, that would help ensure the agency is tracking all CRAs that meet the larger participant threshold. (Recommendation 1)

The Director of CFPB should assess whether its process for prioritizing CRA examinations sufficiently incorporates the data security risks CRAs pose to consumers, and take any needed steps identified by the assessment to more sufficiently incorporate these risks. (Recommendation 2)

## AGENCY COMMENTS AND OUR EVALUATION

We provided a draft of this chapter to CFPB, the Board of Governors of the Federal Reserve System, the Federal Deposit Insurance Corporation, FTC, and the Office of the Comptroller of the Currency. All of the agencies provided technical edits, which we incorporated as appropriate. In addition, we received written comments from CFPB, which are reprinted in appendix II.

CFPB neither agreed nor disagreed with our recommendations. Regarding our recommendation that it identify additional sources of information that would help ensure that it is tracking all CRAs that meet the larger market participant threshold, CFPB noted that it cannot require CRAs to register with the bureau without first undertaking a rulemaking. While we acknowledge the challenges of tracking larger participant CRAs, we maintain that CFPB should be able to identify and monitor them consistently. In its letter, CFPB stated that this may be feasible. The agency noted that, short of rulemaking, there may be cost-effective ways to better ensure that it is appropriately tracking larger participant CRAs and added that they intend to track these CRAs by exploring ways to leverage state registration information. These actions, if fully implemented, would meet the intent of our recommendation.

With respect to the recommendation that CFPB assess whether its process for prioritizing CRA examinations sufficiently incorporates data security risks, CFPB said it will continue to evaluate risks to consumers, including data security risks, as part of its prioritization process. CFPB also said it will assess whether that process should incorporate data security risks CRAs pose to consumers. However, CFPB expressed concern with the scope of its statutory authority, such as its lack of authority to supervise for compliance with GLBA safeguard provisions.

CFPB noted that we did not adequately consider or discuss its limited statutory authority in the area of data security. Specifically, CFPB stated that it does not have authority to supervise for, enforce compliance with, or write regulations implementing GLBA's safeguards provisions or FCRA's records disposal provision. In response, we added language in the report to clarify CFPB's lack of certain authorities over these data security provisions. Nonetheless, as we discuss in the report, CFPB has conducted data security examinations of some CRAs under its existing authority, including its authority to assess compliance with the requirements of federal consumer financial law. We continue to believe that effective supervision of CRAs and the protection of consumer information require that CFPB consider data security risks in its prioritization of CRA examinations.

As agreed with your offices, unless you publicly announce the contents of this chapter earlier, we plan no further distribution until 30 days from the report date. At that time, we will send copies to the appropriate congressional committees, CFPB, the Board of Governors of the Federal Reserve System, the Federal Deposit Insurance Corporation, FTC, and the Office of the Comptroller of the Currency.

Michael Clements
Director, Financial Markets and Community Investment

Nick Marinos
Director, Information Technology and Cybersecurity

## APPENDIX I: OBJECTIVES, SCOPE, AND METHODOLOGY

Our objectives were to examine (1) the federal laws and regulations governing consumer reporting agencies' (CRA) collection, use, and protection of consumer information; (2) measures the Federal Trade Commission (FTC) has taken to enforce CRA compliance with requirements to protect consumer information; (3) measures the Consumer Financial Protection Bureau(CFPB) has taken to ensure that CRAs protect consumer information; and (4) FTC's and CFPB's roles in assisting consumers following a data breach and actions consumers can take following a data breach of a CRA.[72]

To examine the laws governing CRAs, we identified the relevant laws, including the Fair Credit Reporting Act, the Gramm-Leach-Bliley Act, and statutes related to unfair or deceptive acts or practices. We reviewed these laws for their application to CRAs and their collection, use, and protection of consumer information. We interviewed

[72] We were also requested to examine consumer options to address risks of harm from data breaches, and the impact of data breaches at CRAs on federal programs. In addition, section 308 of the Economic Growth, Regulatory Relief, and Consumer Protection Act requires us to further examine issues related to the oversight of CRAs. *See* Pub. L. No. 115-174, § 308, 132 Stat.1296, 1347 (2018). We currently have additional audit work underway to address these topics and plan to issue separate reports on the results of those audits.

representatives of relevant federal agencies, including CFPB and FTC, about these laws and regulations and how they apply to CRAs. We also reviewed documents from and interviewed federal banking regulators on their role in overseeing financial institutions' management of third-party risk, including those of CRAs. We selected four states with existing or proposed information protection laws or regulations that vary from federal requirements (California, Illinois, Massachusetts, and New York); reviewed related documentation; and interviewed Attorneys General from these states about their enforcement of state laws. In addition, we interviewed and reviewed documentation from the three nationwide CRAs and interviewed three other CRAs that produce or compile consumer reporting information. We selected these CRAs because they are not sector-specific and hold information on a broad segment of the population. We conducted a site visit to Equifax's Alpharetta, Georgia data center to learn more about steps the company takes to comply with relevant consumer protection laws. We also interviewed representatives of furnishers and users of CRA consumer information—the American Bankers Association, the Property Casualty Insurance Association of America, and the National Retail Federation—about their roles in the collection, use, and protection of consumer data, and steps their members take to comply with relevant laws.

To assess FTC's and CFPB's measures to enforce information protection provisions and to ensure CRAs' proper collection, use, and protection of consumer information, we reviewed agency documentation and interviewed agency officials on their oversight activities. We reviewed the types of enforcement actions available to FTC and CFPB for violations of laws related to consumer reporting, as well as specific enforcement actions these agencies have brought against CRAs, data furnishers, and users of consumer reports. We also interviewed agency staff about FTC enforcement actions against CRAs and how it determines when to pursue such actions. We reviewed CFPB documentation on the scope of its supervisory examinations of larger market participant CRAs since 2015, as well as findings from recent CRA examinations. In addition, we reviewed CFPB examination guidance for supervising these CRAs, including CFPB's internal guidelines for conducting data security examinations. We also reviewed documents related to CFPB's process for prioritizing which institutions and which product lines (specific product offerings) should receive supervisory examination, and we interviewed CFPB staff about this process. Finally, we interviewed representatives of industry, consumer, and privacy groups for their views on the supervision of CRAs. These included the three nationwide CRAs, three other CRAs, the Consumer Data Industry Association, National Consumer Law Center, Consumer Federation of America, Consumers Union, World Privacy Forum, ID Theft Resource Center, and Consumer Action.

To assess FTC and CFPB roles in assisting consumers, and actions consumers can take following a data breach of a CRA, we reviewed the two agencies' efforts to inform and educate consumers following breaches. Specifically, we reviewed consumer education materials on FTC's and CFPB's websites related to data breaches and identify theft in general, as well as specific information posted after the Equifax data breach. We also interviewed staff from these agencies about their roles in assisting consumers following a breach. To identify actions consumers can take following a data breach, we reviewed our prior related reports and spokc with representatives of the industry and consumer representatives noted above.[73]

We conducted this performance audit from November 2017 to February 2019 in accordance with generally accepted government auditing standards. Those standards require that we plan and perform the audit to obtain sufficient, appropriate evidence to provide a reasonable basis for our findings and conclusions based on our audit objectives. We believe that the evidence obtained provides a reasonable basis for our findings and conclusions based on our audit objectives.

## APPENDIX II: COMMENTS FROM THE BUREAU OF CONSUMER FINANCIAL PROTECTION

Bureau of Consumer Financial Protection
1 700 G Street NW
Washington, D.C. 20552

January 22, 2019

Michael Clements
Director, Financial Markets and Community Investment
Government Accountability Office
441 G Street, NW
Washington DC, 20548

Dear Mr. Clements,

Thank you for the opportunity to review and comment on the draft report by the Government Accountability Office (GAO), titled *Consumer Data Protection: Activities Needed to Strengthen Oversight of Consumer Reporting Agencies* (19-196). The Bureau greatly appreciates GAO's work over the course of this engagement and believes the report provides the public important information regarding federal oversight of the protection of consumer information by consumer reporting agencies (CRAs) and actions consumers can take after a data breach.

---

[73] Prior GAO reports included GAO, Identity Theft Services: Services Offer Some Benefits but Are Limited in Preventing Fraud, GAO-17-254 (Washington, D.C: Mar. 30, 2017) and GAO, Personal Information: Key Federal Privacy Laws Do Not Require Information Resellers to Safeguard All Sensitive Data, GAO-06-674 (Washington, D.C.: June 26, 2006).

Oversight of the credit reporting market has been a top priority at the Bureau because credit reporting plays a critical role in the overall consumer financial services market and has enormous reach and impact; over 200 million Americans have credit files with tradelines furnished voluntarily by over 10,000 providers. For any individual consumer, an accurate consumer report can be critically important, given the significant impact that information can have on the consumer's ability to obtain or pay for financial and other products and services. Despite the impact credit reports can have on a consumer, consumers do not get to choose who collects and sells consumer report information about them.

In both its supervision and enforcement work in connection with CRAs, the Bureau has, to date, focused the bulk of its oversight on assessing compliance with the accuracy, dispute investigation, and permissible purpose obligations outlined in the Fair Credit Reporting Act (FCRA). Those were the areas that were both committed to the Bureau's jurisdiction and presented risk to consumers that could be assessed through the supervisory process.

Those reviews helped further FCRA compliance. As discussed in the March 2017 special edition of its *Supervisory Highlights*, as a result of the numerous supervisory reviews in this area, CRAs made specific improvements in data accuracy and dispute resolution, including: implementing quality control programs of compiled consumer reports; monitoring of furnisher dispute metrics to identify and correct root causes of inaccuracies; conducting reasonable reinvestigations of consumer disputes, including review of relevant information provided by consumers; and improving communication to consumers about dispute results. CRAs also enhanced their management and compliance programs to address FCRA requirements that consumer reports are issued and used for permissible purposes.

In addition to its supervisory work, the Bureau has brought actions and entered into settlements to enforce the FCRA's accuracy requirements, the statutory requirements regarding investigation of disputed information, and the permissible purpose requirements to obtain consumer reports.

The GAO's report discusses the FTC's and Bureau's respective authorities over CRAs as they relate to data security. Although the Bureau does have certain authorities in this regard, the report does not adequately consider or discuss the statutory authorities relating to data security Congress did not provide the Bureau. Critically, Congress specifically excluded important statutory provisions related to data security from the Bureau's purview. The Bureau does not have any authority to supervise for, enforce compliance with, or write regulations implementing the Gramm-Leach-Bliley Act's (GLBA) safeguards provision or the FCRA's records disposal provision.[1] The GLBA safeguards provision and the FTC's implementing rule require CRAs to develop, implement, and maintain comprehensive information security programs that contain administrative, technical, and physical safeguards. The FCRA records disposal provision and the FTC's implementing rule requires CRAs to take reasonable measures to protect against unauthorized access to or use of consumer information in connection with its disposal.

---

[1] The Bureau also does not have any authority over the FCRA's red flags provision and the FTC's implementing rule requiring that certain entities implement written Identity Theft Prevention Programs designed to detect, prevent, and mitigate identity theft. The red flags provision remains under FTC's jurisdiction with respect to entities under its enforcement authority, but only applies to financial institutions and creditors (as defined in statute). *See* 15 U.S.C. §§ 1681m(e), 1681s(a)(1) and 1681w(a)(1) and 16 C.F.R. pts. 681 and 682.

Accordingly, the Bureau lacks authority to implement, supervise for, or enforce data security standards under these statutory provisions.

GAO makes two recommendations to the Bureau:

- The Director of the CFPB should identify additional sources of information, such as through registering CRAs or leveraging state information, that would help ensure the agency is tracking all CRAs that meet the larger participant threshold; and
- The Director of the CFPB should assess whether its process for prioritizing CRA examinations sufficiently incorporates the data security risks CRAs pose to consumers, and take any needed steps identified by the assessment to more sufficiently incorporate these risks.

The Bureau does not object to the first recommendation. With respect to the first recommendation, the Bureau notes that it cannot require larger participant CRAs to register with the Bureau at this time. Registration would require a rulemaking and is not something that the Bureau has required of participants in other markets for which the Bureau issued a larger participant rule. To undertake such a rulemaking, the Bureau would need to consider the potential benefits and costs to consumers and covered persons.

As the report notes, the Bureau prioritizes its exams based on the entities and product lines that pose the greatest risk to consumers. To assess risks to consumers, the Bureau looks at a host of quantitative and qualitative information. Because an institution's size is a significant factor in the Bureau's risk analysis, the Bureau has focused its supervision of larger participants in the CRA market on the largest market participants, which are well known to the Bureau. Identifying potential additional larger participant CRAs may not materially alter any of the Bureau's prioritization decisions.

Nevertheless, the Bureau recognizes that there may be cost-effective ways short of a rulemaking to better ensure the Bureau is appropriately tracking larger participant CRAs. As the report notes, several states, such as New York and Maine, have begun requiring CRA registration. The Bureau is aware of these efforts and intends to explore ways of leveraging state registration information, recognizing that states may be requiring registration of all CRAs and not just those that meet the Bureau's larger participant threshold.

With respect to the second recommendation, the Bureau will continue to evaluate risks to consumers as part of its process to prioritize examinations and other supervisory work. As part of that evaluation, the Bureau will assess whether that process should incorporate data security risks CRAs pose to consumers in light of all of its supervisory responsibilities, including consideration of other risks to consumers, available resources, and the scope of its statutory authority, such as the Bureau's lack of authority to supervise for compliance with GLBA safeguards provisions.

The Bureau looks forward to continuing to work with GAO on this important topic.

Sincerely,

Kathleen L. Kraninger
Director

In: Consumer Protection
Editor: Ralf Schaefer

ISBN: 978-1-53615-876-2


*Chapter 8*

# CONSUMER PROTECTION: GENDER-RELATED PRICE DIFFERENCES FOR GOODS AND SERVICES*

*United States Government Accountability Office*

## ABBREVIATIONS

| | |
|---|---|
| APR | annual percentage rate |
| BCFP | Bureau of Consumer Financial Protcction |
| DOJ | Department of Justice |
| ECOA | Equal Credit Opportunity Act |
| FDIC | Federal Deposit Insurance Corporation |
| Federal Reserve | Board of Governors of the Federal Reserve System |
| FHA | Fair Housing Act |
| FTC | Federal Trade Commission |
| HMDA | Home Mortgage Disclosure Act of 1975 |
| HUD | Department of Housing and Urban Development |
| Nielsen | Nielsen Company |
| SCF | Survey of Consumer Finances |
| SSBF | Survey of Small Business Finances |

* This is an edited, reformatted and augmented version of United States Government Accountability Office; Report to Congressional Requesters, Publication No. GAO-18-500, dated August 2018.

## WHY GAO DID THIS STUDY

Gender-related price differences occur when consumers are charged different prices for the same or similar goods and services because of factors related to gender. While variation in costs and consumer demand may give rise to such price differences, some policymakers have raised concerns that gender bias may also be a factor. While the Equal Credit Opportunity Act and Fair Housing Act prohibit discrimination based on sex in credit and housing transactions, no federal law prohibits businesses from charging consumers different prices for the same or similar goods targeted to different genders.

GAO was asked to review gender-related price differences for consumer goods and services sold in the United States. This chapter examines, among other things, (1) how prices compared for selected goods and services marketed to men and women, and potential reasons for any price differences; (2) what is known about price differences for men and women for products not differentiated by gender, such as mortgages; and (3) the extent to which federal agencies have identified and addressed any concerns about gender-related price differences.

To examine these issues, GAO analyzed retail price data, reviewed relevant academic studies, analyzed federal consumer complaint data, and interviewed federal agency officials, industry experts, and academics.

## WHAT GAO FOUND

Firms differentiate many consumer products to appeal separately to men and women by slightly altering product attributes like color or scent. Products differentiated by gender may sell for different prices if men and women have different demands or willingness to pay for these product attributes. Of 10 personal care product categories (e.g., deodorants and shaving products) that GAO analyzed, average retail prices paid were significantly higher for women's products than for men's in 5 categories. In 2 categories—shaving gel and nondisposable razors—men's versions sold at a significantly higher price. One category—razor blades--had mixed results based on two price measures analyzed, and two others—disposable razors and mass-market perfumes— showed no significant gender price differences. GAO found that the target gender for a product is a significant factor contributing to price differences identified, but GAO did not have sufficient information to determine the extent to which these gender-related price differences were due to gender bias as opposed to other factors, such as different advertising costs. Though the analysis controlled for several observable product attributes, such as product size and packaging type, all underlying differences in costs and demand for products targeted to different genders could not be fully observed.

Studies GAO reviewed found limited evidence of gender price differences for four products or services not differentiated by gender—mortgages, small business credit, auto purchases, and auto repairs. For example, with regard to mortgages, women as a group paid higher average mortgage rates than men, in part due to weaker credit characteristics, such as lower average income. However, after controlling for borrower credit characteristics and other factors, three studies did not find statistically significant differences in borrowing costs between men and women, while one found women paid higher rates for certain subprime loans. In addition, one study found that female borrowers defaulted less frequently than male borrowers with similar credit characteristics, and the study suggested that women may pay higher mortgage rates than men relative to their default risk. While these studies controlled for factors other than gender that could affect borrowing costs, several lacked important data on certain borrower risk characteristics, such as credit scores, which could affect analysis of gender disparities. Also, several studies analyzed small samples of subprime loans that were originated in 2005 or earlier, which limits the generalizability of the results.

In their oversight of federal antidiscrimination statutes, the Bureau of Consumer Financial Protection, Federal Trade Commission, and Department of Housing and Urban Development have identified limited consumer concerns based on gender-related pricing differences. GAO's analysis of complaint data received by the three agencies from 2012–2017 found that they had received limited consumer complaints about gender-related price differences. The agencies provide general consumer education resources on discrimination and consumer awareness. However, given the limited consumer concern, they have not identified a need to incorporate additional materials specific to gender-related price differences into their existing consumer education resources.

August 9, 2018

The Honorable Robert P. Casey, Jr.
United States Senate

The Honorable Carolyn B. Maloney
Ranking Member
Joint Economic Committee
House of Representatives

Gender-related price differences can occur when manufacturers differentiate their products to appeal separately to female and male consumers, such as with clothing, personal care products, toys, and other consumer goods. In addition, businesses may offer different prices to female and male consumers for services, such as dry cleaning or haircuts, to account for different costs, different consumer preferences, or other factors associated with providing services to different genders. While manufacturing, marketing, or other cost differences may contribute to gender-related price differences, some policymakers have raised concerns that gender bias may play a role.[1] Moreover, if female and male consumers pay different prices for similar products that they purchase frequently, such as personal care products, this could result in substantial differences in expenditures by gender over time. A consumer's annual spending on a product category can be significant, even when prices for products within that category are low.[2]

You asked us to review gender-related price differences for goods and services sold in the U.S. marketplace. This chapter examines (1) how prices compared for selected categories of consumer goods that are differentiated for men and women, and potential reasons for any significant price differences; (2) what is known about the extent to which men and women may pay different prices in, or experience different levels of access to, markets for credit and goods and services that are not differentiated based on gender; (3) the extent to which federal agencies have identified and taken steps to address any concerns about gender-related price differences; and (4) state and local government efforts to address concerns about gender-related price differences.[3]

To address our first objective, we purchased and analyzed Nielsen Company (Nielsen) data on retail prices paid for 10 personal care product categories for calendar year 2016.[4] The product categories included underarm deodorants, body deodorants, disposable razors, nondisposable razors, razor blades, shaving creams, shaving gels, and three categories of fragrances. We selected these categories because they are commonly-purchased consumer goods that were categorized by gender in the Nielsen data. The women's and men's versions of personal care products we selected are generally more similar in terms of the form, size, and packaging in comparison to certain other consumer product categories that are also differentiated by gender, such as clothing. We used regression models to analyze data on retail prices paid for 10 categories of personal care products differentiated for men and women. We assessed the reliability of the Nielsen

---

[1] For example, one U.S. state and some local governments have enacted laws intended to address perceived gender bias in the offering of services such as haircuts or dry cleaning, as discussed later in this chapter. One of these local governments examined differences in advertised prices for men's and women's products. *See* New York City Department of Consumer Affairs, *From Cradle to Cane: The Cost of Being a Female Consumer, A Study of Gender Pricing in New York City* (New York City, N.Y.: December 2015).

[2] For example, U.S. household spending on personal care products and services averaged more than $700 annually in 2016. *See* Bureau of Labor Statistics, *Consumer Expenditure Survey* (Washington, D.C.: 2017). Personal care products and services include products for the hair, oral hygiene products, shaving needs, cosmetics and bath products, electric personal care appliances, and other products and services.

[3] Our first objective examines price differences for products that are commonly differentiated to appeal either to men or women. It examines the products themselves and not the gender of the consumer actually purchasing them.

[4] In addition to the retail price paid, the data we purchased from Nielsen include data fields for product brand, package size, package design, product scent, and product color, among other product characteristics. Nielsen collected these retail price data from over 200 national retailers, including grocery stores, pharmacies, mass merchandizers, and club stores. According to Nielsen, together these retailers encompass 82 percent of all U.S. sales for 2016. The prices were collected from participating retailers when an item was scanned at the cash register during check out.

data by reviewing relevant documentation and conducting interviews with Nielsen representatives to review steps they took to collect and ensure the reliability of the data. In addition, we electronically tested data fields for missing values, outliers, and obvious errors. We determined that these data were sufficiently reliable for our purposes. For more details on the methodology for, and limitations of, our analysis of these retail price data, see appendix I.

We also manually collected listed prices for 16 pairs of selected personal care products from four different retailer websites over two 7-day periods in January and March 2018. We selected comparable pairs of similar men's and women's products that were differentiated by product attributes, such as scent or color, and were commonly sold across retailers. We included product pairs from similar categories used in our analysis of the Nielsen data. For more details on our online price data collection and the limitations associated with interpreting the results, see appendix II.

To address our second objective, we identified and reviewed studies that examined differences between the prices men and women paid for, or their access to, consumer services and goods that are not differentiated by gender—specifically interest rates, pricing, or access for mortgages or other loan types while controlling for the effects of factors other than gender or sex. We also identified and reviewed three studies on differences in price for autos and auto repair services. We found the studies we reviewed to be reliable for purposes of determining what is known about price differences for the same products, though several studies analyzed nonrepresentative data samples, such as subprime mortgage loans, and thus the results are not generalizable.

For our third objective, we reviewed relevant federal antidiscrimination statutes and agency documentation related to oversight and enforcement of these statutes. To learn about the potential extent of consumer concerns about price differences that could be based solely on gender or sex, we analyzed federal data on consumer complaints and investigations. We selected a random sample of gender-related consumer complaints from three databases managed by the Bureau of Consumer Financial Protection (BCFP), the Federal Trade Commission (FTC), and the Department of Housing and Urban Development (HUD), respectively, and counted the number of complaints alleging a perceived gender-related price difference.[5] We assessed the reliability of these data by reviewing documentation and interviewing agency officials about these databases. We determined that these data were sufficiently reliable for our purposes of identifying complaints of gender-related price differences. In addition, we interviewed agency officials from BCFP, FTC, HUD, and the Department of Justice (DOJ), as well as industry experts and academics, on gender-related price differences.

---

[5] In the years following its creation, BCFP has referred to itself and been commonly known as the Consumer Financial Protection Bureau, or CFPB. According to BCFP officials, BCFP is in the process of discontinuing use of that name and acronym.

To address our fourth objective, we identified and reviewed three examples of state and local laws that specifically address gender-related price differences. We also interviewed officials from the state and localities that had enacted these laws. See appendix III for more information on our scope and methodology.

We conducted this performance audit from October 2016 to August 2018 in accordance with generally accepted government auditing standards. Those standards require that we plan and perform the audit to obtain sufficient, appropriate evidence to provide a reasonable basis for our findings and conclusions based on our audit objectives. We believe that the evidence obtained provides a reasonable basis for our findings and conclusions based on our audit objectives.

## BACKGROUND

Many consumer products—such as deodorants, shaving products, and hair care products—are differentiated to appeal specifically to men or women through differences in packaging, scent, or other product characteristics (see Figure 1). These differences related to gender can affect manufacturing and marketing costs that may contribute to price differences in products targeted to different genders.

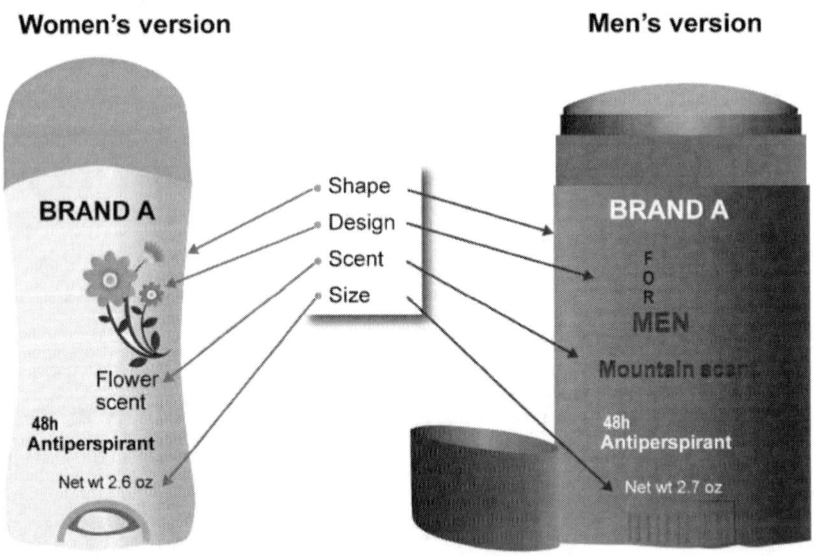


Source: GAO analysis. | GAO-18-500.

Figure 1. Illustrative Example of Similar Products Differentiated to Appeal to Men and Women.

However, firms may also charge consumers different prices for the same (or very similar) goods and services even when there are no differences in costs to produce.[6] To maximize profits, firms use a variety of techniques to charge prices close to the highest price different consumers are willing to pay.[7] Firms may attempt to get segments of the consumer market to pay a higher price than another segment by slightly altering or differentiating the product. Based on the differentiated products, consumers self-select into different groups according to their preferences and what they are willing to pay.[8] For example, some consumer goods have different versions of what is essentially the same product—except for differences in packaging or features, such as scent—with one version intended for women and another version intended for men. The two products may be priced differently because the firm expects that one gender will be willing to pay more for the product than the other based on preference for certain product attributes.

Firms may also use some group characteristic, such as age or gender, to charge different prices because some groups may have differences in willingness or ability to pay.[9] For example, a firm may offer discounted movie tickets to students or seniors, as they may have less disposable income. For the seller the cost of providing the movie is the same for any customer, but the seller is able to maximize its profits by offering tickets to different groups of customers at different prices. A firm's ability to differentiate prices depends on multiple factors, such as the firm's market power (so that competitors cannot put downward pressure on prices to eliminate the price differences), the presence of consumer segments with different demands and willingness to pay, and control over the sale of its product so it cannot be easily resold to exploit price differences.[10]

In addition, the extent to which consumers pay different prices for the same or similar goods can depend on other factors, such as consumers':

- willingness to purchase an item they believe may be priced higher for one gender,
- ability to compare prices and product characteristics and choose a product based on its characteristics rather than its price,
- choices about whether to purchase a more expensive version of the product (e.g., a branded item versus a cheaper store brand),

---

[6] The practice of charging consumers different prices, when the differences in price are not completely attributable to differences in cost, is often referred to as "price discrimination" by economists. For the purposes of our report we refer to this practice as price differentiation, so as not to confuse this term with statutorily prohibited discrimination based on sex.

[7] In theory, firms would like to charge each customer the maximum amount that customer is willing and able to pay. This is known in economics as first degree price discrimination, and it occurs when a different price is charged to each consumer.

[8] Economists refer to this as second degree price discrimination.

[9] Economists refer to this as third degree, or group-based, price discrimination.

[10] One condition for a firm to be able to implement a strategy of price differentiation is that it must be able to segment consumers such that one segment of consumers is not able to buy a product at a lower price and resell at a higher price, or is not able to purchase the product that is meant for the other group. This is referred to as "arbitrage" in economic literature.

- choices about where to purchase the item (i.e., when different retailers sell the same item at different prices), and
- use of coupons or promotions.

No federal law expressly prohibits businesses from charging different prices for the same or similar consumer goods and services targeted to men and women.[11] However, consumer protection laws do prohibit sex discrimination in credit and real estate transactions. Specifically, the Equal Credit Opportunity Act (ECOA) prohibits creditors from discriminating against credit applicants based on sex or certain other characteristics and the Fair Housing Act (FHA) prohibits discrimination in the housing market on the basis of sex or certain other characteristics.[12]

ECOA and FHA (collectively known as the fair lending laws) prohibit lenders from, among other things, refusing to extend credit or using different standards in determining to extend credit based on sex.[13] Credit, such as a credit card account or mortgage loan, is generally made available and priced based on a number of risk factors, including credit score, income, and employment history. A borrower with a lower credit score is likely to pay a higher interest rate on a loan, reflecting the greater risk to the lender that the borrower could default on the loan.[14] In addition to the interest rate, borrowing costs for consumers can also include fees and other costs charged by lenders or brokers.[15] However, there may be differences in average outcomes for men and women—such as for availability of credit or interest rates—if there are differences related to gender in the

---

[11] The Robinson-Patman Act, Pub. L. No. 74-692, 49 Stat. 1526 (1936), prohibits price discrimination by producers in the sale of goods to distributors when the effect of such pricing is to reduce competition and also prohibits certain discriminatory allowances or services furnished or paid to customers. Because this chapter focuses on gender-based price differences, the actions prohibited by the act are outside our scope. Section 5 of the Federal Trade Commission Act prohibits unfair methods of competition and unfair or deceptive acts or practices in or affecting commerce. *See* 15 U.S.C § 45(a)(1). According to an FTC official, a company may violate this section if it mispresents its practices or if those practices cause or are likely to cause substantial consumer injury that is not reasonably avoidable by consumers or outweighed by benefits to consumers or competition.

[12] In addition to prohibiting discrimination based on sex, ECOA prohibits discrimination in the credit market on the basis of race, color, religion, national origin, marital status, or age. *See* 15 U.S.C. § 1691(a)(1). The statute and its implementing regulation, Regulation B, also prohibit discrimination against an applicant because that applicant receives income from a public assistance program, or because an applicant has in good faith exercised any right under the Consumer Credit Protection Act or any state law upon which an exemption has been granted by BCFP. *See* 15 U.S.C. § 1691(a)(2)-(3) and 12 C.F.R. § 1002.2(z). In addition to prohibiting discrimination based on sex, FHA prohibits discrimination in the housing market based on race, color, religion, handicap, familial status, or national origin. *See* 42 U.S.C. § 3604.

[13] 15 U.S.C. § 1691(a)(1); 42 U.S.C. § 3605(a). Lenders in the housing market are also prohibited from varying the terms of credit offered, including the amount, interest rate, duration, or type of loan based on sex or certain other characteristics. *See* 24 C.F.R. § 100.130.

[14] A credit score predicts how likely a borrower is to pay back a loan on time. Credit reporting agencies use a mathematical scoring model with information from a person's credit report to create a credit score. Factors that make up a typical credit score include bill-paying history, current outstanding debt, and the number and type of loan accounts a person has. Lenders use credit scores to make decisions such as whether to offer you a mortgage, credit card, auto loan, or other credit product, and on what terms.

[15] The Truth in Lending Act and its implementing Regulation Z require that, for certain credit transactions, borrowers receive written disclosures about important terms relating to the costs of credit, which includes an annual percentage rate (APR) that reflects, among other things, the interest rate charged. *See* 12 C.F.R. pt. 1026.

factors that determine creditworthiness, such as income. BCFP, FTC, the federal prudential regulators, and DOJ have the authority to investigate alleged violations of ECOA and are primarily responsible for enforcing the act's requirements, while HUD and DOJ share responsibility for enforcing the provisions of FHA.[16] Further, BCFP and the prudential regulators oversee regulated entities for compliance with ECOA by, among other things, collecting complaints from the public and through routine inspections of the financial institutions they oversee. HUD and DOJ have the authority to bring enforcement actions for alleged violations of FHA.

## PRICES DIFFERED SIGNIFICANTLY FOR SELECTED MEN'S AND WOMEN'S PERSONAL CARE PRODUCTS, BUT WE COULD NOT ATTRIBUTE THE DIFFERENCES TO BIAS AS OPPOSED TO OTHER FACTORS

In 5 out of 10 product categories we analyzed, personal care products targeted to women sold at higher average prices than those targeted to men after controlling for certain observable factors.[17] For 2 of the 10 product categories, men's versions sold at higher average prices. While the factors we controlled for likely proxy for various costs and consumer preferences, we could not fully observe all underlying differences in costs and demand for products targeted to different genders. As a result, we could not determine the extent to which the gender-based price differences we observed may be attributed to gender bias as opposed to other factors.

### For 5 of 10 Product Categories Analyzed, Women's Products Sold at Higher Average Prices Than Men's after Controlling for Some Observable Factors

Women's versions of personal care products sold at a statistically significant higher average price than men's versions for 5 of the 10 personal care product categories we

---

[16] The other agencies responsible for enforcing ECOA include the Board of Governors of Federal Reserve System (Federal Reserve), the Federal Deposit Insurance Corporation (FDIC), the Office of the Comptroller of the Currency, the National Credit Union Administration, the Farm Credit Administration, the Department of Transportation, the Securities and Exchange Commission, the Small Business Administration, and the Grain Inspection, Packers, and Stockyards Administration of the Department of Agriculture. *See* 15 U.S.C. § 1691c.

[17] Throughout this chapter section, we refer to products targeted to men and women, but we could not observe the gender of the consumers who actually bought the products in the dataset. Instead, we could only observe the target gender for the product based on Nielsen's categorization of the product as a men's or women's product. In other words, our analysis compares the prices at which products targeted to men or women were sold. We could not determine the extent to which men or women bought products designed for a different gender (e.g., a woman choosing to buy a deodorant targeted to men) or buy on behalf of another gender (e.g., buying for a spouse of the opposite gender).

analyzed—using two different price measures and after controlling for observable factors that could affect price, such as brands, product size or quantity, promotional expenses (see table 1) and other product-specific attributes (e.g., scent, special claims, form).[18] Because women's and men's versions of the same product were frequently sold in different sizes, we compared prices using two price measures: average item price and average price per ounce or count of product.[19] For 2 of the 10 product categories—shaving gel and nondisposable razors—men's versions sold at a statistically significant higher price using both price measures.

**Table 1. Comparison of Average Prices Paid for Men's and Women's Personal Care Products after Controlling for Observable Product Characteristics**

| Product | Higher average item price for products targeted to[a] | Higher average price per ounce or count for products targeted to[a] |
|---|---|---|
| Underarm deodorants | Women | Women |
| Body deodorants | Women | Women |
| Shaving cream | Women | Women |
| Shaving gel | Men | Men |
| Disposable razors | No difference | No difference |
| Nondisposable razors | Men | Men |
| Razor blades | No difference | Women |
| Designer perfume | Women | Women |
| Mass-market perfume | No difference | No difference |
| Mass-market body sprays | Women | Women |

Source: GAO analysis of Nielsen Company data. | GAO-18-500.

Notes: 1 We selected these categories of personal care products because they are commonly-purchased consumer goods that were categorized by gender in the Nielsen Company's data. Our analysis is limited to the set of personal care products that we analyzed. Our findings are not generalizable or applicable to other consumer goods. The average item price is the total dollar sales for a product category divided by the total number of items sold for that category. The average price per ounce or count is the item price divided by the quantity of product and weighted by the item's proportional share of total volume sales, where quantity depicts the number of ounces as in the case of fragrances or the count of blades in razor blade packs.

2 All price comparisons are for similar products after controlling for size, promotional activity, owner brands, product packaging features, and other product attributes.

[a]Statistically significant at the 95 percent level.

---

[18] We used regression models to analyze data on retail prices paid for 10 categories of personal care products differentiated for women and men and determined the significance of price differences at 5 percent or lower level. For more information on our regression analysis, see appendix I.

[19] The average item price is the total dollar sales for a product category divided by the total number of items sold for that category. This measure of price automatically incorporates all prices, including sale prices and other discounts, and is mathematically equivalent to the weighted average of all individual item prices, where the weights are each item's proportional share of the total volume sales. The average price per ounce or count is the item price divided by the quantity of product and weighted by the proportional share of items sold, where quantity or size depicts the number of ounces as in the case of fragrances or the count of blades in razor blade packs. Sizes for women's products were generally smaller than for similar men's products. For information about how these two price measures compared for women's and men's products—without controlling for other observable factors that may also affect price—see appendix IV.

For one category (razor blades), women's versions sold at a statistically significant higher average price per count, but there was no gender price difference using average item prices. Additionally, for two product categories—disposable razors and mass-market perfumes—there were no statistically significant price differences between men's and women's products using either price measure.

In addition to this analysis of retail price scanner data, we also manually collected advertised online prices for a limited selection of personal care products targeted to women and men from several online retailers.[20] Some price comparisons of advertised online prices for men's and women's versions of a product were similar to comparisons of average prices paid based on the Nielsen retail price scanner data. For example, for three pairs of comparable underarm deodorants, the women's deodorant was listed at a higher price per ounce on average than the men's deodorant (see app. II).[21] In addition, for one pair of shaving gel products we analyzed, the men's shaving gel was listed at a higher price per ounce on average. However, for both pairs of nondisposable razors we analyzed, the women's razors were listed at a higher average price per count than the men's razors. This contrasted with the Nielsen data showing that men's nondisposable razors sold at higher prices on average than women's. An important limitation of our analysis of these advertised prices is that we were unable to determine the extent to which consumers actually paid these prices and in what volume the products were sold, and our results are not generalizable to the broader universe of prices for these products sold at other times or by other online retailers.

## We Could Not Determine the Extent to Which Price Differences May Be due to Market Factors as Opposed to Gender Bias

Though we found that the target gender for a product is a significant factor contributing to price differences we identified, we do not have sufficient information to determine the extent to which these gender-related price differences were due to gender bias as opposed to other factors. Versions differentiated to appeal to men and women can result in different costs for the manufacturer. Our econometric analysis controlled for many observable factors related to costs, such as product size, promotional activity, and packaging type.

---

[20] We collected prices for 16 pairs of selected personal care products sold on 4 selected websites for 7 consecutive days in January 2018 and again in March 2018. Generally, we selected pairs of products that had the same brand, packaging type, and other characteristics but were marketed to appeal separately to female and male consumers. We collected the online price data and Nielsen retail price data during different periods of time. Market shifts in demand or other factors that may change over time could account for differences between the online price data and Nielsen retail price data. See appendix II for further details.

[21] For one comparison pair of underarm deodorants, the men's and women's version were listed at the same price or close to the same price on average.

We also controlled for many product attributes such as forms, scents, and special claims that products make to account for underlying manufacturing cost differences.[22] In addition, we controlled for brands, which can reflect consumer preferences. However, we do not have firm-level data on all cost differences—for example, those related to advertising and packaging. As a result, we could not determine the extent to which the price differences we observed may be explained by remaining cost differences between men's and women's products.

We also do not have the data to determine the extent to which men and women have different demands and willingness to pay for a product, which would be expected to affect the prices firms charge for differentiated products. For example, some academic experts we spoke with said that women may value some product attributes, such as design and scent, more than men do. If products differentiated to incorporate those attributes do not result in different costs, then differences in prices could be part of a firm's pricing strategy based on the willingness of one gender to pay more than another.

The conditions necessary for firms to be able to implement a strategy of price differentiation likely exist for the personal care products we analyzed.[23] First, our analysis suggests that due to industry concentration, there is limited market competition for the 10 personal care products we analyzed. With more market power, firms can more easily set different prices for different consumer segments. Second, firms have the ability to segment the market for personal care products by tailoring product characteristics related to gender, such as by labeling the product as women's deodorant or men's deodorant, or by altering scent or colors. Third, while men and women are able to freely purchase a product targeted to the opposite gender, certain factors may limit the extent to which this occurs.[24] For example, some product differences such as scents may discourage one gender from buying products targeted to another gender.[25] In addition, consumers may find it difficult and time-consuming to compare prices for similar men's and women's products because of the ways they are differentiated (such as product size and scents) and because they may be sold in different parts of a store.

---

22 Some academic experts and industry representatives we spoke with suggested that cost differences for some product attributes that firms use to differentiate products, such as scent and colors, may have negligible manufacturing cost differences.

23 As mentioned previously, the extent to which firms are able to implement a strategy of price differentiation depends on the extent of the firm's market power, whether the firm can easily segment the market, and whether the firm has some control over the sale of its product.

24 In other words, an opportunity to exploit price differences by reselling lower-priced products at a higher price exists, but certain factors limit this opportunity.

25 Some research suggests social conditioning and expectations can affect women's willingness to purchase products targeted to men. See Megan Duesterhas, Liz Grauerholz, Rebecca Weichsel, and Nicholas A. Guittar, "The Cost of Doing Femininity: Gendered Disparities in Pricing of Personal Care Products and Services," *Gender Issues*, vol. 28 (2011), 175-191.

# Studies We Reviewed Found Limited Evidence of Price Differences for Men and Women for Mortgages, Small Business Credit, and Auto Purchases

We reviewed studies that compared prices for men and women in four markets where the product or service is not differentiated by gender: mortgages, small business credit, auto purchases, and auto repairs.[26] First, we reviewed studies on mortgage and small business credit that analyzed interest rates and access to credit to identify any differences for men and women. Second, we reviewed studies that compared prices quoted to men and women in auto purchase and repair markets. However, several of these studies have important limitations, such as using nonrepresentative data samples, and the results are not generalizable.

## Studies on Mortgages Found Mixed Evidence of Disparities in Borrowing Costs between Men and Women

Studies we reviewed found that women as a group pay higher interest rates on average than men in part due to weaker credit characteristics. After controlling for borrower credit characteristics and other factors, three studies did not find statistically significant differences in interest rates between men and women for the same type of mortgage, while one study found that women paid higher mortgage rates for certain subprime loans. In addition, one study found that female borrowers defaulted less frequently on their loans than male borrowers with similar credit characteristics, suggesting that women as a group may pay higher mortgage rates than men relative to their default risk. While these studies attempted to control for factors other than gender or sex that could affect borrowing costs, several lacked important data on certain borrower risk characteristics. For example, several studies we reviewed rely on Home Mortgage Disclosure Act of 1975 (HMDA) data, which did not include data on risk factors such as borrower credit scores that could affect analysis of disparities between men and women.[27]

---

[26] Transactions for these products and services generally can involve some negotiation between buyers and sellers. Some experts and academics, as well as agency officials with whom we spoke, have noted that disparate treatment based on gender can take place in transactions involving negotiations, in part, because buyers may not know the price other consumers have paid for a product or service.

[27] We previously identified limitations of HMDA data, such as a lack of information on the credit risks of mortgage borrowers, which could affect the ability of agencies and regulators to identify discrimination violations of fair lending laws. See GAO, *Fair Lending: Data Limitations and the Fragmented U.S. Financial Regulatory Structure Challenge Federal Oversight and Enforcement Efforts* GAO-09-704 (Washington, D.C.: July 15, 2009). Effective January 1, 2018, some financial institutions are required to report additional data points, including borrower credit scores, for certain credit transactions covered by HMDA. See 12 C.F.R. pt. 1003. In addition, some research suggests that controlling for certain variables not related to gender may be inappropriate if those variables themselves may reflect outcomes related to gender discrimination. For

Also, several studies analyzed nonrepresentative samples of loans, such as subprime loans or loans originated more than 10 years ago, which limits the generalizability of the results (see Table 2).

Three of the studies we reviewed found that while women on average were charged higher interest rates on mortgage loans than men, this difference was not statistically significant after controlling for other factors. For example, one study found that differences in mortgage interest rates between men and women became insignificant after controlling for differences in how men and women shop for mortgage rates.[28] The authors used data from the 2004 Survey of Consumer Finances (SCF) to analyze the effect on interest rates of mortgage features, borrower characteristics such as gender, and market conditions.[29] However, their analysis did not include data on some borrower credit characteristics such as credit score and debt-to-income ratio that could affect borrowing costs.[30] Another study found that women were charged higher interest rates for subprime loans made in 2005, but once the authors controlled for observed risk characteristics there was no evidence of disparity in interest rates by gender of the borrower in the subprime market.[31]

However, the authors' data did not include any fees paid at loan origination, which could affect the overall cost of borrowing. A third study that examined disparities between men and women in subprime loans found no significant evidence that gender affected the cost of borrowing within the subprime market, though it did find that women—particularly African American women—were more likely to have subprime

---

example, see Ian Ayres, "Testing for Discrimination and the Problem of 'Included Variable Bias,'" unpublished working paper, Yale Law School (2010), accessed on June 4, 2018, at https://ianayres.yale.edu/sites/default/files/files/Testing %20for%20Discrimination.pdf.

28 Ping Cheng, Zhenguo Lin, and Yingchun Liu, "Do Women Pay More for Mortgages?" *The Journal of Real Estate Finance and Economics*, vol. 43 (2011), 423-440. The authors concluded that men are likely to pay lower rates on mortgages because they tended to search for the lowest rates, and search is rewarded by the market, whereas women are more likely to receive higher rates—and subprime loans—because they are more likely to rely on referrals from people they know. In May 2018, BCFP published a series of briefs on the effect of shopping for a mortgage on interest rates, accessed on July 17, 2018, at https://www.consumerfinance.gov/data-research/research-reports/know-before-you-owemortgage-shopping-study/.

29 SCF is a triennial survey of the various financial and demographic characteristics of U.S. families. The study is sponsored by the Federal Reserve in cooperation with the Department of the Treasury. The SCF is conducted among a representative sample of U.S. households. It contains information on mortgages as well as on broader household finances and demographics, but it does not contain data on credit scores, discount points or fees, or other factors that could affect interest rates.

30 In a separate study, the same authors also used SCF data to look for racial disparity and found that African American borrowers pay more than white borrowers. They also found that the disparity between African American and white borrowers is more pronounced for women than it is for men. They did not conduct any analysis directly comparing rates between African American men and women. See Ping Cheng, Zhenguo Lin, and Yingchun Liu, "Racial Discrepancy in Mortgage Interest Rates," *The Journal of Real Estate Finance and Economics*, vol. 51 (2015), 101-120.

31 Andrew Haughwout et al., "Subprime Mortgage Pricing: The Impact of Race, Ethnicity, and Gender on the Cost of Borrowing," *Brookings-Wharton Papers on Urban Affairs* (2009), 33-63. The authors examined the mortgage rates charged to a group of subprime mortgage borrowers in 2005 on a particular type of mortgage. The risk characteristics that the authors controlled for were the borrower's credit score (FICO score), the initial combined loan-to-value and debt-to-income ratios, level of documentation used in the underwriting, whether the mortgage is for a purchase or a refinance, the loan amount, the presence and duration of a prepayment penalty, the type of property used as collateral, and the loan type.

loans.[32] The authors found that, even after controlling for some financial characteristics and loan terms, single African American women were more likely than non-Hispanic white couples to have subprime loans.

**Table 2. Summary of Selected Studies on the Effect of Gender or Sex on Mortgage Borrowing Costs**

| Study authors | Data sources | Scope of data analyzed | Identified effects of gender or sex on borrowing costs | Example of data limitations |
|---|---|---|---|---|
| Cheng, Lin, and Liu (2011) | Survey of Consumer Finances, 2004 | Sample of 1,511 loans originated between 2000 and 2004 | No significant effect of gender or sex on mortgage loan interest rates | Did not control for credit score and debt-to-income ratio |
| Goodman, Zhu, and Bai (2016) | Home Mortgage Disclosure Act (HMDA), 2004-2014; Core Logic, 2004-2014 | All loans matched between datasets originated between 2004 and 2014 | Women default less than men with similar credit characteristics | HMDA and Core Logic data track loans by different geographic measures, requiring some estimation to match loans between datasets |
| Haughwout et al. (2009) | HMDA, 2005; First American Loan Performance, 2005 | Sample of adjustable rate subprime loans originated in 2005 | No significant effect of gender or sex on mortgage loan interest rates | Did not control for any fees paid at loan origination |
| Van Rensselaer et al. (2014) | Mortgage data from one large subprime lending company, 1997-2007 | Random sample of 30-year fixed rate subprime loans originated between 2003 and 2005 | Women had significantly higher borrowing costs compared to men | Did not control for education level and shopping behavior |
| Wyly and Ponder (2011) | HMDA, 2006; National Mortgage Data Repository, 1994-2008 | 619 subprime loans originated between 1994 and 2008 | No significant effect of gender or sex on mortgage loan interest rates | Did not control for credit score |

Source: GAO analysis of selected studies that evaluate the effects of gender on mortgage borrowing costs. | GAO-18-500.

One study analyzed subprime loans made by one large lender from 2003 through 2005 and found that women paid more for subprime mortgages than men after controlling for some risk factors.[33] This study found that women had higher average borrowing costs—as measured by annual percentage rate—than men, and controlling for credit characteristics such as credit scores and debt-to-income ratios did not fully explain the

[32] Elvin Wyly and C.S. Ponder, "Gender, age, and race in subprime America," *Housing Policy Debate*, vol. 21, no. 4 (2011), 529-564. The authors also used data that combine demographic information with detailed financial circumstances of mortgage transactions for approximately 600 subprime loans that originated between 1994 and 2008.

[33] Kristy N. Van Rensselaer et al., "Mortgage Pricing and Gender: A Study of New Century Financial Corporation," *Academy of Accounting and Financial Studies Journal*, vol. 18, no. 4 (2014), 95-110. Generally, a borrower with a higher debt-to-income ratio is more likely to default.

differences.[34] However, the authors did not control for other factors that could also affect borrowing costs, such as differences in education, shopping behaviors, and geographic location.

Additionally, a research paper found that female-only borrowers—that is, where the only borrower is a woman—default less than male-only borrowers with similar loans and credit characteristics.[35] The authors found that female-only borrowers on average pay more for their mortgage loans because they generally have weaker credit characteristics, such as lower income, and also because a higher percentage of these mortgage loans are subprime.[36] However, after controlling for credit characteristics such as credit score, loan term, and loan-to-value ratio, among others, the analysis showed that these weaker credit characteristics do not accurately predict how well women pay their mortgage loans. Since pricing is tied to credit characteristics and not performance, women may pay more relative to their actual risk than do similar men.

## Studies on Small Business Credit Did Not Identify Gender Differences in Borrowing Costs but Found Mixed Evidence of Differences for Access to Credit

Studies we reviewed on small business loans generally did not find differences in interest rates, though some found differences in denial rates and other accessibility issues between female- and male-owned firms.[37] Most of the studies we reviewed used data from the 1993, 1998, or 2003 Survey of Small Business Finances (SSBF), which could limit the applicability or relevance of their findings today.[38] A study that analyzed data from the 1993 SSBF did not find evidence that businesses owned by women paid more

---

[34] According to BCFP, the annual percentage rate (APR) is a broader measure of the cost of borrowing money since it reflects not only the interest rate but certain other credit costs. The higher the APR, the more costs over the life of the loan. *See* Consumer Financial Protection Bureau, "What is the difference between an interest rate and the Annual Percentage Rate (APR) in an auto loan?" *Ask CFPB*, accessed on July 30, 2018, at https://www.consumerfinance.gov/ask-cfpb/what-is-the-difference-between-an-interestrate-and-the-annual-percentage-rate-apr-in-an-auto-loan-en-733/.

[35] Laurie Goodman, Jun Zhu, and Bing Bai, "Women Are Better than Men at Paying Their Mortgages," *Urban Institute*, Research Report (2016).

[36] The authors also found that women faced higher denial rates than men.

[37] Most of these studies looked only at white women due to lack of data on minority-owned firms, thus limiting their generalizability.

[38] The SSBF, conducted by the Federal Reserve, collected information on small businesses (fewer than 500 employees) in the United States, such as owner characteristics, firm size, use of financial services, and the income and balance sheets of firms, among others. This survey has been suspended since 2003. In 2010, the Federal Reserve Bank of New York established the Small Business Credit Survey to annually survey firms about business performance, financing needs and choices, and borrowing experiences. The 2016 survey was the first iteration to be conducted on a nationwide level with the involvement of all 12 Federal Reserve Banks. For its report on women-owned firms, see Federal Reserve Banks of New York and Kansas City, *Small Business Credit Survey: Report on Women-Owned Firms* (New York City, N.Y.: Nov. 2017), accessed on July 9, 2018, at https://www.newyorkfed.org/medialibrary/media/smallbusiness/2016/SBCS-ReportWomen Owned Firms-2016.pdf.

for credit than firms owned by white men.[39] However, when the authors took into account the market concentration and competition, they found that white female-owned firms experienced increased denial rates in less competitive markets.[40] In addition, the study found that women may avoid applying for credit in those markets because of the fear of being denied. For example, almost half of all small business owners who needed credit reported that they did not apply for credit, and these rates were even higher for businesses owned by women and minorities.

Other studies found that women may have less access to small business credit than men, in part because of higher denial rates and because they may not apply for credit out of fear of rejection. For example, one study found that women-owned firms have higher loan denial rates compared with men; however, this is mainly due to differences in business characteristics of female- and male-owned firms.[41] The authors also found that even when denial rates are the same for small businesses with similar characteristics, women's loan application rates are lower, suggesting that women may be discouraged from applying for credit by the higher overall denial rates for female-owned firms.[42] Another study by one of the same authors examined the reasons why female borrowers may be discouraged from applying for a business loan compared to male business owners and found that it was mainly because they fear that their application will be rejected.[43] A third study by the same author found that women in general did not have less access to credit than men, though newer female-owned firms received significantly lower loan amounts than requested compared to their male-owned counterparts.[44] Similarly, the study also found that women with few years of experience managing or owning a business received significantly lower loan amounts compared with men with similar

---

[39] Ken S. Cavalluzzo, Linda C. Cavalluzzo, and John D. Wolken, "Competition, Small Business Financing, and Discrimination," *The Journal of Business*, vol. 75, no. 4 (2002).

[40] A concentrated market has fewer firms and therefore generally less competition. In a more competitive market, discriminatory practices that could hurt a firm's profits are more likely to be eliminated.

[41] Naranchimeg Mijid and Alexandra Bernasek, "Gender and the credit rationing of small businesses," *The Social Science Journal*, vol. 50 (2013). At the same time, another study looking at data from three SSBFs did not find gender of the owner to have an effect on a firm being discouraged to apply for a loan or on being denied. See Rebel Cole and Tatyana Sokolyk, "Who Needs Credit and Who Gets Credit? Evidence from the Surveys of Small Business Finances," *Journal of Financial Stability*, vol. 24 (2016), 40-60. An older paper looking at a different survey found that women-owned businesses were significantly less likely to apply for a bank loan as well as obtain a lower loan amount compared with men even after controlling for important business characteristics. However, they say that these results may be due to women owners having different concerns about how much control they would like to have over their business, and their analysis did not include any variable to account for this difference. See Monica Zimmerman Treichel and Jonathan A. Scott, "Women-Owned Businesses and Access to Bank Credit: Evidence from Three Surveys Since 1987," *Venture Capital*, vol. 8, no. 1 (2006), 51-67. The data in this study come from the Credit, Banks and Small Business survey conducted by the National Federation of Independent Business in 1987, 1995, and 2001.

[42] The study suggests that "non-application" arising out of fear of rejection is a form of credit rationing, or limiting by lenders of the amount of credit made available to borrowers, and therefore included these discouraged borrowers in its model to analyze the effects of the gender on credit rationing of small businesses.

[43] Naranchimeg Mijid, "Why are female small business owners in the United States less likely to apply for bank loans than their male counterparts?" *Journal of Small Business & Entrepreneurship*, vol. 27, no. 2 (2015), 229-249.

[44] Naranchimeg Mijid, "Gender differences in Type 1 credit rationing of small businesses in the US." *Cogent Economics & Finance*, vol. 3 (2015).

years of experience. A fourth study looked at six different types of loans, including lines of credit, and found that white women were significantly more likely than white men to avoid applying for a loan because they assume they would be denied.[45] However, once the authors' model controlled for education differences, all gender disparities in applying for credit disappeared, though white women were still less likely than white men to have loans.[46]

## Studies Found That Men and Women Paid or Were Quoted Different Prices for Auto Purchases and Auto Repairs

Studies we reviewed on auto purchases and repairs found that a seller's expectation of what customers are willing to pay and how informed they seemed can differ by gender, which can affect the price customers are quoted. However, these studies were published in 1995 and 2001, which may limit the applicability or relevance of their findings today. The 2001 study we reviewed on auto purchases found that though women paid higher prices than men for car purchases on average, these differences declined when cars were purchased online.[47] The authors suggest that this may be because Internet consumers can effectively convey their level of price knowledge and therefore may seem better informed to the sellers. They also suggest it could be because the dealerships have less information about online consumers and their willingness to pay, which may limit the extent of price differentiation.[48] The 1995 study on auto purchases found that the dealers quoted significantly lower prices to white males than to female or African American test buyers using identical, scripted bargaining strategies in part because dealers may have made assumptions about women's willingness to bargain for lower prices.[49]

We also reviewed one study on auto repairs that found that women were quoted higher prices than men if they seemed uninformed about the cost of car repair when requesting a quote, but the price differences disappeared if the study participant

---

45 Susan Coleman, "Access to Debt Capital for Women- and Minority-Owned Small Firms: Does Educational Attainment Have an Impact?" *Journal of Developmental Entrepreneurship*, vol. 9, no. 2 (2004), 127-143.

46 The study found that white women were no less likely to apply for loans or be denied.

47 Fiona Scott Morton, Florian Zettelmeyer, and Jorge Silva-Risso, "Consumer Information and Price Discrimination: Does the Internet Affect the Pricing of New Cars to Women and Minorities?" *National Bureau of Economic Research*, Working Paper 8668 (2001).

48 The authors analyzed data on every new car transaction at selected dealerships from January 1, 1999 to February 28, 2000, to examine the relationship between car prices and demographics for both online and offline purchases, and they controlled for transactional and car-related factors that may affect the price of a car.

49 Ian Ayres and Peter Siegelman, "Race and Gender Discrimination in Bargaining for a New Car," *The American Economic Review*, vol. 85, no. 3. (1995), 304-321, accessed on November 7, 2016, at http://links.jstor.org/sici?sici=0002- 8282%28199506%2985%3A3%3C304%3ARAGDIB%3E2.0.CO%3B2-W. The authors sent 38 testers to bargain for 306 cars at 153 new-car dealerships in the Chicago area.

mentioned an expected price.[50] The study suggests that a potential explanation for this result could be that auto repair shops expect women to accept a price that is higher than the market average and men to accept a price below it.

## FEDERAL AGENCIES HAVE IDENTIFIED LIMITED OR NO CONSUMER CONCERNS ABOUT PRICE DIFFERENCES BASED ON SEX OR GENDER

### Federal Agencies Monitor Consumer Complaints and Identified Limited Examples of Concerns of Price Differences Based on the Consumer's Sex or Gender

BCFP and HUD have responsibilities to monitor consumer complaints in the consumer credit and housing markets, respectively.[51] Additionally, FTC monitors complaints about the consumer credit and consumer goods markets. All three agencies play a role in potentially monitoring or addressing issues of gender-related price differences and have online complaint forms for submission of consumer complaints:[52]

- BCFP collects and reviews consumer complaints about financial products and services and provides complaints and related data in its Consumer Complaint Database. In 2017 BCFP received approximately 320,200 consumer complaints. The products that generated the most complaints in 2017 were "Credit or consumer reporting," "Debt collection," and "Mortgage."[53] According to BCFP officials, BCFP also analyzes loan and demographics data collected through HMDA and other data sources to monitor and identify market trends. In addition, BCFP and the federal financial regulators examine fair lending practices of the

[50] Meghan R. Busse, Ayelet Israeli, and Florian Zettelmeyer, "Repairing the Damage: The Effect of Price Expectations on Auto Repair Price Quotes," *National Bureau of Economic Research*, Working Paper 19154 (2013).

[51] Agency monitoring of market trends and consumer concerns is important because consumers cannot easily identify discrimination. For example, we reported that some marketplace lenders, which consumers can use to cover personal expenses (such as home or medical expenses), may use less traditional data during the underwriting process. See GAO, *Financial Technology: Information on Subsectors and Regulatory Oversight,* GAO-17-361 (Washington, D.C.: April 19, 2017). The use of less traditional data, such as utilities, rent, telephone bills, and educational history, introduces the risk that the data used are inaccurate and raises concerns that consumers may not have sufficient recourse if the information being used is incorrect.

[52] In addition to their online complaint forms, consumers can also submit complaints by phone or mail. All three agencies also receive complaints through other means, such as from other federal agencies (in the case of BCFP and FTC) or partner organizations, among others. See appendix V for more information on these agencies' consumer complaints processes.

[53] Bureau of Consumer Financial Protection, *Consumer Response Annual Report January 1-December 31, 2017,* accessed on June 26, 2018, at https://s3.amazonaws.com/files.consumerfinance.gov/f/documents/cfpb_consumerresponse-annual-report_2017.pdf.

institutions they regulate, and these examinations have uncovered sex discrimination in credit products by FDIC and NCUA.[54]

- FTC receives complaints and the complaints are stored in the Consumer Sentinel Network, a database of consumer complaints received by FTC, as well as those filed with other federal and state agencies and organizations, such as mass marketing fraud complaints from the Council of Better Business Bureaus. The complaints in the Consumer Sentinel Network focus on consumer fraud, identity theft, and other consumer protection matters, such as debt collection, and can include complaints related to consumer credit markets.
- HUD receives consumer complaints about potential FHA violations through its website, via its toll-free phone hotline, and in writing. HUD monitors those complaints through its online HUD Enforcement Management System. HUD investigates all complaints for which it has jurisdictional authority. HUD may monitor complaints to identify trends, but HUD officials stated that the agency does not generally monitor consumer credit and housing market data, absent a specific complaint. In cases where HUD has jurisdictional authority under FHA, HUD offers conciliation between the parties. If resolution is not reached, and HUD determines there is reasonable cause to believe a violation has occurred, the parties may elect to have the matter heard in U.S. District Court or at HUD.

In their oversight of federal antidiscrimination statutes, BCFP officials said they have not identified significant consumer concerns about price differences based on a consumer's sex or gender. FTC and HUD officials identified some examples of concerns of this nature. For example, FTC has taken enforcement actions alleging unlawful race- and gender-related price differences.[55] HUD has also identified several cases where pregnant women and their partners applied for a mortgage while the woman was on maternity leave, and the couple's mortgage loan application was denied.[56]

---

[54] For example, according to FDIC officials, from January 2012 to December 2017, FDIC cited three ECOA violations related to sex. FDIC officials stated that all three involved female loan applicants being charged higher prices than comparable males. The violations were identified in examinations that occurred, respectively, in 2013, 2015, and 2015. In two of the cases, restitution was provided. The third case was referred to DOJ. According to DOJ officials, after considering the matter, DOJ deferred to FDIC for administrative enforcement.

[55] For example, in *United States v. Delta Funding Corp.*, No. 00-1872 (E.D.N.Y. 2000), the complaint alleged that higher mortgage broker fees were charged to African American females than to white males in violation of ECOA and FHA.

[56] According to HUD, refusing to provide a mortgage loan or mortgage insurance because a woman is pregnant or on family leave violates FHA's prohibition against sex and familial-status discrimination, which includes discrimination against individuals who have or are expecting a child. As of May 2017, HUD received nearly 150 complaints alleging maternity leave discrimination and has obtained more than $8 million in compensation for victims.

## Our Analysis of Federal Agency Data Identified Few Consumer Complaints about Price Differences Based on Sex or Gender

### Table 3. Consumer Complaints about Price Differences Related to Gender or Sex by Agency, 2012–2017

| Agency | Number of gender or sex-related complaints[a] | Sample of gender or sex-related complaints reviewed | Estimate of gender or sex-related complaints about price differences (percent) | 95 percent confidence interval |
|---|---|---|---|---|
| Bureau of Consumer Financial Protection (BCFP) | 6,117 | 100 | 0.0 | 0.0 –3.0 |
| Department of Housing and Urban Development (HUD) | 5,421 | 100 | 4.0 | 1.1 –9.9 |
| Federal Trade Commission (FTC) | 10,472 | 100 | 1.0 | 0.0 –5.4 |

Source: GAO analysis of BCFP, HUD, and FTC consumer complaints data from 2012 - 2017. | GAO-18-500.

Note: We drew a stratified random probability sample of 100 gender-related consumer complaints with narratives from BCFP's, FTC's, and HUD's consumer complaint databases. With this probability sample, each member of the study population had a nonzero probability of being included, and that probability could be computed for any member. All estimates in this table have a margin of error at 5.9 percentage points or fewer at a 95 percent confidence level.

[a]To identify our universe of gender-related consumer complaints in BCFP's and FTC's databases, we used search terms that targeted sex or gender discrimination (e.g., gender, sex, female, male, treatment, discrimination). See our complete list of search terms in appendix III. HUD's consumer complaint database is categorized by protective class (e.g., race, sex, national origin), and we did not need to use search terms to identify gender-related complaints.

BCFP, FTC, and HUD have received few consumer complaints about price differences related to sex or gender, according to our analysis of a sample of each agency's 2012–2017 complaint data (see Table 3).[57] In separate samples of 100 gender-related complaints at BCFP, HUD, and FTC, we found that 0, 4, and 1 complaint, respectively, were related to price differences based on sex or gender.[58] Three of the complaints from HUD also cited differences in price based on other protected classes (such as race or ethnicity).

Half of the academic experts and consumer groups we interviewed told us that in some markets it is difficult for consumers to observe and compare prices paid by other consumers, such as when prices are not posted or can be negotiated (e.g., car sales). In such cases, consumers may not know if other consumers are paying a higher or lower price than the price quoted to them. Most academic experts also told us that when consumers are aware that price differences could exist, they may make different decisions when making purchases. Additionally, officials from BCFP noted that price differences

---

[57] We drew a stratified random probability sample of 100 gender-related consumer complaints with narratives from each database. With this probability sample, each member of the study population had a nonzero probability of being included, and that probability could be computed for any member.

[58] Examples of gender-related complaints about price differences include being charged more for an auto lease and paying more for rental housing and home repairs.

related to gender may be difficult for consumers to identify, or that consumers may not know where to complain.

### Agencies Provide Resources on Discrimination and Have Not Developed Other Consumer Education Efforts on Gender in Part due to Limited Public Complaints

The consumer education resources of BCFP, FTC, and HUD provide general consumer education resources on discrimination (i.e., consumer user guide or a website) and consumer awareness. Officials from BCFP and HUD said they have not identified a need to develop other consumer education resources specific to gender-related price differences. For example, BCFP's print and online consumer education materials are intended to inform consumers of their rights and protections related to credit discrimination, which includes discrimination based on sex or gender. The three agencies' consumer education materials also provide advice that could help consumers avoid paying higher prices regardless of their gender—such as home-buying resources and resources on comparison shopping. However, the agencies have not developed additional educational resources focused specifically on potential gender-related price differences in part because few complaints on this topic have been collected in their databases, agency officials told us. FTC officials noted that it tries to focus its education efforts on topics that will have the greatest benefit to consumers, often determined by information it gathers through complaints and investigations.

Representatives of five consumer groups and industry associations told us that they have received few complaints about gender-related price differences. However, four consumer groups noted that low concern could be the result of consumers being unaware of price differences related to gender. For example, as indicated above, price differences related to gender may be difficult for consumers to identify when they cannot determine whether they are paying a higher price than others. Representatives of two retailing industry associations similarly stated that they have not heard concerns about price differences related to gender.

## Some State and Local Governments Have Passed Laws to Address Concerns about Gender-Related Price Differences

In response to consumer complaints or concerns about gender disparities in pricing, at least one state (California) and two municipalities (Miami-Dade County and New York

City) have passed laws or ordinances to prohibit businesses from charging different prices for the same or similar goods or services solely based on gender (see Table 4).[59]

**Table 4. Examples of State and Local Gender-Related Pricing Laws in the United States**

| U.S. state or locality | Law or ordinance | Exceptions | Enforcement |
|---|---|---|---|
| California | *Gender Tax Repeal Act of 1995.* Prohibits any business establishment from charging different prices for the same or similar services based solely on a consumer's gender. It also requires businesses that provide clothing alteration, hair care, dry cleaning, or laundry services to publicly display the prices they charge or disclose the prices to consumers upon request. | Excludes insurance, and prices can differ for women and men based on the amount of time, difficulty, or cost to provide services to those specific demographics. | The State Attorney General or an individual can file a complaint in court. Individuals can also submit complaints to California's Department of Fair Employment and Housing, Violators receive written notice to correct the violation within 30 days; if the price is not changed, violators could be liable for a civil penalty of $4,000. |
| Miami-Dade County, Florida | *Gender Pricing Ordinance, enacted in 1997.* Prohibits businesses from charging different prices for goods or services based solely on a consumer's gender. *Dry Cleaning and Laundering Ordinance*, enacted in 1997. Prohibits cleaners from discriminating against a customer because of a customer's gender with respect to the price charged for like cleaning. | Excludes insurance, and prices can differ based on the amount of time, difficulty, or cost involved in providing goods and services to consumers of different genders; and discounts can be based on gender as long as they do not exclude others from the program. | Office of Consumer Protection in the Department of Regulatory and Economic Resources, Business Affairs Division. Consumers can sue in Small Claims Court; Office of Consumer Protection can issue citations, but does not have capacity to seek and identify violations. |
| New York City, N.Y. | *City Council Bill Number 804-A, 1998.*Prohibits businesses that provide services, such as hair cutting and dry cleaning, from basing prices solely on gender. | Applicable to retail service establishments only. | New York City Department of Consumer Affairs can issue violations that can be discovered during routine inspections. Violators must pay a civil penalty of between $50 and $250 for first offense and for each successive offense, the penalty is between $100 and $500. |

Source: GAO analysis and interviews with state and local officials. | GAO-18-500.

[59] In addition to these jurisdictions, the U.S. territory of Guam also prohibits charging consumers different prices for the same goods or services based on, among other factors, the sex of the consumer.

In addition, two of these laws included requirements related to promoting price transparency. California enacted the Gender Tax Repeal Act of 1995, which prohibits businesses from charging different prices for the same or similar services based on a consumer's gender. The law also requires certain businesses to display price information and disclose prices upon request, according to state officials with whom we spoke. Similarly, in 1997, Miami-Dade County passed the Gender Pricing Ordinance, which prohibits businesses from charging different prices based solely on a consumer's gender (though businesses are permitted to charge different prices if the goods or services involve more time, difficulty, or cost). In the same year, it also passed an ordinance that prohibits dry cleaning businesses from charging different prices for similar services based on gender. This ordinance also requires those businesses to post all prices on a clear and conspicuous sign, according to county officials with whom we spoke. State and local officials we interviewed identified benefits and challenges associated with these laws. For example, California, New York City, and Miami-Dade County officials noted that these laws give them the ability to intervene to address pricing practices that may lead to discrimination based on gender. In addition, California state officials said that the state's efforts to implement the Gender Tax Repeal Act helped to improve consumer awareness about gender price differences. However, officials from California and Miami-Dade County cited challenges associated with tracking relevant complaints. For example, Miami-Dade County's online complaint form includes a narrative section but does not ask for the complainant's gender. Consumers do not always identify their gender in the narrative or state that that was the reason for their treatment.

Additionally, officials from California and Miami-Dade County stated that seeking out violations would be very resource-intensive, and they rely on residents to submit complaints about violations.

## AGENCY COMMENTS

We provided a draft of this chapter to BCFP, DOJ, FTC, and HUD. BCFP, FTC, and HUD provided technical comments on the report draft, which we incorporated where appropriate.

As agreed with your offices, unless you publicly announce the contents of this chapter earlier, we plan no further distribution until 30 days from the report date.

Alicia Puente Cackley
Director, Financial Markets and Community Investment

# APPENDIX I: NIELSEN RETAIL PRICE DATA ANALYSIS METHODOLOGY

We used a multivariate regression model to estimate the effect of gender (to which a product is targeted to) on the price of that product while controlling for other factors that may also affect the product's price. The factors that we controlled for were the product size, promotional and packaging costs, and other product characteristics discussed in detail later. We used scanner data from the Nielsen Company (Nielsen) for calendar year 2016 and analyzed the following 10 product categories: (1) underarm deodorants, (2) body deodorants, (3) shaving cream, (4) shaving gel, (5) disposable razors, (6) nondisposable razors, (7) razor blades, (8) designer perfumes, (9) mass-market perfumes, and (10) mass-market body sprays.[60] We estimated the following regression model for each of our 10 product categories:

$$P=\alpha+\beta^*\text{Male} + \lambda^*\ \text{Size} + \theta^*\text{Owneri} +\eta^*\text{Promotion}+ \mu^*X_j + \delta^*Y_k + \varepsilon$$

The dependent variable P in the above equation represents price. For our analysis, we constructed two measures of price. The first is the item price, estimated as the total dollar sales of an item (each item is depicted by a unique Universal Product Code (UPC) in the Nielsen data), divided by the total units sold of that item. The second measure of price that we use is price per ounce or price per count. This is estimated as the item price divided by the total quantity of product, where quantity or size depicts the number of ounces (as in the case of fragrances) or the count of blades in razor blade packs. The total quantity of the product is the ounces or counts of one item multiplied by the number of items included in a specific product configuration. For example, a 2-pack of deodorant sticks where each deodorant stick is 2.7 ounces would be a total quantity of 5.4 ounces.

The variable *Male* in the above equation is an indicator variable depicting whether the product is designated as a "men's" product in the Nielsen data. It is represented as a value of "1" for men's products and a value of "0" for women's products. The co-efficient for this variable, parameter β, would therefore show the price difference between a men's and women's product. A negative value would imply a lower price for products designated as men's products.

---

[60] The prices were collected from participating retailers when an item was scanned at the cash register during check out.

The variable *Size* represents the most appropriate specification of the size of the product.[61]

*Owneri* is a set of indicator variables representing all the brand owners selling a particular product. The brand of a product can be expected to have a substantial effect on prices for the kind of products we analyze because brands can be a proxy for quality for some consumers. However, we also found that firms often create gender-specific brands, so holding brands constant rendered most gender-based price comparisons infeasible. To overcome this, we hold owners instead of brands constant for our price comparison analysis.

The variable *Promotion* represents the percentage of dollar sales that were sold on any type of promotion.[62] This variable proxies for promotional costs to some extent based on the assumption that the greater the proportion of sales due to promotional activity, the greater the promotional costs.

The variables *Xi* represent a set of indicator variables for packaging characteristics such as package delivery method (for example, roll-on or aerosol spray deodorants) or package shape (for example, bottle, tube, or can). We expect these characteristics to proxy for different costs associated with different packaging methods.

The variables *Yk* represent a set of indicator variables representing different product characteristics (for example, forms such as gel stick or smooth solid and claims such as "active cooling" or "anti-wetness" for underarm deodorants, and blade types such as "triple edge" and "flexible six" for razors). These product characteristics may proxy for some underlying manufacturing costs or even consumer preferences. Since firms may create gender-specific product attributes—scents like "sweet petals" and "pure sport" or razor head types and colors to differentiate products between genders—we did not always keep every product attribute constant when comparing prices.[63]

---

[61] We tried four different potential functional forms for size—size, square-root of size, log(size) and a quadratic term (size plus size-squared)—for each of our two prices. Since size may affect prices differently for different products (for example, the number of disposable razors in a plastic bag versus number of ounces of designer perfume), we chose different size specifications for different products. We used Akaike's information criterion to choose the model with the best fit.

[62] According to Nielsen, these promotions comprise feature w/o Display, Display w/o Feature, Feature & Display or Temporary Price Reduction. Nielsen also reports the total number of weeks a product has been on promotion. We chose not to include both of these variables as they are highly correlated. We chose the former as we expect average prices to be directly influenced more by how much sold at promotional prices versus the amount of time the product was on promotion.

[63] Firms may use different product characteristics to differentiate one product from another in the expectation that different segments of consumers (in this case, men and women) will self-select into different groups. Thus, firms may create gender-specific scents, razor head types, and even brands. Therefore when we control for the differentiating attribute, the products may not remain comparable, and any price differences become insignificant in our analyses. When controlling for some attribute made price differences insignificant, we explored further to see whether there was enough overlap between men's and women's products for that particular attribute. If there was no overlap or if it was limited to only a couple of products with insignificant sales, it did not make sense to conclude that lack of significant price differences implied no gender-related price differences for those products.

## Table 5. Regression Results for Analysis of Selected Personal Care Products, 2016

| | **Underarm deodorants** | **Body deodorants** | **Shaving cream** | **Shaving gel** | **Disposable razors** | **Nondis-posable razors** | **Razor blades** | **Designer perfume** | **Mass-market perfume** | **Mass-market body sprays** |
|---|---|---|---|---|---|---|---|---|---|---|
| Number of observations | 2014 | 64 | 193 | 435 | 1237 | 417 | 567 | 3945 | 2003 | 523 |
| R-square[a] | 0.77 and 0.90 | 0.99 and 0.99 | 0.98 and 0.99 | 0.79 and 0.71 | 0.87 and 0.91 | 0.92 and 0.93 | 0.69 and 0.73 | 0.60 and 0.61 | 0.64 and 0.75 | 0.92 and 0.87 |
| Co-efficient | -0.275* | -0.77* | -0.568* | 0.567* | -0.0.31 | 2.04* | 0.303 | -1.73** | 0.792 | -0.503* |
| for "male" in item price regressions | (0.120) | (0.178) | (0.096) | (0.146) | (0.229) | (0.482) | (0.971) | (1.02) | (0.798) | (0.144) |
| Co-efficient | -0.081* | -0.139* | -0.029* | 0.071* | -.004 | 1.44* | -0.335* | -2.678* | 0.326 | -0.166* |
| for "male" in ounce or count price regressions | (0.038) | (0.029) | (0.005) | (0.020) | (0.062) | (0.507) | (0.146) | (0.636) | (0.534) | (.049) |
| Brands or owners | √ | √ | √ | √ | √ | √ | √ | √ | √ | √ |
| Promotional expenditure | √ | √ | √ | √ | √ | √ | √ | √ | √ | √ |
| Packaging general shape | √ | √ | √ | √ | √ | √ | √ | √ | √ | √ |
| Packaging delivery method | √ | √ | √ | √ | n/a | n/a | n/a | √ | √ | √ |
| Size transformation in regressions with: | | | | | | | | | | |
| Item price | Square root (size) | (size + square (size)) | Size | (size + square (size)) | (size + square (size)) | (size+ square (size)) | Size | Size | Size | Log (size) |
| Ounce or count price | Log(size) | Log(size) | (size + square (size)) | Log(size) | Log(size) | Log (size) | (size + square (size)) | (size + square (size)) | (size + square (size)) | Log (size) |
| Attributes included | | | | | | | | | | |
| Form | X | n/a | n/a | n/a | n/a | n/a | n/a | n/a | n/a | n/a |
| Claim | X | √ | X | X | X | n/a | n/a | n/a | n/a | n/a |
| Scent | X | X | X | X | n/a | n/a | n/a | X | X | X |

## Table 5. (Continued)

| | Underarm deodorants | Body deodorants | Shaving cream | Shaving gel | Disposable razors | Nondis-posable razors | Razor blades | Designer perfume | Mass-market perfume | Mass-market body sprays |
|---|---|---|---|---|---|---|---|---|---|---|
| Color | n/a | n/a | n/a | n/a | X | X | X | n/a | n/a | n/a |
| Razor blade type | n/a | n/a | n/a | n/a | √ | X | X | n/a | n/a | n/a |
| Razor head type | n/a | n/a | n/a | n/a | √ | √ | n/a | n/a | n/a | n/a |

Legend: √ = included; X = not included; n/a = data not available or relevant

* denotes significance at 5 percent or less. ** denotes significance at 10 percent.

Source: GAO analysis of Nielsen Company data. | GAO-18-500

Notes:

1. Standard errors for the coefficients are in brackets.
2. Body deodorants: We have under 100 observations for body deodorants and therefore the significance tests conducted may not have very high power.
3. Shaving cream and shaving gel: Shaving cream data provided by Nielsen included both "creams" and "gels." Upon examining the data, we observed that gels are typically more expensive than creams. Therefore, we decided to treat these as separate products for our regression analysis.
4. Disposable razors: Our data show that consumers buy a larger quantity of more expensive razors targeted to men in general. For example, in the price category of $20 and above, consumers mostly buy razors targeted to men. These higher-priced razors are usually the ones that include more razors in that product configuration. For this reason, we repeated our analysis only for products that had an average price of less than $10 and the results remained qualitatively similar.
5. Nondisposable razors: Looking at the distribution of buying behavior, it seemed that in the range of prices above $12.50, consumers buy razors targeted to men. We therefore split our sample into average prices above $12.50 and below $12.50 to analyze the relative prices. For prices below $12.50, it seemed there were no significant differences in prices even after we controlled for owners and packaging shape. Controlling for blade-type however made prices for razors targeted to women significantly lower. For prices above $12.50 we do not have many observations to make reasonable comparisons.
6. Fragrances: We chose to analyze products in the designer and mass-market segments separately as they are at very different price points and cannot be considered substitutes for each other. We also dropped the gift-pack segment as these may comprise different product and packaging details that we could not account for from our data. The other common segment between men and women is fragrance soap, which we chose not to analyze due to insignificant sales in the women's segment. Fragrances are also further divided into several products such as body splash, fragrant soap, after-shave, eau de parfum, powder, etc. To keep our analysis meaningful and manageable, we decided to select only the few products that represented at least 5 percent of that segment in sales. Based on our analysis of types of products, price points, and common owners, we decided to group the fragrance products into three product categories:
   (1) designer perfumes = designer eau de toilette + designer eau de parfum + designer cologne;
   (2) mass-market perfumes = mass-market eau de toilette + mass-market eau de parfum + mass-market cologne; and (3) mass-market body spray = body spray + fragrance body spray.

[a]The first R-square value is from the item price regressions and the second one is from the per unit price regressions.

The idiosyncratic error term is represented by $\varepsilon$. All of our regressions are weighted, with the proportion of units sold for a particular item in that year as the weight. This is because, for personal care products, there are large differences in units sold of various product types and brands, and therefore it not useful to compare simple unweighted average prices. For example, for one company the highest selling men's deodorant stick sold almost 12 million units in 2016, and the highest selling women's deodorant stick sold over 8 million units. The average units sold for underarm deodorants as a whole was just over 300,000 units, and 1,000 products out of a total of almost 3,000 products had less than 100 units sold in 2016.

The linear model we used has the usual shortcomings of being subject to specification bias to the extent the relationship between price and each of the independent variables is not linear. The model also does not include complete data on costs, such as advertising and packaging, or consumers' willingness to pay, both of which have an effect on the price differences. The model may thus also be subject to omitted variable bias. In addition, the model may have some endogeneity issues to the extent the product characteristics themselves are influenced by consumers' willingness to pay for some of those product features. To reduce the impact of any model misspecifications or heteroscedasticity, we used the robust (or Huber-White sandwich) estimator.[64]

We estimated the regression model above for each of the 10 products separately and for each of the two measures of price. We used Nielsen's in-store, retail price scanner data, which include information on total volume sold and dollar sales for items purchased at 228 retailers including grocery stores, drug stores, mass merchandisers (such as Target), dollar stores, club stores (such as Sam's Club), and convenience stores. The data capture 82 percent of all U.S. sales. Nielsen also projects sales for the remaining noncooperating retailers, and that information is included in this dataset. We excluded some very small brands that did not have enough units sold from our regression analysis in order to avoid outliers. These brands usually had less than 50,000 units sold over the entire year, and for some products they represented less than 1 percent of all units sold.

We found that average retail prices paid were significantly higher for women's products than for men's in 5 out of 10 personal care products. In 2 categories, men's versions sold at a significantly higher price.

---

[64] Using this estimator helps to forgo model-based variance estimates in favor of the more model-agnostic "robust" variances, which give more accurate assessments of the sample-to-sample variability of the parameter estimates even when the model is mis-specified.

One category had mixed results based on two price measures analyzed, and two others showed no significant gender price differences.

A summary of our regression results is presented in Table 5.

# APPENDIX II: COLLECTION OF ONLINE PRICES FOR SELECTED PERSONAL CARE PRODUCTS

We manually collected prices for 16 pairs of selected personal care products from the websites of four online retailers that also operated physical store locations.[414] We selected comparable pairs of similar men's and women's products that were differentiated by product attributes, such as scent or color, and were sold at most or all of the four retailers. The products were selected based on several comparability factors such as brand, product claims, and number of blades in a razor. For two 1-week time periods in January and March 2018, we collected prices manually between 1:00 p.m. and 7:00 p.m. (ET) over two 7-day time periods. We collected listed prices and did not adjust the prices for any promotions that were available, such as online coupons or buy-one-get-one-free offers.

Table 6 presents the results of our online price collection. These results have important limitations:

- The average prices shown are not generalizable to the broader universe of prices for these products sold at other times or by other online retailers.
- The data reflect prices advertised to consumers rather than the prices consumers actually paid.
- The data do not capture the volume of sales for each item for each retailer; in our analysis, we weighted all advertised prices equally across the retailers. As a result, differences we found within these advertised prices may not have translated into comparable differences in prices female and male consumers paid for these products online.
- The prices do not reflect any promotional discounts, volume discounts, or other discounts that may have been available to some or all consumers.

[414] The retailers consisted of two large national drugstores and two national mass merchandisers.

## Table 6. Average Online Prices Collected for Selected Personal Care Products on Four Retailer Websites, 2018

| | Average item price (dollars) | | | | Average price per ounce or count (dollars) | | | | Average product size (ounces or count) | |
|---|---|---|---|---|---|---|---|---|---|---|
| | January 2018 | | March 2018 | | January 2018 | | March 2018 | | January and March 2018 | |
| Product | Men's | Women's | Men's | Women's | Men's | Women's | Men's | Women's | Men's | Women's |
| Body Spray Pair 1 | 5.14 | 5.53 | 4.87 | 5.96 | 1.29 | 1.38 | 1.22 | 1.49 | 4.0 | 4.0 |
| Body Spray Pair 2 | 4.98 | 7.49 | 4.87 | 6.08 | 1.25 | 0.94 | 1.22 | 0.94 | 4.0 | 7.2 |
| Body Spray Pair 3 | 25.41 | 22.48 | 27.08 | 27.62 | 10.16 | 13.22 | 11.40 | 16.25 | 2.5 | 1.7 |
| Deodorant Pair 1 | 5.45 | 5.79 | 5.23 | 5.84 | 2.02 | 2.23 | 1.94 | 2.25 | 2.7 | 2.6 |
| Deodorant Pair 2 | 4.22 | 4.28 | 4.25 | 4.26 | 1.56 | 1.64 | 1.58 | 1.64 | 2.7 | 2.6 |
| Deodorant Pair 3 | 5.45 | 5.45 | 5.17 | 5.31 | 2.42 | 2.42 | 2.30 | 2.36 | 2.3 | 2.3 |
| Deodorant Spray Pair 1 | 5.48 | 5.32 | 5.28 | 5.32 | 1.37 | 1.33 | 1.32 | 1.33 | 4.0 | 4.0 |
| Deodorant Spray Pair 2 | 6.28 | 6.28 | 6.08 | 6.15 | 1.65 | 1.65 | 1.60 | 1.62 | 3.8 | 3.8 |
| Disposable Razors Pair 1 | 7.10 | 7.57 | 6.65 | 7.03 | 1.44 | 1.55 | 1.38 | 1.49 | 5.1 | 5.1 |
| Disposable Razors Pair 2 | 4.17 | 3.84 | 5.08 | 3.88 | 0.42 | 0.36 | 0.51 | 0.36 | 10.0 | 10.9 |
| Nondisposable Razors Pair 1 | 10.55 | 11.49 | 10.48 | 11.04 | 10.55 | 11.49 | 10.48 | 11.04 | 1.0 | 1.0 |
| Nondisposable Razors Pair 2 | 9.64 | 10.12 | 9.93 | 11.41 | 9.64 | 10.12 | 9.93 | 11.41 | 1.0 | 1.0 |
| Razor Blades Pair 1 | 9.43 | 13.85 | 11.48 | 12.90 | 2.36 | 2.96 | 2.87 | 2.69 | 4.0 | 5.0 |
| Razor Blades Pair 2 | 19.05 | 21.19 | 14.99 | 21.23 | 3.64 | 4.06 | 3.31 | 4.13 | 5.[illegible] | 5.3 |
| Shaving Gel Pair 1 | 4.34 | 2.38 | 4.43 | 2.32 | 0.62 | 0.34 | 0.63 | 0.33 | 7.0 | 7.0 |
| Shaving Gel Pair 2 | 3.24 | 3.21 | 3.24 | 3.24 | 0.46 | 0.46 | 0.46 | 0.46 | 7.0 | 7.0 |

Source: GAO analysis. | GAO-18-500.

Note: We manually collected prices for 16 pairs of selected personal care products from websites of four online retailers. We selected comparable pairs of similar men's and women's products that were differentiated by product attributes, such as scent or color, and were commonly sold at most or all of the four retailers. The products were selected based on several comparability factors such as brand, product claims, and number of blades in a razor. The selected online retailers were retailers that also operated physical store locations. For two 1-week time periods in January and March 2018, we collected prices manually between 1:00 p.m. and 7:00 p.m. (ET). We collected listed prices and did not adjust the prices for any promotions that were available, such as online coupons or buy-one-getone-free offers. The data are presented for illustrative purposes only and are not generalizable to any other personal care products or retailer websites.

# APPENDIX III: OBJECTIVES, SCOPE, AND METHODOLOGY

This chapter examines (1) how prices compared for selected categories of consumer goods that are differentiated for men and women, and potential reasons for any significant price differences; (2) what is known about the extent to which men and women may pay different prices in, or experience different levels of access to, markets for credit and goods and services that are not differentiated based on gender; (3) the extent to which federal agencies have identified and taken steps to address any concerns about gender-related price differences; and (4) state and local government efforts to address concerns about gender-related price differences.

To compare prices for selected goods that are differentiated for men and women, we purchased and analyzed Nielsen Company (Nielsen) data on retail prices paid for 10 personal care product categories for calendar year 2016.[65] The product categories included underarm deodorants, body deodorants (typically sold as a spray), disposable razors, nondisposable razors, razor blades, shaving creams, shaving gels, and three categories of fragrances. We selected these categories of personal care products because they are commonly purchased consumer goods that were categorized by gender in the Nielsen data. The women's and men's versions of personal care products we selected are generally more similar in terms of the form, size, and packaging in comparison to certain other consumer product categories that are also differentiated by gender, such as clothing. We used regression models to analyze data on retail prices paid for the 10 categories of personal care products differentiated for women and men. To assess the reliability of the Nielsen data, we reviewed relevant documentation and conducted interviews with Nielsen representatives to review steps they took to collect and ensure the reliability of the data. In addition, we electronically tested data fields for missing values, outliers, and obvious errors. We determined that these data were sufficiently reliable for our purposes. For more details on the methodology for, and limitations of, our analysis of these retail price data, see appendix I.

We also manually collected listed prices for 16 pairs of selected personal care products from four different retailer websites over two 7-day periods in January and March 2018. For each pair, we selected comparable men's and women's products that were differentiated by product attributes, such as scent or color, and were commonly sold across retailers. For more details on our online price data collection and the limitations associated with interpreting the results, see appendix II.

---

[65] In addition to the retail price paid, the data we purchased from Nielsen include data fields for product brand, package size, package design, product scent, and product color, among other product characteristics. Nielsen collected these retail price data from over 200 national retailers, including grocery stores, pharmacies, mass merchandizers, and club stores. Together these retailers encompass 82 percent of all U.S. sales for 2016. The prices were collected from participating retailers when an item was scanned at the cash register during check out.

To examine what is known about the extent to which men and women may be offered different prices or access for the same goods or services, we reviewed academic literature identified through a literature search covering the last 25 years. To identify existing studies from peer-reviewed journals, we conducted searches using subject and keyword searches of various databases, such as EconLit, Scopus, ProQuest, and Social SciSearch. We also used a snowball search technique—meaning we reviewed relevant academic literature cited in our selected studies—to identify additional studies. We performed these searches and identified articles from December 2016 to April 2018. From these searches, we identified 21 studies that appeared in peer-reviewed journals or research institutions' publications from 1995 through 2016 and were relevant to gender-related price differences for the same products. We reviewed and assessed each study's evaluation methodology based on generally accepted social science standards. See the bibliography at the end of this chapter for a list of the 21 studies.

We then summarized the research findings. A GAO economist read and assessed each study, using the same data collection instrument. The assessment focused on information such as the types of disparities examined, the research design and data sources used, and methods of data analysis. The assessment also focused on the quality of the data used in the studies as reported by the researchers and any limitations of data sources for the purposes for which they were used. A second GAO economist reviewed each completed data collection instrument to verify the accuracy of the information included. As a result, the 21 studies that we selected for our review met our criteria for methodological quality. We found the studies we reviewed to be reliable for purposes of determining what is known about price differences for the same products. However, these studies have important limitations, such as using nonrepresentative data samples, and the results are not generalizable.

To examine the federal role in overseeing gender-related price differences, we reviewed relevant federal statutes and agency guidance, and interviewed officials from the Federal Trade Commission (FTC), Bureau of Consumer Financial Protection (BCFP), the Department of Housing and Urban Development (HUD), and the Department of Justice (DOJ). To help identify the extent of concerns about gender-related price differences, we interviewed representatives from eight consumer groups, three industry associations, and four academic experts. Additionally, we reviewed a sample of consumer complaints from databases managed by BCFP, FTC, and HUD (Consumer Complaint Database, Consumer Sentinel Network, and Enforcement Management System, respectively). Complaints were submitted by consumers across the United States about various financial products, housing grievances, and other consumer protection concerns.

To identify our universe of gender-related consumer complaints in BCFP and FTC databases, we used the following search terms that targeted sex or gender discrimination: discriminate, unfair, treat, deception, abuse, female, woman, women, man, men, male, gender, sex, female, woman, women, man, men, male, gender, and sex. HUD's consumer complaint database is categorized by protected class (e.g., race, sex, national origin), so we did not need to use search terms to identify gender-related complaints.

For the years 2012 through 2017, we identified 6,117 BCFP consumer complaint narratives; 10,472 FTC consumer complaints narratives; and 5,421 HUD consumer complaint narratives that were relevant to our scope. We then drew a stratified random probability sample of 100 gender-related consumer complaints from each database. To determine which complaints in our samples were about price differences related to gender or sex, two team members read through each complaint narrative and coded whether or not the complainant's narrative indicated that they felt that they paid or were charged more because of their gender or sex. A third team member conducted a final review of the results, and made a final determination in cases where there were differences in the first two team member's assessments.

With this probability sample, each member of the study population had a nonzero probability of being included, and that probability could be computed for any member. We followed a probability procedure based on random selections and our sample is only one of a large number of samples that we might have drawn. Since each sample could have provided different estimates, we express our confidence in the precision of our particular sample's results as a 95 percent confidence interval (with a margin of error of 5.9 percent). This is the interval that would contain the actual population value for 95 percent of the samples we could have drawn. We assessed the reliability of these data by reviewing documentation and interviewing agency officials about the databases used to collect these complaints. We determined that these data were sufficiently reliable for our purposes of identifying complaints of gender-related price differences.

To explore state and local efforts to address concerns about gender-related price differences, we conducted a literature search and identified three state or local laws or ordinances that specifically address gender-related price differences: California, Miami-Dade County, Florida, and New York City, New York. We reviewed these laws and ordinances and interviewed officials from these jurisdictions to discuss motivations for, oversight of, and the impact of these laws.

We conducted this performance audit from October 2016 to August 2018 in accordance with generally accepted government auditing standards. Those standards require that we plan and perform the audit to obtain sufficient, appropriate evidence to provide a reasonable basis for our findings and conclusions based on our audit objectives. We believe that the evidence obtained provides a reasonable basis for our findings and conclusions based on our audit objectives.

# APPENDIX IV: DESCRIPTIVE STATISTICS OF NIELSEN RETAIL PRICE DATA

For each of 10 personal care product categories we analyzed, we compared the overall average prices for women's products and men's products using two measures of average price: average item price and average price per ounce or count. While the second price measure adjusts the average price for quantity of product, these comparisons did not take into account the effect on price of differences in product brand, packaging, and other characteristics.

**Table 7. Comparison of Average Retail Prices Paid in 2016 for Men's and Women's Products for 10 Selected Personal Care Product Categories**

| | **Average item price[a] (dollars)** | | | **Average price per ounce or count[b] (dollars)** | | |
|---|---|---|---|---|---|---|
| Product | Products targeted to women (w) | Products targeted to men (m) | Difference (percent) (w-m) / m | Products targeted to women (w) | Products targeted to men (m) | Difference (percent) (w-m) / m |
| Underarm deodorants | 4.14 | 3.98 | 4 | 1.70 | 1.22 | 39* |
| Body deodorants | 2.59 | 5.72 | -55* | 1.63 | 1.18 | 38* |
| Shaving cream | 2.80 | 1.95 | 44* | 0.37 | 0.27 | 37 |
| Shaving gel | 2.90 | 3.35 | -13 | 0.41 | 0.48 | -15* |
| Disposable razors | 5.02 | 5.64 | -11 | 1.34 | 1.13 | 19 |
| Nondisposable razors | 9.66 | 10.95 | -12** | 2.87 | 4.34 | -34** |
| Razor blades | 17.63 | 18.49 | -5 | 3.77 | 3.26 | 16 |
| Designer perfume | 24.91 | 27.32 | -9* | 21.62 | 18.63 | 16* |
| Mass-market perfume | 11.59 | 11.28 | 3 | 8.04 | 6.48 | 24** |
| Mass-market body spray | 2.68 | 4.33 | -38* | 1.21 | 0.97 | 25* |

Legend: * = statistically significant at the 95 percent level (p-value < 0.05); ** = statistically significant at the 90 percent level (p-value < 0.1)

Source: GAO analysis of Nielsen Company data. | GAO-18-500.

Note: We selected these categories of personal care products because they are commonly-purchased consumer goods that were categorized by gender in the Nielsen Company's data. Our analysis is limited to the set of personal care products that we analyzed. Our findings are not generalizable or applicable to other consumer goods.

[a]The average item price is the total dollar sales for a product category divided by the total number of items sold for that category.

[b]The average price per ounce or count is the item price divided by the quantity of product and weighted by the proportional share of items sold, where quantity depicts the number of ounces, as in the case of fragrances or the count of blades in razor blade packs.

As shown in Table 7, adjusting the average item price to account for differences in product quantity (ounces or count) significantly affected the size and magnitude of gender price differences for several product categories.[66] This is because men's products

[66] However, comparing average price per ounce or count does not capture quantity discounts that may be associated with larger quantities or counts of products. We account for this in our regression models for analyzing comparative prices.

in the dataset were frequently larger in size or count compared with women's products in the same category. For example, women's disposable razors sold for 11 percent less than those targeted to men when we compared average item prices. However, when we compared average price per count of razors, women's disposable razors sold for 19 percent more on average than men's. This is because women's disposable razors had on average about one fewer razor per package. In 5 out of 10 product categories, women's versions of the product on average sold for a higher price per ounce or count than men's and these differences were statistically significant at the 95 percent confidence level for 4 products and at the 90 percent level for one product.

Information about sales and relative sizes of different products targeted to men and women are presented in table 8 below.

**Table 8. Total Sales and Units Sold for Selected Personal Care Products, 2016**

| | **Total sales (dollars in millions)** | | **Units sold (millions)** | | **Ounces or count sold (millions)** | | **Average size (ounces or count)** | |
|---|---|---|---|---|---|---|---|---|
| Product | Men's | Women's | Men's | Women's | Men's | Women's | Men's | Women's |
| Underarm deodorants | 1,474 | 930 | 370 | 225 | 1,362 | 632 | 4.21 | 3.72 |
| Body deodorants | 15 | 10 | 1.7 | 5.5 | 9.2 | 10.5 | 7.13 | 4.26 |
| Shaving cream | 80 | 64 | 41 | 23 | 366 | 185 | 9.10 | 8.71 |
| Shaving gel | 195 | 115 | 58 | 40 | 443 | 322 | 9.63 | 11.38 |
| Disposable razors | 639 | 498 | 113 | 99 | 815 | 523 | 7.13 | 6.12 |
| Nondisposable razors | 308 | 214 | 28 | 22 | 158 | 113 | 5.44 | 5.82 |
| Razor blades | 803 | 333 | 44 | 19 | 276 | 107 | 7.25 | 5.72 |
| Designer perfume | 142 | 138 | 5 | 6 | 10 | 8 | 2.42 | 1.98 |
| Mass-market perfume | 73 | 88 | 6.5 | 7.6 | 19 | 18 | 2.71 | 2.14 |
| Mass-market body spray | 62 | 57 | 14 | 21 | 74 | 74 | 8.18 | 8.03 |

Source: GAO analysis of Nielsen Company data. | GAO-18-500.

Note: We selected these categories of personal care products because they are commonly-purchased consumer goods that were categorized by gender in the Nielsen Company's data. Our analysis is limited to the set of personal care products that we analyzed. Our findings are not generalizable or applicable to other consumer goods. The average item price is the total dollar sales for a product category divided by the total number of items sold for that category. The average price per ounce or count is the item price divided by the quantity of product and weighted by the item's proportional share of total volume sales, where quantity depicts the number of ounces as in the case of fragrances or the count of blades in razor blade packs.

# APPENDIX V: SELECTED FEDERAL AGENCY CONSUMER COMPLAINT PROCESSES

This appendix provides additional details about the consumer complaint processes at the Bureau of Consumer Financial Protection (BCFP), Federal Trade Commission (FTC), and Department of Housing and Urban Development (HUD).

**Table 9. Summary of Agencies' Efforts to Collect Consumer Complaints**

| | Bureau of Consumer Financial Protection (BCFP) | Federal Trade Commission (FTC) | Department of Housing and Urban Development (HUD) |
|---|---|---|---|
| How agencies collect or receive complaints | •Consumers can submit their complaint through an online complaint form to the Consumer Complaint Database on BCFP's website.<br>•Phone<br>•Mail or fax<br>•Other financial regulators | •Consumers can submit their complaint through an online complaint form to the Consumer Sentinel Network on FTC's website.<br>•Phone<br>•Mail<br>•FTC also imports complaints from other federal agencies (e.g., BCFP)<br>•State level agencies (e.g., State attorneys general)<br>•Other entities, such as the Council of Better Business Bureaus, consumer groups, and certain companies (e.g., Publishers Clearing House) | •Consumers can submit their complaint through an online complaint form to the HUD Enforcement Management System on HUD's website.<br>•Phone<br>•Mail<br>•HUD Regional offices<br>•Partner organizations |
| How complaints are handled | •Complaints are reviewed to determine if the complaint can be sent to a company for response or should be referred to another regulator. Complaints are categorized by consumer-selected product and sub-product.<br>•Complaints sent to companies for response are published in the publicly available Consumer Complaint Database after the company has responded, or after the company has had the complaint for 15 calendar days, whichever comes first. | •Complaints are sorted into three broad categories: Fraud, Identity Theft, and Other Consumer Protection Problems.<br>•Complaints marked as "other" are categorized by FTC staff.<br>•All complaints are made available to members of the Consumer Sentinel Network, which include 2,300 law enforcement members across the country who use the data to investigate targets, identify witnesses, and spot trends. | •Complainants are interviewed to collect facts about alleged discrimination by HUD staffto determine if HUD has jurisdiction over the complaint.<br>•If HUD has the authority to investigate, it will file the complaint and begin an investigation of the alleged discrimination. |
| How complaints are responded to and monitored | •BCFP monitors complaints and company responses to identify trends. | •FTC makes the complaints available to law enforcement partners across the country. However, FTC does not intervene in individual disputes between consumers and merchants.<br>•FTC monitors its complaint database to identify emerging consumer concern trends. | •HUD offers conciliation between the parties in cases of violations. If resolution is not reached, and HUD determines there is reasonable cause to believe a violation has occurred, the parties may elect to have the matter heard in U.S. District Court or at HUD.<br>•HUD monitors the complaint database to identify trends. |

Source: GAO analysis of BCFP, FTC, and HUD consumer complaint processes. | GAO-18-500.

Consumers with a complaint about unfair treatment related to gender could submit a complaint to one of these agencies. BCFP and FTC monitor consumer complaints related to violations under the Equal Credit Opportunity Act, while HUD and the Department of Justice (DOJ) investigate housing discrimination complaints under the Fair Housing Act. These complaints could be about price differences because of gender.[67]

## APPENDIX VI: BIBLIOGRAPHY

We reviewed literature to identify what is known about the extent to which female and male consumers may face different prices or access in markets for credit and goods and services that are not differentiated based on gender. This bibliography contains citations for the 20 studies and articles that we reviewed that compared prices or access for female and male consumers in markets where the product is not differentiated by gender (mortgages, small business credit, auto purchases, and auto repairs).

Asiedu, Elizabeth, James A. Freeman, and Akwasi Nti-Addae. "Access to Credit by Small Businesses: How Relevant Are Race, Ethnicity, and Gender?" *The American Economic Review*, vol. 102, no. 3 (2012): 532- 537.

Ayers, Ian and Peter Siegelman. "Race and Gender Discrimination in Bargaining for a New Car." *The American Economic Review*, vol. 85, no. 3. (1995): 304-321.

Blanchard, Lloyd, Bo Zhaob, and John Yinger. "Do lenders discriminate against minority and woman entrepreneurs?" *Journal of Urban Economics* 63 (2008): 467–497.

Blanchflower, David G., Phillip B. Levine, and David J. Zimmerman. "Discrimination in the Small-Business Credit Market." *The Review of Economics and Statistics*, vol. 85, no. 4 (2003): 930-943.

Busse, Meghan R., Ayelet Israeli, and Florian Zettelmeyer. "Repairing the Damage: The Effect of Price Expectations on Auto Repair Price Quotes." *National Bureau of Economic Research*, Working Paper 19154 (2013).

Cavalluzzo, Ken S., Linda C. Cavalluzzo, and John D. Wolken. "Competition, Small Business Financing, and Discrimination: Evidence from a New Survey." *The Journal of Business*, vol. 75, no. 4 (2002): 641- 679.

Cheng, Ping, Zhenguo Lin, and Yingchun Liu. "Do Women Pay More for Mortgages?" *The Journal of Real Estate Finance and Economics*, vol. 43 (2011): 423-440.

Cheng, Ping, Zhenguo Lin, and Yingchun Liu. "Racial Discrepancy in Mortgage Interest Rates." *The Journal of Real Estate Finance and Economics*, vol. 51 (2015): 101-120.

[67] Depending on the scope and magnitude, complaints may be referred to DOJ if they indicate a potential pattern or practice of illegal discrimination. According to DOJ officials, from 2012 through 2016, the Civil Rights Division investigated 69 lending matters, including matters referred to DOJ by the financial regulators, of which15 involved gender-related price differences.

Cole, Rebel, and Tatyana Sokolyk. "Who Needs Credit and Who Gets Credit? Evidence from the Surveys of Small Business Finances." *Journal of Financial Stability*, vol. 24 (2016), 40-60.

Coleman, Susan. "Access to Debt Capital for Women- and Minority-Owned Small Firms: Does Educational Attainment Have an Impact?" *Journal of Developmental Entrepreneurship*, vol. 9, no. 2 (2004): 127-143.

Duesterhas, Megan, Liz Grauerholz, Rebecca Weichsel, and Nicholas A. Guittar. "The Cost of Doing Femininity: Gendered Disparities in Pricing of Personal Care Products and Services," *Gender Issues*, vol. 28, (2011): 175-191.

Goodman, Laurie, Jun Zhu, and Bing Bai. "Women Are Better than Men at Paying Their Mortgages." *Urban Institute*, Research Report (2016).

Haughwout, Andrew, et al. "Subprime Mortgage Pricing: The Impact of Race, Ethnicity, and Gender on the Cost of Borrowing." *Brookings-Wharton Papers on Urban Affairs* (2009): 33-63.

Mijid, Naranchimeg. "Gender differences in Type 1 credit rationing of small businesses in the US." *Cogent Economics & Finance*, vol. 3 (2015).

Mijid, Naranchimeg. "Why are female small business owners in the United States less likely to apply for bank loans than their male counterparts?" *Journal of Small Business & Entrepreneurship*, vol. 27, no. 2 (2015): 229- 249.

Mijid, Naranchimeg and Alexandra Bernasek. "Gender and the credit rationing of small businesses." *The Social Science Journal*, vol. 50 (2013): 55-65.

Morton, Fiona Scott, Florian Zettelmeyer, and Jorge Silva-Risso. "Consumer Information and Price Discrimination: Does the Internet Affect the Pricing of New Cars to Women and Minorities?" *National Bureau of Economic Research*, Working Paper 8668 (2001).

O'Connor, Sally. "The Impact of Gender in the Mortgage Credit Market." *University of Wisconsin-Milwaukee Doctoral Dissertation* (1996).

Van Rensselaer, Kristy N., et al. "Mortgage Pricing and Gender: A Study of New Century Financial Corporation." *Academy of Accounting and Financial Studies Journal*, vol. 18, no. 4 (2014): 95-110.

Wyly, Elvin and C.S. Ponder. "Gender, age, and race in subprime America." *Housing Policy Debate*, vol. 21, no. 4 (2011): 529-564.

Zimmerman Treichel, Monica and Jonathan A. Scott. "Women-Owned Businesses and Access to Bank Credit: Evidence from Three Surveys Since 1987." *Venture Capital*, vol. 8, no. 1 (2006): 51-67.

In: Consumer Protection
Editor: Ralf Schaefer

ISBN: 978-1-53615-876-2


*Chapter 9*

# ECONOMIC GROWTH, REGULATORY RELIEF, AND CONSUMER PROTECTION ACT (P.L. 115-174) AND SELECTED POLICY ISSUES*

***David W. Perkins, Darryl E. Getter, Marc Labonte, Gary Shorter, Eva Su and N. Eric Weiss***

## SUMMARY

Some observers assert the financial crisis of 2007-2009 revealed that excessive risk had built up in the financial system, and that weaknesses in regulation contributed to that buildup and the resultant instability. In response, Congress passed the Dodd-Frank Wall Street Reform and Consumer Protection Act (P.L. 111-203; the Dodd-Frank Act), and regulators strengthened rules under existing authority. Following this broad overhaul of financial regulation, some observers argue certain changes are an overcorrection, resulting in unduly burdensome regulation.

The Economic Growth, Regulatory Relief, and Consumer Protection Act (S. 2155, P.L. 115-174) was signed into law by President Donald Trump on May 24, 2018. P.L. 115-174 modifies Dodd-Frank provisions, such as the Volcker Rule (a ban on proprietary trading and certain relationships with investment funds), the *qualified mortgage* criteria under the Ability-to-Repay Rule, and enhanced regulation for large banks; provides smaller banks with an "off ramp" from Basel III capital requirements—standards agreed to by national bank regulators as part of an international bank regulatory framework; and makes other changes to the regulatory system.

Most changes made by P.L. 115-174 can be grouped into one of five issue areas: (1) mortgage lending, (2) regulatory relief for "community" banks, (3) consumer protection, (4) regulatory relief for large banks, and (5) regulatory relief for capital formation.

---

* This is an edited, reformatted and augmented version of Congressional Research Service, Publication No. R45073, dated June 6, 2018.

Title I of P.L. 115-174 relaxes or provides exemptions to certain mortgage lending rules. For example, it creates a new compliance option for mortgages originated and held by banks and credit unions with less than $10 billion in assets to be considered qualified mortgages for the purposes of the Ability-to-Repay Rule. In addition, P.L. 115-174 exempts certain insured depositories and credit unions that originate few mortgages from certain Home Mortgage Disclosure Act reporting requirements.

A number of Title II provisions provide regulatory relief to community banks. For example, banks with under $10 billion in assets are exempt from the Volcker Rule, and certain banks that meet a new *Community Bank Leverage Ratio* are exempt from other risk-based capital ratio and leverage ratio requirements.

Title III enhances consumer protections in targeted areas. For example, it subjects credit reporting agencies (CRAs) to additional requirements, including requirements to generally provide fraud alerts for consumer files for at least a year and to allow consumers to place security freezes on their credit reports. In addition, it requires CRAs to exclude certain medical debt from veterans' credit reports.

Title IV alters the criteria used to determine which banks are subject to *enhanced prudential regulation* from the original $50 billion asset threshold original set by Dodd-Frank. Banks designated as *global systemically important banks* and banks with more than $250 billion in assets are still automatically subjected to enhanced regulation. However, under P.L. 115-174 banks with between $100 billion and $250 billion in assets are automatically subject only to supervisory stress tests, while the Federal Reserve (Fed) has discretion to apply other individual enhanced prudential provisions to these banks. Banks with assets between $50 billion and $100 billion will no longer be subject to enhanced regulation, except for the risk committee requirement. In addition, P.L. 115-174 relaxes leverage requirements for large custody banks, and allows certain municipal bonds to be counted toward large banks' liquidity requirements.

Title V provides regulatory relief to certain securities regulations to encourage capital formation. For example, it exempts more securities exchanges from state securities regulation and subjects certain investment pools to fewer registration and disclosure requirements.

Title VI provides enhanced consumer protection for borrowers of student loans. For example, it requires CRA to exclude certain defaulted private student loan debt from credit reports.

Proponents of P.L. 115-174 assert it provides necessary and targeted regulatory relief, fosters economic growth, and provides increased consumer protections. Opponents of the legislation argue it needlessly pares back important Dodd-Frank protections to the benefit of large and profitable banks.

## INTRODUCTION

The Economic Growth, Regulatory Relief, and Consumer Protection Act (S. 2155) was reported out by the Senate Committee on Banking, Housing, and Urban Affairs on December 18, 2017. It was then passed by the Senate on March 14, 2018, following the inclusion of a manager's amendment that added a number of provisions to the bill as reported.[1] The House passed P.L. 115-174 on May 22, 2018, and President Donald Trump signed it into law on May 24, 2018.

P.L. 115-174 changes a number of financial regulations; its six titles alter certain aspects of the regulation of banks, capital markets, mortgage lending, and credit reporting agencies. Many of the provisions can be categorized as providing regulatory relief to banks and certain companies accessing capital markets. Others are designed to relax mortgage lending rules and provide additional protections to consumers, including protections related to credit reporting, veterans' mortgage refinancing, and student loans.

Some P.L. 115-174 provisions amend the Dodd-Frank Wall Street Reform and Consumer Protection Act (Dodd-Frank Act; P.L. 111-203), regulatory reform legislation enacted following the 2007-2009 financial crisis that initiated the largest change to the financial regulatory system since at least 1999.[2] Other provisions amend certain rules implemented by bank regulators under existing authorities and which closely adhere to the Basel III Accords—the international bank regulation standards-setting agreement. Finally, other provisions address long-standing or more recent issues not directly related to Dodd-Frank or Basel III.

Proponents of the legislation assert it provides targeted financial regulatory relief that eliminates a number of unduly burdensome regulations, fosters economic growth, and strengthens consumer protections.[3] Opponents of the legislation argue it needlessly pares back important Dodd-Frank safeguards and protections to the benefit of large and profitable banks.[4]

Prior to passage of P.L. 115-174, the House and the Administration had also proposed wide-ranging financial regulatory relief plans. In terms of the policy areas addressed, some of the changes in P.L. 115-174 are similar to those proposed in the Financial CHOICE Act (FCA; H.R. 10), which passed the House on June 8, 2017 (see Appendix B).[5] However, the two bills generally differ in the scope and degree of proposed regulatory relief. The FCA calls for widespread changes to the regulatory framework across the entire financial system, whereas P.L. 115-174 is more focused on the banking industry, mortgages, capital formation, and credit reporting. Likewise, many of the provisions found in P.L. 115-174 parallel regulatory relief recommendations made in the Treasury Department's series of reports pursuant to Executive Order 13772,

---

[1] Previous versions of this report examined S. 2155, as reported. This updated version of the report examines P.L. 115 174, as passed by the Senate and House and signed into law by the President.

[2] For more information, see CRS Report R41350, *The Dodd-Frank Wall Street Reform and Consumer Protection Act: Background and Summary*, coordinated by Baird Webel.

[3] Senate Committee on Banking, Housing, and Urban Affairs, "Senators Announce Agreement on Economic Growth Legislation," majority press release, November 13, 2017, at https://www.banking.senate.gov/ public/index.cfm/ republican-press-releases.

[4] Senate Committee on Banking, Housing, and Urban Affairs, "Brown Opposes Legislation to Roll Back Dodd-Frank Protections," minority press release, November 13, 2017, at https://www.banking.senate.gov/ public/index.cfm/ democratic-press-releases.

[5] For more information, see CRS Report R44839, *The Financial CHOICE Act in the 115th Congress: Selected Policy Issues*, by Marc Labonte et al.

particularly the first report on banks and credit unions.[6] The Treasury reports are more wide-ranging than P.L. 115-174, however, and more focused on changes that can be made by regulators without congressional action.

The Congressional Budget Office (CBO) estimated that P.L. 115-174 would reduce the budget deficit by $23 million over 10 years.[7] CBO estimated that only one provision would reduce the deficit—Section 217 requires the Federal Reserve (Fed) to transfer $675 million from its surplus account to the Treasury, where it is added to general revenues. CBO estimated that this provision would increase revenues by $478 million on net over 10 years.[8] CBO assumed when making the estimate that the Fed would finance the transfer by selling Treasury securities, which otherwise would have earned $177 million in income that would have been remitted to the Treasury in the next 10 years. Thus, the provision can be thought of as shifting Fed remittances from the future to the present, as opposed to representing new economic resources available to the federal government. Various other provisions are forecast to increase the deficit, with the three provisions with the largest effect on the deficit being the community bank leverage ratio (Section 201), changes to the enhanced regulation threshold (Section 401), and changes to the supplementary leverage ratio for custody banks (Section 402).[9]

This chapter summarizes P.L. 115-174 as enacted and highlights major policy proposals of the legislation. Most changes proposed by P.L. 115-174, as passed, can be grouped into one of five issue areas: (1) mortgage lending, (2) regulatory relief for "community" banks, (3) consumer protection, (4) regulatory relief for large banks, and (5) regulatory relief in securities markets. The report provides background on each policy area, describes the P.L. 115-174 provisions that make changes in these areas, and examines the prominent policy issues related to those changes. In its final section, this chapter also provides an overview of provisions that do not necessarily relate directly to these five topics. This chapter also includes a summary of various exemption thresholds created or raised by P.L. 115-174 in Appendix A, and a list of provisions in P.L. 115-174 that address similar issues as a number of House bills in Appendix B.

---

[6] U.S. Department of the Treasury, *A Financial System That Creates Opportunities: Banks and Credit Unions*, June 2017, at https://www.treasury.gov/press-center/press-releases/Documents/A%20Financial%20System.pdf. For a summary, see CRS Insight IN10720, *First Treasury Report on Regulatory Relief: Depository Institutions*, by David W. Perkins.

[7] Congressional Budget Office, *Estimates of the Direct Spending and Revenue Effects of Amendment Number 2151*, March 8, 2018, at https://www.cbo.gov/system/files/115th-congress-2017-2018/costestimate/s2155amendmentnumber2151.pdf.

[8] Congressional Budget Office, *Estimates of the Direct Spending and Revenue Effects of Amendment Number 2151*, March 8, 2018, at https://www.cbo.gov/system/files/115th-congress-2017-2018/costestimate/s2155amendmentnumber2151.pdf.

[9] Congressional Budget Office, Cost Estimate, P.L. 115-174, March 5, 2018, at https://www.cbo.gov/system/files/115th-congress-2017-2018/costestimate/s2155.pdf.

# AMENDING MORTGAGE RULES

Title I of P.L. 115-174 is intended to reduce the regulatory burden involved in mortgage lending and to expand credit availability, especially in certain market segments. Following the financial crisis, in which lax mortgage standards are believed by certain observers to have played a role, new mortgage regulations were implemented and some existing regulations were strengthened. Some analysts are now concerned that certain new and long-standing regulations unduly impede the mortgage process and unnecessarily restrict the availability of mortgages. To address these concerns, several provisions in P.L. 115-174 are designed to relax mortgage rules, including by providing relief to small lenders and easing rules related to specific mortgage types or markets.

Other analysts argue that market developments have contributed to a tightening of mortgage credit and, though some changes to regulations may be desirable, the regulatory structure in place prior to the enactment of P.L. 115-174 generally provided important consumer protections.

## Background[10]

The bursting of the housing bubble in 2007 preceded the December 2007-June 2009 recession and a financial panic in September 2008. As shown in Figure 1, house prices rose significantly between 1991 and 2007 and then declined sharply for several years. Nationwide house prices did not return to their peak levels until the end of 2015. The decrease in house prices reduced household wealth and resulted in a surge in foreclosures. This had negative effects on homeowners and contributed to the financial crisis by straining the balance sheets of financial firms that held nonperforming mortgage products.

Many factors contributed to the housing bubble and its collapse, and there is significant debate about the underlying causes even a decade later. Many observers, however, point to relaxed mortgage underwriting standards, an expansion of nontraditional mortgage products, and misaligned incentives among various participants as underlying causes.[11]

Mortgage lending has long been subject to regulations intended to protect homeowners and to prevent risky loans, but the issues evident in the financial crisis spurred calls for reform. The Dodd-Frank Act made a number of changes to the mortgage

---

[10] For more information, see CRS In Focus IF10126, *Introduction to Financial Services: The Housing Finance System*, by Katie Jones and N. Eric Weiss.

[11] The Financial Crisis Inquiry Commission, *The Financial Crisis Inquiry Report*, January 2011, pp. 213-230, https://www.gpo.gov/fdsys/pkg/GPO-FCIC/pdf/GPO-FCIC.pdf.

system, including establishing the Consumer Financial Protection Bureau (CFPB)[12]—which consolidated many existing authorities and established new authorities, some of which pertained to the mortgage market—and creating numerous consumer protections in Dodd-Frank's Title XIV, which was called the Mortgage Reform and Anti-Predatory Lending Act.[13]

A long-standing issue in the regulation of mortgages and other consumer financial services is the perceived trade-off between consumer protection and credit availability. If regulation intended to protect consumers increases the cost of providing a financial product, some lenders may charge a higher price and provide the service more selectively.[14] Those who still receive the product may benefit from the enhanced disclosure or added legal protections of the regulation, but that benefit may result in a higher price for the product.

Some policymakers generally believe that the postcrisis mortgage rules have struck the appropriate balance between protecting consumers and ensuring that credit availability is not restricted due to overly burdensome regulations. They contend that the regulations are intended to prevent those unable to repay their loans from receiving credit and have been appropriately tailored to ensure that those who can repay are able to receive credit.[15]

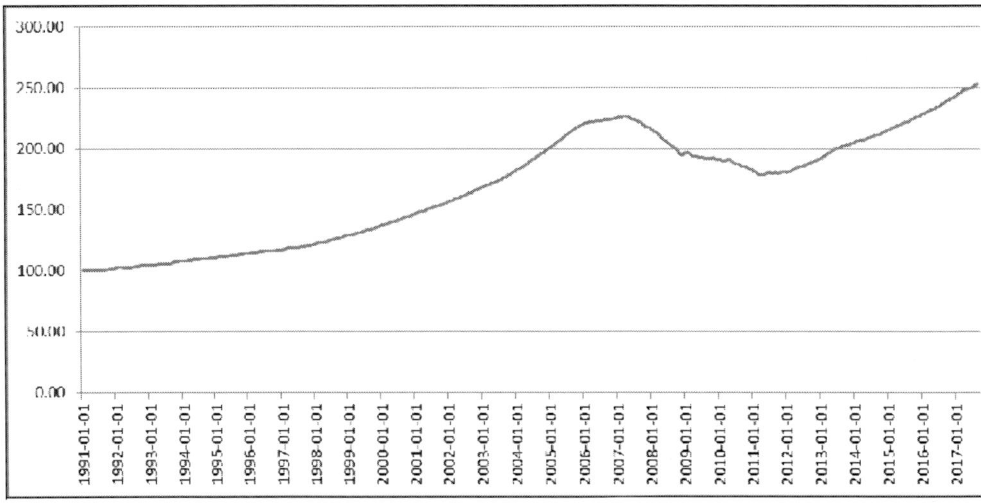


Source: Figure created by CRS using data from the Federal Housing Finance Agency House Price Index (Seasonally Adjusted Purchase-Only Index).

Note: January 1991 is set to 100 for this index.

Figure 1. House Prices, 1991-2017.

---

[12] P.L. 111-203 Title X.

[13] P.L. 11-203 Title XIV.

[14] House Financial Services Committee, *The Financial CHOICE Act*, A Republican Proposal to Reform The Financial Regulatory System, April 24, 2017, pp. 6-7, 51-52.

[15] H.Rept. 115-153, Part 1, Book 2, "Minority View," pp. 968-971.

Critics counter that some rules have imposed compliance costs on lenders of all sizes, resulting in less credit available to consumers and restricting the types of products available to them. Some assert this is especially true for certain nonstandard types of mortgages, such as mortgages for homes in rural areas or for manufactured housing. They further argue that the rules for certain types of lenders, usually small lenders, are unduly burdensome.[16]

A variety of experts and organizations attempt to measure the availability of mortgage credit, and although their methods vary, it is generally agreed that mortgage credit is tighter than it was in the years prior to the housing bubble and subsequent housing market turmoil. Figure 2 shows that mortgage originations to borrowers with FICO credit scores below 720 have decreased in absolute and percentage terms. However, no consensus exists on whether or to what degree mortgage rules have unduly restricted the availability of mortgages, in part because it is difficult to isolate the effects of rules and the effects of broader economic and market forces. For example, the supply of homes on the market, demand for those homes, and demographic trends may also be playing a role.[17] In addition, whether a tightening of credit should be interpreted as a desirable correction to precrisis excesses or an unnecessary restriction on credit availability is subject to debate.

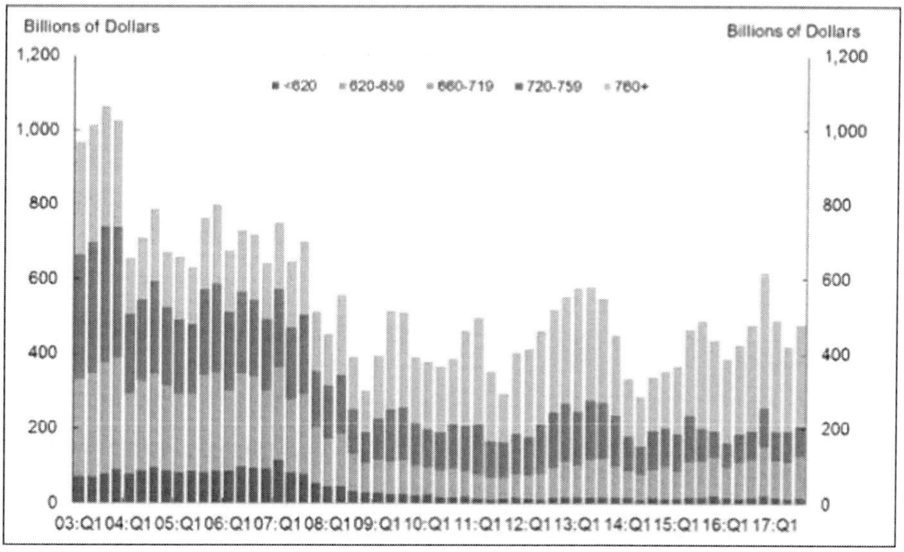


**Source:** Federal Reserve Bank of New York, *Quarterly Report on Household Debt and Credit, 2017 Q3*, p. 6, at https://www.newyorkfed.org/medialibrary/interactives/householdcredit/data/pdf/HHDC_2017Q3.pdf.

Figure 2. Mortgage Originations by Credit Score.

[16] House Financial Services Committee, *The Financial CHOICE Act*, A Republican Proposal to Reform The Financial Regulatory System, April 24, 2017, pp. 6-7, 51-52.

[17] For example, see Joint Center for Housing Studies, *The State of the Nation's Housing 2015*, pp. 8-9.

## Provisions and Selected Analysis

Title I contains 10 sections that amend various laws that affect relatively small segments of the nation's mortgage market. Some sections pertain to consumer protection, and are generally intended to relax consumer protections in areas and markets in which the costs of these regulations are thought by some observers to be high relative to the rest of the mortgage market. In some cases, the legislation removes perceived regulatory barriers to the efficient functioning of specific segments of the mortgage market. Other provisions aim to balance safety and soundness concerns with concerns about access to credit.

### *Section 101—Qualified Mortgage Status for Loans Held by Small Banks Provision*

Section 101 creates a new qualified mortgage (QM) compliance option for mortgages that depositories with less than $10 billion in assets originate and hold in portfolio. To be eligible, the lender has to consider and document a borrower's debts, incomes, and other financial resources, and the loan has to satisfy certain product-feature requirements.

### Analysis

Title XIV of the Dodd-Frank Act established the ability-to-repay (ATR) requirement to address problematic market practices and policy failures that some policymakers believe fueled the housing bubble that precipitated the financial crisis. Under the ATR requirement, a lender must verify and document that, at the time a mortgage is made, the borrower has the ability to repay the loan. Lenders that fail to comply with the ATR rule could be subject to legal liability, such as the payment of certain statutory damages.[18]

The CFPB issued regulations in January 2013 implementing the ATR requirement. A lender can comply with the ATR requirement in different ways, one of which is by originating a QM. When a lender originates a QM, it is presumed to have complied with the ATR requirement, which consequently reduces the lender's potential legal liability for its residential mortgage lending activities. The definition of a QM, therefore, is important to a lender seeking to minimize the *legal risk* of its residential mortgage lending activities, specifically its compliance with the statutory ATR requirement.

The Dodd-Frank Act provides a general definition of a QM, but also authorizes CFPB to issue "regulations that revise, add to, or subtract from" the general statutory definition.[19] The CFPBissued QM regulations establish a *Standard QM* that meets all of the underwriting and product-feature requirements outlined in the Dodd-Frank Act. However, the QM regulations also establish several additional categories of QMs, one of

---

[18] Consumer Financial Protection Bureau (CFPB), "Ability-to-Repay and Qualified Mortgage Standards Under the Truth in Lending Act," 78 *Federal Register* 6416, January 30, 2013, at https://www.gpo.gov/fdsys/pkg/FR-2013-01-30/ pdf/2013-00736.pdf.

[19] 15 U.S.C. §1639c.

which is the *Small Creditor Portfolio QM,* which provide lenders the same presumption of compliance with the ATR requirement as the Standard QM. Compared with the Standard QM compliance option, the Small Creditor Portfolio QM has less prescriptive underwriting requirements. It is intended to reduce the regulatory burden of the ATR requirement for certain small lenders.

A mortgage can qualify as a Small Creditor Portfolio QM if three broad sets of criteria are satisfied.[20] First, the loan must be held in the originating lender's portfolio for at least three years (subject to several exceptions). Second, the loan must be held by a *small creditor*, which is defined as a lender that originated 2,000 or fewer mortgages in the previous year and has less than $2 billion in assets. Third, the loan must meet the underwriting and product-feature requirements for a Standard QM except for the debt-to-income ratio.

Some argue that the QM definition has led to an unnecessary constriction of credit and has been unduly burdensome for lenders. In particular, critics argue that not all of the lender and underwriting requirements included in the Small Creditor Portfolio QM are essential to ensuring that a lender will verify a borrower's ability to repay, and instead argue that holding the loan in portfolio is sufficient to encourage thorough underwriting.[21]

By keeping the loan in portfolio, lenders have added incentive to consider whether the borrower will be able to repay the loan. Keeping the loan in portfolio means that the lender retains the default risk and could be exposed to losses if the borrower does not repay. This retained risk, the argument goes, encourages small creditors to provide additional scrutiny during the underwriting process, even in the absence of a legal requirement to do so. The expanded portfolio option, according to supporters, will spur lenders to offer more mortgages and reduce the burden associated with the more prescriptive underwriting standards of the existing QM options. The less prescriptive standards could most benefit creditworthy borrowers with atypical financial situations, such as self-employed individuals or seasonal employees, who may have a difficult time conforming to the existing standards.

As summarized in Table 1, P.L. 115-174 creates a new compliance option for lenders who keep a mortgage in portfolio in addition to the existing Small Creditor Portfolio QM. Compared with the CFPB's Small Creditor Portfolio QM, P.L. 115-174 allows larger lenders to use the portfolio compliance option (raising the asset threshold from $2 billion to $10 billion and eliminating the origination limits) but limits the new option to insured depositories (banks and credit unions) rather than to both depository and nondepository lenders. The new portfolio option created by P.L. 115-174 has more restrictive portfolio requirements, requiring lenders to hold the loan in portfolio for the life of the loan (with certain exceptions) rather than for just three years. However, the P.L. 115-174 option has

---

[20] 12 C.F.R. §1026.43.

[21] For example, see Rep. Andy Barr, "Barr Introduces Legislation to Help Homebuyers, Prevent Bailouts," press release, February 27, 2015, at https://barr.house.gov/media-center/press-releases/barr-introduces-legislation-to-helphomebuyers-prevent-bailouts.

more relaxed loan criteria. Lenders have to comply with some product-feature restrictions, but those restrictions are generally less stringent than under the other compliance option. In addition, P.L. 115-174 relaxes underwriting criteria, requiring lenders to consider and document a borrower's debts, incomes, and other financial resources in accordance with less prescriptive guidance than is required under certain other QM option criteria.

**Table 1. Comparison of P.L. 115-174 to the CFPB's Small Creditor Portfolio QM**

| | CFPB's Small Creditor Portfolio QM | P.L. 115-174 |
|---|---|---|
| Portfolio Requirements | Mortgage must be held in portfolio for three years. It may be transferred to another small lender and retain QM status. | Mortgage must be held in portfolio by the originator. It may be transferred and retain QM status under certain limited circumstances. |
| Lender Restrictions | Limited to small lenders (depositories and nondepositories) with less than $2 billion in assets and fewer than 2,000 originations a year (excluding those held in portfolio). | Limited to small insured depositories (banks and credit unions) with less than $10 billion in assets. |
| Loan Criteria | Loan must satisfy the underwriting and product feature requirements of the Standard QM Option, with the exception of the Standard QM Option's DTI requirement. | Loan must satisfy fewer product feature restrictions and less prescriptive underwriting guidance than the CFPB's Small Creditor Portfolio QM. |

Source: Table created by the Congressional Research Service.

Notes: QM = qualified mortgage. DTI = debt-to-income ratio. CFPB Small Creditor Portfolio QM refers to compliance option available in 12 C.F.R. §1026.43.

Although supporters of the expanded portfolio QM option in P.L. 115-174 argue that the new compliance option will expand credit availability and appropriately align the incentives of the borrower and lender, critics of the proposal counter that the incentives of holding the loan in portfolio are insufficient to protect consumers and that the protections in the rule in place prior to the enactment of P.L. 115-174 are needed to ensure that the hardships caused by the housing crisis are not repeated.

### *Section 102—Charitable Tax Deduction for Appraisals*

Under current law,[22] appraisers who meet certain criteria (such as an appraiser who is not an employee of the mortgage loan originator) are required to be compensated at a rate that is customary and reasonable for appraisal services in the market in which the appraised property is located. During the buildup of the housing bubble and its subsequent bust, house prices rose quickly and then fell steeply in many parts of the country, causing some policymakers to question the accuracy of the appraisals that supported the mortgage loans during the housing bubble, and the independence of the appraisers. The customary-and-reasonable fee requirement in current law is intended to help ensure that appraisers are acting with appropriate independence and not in the

[22] 15 U.S.C. §1639e.

interest of the lender, seller, borrower, or other interested party. However, some have argued that the requirement for appraisers to receive a customary and reasonable fee made it difficult for them to donate their services to charitable organizations. Section 102 allows appraisers to donate their appraisal services to a charitable organization eligible to receive tax-deductible charitable contributions, such as Habitat for Humanity, by clarifying that a donated appraisal service to a charitable organization would not be in violation of the customary-and-reasonable fee requirement.

### *Section 103—Exemption from Appraisals in Rural Areas*

#### Provision

The Dodd-Frank Act strengthened appraisal requirements after concerns were raised about the role that inaccurate appraisals played in the housing crisis. In recent years, there have been reports of shortages of qualified appraisers, especially in rural areas.[23] Section 103 waives the general requirement for independent home appraisals for federally related mortgages in rural areas where the lender has contacted three state-licensed or state-certified appraisers who could not complete an appraisal in "a reasonable amount of time."[24] An originator who makes a loan without an appraisal could sell the mortgage only under certain circumstances, such as bankruptcy.

### *Section 104—Home Mortgage Disclosure Act Adjustment*

#### Provision

Section 104 exempts banks and credit unions from certain Home Mortgage and Disclosure Act (HMDA; P.L. 94-200) reporting requirements—generally new requirements implemented by the Dodd-Frank Act.[25] Lenders that have originated fewer than 500 closed-end mortgage loans in each of the preceding two years qualify for reduced reporting on those loans and lenders originating fewer than 500 open-end lines of credit in each of the preceding two years qualify for reduced reporting on those loans, provided they achieve certain Community Reinvestment Act compliance scores.

HMDA, which was originally enacted in 1975, requires most lenders to report data on their mortgage business so that the data can be used to assist (1) "in determining whether financial institutions are serving the housing needs of their communities"; (2) "public officials in distributing public-sector investments so as to attract private

---

[23] For example, see Federal Reserve System, FDIC, NCUA, OCC, *Interagency Advisory on the Availability of Appraisers*, May 31, 2017, at https://www.occ.gov/news-issuances/news-releases/2017/nr-ia-2017-60a.pdf.

[24] For more on the regulation of real estate appraisers, see CRS Report RS22953, *Regulation of Real Estate Appraisers*, by N. Eric Weiss.

[25] Regulation pursuant to Section 1094 of Dodd-Frank was fully effective on January 1, 2018. See Bureau of Consumer Financial Protection, "Home Mortgage Disclosure (Regulation C)," 80 *Federal Register* 208, October 28, 2015.

investment to areas where it is needed"; and (3) "in identifying possible discriminatory lending patterns."[26] The Dodd-Frank Act required lenders to collect additional data through HMDA, such as points and fees payable at origination, the term of the mortgage, and certain information about the interest rate. Currently, depository lenders generally have to comply with the HMDA reporting requirements if they have $45 million or more of assets, originated at least 25 home purchase loans in each of the previous two years, and satisfied other criteria.[27] Section 104 exempts additional depository lenders from most of the HMDA requirements that were added by the Dodd-Frank Act.

### *Section 105—Credit Union Loans for Nonprimary Residences*

#### Provision

Section 105 excludes loans made by a credit union for a single-family home that is not the member's primary residence from the definition of a *member business loan*.[28] Credit unions face certain restrictions on the type and volume of loans that they can originate. One such restriction relates to member business loans. A member business loan means "any loan, line of credit, or letter of credit, the proceeds of which will be used for a commercial, corporate or other business investment property or venture, or agricultural purpose," with some exceptions, made to a credit union member.[29] The aggregate amount of member business loans made by a credit union must be the lesser of 1.75 times the credit union's actual net worth, or 1.75 times the minimum net worth amount required to be well capitalized. A loan for a single-family home that is a primary residence is not considered a member business loan, but a similar loan for a nonprimary residence, such as an investment property or vacation home, was considered a member business loan prior to the enactment of P.L. 115-174. Section 105 modifies the definition such that nonprimary residence transactions are excluded from the member business loan definition.

### *Section 106—Mortgage Loan Originator Licensing and Registration*

#### Provision

Section 106 allows certain state-licensed mortgage loan originators (MLOs) who are licensed in one state to temporarily work in another state while waiting for licensing

---

[26] FFIEC, "HMDA: Background and Purpose," at https://www.ffiec.gov/hmda/history.htm. The 500-loan exemption from HMDA reporting requirements does not apply to a lender that receives "needs improvement" or lower rating in both of their two most recent Community Reinvestment Act examinations.

[27] Asset threshold is adjusted annually for inflation. 12 C.F.R. §1003.2 *Financial Institution*(1). For the 2018 asset threshold, see Bureau of Consumer Financial Protection, "Home Mortgage Disclosure (Regulation C) Adjustment to Asset-Size Exemption Threshold," 82 *Federal Register* 61145, December 27, 2017. In addition, nondepository lenders must comply if they have $10 million or more in assets or originated 100 or more home purchase loans. See 12 C.F.R. §1003.2 *Financial Institution*(2).

[28] For more on member business loans, see CRS Report R43167, *Policy Issues Related to Credit Union Lending*, by Darryl E. Getter.

[29] 12 U.S.C. §1757a.

approval in the new state. It also grants MLOs who move from a depository institution (where loan officers do not need to be state licensed) to a nondepository institution (where they do need to be state licensed) a grace period to complete the necessary licensing.

Under the Secure and Fair Enforcement for Mortgage Licensing Act of 2008 (P.L. 110-289; SAFE Act),[30] MLOs who work for a bank must register with the National Mortgage Licensing System and Registry (NMLS), and those working for a nonbank mortgage lender must be licensed and registered in their state. Supporters of the original 2008 legislation argued that without registration and licensing, unscrupulous or incompetent MLOs may be able to move from job to job to escape the consequences of their actions. For MLOs at nonbank lenders, the process of becoming licensed and registered in a state can be time intensive, involving criminal background checks and prelicensing education. This could potentially be problematic for individuals moving (1) from a bank lender to a nonbank lender, or (2) from a nonbank lender in one state to a nonbank lender in another state. To address transition issues, Section 106 provides grace periods to allow individuals who are transferring positions in the situations mentioned above (and meet other performance criteria, such as not having previously had his or her license revoked or suspended) to become appropriately licensed and registered.

### *Section 107—Manufactured Homes Retailers*

#### Provision

In response to problems in the mortgage market when the housing bubble burst, the SAFE Act and the Dodd-Frank Act established new requirements for mortgage originators' licensing, registration, compensation, and training, among other practices. A mortgage originator is someone who, among other things, "(i) takes a residential mortgage loan application; (ii) assists a consumer in obtaining or applying to obtain a residential mortgage loan; or (iii) offers or negotiates terms of a residential mortgage loan."[31] The definition used in implementing the regulation in place at the time of the enactment of P.L. 115-174 excluded employees of manufactured-home retailers under certain circumstances, such as "if they do not take a consumer credit application, offer or negotiate credit terms, or advise a consumer on credit terms."[32] Section 107 expands the exception such that retailers of manufactured homes or their employees are not be considered mortgage originators if they do not receive more compensation for a sale that

---

[30] 12 U.S.C. §5106.

[31] 15 U.S.C. §1602(cc). The definition of mortgage originator has multiple exemptions, such as for those who perform primarily clerical or administrative tasks in support of a mortgage originator or those who engage in certain forms of seller financing.

[32] CFPB, *Manufactured-Housing Consumer Finance in the United States*, September 2014, p. 51, at http://files.consumerfinance.gov/f/201409_cfpb_report_manufactured-housing.pdf.

included a loan than for a sale that did not include a loan, and if they provide customers certain disclosures about their affiliations with other creditors.

### *Section 108—Escrow Requirements Relating to Certain Consumer Credit Transactions*

#### Provision

Section 108 exempts any loan made by a bank or credit union from certain escrow requirements if the institution has assets of $10 billion or less, originated fewer than 1,000 mortgage loans in the preceding year, and meets certain other criteria.

An escrow account is an account that a "mortgage lender may set up to pay certain recurring property-related expenses ... such as property taxes and homeowner's insurance."[33] Escrow accounts may only be used for the purpose they were created. For example, a mortgage escrow account can only be used to pay for expenses (such as property taxes) for that mortgage, not for the mortgage lender's general expenses. Escrow accounts provide a way for homeowners to make monthly payments for annual or semi-annual expenses. Maintaining escrow accounts for borrowers are potentially costly for some banks, such as certain small institutions.

Higher-priced mortgage loans have been required to maintain an escrow account for at least one year pursuant to a regulation that was implemented before the Dodd-Frank Act.[34] The Dodd-Frank Act, among other things, extended the amount of time an escrow account for a higher-priced mortgage loan must be maintained from one year to five years, although the escrow account can be terminated after five years if certain conditions are met. It also provided additional disclosure requirements.[35]

The Dodd-Frank Act gave the CFPB the discretion to exempt from certain escrow requirements lenders operating in rural areas if the lenders satisfied certain conditions.[36] The CFPB's escrow rule included exemptions from escrow requirements for lenders that (1) operate in rural or underserved areas; (2) extend 2,000 mortgages or fewer; (3) have less than $2 billion in total assets; and (4) do not escrow for any mortgage they service (with some exceptions).[37] Additionally, a lender that satisfies the above criteria must

---

[33] CFPB, "What Is an Escrow or Impound Account?" at http://www.consumerfinance.gov/askcfpb/140/what-is-an-escrow-or-impound-account.html.

[34] A higher-priced mortgage loan is a loan with an APR "that exceeds an 'average prime offer rate' for a comparable transaction by 1.5 or more percentage points for transactions secured by a first lien, or by 3.5 or more percentage points for transactions secured by a subordinate lien." CFPB, "Escrow Requirements Under the Truth in Lending Act (Regulation Z)," 78 *Federal Register* 4726, January 22, 2013. If the first lien is a jumbo mortgage (above the conforming loan limit for Fannie Mae and Freddie Mac), then it is considered a higher-priced mortgage loan if its APR is 2.5 percentage points or more above the average prime offer rate.

[35] CFPB, *Small Entity Compliance Guide: TILA Escrow Rule*, April 18, 2013, p. 4, at http://files. consumerfinance.gov/ f/201307_cfpb_updated-sticker_escrows-implementation-guide.pdf.

[36] P.L. 111-203, §1461.

[37] See 12 C.F.R. §1026.35 and CFPB, "Escrow Requirements Under the Truth in Lending Act (Regulation Z)," 78 *Federal Register* 4726, January 22, 2013. In a September 2015 rule the CFPB amended certain escrow requirements; see CFPB, "Amendments Relating to Small Creditors and Rural or Underserved Areas Under

intend to hold the loan in its portfolio to be exempt from the escrow requirement for that loan. Section 108 amends the exemption criteria such that a bank or credit union also are exempt from maintaining an escrow account for a mortgage as long as it has assets of $10 billion or less, originated fewer than 1,000 mortgage loans in the preceding year, and met certain other criteria.

### *Section 109—Waiting Period Requirement for Lower-Rate Mortgage*

**Provision**

The Dodd-Frank Act directed the CFPB to combine mortgage disclosures required under the Truth in Lending Act (P.L. 90-321; TILA) and Real Estate Settlement Procedures Act (P.L. 93 533; RESPA) into a TILA-RESPA Integrated Disclosure (TRID) form. On November 20, 2013, the CFPB issued the TRID final rule that would require lenders to use the streamlined disclosure forms. Under current law,[38] a borrower generally must receive the disclosures at least three days before the closing of the mortgage. After receiving their required disclosures, borrowers have in some cases been offered new mortgage terms by their lender, which requires new disclosures and potentially delays their mortgage closing. Section 109 waives the three-day waiting period between a consumer receiving a mortgage disclosure and closing on the mortgage if a consumer receives an amended disclosure that includes a lower interest rate than was offered in the previous disclosure.

Section 109 also expresses the sense of Congress that the CFPB should provide additional guidance on certain aspects of the final rule, such as whether lenders receive a safe harbor from liability if they use model disclosures published by the CFPB that do not reflect regulatory changes issued after the model forms were published.

## REGULATORY RELIEF FOR COMMUNITY BANKS

Title II of P.L. 115-174 is focused on providing regulatory relief to community banks. Although small banks qualify for various exemptions from certain regulations, whether the regulations have been appropriately tailored is the subject of debate. Certain Title II provisions raise previous asset thresholds or create new ones at which banks and other depositories are exempt from regulation or otherwise qualify for reduced regulatory obligations.

---

the Truth in Lending Act (Regulation Z)," at http://files.consumerfinance.gov/f/201509_cfpb_amendments-relating-to-small-creditors-and-ruralor-underserved-areas-under-the-truth-in-lending-act-regulation-z.pdf.

[38] 15 U.S.C. §1639(b).

## Background[39]

The term community bank typically refers to a small bank focused on a traditional commercial bank business of taking deposits and making loans to meet the financial needs of a particular community. Although conceptually size does not necessarily have to be a determining factor, community banks are nevertheless often identified as such based on having a small asset size. No consensus exists on what size limit is compatible with the community bank concept, and some observers doubt the effectiveness of size-based measures in identifying community banks.[40]

Community banks are more likely to be concentrated in core commercial bank businesses of making loans and taking deposits and less concentrated in other activities like securities trading or holding derivatives. Community banks also tend to operate within a smaller geographic area. Also, these banks are generally more likely to practice *relationship lending*, wherein loan officers and other bank employees have a longer-standing and perhaps more personal relationship with borrowers.[41]

Due in part to these characteristics, proponents of community banks assert that these banks are particularly important credit sources to local communities and otherwise underserved groups, as big banks may be unwilling to meet the credit needs of a small market of which they have little direct knowledge. If this is the case, imposing burdens on small banks that potentially restrict the amount of credit they make available could have a cost for these groups. In addition, relative to large banks, small banks individually pose less of a systemic risk to the broader financial system, and are likely to have fewer employees and resources to dedicate to regulatory compliance.[42] Arguably, this means regulation aimed at systemic stability might produce little benefit at a high cost when applied to these banks.[43]

Thus, one rationale for easing the regulatory burden for community banks would be that regulation intended to increase systemic stability need not be applied to such banks since they individually do not pose a risk to the entire financial system. Sometimes the argument is extended to assert that because small banks did not cause the 2007-2009 crisis and pose less systemic risk, they need not be subject to new regulations.

Another potential rationale for easing regulations on small banks would be if there are economies of scale to regulatory compliance costs, meaning that as banks become

---

[39] For more information, see CRS Report R44855, *Banking Policy Issues in the 115th Congress*, by David W. Perkins.

[40] Federal Deposit Insurance Corporation, *FDIC Community Banking Study*, December 2012, at https://www.fdic.gov/ regulations/resources/cbi/report/cbi-full.pdf.

[41] Federal Deposit Insurance Corporation, *FDIC Community Banking Study*, December 2012, at https://www.fdic.gov/ regulations/resources/cbi/report/cbi-full.pdf.

[42] Drew Dahl, Andrew Meyer, and Michelle Neely, "Scale Matters: Community Banks and Compliance Costs," *Federal Reserve Bank of St. Louis, The Regional Economist*, July 2016, at https://www.stlouisfed.org/~/media/ Publications/Regional-Economist/2016/July/scale_matters.pdf.

[43] CRS Report R43999, *An Analysis of the Regulatory Burden on Small Banks*, by Sean M. Hoskins and Marc Labonte.

bigger, their costs do not rise as quickly as asset size. From a cost-benefit perspective, if regulatory compliance costs are subject to economies of scale, then the balance of costs and benefits of a particular regulation will depend on the size of the bank. Although regulatory compliance costs are likely to rise with size, those costs as a percentage of overall costs or revenues are likely to fall. In particular, as regulatory complexity increases, compliance may become relatively more costly for small firms.[44] Empirical evidence on whether compliance costs are subject to economies of scale is mixed.[45] Some argue for reducing the regulatory burden on small banks on the grounds that they provide greater access to credit or offer credit at lower prices than large banks for certain groups of borrowers. These arguments tend to emphasize potential market niches small banks occupy that larger banks may be unwilling to fill.[46] For these reasons, community banks differ from large institutions in a number of ways besides size that arguably could result in their being subject to certain regulations that are *unduly burdensome*—meaning the benefit of the regulation does not justify the cost.

Other observers assert that the regulatory burden facing small banks is appropriate, citing the special regulatory emphasis already given to minimizing small banks' regulatory burden. For example, during the rulemaking process, bank regulators are required to consider the effect of rules on small banks.[47] In addition, they note that many regulations already include an exemption for small banks or are tailored to reduce the cost for small banks to comply. Supervision is also structured to put less of a burden on small banks than larger banks, such as by requiring less frequent bank examinations for certain small banks.[48] Furthermore, they counter that although small institutions were not a major cause of the past crisis, they did play a prominent role in the savings and loan crisis of the late 1980s, a systemic event that cost taxpayers $124 billion, according to one analysis.[49] Also, they note that systemic risk is only one of the goals of regulation, along with prudential regulation and consumer protection, and argue that the failure of

---

[44] Drew Dahl, Andrew Meyer, and Michelle Neely, "Scale Matters: Community Banks and Compliance Costs," *Federal Reserve Bank of St. Louis, The Regional Economist*, July 2016, at https://www.stlouisfed.org/~/media/Publications/Regional-Economist/2016/July/scale_matters.pdf.

[45] For example, see FDIC, *FDIC Community Banking Study*, p. B-2, December 2012; FDIC Office of Inspector General, *The FDIC's Examination Process for Small Community Banks*, AUD-12-011, August 2012; CFPB, *Understanding the Effects of Certain Deposit Regulations on Financial Institutions' Operations*, November 2013, p. 113; and Independent Community Bankers of America, *2014 ICBA Community Bank Call Report Burden Survey*.

[46] See FDIC, *FDIC Community Banking Study*, pp. 3-6, December 2012, at https://www.fdic.gov/regulations/resources/ cbi/report/cbi-full.pdf.

[47] See Regulatory Flexibility Act of 1980 (P.L. 96-354), 5 U.S.C. §§601-612; and the Riegle Community Development and Regulatory Improvement Act (P.L. 103-325), 12 U.S.C. §4802(a).

[48] For example, see Federal Reserve System, "Inspection Frequency and Scope Requirements for Bank Holding Companies and Savings and Loan Holding Companies with Total Consolidated Assets of $10 Billion or Less," SR 13 21, December 17, 2013, at http://www.federalreserve.gov/bankinforeg/srletters/sr1321.htm.

[49] Timothy Curry and Lynn Shibut, "The Cost of the Savings and Loan Crisis: Truth and Consequences," *FDIC Banking Review*, vol. 13, no. 2 (Fall 2000).

hundreds of banks during the crisis illustrates that precrisis prudential regulation for small banks was not stringent enough.[50]

## Provisions and Selected Analysis

This section reviews eight provisions in Title II that amend various laws and regulations that affect depositories, including banks, federal savings associations, and credit unions. Although some provisions relax certain regulations for all banks, Title II provisions are generally aimed at providing regulatory relief to institutions under certain asset thresholds. Several sections amend prudential regulation rules, including minimum capital requirements and the Volcker Rule, whereas others are designed to reduce supervisory requirements by decreasing exam frequency and reporting requirements for small banks. Other sections in Title II are related to public housing, insurance, and the National Credit Union Administration and are described in the "Miscellaneous Proposals in P.L. 115-174" section.

### *Section 201—Community Bank Leverage Ratio*

#### Provision

Section 201 directs regulators to develop a *Community Bank Leverage Ratio* (CBLR) and set a threshold ratio of between 8% and 10% capital to unweighted assets—compared with the general leverage ratio requirement of 5%—to be considered well capitalized. If a bank with less than $10 billion in assets maintains a CBLR above that threshold, it will be exempt from all other leverage and risk-based capital requirements. Banking regulators may determine that an individual bank with under $10 billion in assets is not eligible to be exempt based on its risk profile.

#### Analysis

Capital—defined by the legislation as tangible equity (e.g., ownership shares)[51]—gives a bank the ability to absorb losses without failing, and regulators set minimum amounts a bank must hold. These capital requirements are expressed as *capital ratio*

---

[50] An FDIC study found that community banks did not account for a disproportionate share of bank failures between 1975 and 2011, relative to their share of the industry. Because community banks account for more than 90% of organizations (by the FDIC definition, which as noted above is not limited to a size threshold), most bank failures are community banks, however. See FDIC, *FDIC Community Banking Study*, pp. 2-10, December 2012, at https://www.fdic.gov/regulations/resources/cbi/report/cbi-full.pdf.

[51] The legislation's definition of capital differs from the definition used in other leverage ratio regulation, which require banks to meet a leverage ratio based on *Tier 1* capital, which includes both Common Equity Tier 1 capital (e.g., common stock and retained earnings) and Additional Tier 1 capital (e.g., noncumulative perpetual preferred stock). For a complete list of instruments included in Tier 1 capital, see FDIC, *Expanded Community Bank Guide to the New Capital Rule for FDIC-Supervised Banks*, pp. 5-11, at https://www.fdic.gov/regulations/capital/capital/ community_bank_guide_expanded.pdf.

*requirements*—ratios of a bank's assets and capital. The ratios are generally one of two main types—a risk-weighted capital ratio or a leverage ratio. Risk-weighted ratios assign a risk weight—a number based on the riskiness of the asset that the asset value is multiplied by—to account for the fact that some assets are more likely to lose value than others. Riskier assets receive a higher risk weight, which requires banks to hold more capital—to better enable them to absorb losses—to meet the ratio requirement.[52] In contrast, leverage ratios treat all assets the same, requiring banks to hold the same amount of capital against the asset regardless of how risky each asset is.

Whether multiple risk-based capital ratios should be replaced with a single leverage ratio is subject to debate. Some observers argue that it is important to have both risk-weighted ratios and a leverage ratio because the two complement each other. Riskier assets generally offer a greater rate of return to compensate the investor for bearing more risk. Without risk weighting, banks may have an incentive to hold riskier assets because the same amount of capital would be required to be held against risky, high-yielding assets and safe, low-yielding assets. Therefore, a leverage ratio alone—even if set at higher levels—may not fully account for a bank's riskiness because a bank with a high concentration of very risky assets could have a similar ratio to a bank with a high concentration of very safe assets.[53]

However, others assert the use of risk-weighted ratios should be optional, provided a high leverage ratio is maintained.[54] Risk weights assigned to particular classes of assets could potentially be an inaccurate estimation of some assets' true risk, especially because they cannot be adjusted as quickly as asset risk might change. Banks may have an incentive to overly invest in assets with risk weights that are set too low (they would receive the high potential rate of return of a risky asset, but have to hold only enough capital to protect against losses of a safe asset), or inversely to underinvest in assets with risk weights that are set too high. Some observers believe that the risk weights in place prior to the financial crisis were poorly calibrated and "encouraged financial firms to crowd into" risky assets, exacerbating the downturn.[55] For example, banks held highly rated mortgage-backed securities (MBSs) before the crisis, in part because those assets offered a higher rate of return than other assets with the same risk weight. MBSs then suffered unexpectedly large losses during the crisis.

---

[52] FDIC, *Risk Management Manual of Examination Policies: Section 2.1 Capital*, pp. 2-9, at https://www.fdic.gov/regulations/safety/manual/section2-1.pdf.

[53] See Former Fed Chair Yellen's comments during U.S. Congress, House Committee on Financial Services, *Monetary Policy and the State of the Economy*, 114th Cong., 2nd sess., June 22, 2016, at http://www.cq.com/doc/ congressionaltranscripts-4915133?2.

[54] House Committee on Financial Services, *The Financial CHOICE Act: A Republican Proposal to Reform the Financial Regulatory System*, June 23, 2016, p. 6, at http://financialservices.house.gov/uploadedfiles/financial_choice_act_comprehensive_outline.pdf.

[55] Ibid., p. 8

Some critics of the current requirements are especially opposed to their application to small banks. They argue that the risk-weighted system involves "needless complexity" and is an example of regulator micromanagement.[56] Furthermore, they say, that complexity could benefit the largest banks that have the resources to absorb the added regulatory cost compared with small banks that could find compliance costs relatively more burdensome. Thus, they contend that a simpler system should be implemented for small banks to avoid giving large banks a competitive advantage over them.

In its cost estimate, CBO assumed that regulators would select a 9% leverage ratio and estimates that 70% of community banks will opt in to the new leverage regime. As a result, they forecasted that some community banks would take on more risk and increase the likelihood that more community banks will fail than would under the general capital and leverage ratio regime. CBO estimated that this will raise costs to the Deposit Insurance Fund by $240 million, about half of which would be offset by higher insurance premiums over the 10-year budget window.[57]

### *Section 202—Allowing More Banks to Accept Reciprocal Deposits*

#### Provision

Section 202 makes *reciprocal deposits*—deposits that two banks place with each other in equal amounts—exempt from the prohibitions against taking *brokered deposits* faced by banks that are not well capitalized (i.e., those that may hold enough capital to meet the minimum requirements, but not by the required margins to be classified as well capitalized), subject to certain limitations.

#### Analysis

Certain deposits at banks are not placed there by individuals or companies utilizing the safekeeping, check writing, and money transfer services the banks provide. Instead, brokered deposits are placed by a third-party broker that places clients' savings in accounts paying higher interest rates. Regulators consider these deposits less stable, because brokers are more willing to withdraw them and move them to another bank than individuals and companies who face higher switching costs and inconvenience when switching banks (e.g., filling out and submitting new direct deposit forms to one's employer, getting new checks, and changing automatic bill payment information). Due to these characteristics, regulators generally prohibit not-well-capitalized banks from

---

[56] House Committee on Financial Services, *The Financial CHOICE Act: A Republican Proposal to Reform the Financial Regulatory System*, June 23, 2016, p. 6, at http://financialservices.house.gov/uploadedfiles/financial_choice_act_comprehensive_outline.pdf.

[57] Congressional Budget Office, Cost Estimate, P.L. 115-174, March 5, 2018, at https://www.cbo.gov/system/files/115th-congress-2017-2018/costestimate/s2155.pdf. CBO's score of this provision did not change in its score of the manager's amendment. Congressional Budget Office, *Estimates of the Direct Spending and Revenue Effects of Amendment Number 2151*, March 8, 2018, at https://www.cbo.gov/system/files/115th-congress-2017-2018/ costestimate/s2155amendmentnumber2151.pdf.

accepting brokered deposits in order to limit potential losses to the Federal Deposit Insurance Corporation (FDIC) in the event the bank fails.

Section 202 allows certain not-well-capitalized banks to accept a particular type of brokered deposit called *reciprocal deposits*, an arrangement between two banks in which each bank places a portion of its own customers' deposits with the other bank. Generally, the purpose of this transaction is to ensure that large accounts stay under the $250,000-per-account deposit insurance limit, with any amount in excess of the limit placed in a separate account at another bank. Like other brokered deposits, reciprocal deposits are funding held by a bank that does not have a relationship with the underlying depositors. However, reciprocal deposits differ from other brokered deposits in that if reciprocal deposits are withdrawn from a bank, the bank receives its own deposits back and thus may better maintain its funding.

CBO estimated that Section 202 would increase the budget deficit by $25 million over 10 years because permitting reciprocal deposits will increase deposit insurance payouts from bank failures, imposing losses on the FDIC insurance fund that would not fully be offset by higher deposit insurance premiums within the 10-year budget window.[58]

### *Section 203 and 204—Changes to the Volcker Rule*

#### Provision

Section 203 creates an exemption from prohibitions on propriety trading—owning and trading securities for the bank's own portfolio with the aim of profiting from price changes—and relationships with certain investment funds for banks with (1) less than $10 billion in assets, and (2) trading assets and trading liabilities less than 5% of total assets. Pursuant to Section 619 of the Dodd-Frank Act, often referred to as the "Volcker Rule," bank organizations generally face these prohibitions.[59] In addition to Section 203's exemption for small banks, Section 204 eases certain Volcker Rule restrictions on all bank entities, regardless of size, related to sharing a name with hedge funds and private equity funds they organize.

#### Analysis

The Volcker Rule generally prohibits banking entities from engaging in proprietary trading or sponsoring a hedge fund or private equity fund. Proponents of the rule argue that proprietary trading adds further risk to the inherently risky business of commercial banking. Furthermore, they assert that other types of institutions are very active in

---

[58] Congressional Budget Office, Cost Estimate, P.L. 115-174, March 5, 2018, at https://www.cbo.gov/system/files/115th-congress-2017-2018/costestimate/s2155.pdf.

[59] The rule is named after Paul Volcker, the former Chair of the Federal Reserve (Fed), former Chair of President Obama's Economic Recovery Advisory Board, and a vocal advocate of a prohibition on proprietary trading at commercial banks.

proprietary trading and better suited for it, so bank involvement in these markets is unnecessary for the financial system.[60] Finally, proponents assert moral hazard is problematic for banks in these risky activities. Because deposits—an important source of bank funding—are insured by the government, a bank could potentially take on excessive risk without concern about losing this funding. Thus, support for the Volcker Rule has often been posed as preventing banks from "gambling" in securities markets with taxpayer-backed deposits.[61]

Some observers doubt the necessity and the effectiveness of the Volcker Rule in general. They assert that proprietary trading at commercial banks did not play a role in the financial crisis, noting that issues that played a direct role in the crisis—including failures of large investment banks and insurers, and losses on loans held by commercial banks—would not have been prevented by the rule.[62] In addition, although the activities prohibited under the Volcker Rule pose risks, it is not clear whether they pose greater risks to bank solvency and financial stability than "traditional" banking activities, such as mortgage lending. Taking on additional risks in different markets potentially could diversify a bank's risk profile, making it less likely to fail.[63] Some contend the rule poses practical supervisory problems. The rule includes exceptions for when bank trading is deemed appropriate—such as when a bank is hedging against risks and marketmaking—and differentiating among these motives creates regulatory complexity and compliance costs that could affect bank trading behavior.[64]

In addition to the broad debate over the necessity and efficacy of the Volcker Rule, whether small banks should be subjected to the rule is also a debated issue. Proponents of the rule contend that the vast majority of community banks do not face compliance obligations under the rule, and so do not face an excessive burden by being subject to it. They argue that those community banks that are subject to compliance obligations can comply simply by having clear policies and procedures in place that can be reviewed during the normal examination process. In addition, they assert the small number of community banks that are engaged in complex trading should have the expertise to comply with the Volcker Rule.[65]

---

[60] Paul Volcker, "How to Reform Our Financial System," *New York Times*, January 30, 2010.

[61] See, for example, House Financial Services Committee, "Waters: Dodd-Frank Repeal Is Truly the Wrong Choice," press release, June 24, 2016, at http://democrats.financialservices.house.gov/news/document single.aspx?DocumentID= 399901.

[62] House Financial Services Committee, *The Financial CHOICE Act: Comprehensive Summary*, June 23, 2016, pp. 81 86, at http://financialservices.house.gov/uploadedfiles/financial_choice_act_comprehensive_outline.pdf.

[63] Anjan V. Thakor, *The Economic Consequences of the Volcker Rule*, U.S. Chamber of Commerce, Center for Capital Markets Competitiveness, Summer 2012, pp. 28-30, at http://www.centerforcapitalmarkets.com/wp-content/uploads/ 2010/04/17612_CCMC-Volcker-RuleFINAL.pdf.

[64] House Financial Services Committee, *The Financial CHOICE Act: Comprehensive Summary*, June 23, 2016, pp. 81 86, at http://financialservices.house.gov/uploadedfiles/financial_choice_act_comprehensive_outline.pdf.

[65] Thomas Hoenig, speech at the National Press Club, April 15, 2015, at https://www.fdic.gov/news/news/speeches/ spapril1515.html.

Others argue that the act of evaluating the Volcker Rule to ensure banks' compliance is burdensome in and of itself. They support a community bank exemption so that community banks and supervisors do not have to dedicate resources to complying with and enforcing a regulation whose rationale is unlikely to apply to smaller banks.[66]

### *Section 205—Financial Reporting Requirements for Small Banks*

**Provision**

Section 205 directs the federal banking agencies to issue regulations to reduce the reporting requirements that banks with assets under $5 billion must comply with in the first and third quarters of the year. Currently, all banks must submit a report of condition and income to the federal bank agencies at the end of every financial quarter of the year, sometimes referred to as a "call report."[67] Completing the call report involves entering numerous values into forms or "schedules" in order to provide the regulator with a detailed accounting of many aspects of each bank's income, expenses, and balance sheet. The filing requires an employee or employees to dedicate time to the exercise and in some cases banks purchase certain software products that assist in the task. Section 205 directs the regulators to shorten or simplify the reports banks with assets under $5 billion file in the first and third quarter.

### *Section 206—Allowing Thrifts to Opt-In to National Bank Regulatory Regime*

**Provision**

Section 206 creates a mechanism for federal savings associations (or "thrifts") with under $20 billion in assets to opt out of the federal thrift regulatory regime and enter the national bank regulatory regime without having to go through the process of changing their charter. An institution that makes loans and takes deposits can have one of several types of charters— including a national bank charter and federal savings association charter, among others—each of which subjects the institutions to regulations that can differ in certain ways.[68] Without this provision, if an institution wanted to switch from one regime to another, it would have to change its charter.

Historically, thrifts were intended to be institutions focused on residential home mortgage lending, and as such they are subject to regulatory limitations on how much of other types of lending they can do.

---

[66] Federal Reserve Gov. Daniel Tarullo, "A Tiered Approach to Regulation and Supervision of Community Banks," speech at the Community Bankers Symposium, Chicago, Illinois, November, 7, 2014, at http://www.federalreserve.gov/newsevents/speech/tarullo20141107a.htm.

[67] 12 U.S.C. §324; 12 U.S.C. §1817; 12 U.S.C. §161; and 12 U.S.C. §1464.

[68] Federal Financial Institutions Examination Council, *Interagency Statement on Regulatory Conversions (FIL-40-2009)*, July 7, 2009.

Certain thrifts may want to expand their lending in other business lines, but be unable to do so because of these limitations. Without the mechanism provided by Section 206, if a thrift wanted to exceed the limitations, it would have to convert its charter to a national bank charter, which could potentially be costly.[69]

### *Section 207—Small Bank Holding Company Policy Statement Threshold*

#### Provision

Section 207 raises the asset threshold in the Federal Reserve Small Bank Holding Company (BHC) and Small Saving and Loan Holding Company Policy Statement from $1 billion to $3 billion in total assets. In the policy statement, the Federal Reserve permits BHCs under the asset threshold to take on more debt in order to complete a merger (provided they meet certain other requirements concerning nonbank activities, off-balance-sheet exposures, and debt and equities outstanding) than would be allowed for a larger BHC.[70] In addition, Section 171 of the Dodd-Frank Act (sometimes referred to as the "Collins Amendment") exempts BHCs subject to this policy statement from the requirement that banking organizations meet the same capital requirements at the holding company level that depository subsidiaries face.[71] The significance of the Collins Amendment arguably depends on the extent to which a BHC has activities in nonbank subsidiaries, and many small banks do not have substantial activities in nonbank subsidiaries.

### *Section 210—Frequency of Examination for Small Banks*

#### Provision

Section 210 raises the asset threshold below which banks can become eligible for an 18-month examination cycle instead of a 12-month cycle from $1 billion to $3 billion. Generally, federal bank regulators must conduct an on-site examination of the banks they oversee at least once in each 12-month period. However, if a bank below the asset threshold meets certain criteria related to capital adequacy and scores received on previous examinations, then it can be examined only once every 18 months.[72] Raising this threshold allows more banks to be subject to less frequent examination.

---

[69] Office of the Comptroller of the Currency, "Summary of Proposed Legislation to Add Flexibility to the Federal Savings Association Charter," November 18, 2014, at https://www.occ.treas.gov/topics/bank-management/mutualsavings-associations/summary-of-proposed-legislation-11-18-2014.pdf.

[70] 12 C.F.R. Appendix C to Part 225.

[71] 12 U.S.C. §5371(b)(5)(C).

[72] 12 U.S.C. §1820(d).

### *Section 213—Identification When Opening an Account Online*

**Provision**

Section 213 permits financial institutions to use a scan of, make a copy of, or receive the image of a driver's license or identification card to record the personal information of a person requesting to open an account or for some other service through the internet.

### *Section 214—Classifying High Volatility Commercial Real Estate Loans*

**Provision**

Section 214 allows banks to classify certain credit facilities (e.g., business loans, revolving credit, and lines of credit) that finance the acquisition, development, or construction of commercial properties as regular commercial real estate exposures instead of *high volatility commercial real estate* (HVCRE) exposures for the purposes of calculating their risk-weighted capital requirements, previously discussed in the Section 201 "Analysis" section. Prior to the enactment of P.L. 115-174, banks generally were required to classify facilities financing commercial real estate projects as HVCRE, unless the developer contributed capital of at least 15% of the estimated "as completed value" of the project. Under that rule, capital included cash, unencumbered readily marketable assets, and out of pocket-expenses. Being classified as HVCRE means the exposure must be given a risk weight of 150% instead of the 100% weight given to other CRE exposures, thus requiring banks to hold more capital to finance those projects.

Section 214 offers a number of additional avenues for commercial real estate exposures to avoid or shed HVCRE status. It allows the appraised value of the property being developed to count as a capital contribution, providing another avenue for projects to reach the minimum 15% threshold. In addition, Section 214 allows certain credit facilities financing the acquisition or improvement of already-income-producing properties to avoid classification as HVCRE, provided the cash flow is sufficient to support the property's debt service and other expenses. Finally, a HVCRE could achieve reclassification when the property development is substantially completed or when it begins generating cash flow sufficient to support the property's debt service and other expenses. A lower capital requirement gives banks greater incentive to make HVCRE loans, but provides banks with less capital cushion against potential losses on what has been historically a risky category of lending.

## CONSUMER PROTECTIONS

Title III, Title VI, and Section 215 of Title II are intended to address various consumer protection challenges facing the credit reporting industry and borrowers in certain credit markets, such as active duty service members, veterans, student borrowers, and borrowers funding energy efficiency projects.

## Background[73]

### *Credit Reporting*

The credit reporting industry collects and subsequently provides information to companies about behavior when consumers conduct various financial transactions. A credit report typically includes information related to a consumer's identity (such as name, address, and Social Security number), existing or recent credit transactions (including credit card accounts, mortgages, and other forms of credit), public record information (such as court judgments, tax liens, or bankruptcies), and credit inquiries made about the consumer.

Credit reports are prepared by credit reporting agencies (CRAs). The three largest CRAs— Equifax, TransUnion, and Experian—are the most well-known, but they are not the only CRAs. Approximately 400 smaller CRAs either are regional or specialize in collecting specific types of information or information for specific industries, such as information related to payday loans, checking accounts, or utilities.

Companies use credit reports to determine whether consumers have engaged in behaviors that could be costly or beneficial to the companies. For example, lenders rely upon credit reports and scoring systems to determine the likelihood that prospective borrowers will repay mortgage and other consumer loans. Insured depository institutions (i.e., banks and credit unions) rely on consumer data service providers to determine whether to make checking accounts or loans available to individuals. Insurance companies use consumer data to determine what insurance products to make available and to set policy premiums.[74] Employers may use consumer data information to screen prospective employees to determine, for example, the likelihood of fraudulent behavior. In short, numerous firms rely upon consumer data to identify and evaluate the risks associated with entering into financial relationships or transactions with consumers.

Much of what is thought of as the business of credit reporting is regulated through the Fair Credit Reporting Act (FCRA; P.L. 91-508).[75] The FCRA requires "that consumer reporting agencies adopt reasonable procedures for meeting the needs of commerce for consumer credit, personnel, insurance, and other information in a manner which is fair

[73] For more information, see CRS Report R44125, *Consumer and Credit Reporting, Scoring, and Related Policy Issues*, by Darryl E. Getter.

[74] See CRS Report RS21341, *Credit Scores: Credit-Based Insurance Scores*, by Baird Webel.

[75] P.L. 91-508. Title VI, §601, 84 Stat. 1128 (1970), codified as amended at 15 U.S.C. §§1681-1681x. For the legal definition, see 12 C.F.R. §1090.104, "Consumer Reporting Market," at http://www.ecfr.gov/cgi-bin/text-idx?SID= c13cb74ad55c0e8d6abf8d2d1b26a2bc&mc=true&node=se12.9.1090_1104&rgn=div8. The Fair Credit Reporting Act, the Fair Debt Collection Practices Act, and the Equal Credit Opportunity Act are all consumer credit protection amendments included in the Consumer Credit Protection Act (P.L. 90-321).

and equitable to the consumer, with regard to the confidentiality, accuracy, relevancy, and proper utilization of such information."[76] The FCRA establishes consumers' rights in relation to their credit reports, as well as permissible uses of credit reports. For example, the FCRA requires that consumers be told when their information from a CRA has been used after an adverse action (generally a denial of a loan) has occurred, and disclosure of that information must be made free of charge.[77] Consumers have a right to one free credit report every year from each of the three largest nationwide credit reporting providers in the absence of an adverse action. Consumers have the right to dispute inaccurate or incomplete information in their report. The CRAs must investigate and correct, usually within 30 days. The FCRA also imposes certain responsibilities on those who collect, furnish, and use the information contained in consumers' credit reports.

Although the FCRA originally delegated rulemaking and enforcement authority to the Federal Trade Commission (FTC), the Dodd-Frank Act transferred that authority to the Consumer Financial Protection Bureau. The CFPB coordinates its enforcement efforts with the FTC's enforcements under the Federal Trade Commission Act.[78] Since 2012, the CFPB has subjected the "larger participants" in the consumer reporting market to supervision.[79] Previously, CRAs were not actively supervised for FCRA compliance on an ongoing basis.

How consumers' personal information is used and protected has been an area of concern. For example, if a fraudster is able to obtain a consumer's personal identifying information he or she could "steal" that person's identity, using it to obtain credit with no intention of repaying. The unpaid debt would then appear on the consumer's credit report, making him or her appear uncreditworthy and potentially resulting in a denial of credit or other adverse outcomes. In September 2017, Equifax announced a security breach[80] in which the sensitive information of an estimated 145.5 million U.S. consumers was potentially compromised, which highlighted the importance of this issue.[81]

---

[76] 15 U.S.C. §1681.

[77] See FTC, *A Summary of your Rights Under the Fair Credit Reporting Act*, at https://www.consumer.ftc.gov/articles/ pdf-0096-fair-credit-reporting-act.pdf.

[78] Memorandum of Understanding Between the Consumer Financial Protection Bureau and the Federal Trade Commission, at https://www.ftc.gov/system/files/120123ftc-cfpb-mou.pdf.

[79] The definition of larger participants includes entities with more than $7 million in annual receipts from consumer reporting activities. When the rule was published in 2012, this definition covered approximately 30 of the 410 consumer reporting agencies. Bureau of Consumer Financial Protection, "12 CFR Part 1090: Defining Larger Participants of the Consumer Reporting Market," 77 *Federal Register* 42874-42900, July 20, 2012.

[80] See Equifax, "Equifax Announces Cybersecurity Incident Involving Consumer Information," press release, September 7, 2017, at https://www.equifaxsecurity2017.com/2017/09/07/equifax-announces-cybersecurity-incidentinvolving-consumer-information/; and Equifax, "Equifax Announces Cybersecurity Firm has Concluded Forensic Investigation of Cybersecurity Incident," press release, October 2, 2017, at https://investor.equifax.com/news-andevents/news/2017/10-02-2017-213238821.

[81] For more information, see CRS Insight IN10792, *The Equifax Data Breach: An Overview and Issues for Congress*, by N. Eric Weiss.

### *Veterans and Active Duty Servicemembers*

Active duty military members are subject to sudden and often times dangerous deployments and assignments that require them to be away from home in a way that is unique from other professions and could adversely affect servicemembers' ability to meet financial obligations. As a result, a number of U.S. laws dating at least as far back as World War I are designed to ease the financial burden on military members and protect them from being financially mistreated.[82] More recently, the Servicemembers Civil Relief Act (SCRA; P.L. 108-189) amended and expanded certain protections for active duty servicemembers. However, some observers assert servicemembers remain inadequately protected in certain transactions and markets, including in the reporting of medical debt to credit reporting agencies, home mortgage refinancing, and mortgage foreclosures.

### *Student Loans*[83]

Aggregate student loan debt in the United States has increased markedly over time. According to the U.S. Department of Education (ED), "[a]verage tuition prices have more than doubled at U.S. colleges and universities over the past three decades, and over this time period a growing proportion of students borrowed money to finance their postsecondary education"[84] The ED's Federal Student Aid Data Center estimated that the total amount of outstanding federal student loan debt exceeded $1.37 trillion at the end of the 2017 fiscal year.[85]

As overall student loan indebtedness has increased, some studies have suggested that repayment burdens facing many borrowers and co-signers have also increased. For example, statistics published by ED suggest that many borrowers face an average educational debt burden that exceeds the "manageable percentage of income that a borrower can" realistically "be expected to devote to loan payment,"[86] although other studies have come to different conclusions.[87] This has led some observers to broadly question whether appropriate protections are in place in this market. A specific area of concern are private student loans, which generally are not required to offer the same

---

[82] More information is in CRS Report RL34575, *The Service Members Civil Relief Act: An Explanation*, by R. Chuck Mason (out-of-print; available to congressional clients upon request).

[83] This section is adapted from CRS Report R45113, *Bankruptcy and Student Loans*, by Kevin M. Lewis.

[84] National Center for Education Statistics, *Stats in Brief: Use of Private Loans by Postsecondary Students: Selected Years 2003-04 Through 2011-12*, U.S. Department of Education, November 2016, at https://nces.ed.gov/pubs2017/ 2017420.pdf.

[85] Federal Student Aid, *Federal Student Loan Portfolio*, U.S. Department of Education, at https://studentaid.ed.gov/sa/ about/data-center/student/portfolio.

[86] National Center for Education Statistics, *Stats in Brief: The Debt Burden of Bachelor's Degree Recipients*, U.S. Department of Education, April 2017, at https://nces.ed.gov/pubs2017/2017436.pdf.

[87] For example, Beth Akers and Matthew M. Chingos, *Is a Student Loan Crisis on the Horizon*, Brown Center on Education Policy at Brookings, June 2014, at https://www.brookings.edu/wp-content/uploads/2016/06/Is-a-StudentLoan-Crisis-on-the-Horizon.pdf.

repayment relief, loan rehabilitation, and loan discharge options that are offered in federal student loans.[88]

## Provisions and Selected Analysis

### *Section 215—Reducing Identity Theft*

#### Provisions

Section 215 directs the Social Security Administration (SSA) to allow certain financial institutions to receive customers' consent by electronic signature to verify their name, date of birth, and Social Security number with SSA. In addition, the section directs SSA to modify their databases or systems to allow for the financial institutions to electronically and quickly request and receive accurate verification of the consumer data.

Some identity thefts use a technique called *synthetic identity theft* in which they apply for credit using a mixture of real, verifiable information of an existing person with fictitious information, thus creating a "synthetic" identity. Often these identity thieves use real Social Security numbers of people they know are unlikely to have existing credit files, such as children or recent immigrants.[89] The SSA Consent-Based Social Security Number Verification system was created to fight identity fraud such as this, but prior to the enactment of P.L. 115-174 it required financial institutions to obtain a physical written signature to make a verification request. Some observers feel this requirement is outdated and time consuming, undermining the effectiveness of the program.[90] Section 215 aims to modernize and make the SSA's verification system more efficient by allowing the use of electronic signatures.

### *Section 301—Fraud Alerts and Credit Report Security Freezes*

#### Provisions

Section 301 amends the FCRA to require credit bureaus to provide fraud alerts for consumer files for at least one year (up from 90 days) when notified by an individual who believes he or she has been or may become a victim of fraud or identity theft. It also provides consumers the right to place (and remove) a security freeze on their credit

[88] For more information on federal student loans, see CRS Report R40122, *Federal Student Loans Made Under the Federal Family Education Loan Program and the William D. Ford Federal Direct Loan Program: Terms and Conditions for Borrowers*, by David P. Smole.

[89] Representative Randy Hultgren, "How to Better Combat Identity Fraud," *Crain's Chicago Business*, March 9, 2018.

[90] Letter from Senators Bill Cassidy, Tim Scott, Claire McCaskill and Gary Peters, to Nancy A. Berryhill, Acting Commissioner of Social Security, February 12, 2018, https://www.cassidy.senate.gov/imo/media/doc/Synthetic%20Identity%20Fraud.pdf.

reports free of charge. In addition, Section 301 creates new protections for the credit reports of minors.

A fraud alert is the inclusion in an individual's report, at the request of the individual, of a notice that the individual has reason to believe they might be the victim of fraud or identity theft. Generally, when a lender receives a credit report on a prospective borrower that includes a fraud alert, the lender must take reasonable steps to verify the identity of the prospective borrower, thus making it more difficult for a fraudster or identity thief to take out loans using the victim's identity. Prior to the enactment of P.L. 115-174, when an individual requested a fraud alert, the CRAs were required to include the alert in the credit report for 90 days, unless the individual asked for its removal sooner. Section 301 increases this period to one year.

A security freeze can be placed on an individual's credit report at the request of the individual (or in the case of a minor, at the request of an authorized representative), and generally prohibits the CRAs from disclosing the contents of the credit report for the purposes of new extensions of credit. If a consumer puts a security freeze on his or her credit report, it would make it harder to fraudulently open new credit lines using that consumer's identity.

**Analysis**

By lengthening the time fraud alerts stay on credit reports and by allowing consumers to place security freezes on their credit reports, Section 301 gives consumers the ability to make it more difficult for identity thieves to get credit using a victim's identity. Reducing the prevalence of erroneous information appearing on credit reports as a result of fraud would reduce the occurrence of defrauded consumers being denied credit on the basis of erroneous information. However, these protections can create some potential costs for lenders and consumers. While a fraud alert is active, the increased verification requirements could potentially increase costs for the lender. A security freeze restricts the use of credit report information in a credit transaction, reducing the information available to lenders and possibly reducing the consumer's access to credit. Although requesting a fraud alert or credit freeze be turned off or "lifted" during a period when a consumer expects to apply for new credit is not especially difficult, doing so is an additional step facing consumers seeking credit and requires some time and attention.[91]

Section 301 also is related to broader debates over the availability, use, and control of personal financial information. Information that financial institutions and service providers have about consumers allows those firms to make better assessments of the consumers' needs and creditworthiness. Credit reports that contain accurate and complete information may improve the efficiency of consumer credit markets, potentially reducing the cost of consumer credit and the frequency of loan default while also increasing the

[91] Lisa Weintraub Schifferle, "Fraud Alert or Credit Freeze—Which Is Right for You?," *Federal Trade Commission Consumer Information*, September 14, 2017.

availability of credit. However, as availability of personal financial information increases, it raises questions about what control individuals have over their own personal, sensitive financial information, particularly in cases in which firms use the information to make adverse decisions against an individual and in which an individual's information is in some way compromised as in the case of fraud. By requiring CRAs to place security freezes at the request of consumers and lengthening the time fraud alerts placed by consumers stay on their reports, Section 301 gives greater control to individuals over how and when their credit reports are used.

### *Section 302—Veteran Medical Debt in Credit Reports*

**Provisions**

Section 302 amends the FCRA to mandate that certain information related to certain medical debt incurred by a veteran be excluded from the veteran's credit report. This medical debt cannot be included in the credit report until one year had passed from when the medical service was provided. The CRAs have already implemented a six-month delay on reporting medical debt for all individuals, so Section 302 gives veterans an additional six months before their medical debts are reported. In addition, Section 302 requires that any information related to medical debt that had been characterized as delinquent, charged off, or in collection be removed once the debt was fully paid or settled. Furthermore, Section 302 establishes a dispute process for veterans wherein a CRA must remove information related to a debt if the veterans notifies and provides documentation to a CRA showing that the Department of Veterans Affairs is in the process of making payment. Finally, Section 302 requires credit reporting agencies to free credit monitoring to active duty military members that would alert them to material changes in their credit scores.

### *Section 303—Whistleblowers on Senior Exploitation*

**Provision**

Section 303 protects certain financial institution employees from liability for disclosing suspected fraudulent or unauthorized use of the resources or assets of a person 65 years of age or older by another individual, such as a caregiver or fiduciary.

### *Section 304—Protecting Tenants at Foreclosure*

**Provision**

Section 304 repeals the sunset provision of the Protecting Tenants at Foreclosure Act (P.L. 111- 22), which expired at the end of 2014, thus restoring certain notification and eviction requirements related to renters living in foreclosed-upon properties.

### *Section 307—Real Property Retrofit Loans*

**Provision**

Section 307 requires the CFPB to issue regulations requiring creditors to assess a borrower's ability to repay a home improvement loan that is financed through a property lien and included in real property tax payments.

Some states have encouraged retrofitting homes through Property Assessed Clean Energy (PACE) financing programs that allow state and local governments to issue bonds and use the funds raised to finance residential, commercial, or industrial energy efficiency and renewable energy projects. The proceeds from PACE bonds are lent to property owners, who use the funds to invest in energy efficiency upgrades or renewable energy property. The loans are added to property tax bills through special assessments and paid off over time. PACE programs offer an alternative to traditional loans and repayments. Some observers have expressed concerns that PACE loans could lead to mortgage defaults, as PACE loans often have relatively high interest rates compared with home-purchase loans.[92] To address this issue, Section 307 extends consumer protections of the ability-to-repay requirement to PACE loans.

### *Section 309—Protecting Veterans from Harmful Mortgage Refinancing*

**Provision**

Section 309 enhances consumer protections for veterans when they refinance housing loans by (1) placing restrictions on the new loan terms to keep refinancing costs reasonable and (2) requiring lenders to provide borrowers with information illustrating how the borrower benefits from a refinancing. These protections are designed to address the practice of offering veterans with VA-backed loans—which have more relaxed credit score standards than other mortgages and typically have no down payment requirement—lower monthly payments but charging them deceptively high upfront fees.[93] Section 309 requires the VA to only insure or guarantee refinancing that met certain standards. For example, the borrower must be able to "recoup" upfront fees in the form of lower monthly payments within 36 months; the new interest rate must be a certain minimum level below the rate of the original loan; and the lender must provide the borrower with a *net tangible benefit test* demonstrating that the borrower would benefit from the refinancing. In addition, Section 309 directs the VA to provide annual reports to Congress on market activity pertaining to certain veteran mortgage refinancing.

---

[92] For example, see Kirsten Grind, "More Borrowers Are Defaulting on Their 'Green' PACE Loans," *Wall Street Journal*, August 15, 2017, at https://www.wsj.com/articles/more-borrowers-are-defaulting-on-their-green-pace-loans1502789401.

[93] Senator Thom Tillis, "Congress Needs to Protect Veterans From Bad Actors in VA Home Loan Financing," *The Hill*, November 9, 2017, at http://thehill.com/blogs/congress-blog/politics/359591-congress-needs-to-protect-veterans-frombad-actors-in-va-home.

## *Section 310—Consider Use of Alternative Credit Scores for Mortgage Underwriting*

### Provisions

Section 310 requires Fannie Mae and Freddie Mac to solicit applications to evaluate additional credit scores to their mortgage underwriting (evaluating) process. In addition, it directs Fannie Mae and Freddie Mac to establish approval criteria in the areas of integrity, reliability, and accuracy. Fannie Mae, Freddie Mac, and the Federal Housing Finance Agency could add additional requirements.

Currently, when determining whether to buy a mortgage, Fannie Mae and Freddie Mac use a particular version of a Fair Isaac Corporation's FICO credit scoring model that was first developed in the late 1990s.[94] This version, sometimes called *classic FICO*, is used to score a homebuyer's credit files from each of the three major credit reporting agencies (Experian, Equifax, and TransUnion). Some observers see shortcomings with how this score is calculated, including its lack of consideration of rent, utility, and cell phone payments, and believe it to be outdated.[95] Fair Isaac has recently developed new credit scores, and a company owned by the three major credit reporting agencies has developed another called the VantageScore. Furthermore FHFA, Fannie Mae, and Freddie Mac are evaluating the merits of the various scores, and FHFA issued a request for feedback about issues that they should consider in evaluating various scoring options, which closed on March 30, 2018.[96] Section 310 directs Fannie Mae and Freddie Mac to create a process by which other credit models can be approved and validated for use in their mortgage purchase decisions.

## *Section 313—Foreclosure Relief Extension for Servicemembers*

### Provisions

Section 313 makes permanent the length of the one-year protection period active duty servicemembers have against the sale, foreclosure, or seizure of their mortgage properties. The Servicemembers Civil Relief Act (SCRA; P.L. 114-142) grants protections pertaining to the sale, foreclosure, or seizure of a servicemember's mortgaged

---

[94] Laurie Goodman, *In Need of an Update: Credit Scoring in the Mortgage Market*, The Urban Institute, July 2017, at https://www.urban.org/sites/default/files/publication/92301/in-need-of-an-update-credit-scoring-in-the-mortgagemarket_2.pdf, and Fannie Mae, *Selling Guide*, April 3, 2018, p. 476, at https://www.fanniemae.com/content/guide/ sel040318.pdf.

[95] Senator Tim Scott, "Senators Scott, Warner Champion Homeownership for the 'Credit Invisible,'" press release, August 1, 2017, at https://www.scott.senate.gov/media-center/press-releases/senators-scott-warner-champion-homeownership-for-the-credit-invisible.

[96] Federal Housing Finance Agency, *Credit Score Request for Input*, December 20, 2017, at https://www.fhfa.gov/Media/PublicAffairs/PublicAffairsDocuments/CreditScore_RFI-2017.pdf, and Federal Housing Finance Agency, *FHFA Extends Deadline to March 30 for Request for Input on Fannie Mae and Freddie Mac Credit Score Requirements*, February 2, 2018, at https://www.fhfa.gov/Media/PublicAffairs/Pages/FHFA-Extends-Deadline-forRFI-on-Fannie-Mae-and-Freddie-Mac-Credit-Score-Requirements.aspx.

property.[97] Specifically, a legal action to enforce a real estate debt against a servicemember on "active duty" or "active service" (or a spouse or dependent of a servicemember) may be stopped by a court if such action occurs within a certain protection period (unless the creditor has obtained a valid court order). The original length of the protection period was 90 days from the servicemember's end of active service. Congress temporarily extended the protection period pursuant to the SCRA to one year at various times, most recently in the National Defense Authorization Act for Fiscal Year 2018 enacted on December 12, 2017 (as P.L. 115-91). Absent the enactment of P.L. 115-174, the protection period would have reverted to 90 days on January 1, 2020.[98]

### *Section 601—Student Loan Protections in the Event of Death or Bankruptcy*

#### Provisions

Section 601 enhances consumer protections for student borrowers and cosigners of student loans by (1) prohibiting lenders from declaring automatic default in the case of death or bankruptcy of the co-signer; and (2) requiring lenders to release cosigners from obligations related to a student loan in the event of the death of the student borrower. Prior to the enactment of P.L. 115-174, a private lender could declare an otherwise performing student loan as being in default if the cosigner—typically a parent of the student who shares the obligation to repay the loan—declares bankruptcy or dies. In addition, whereas a federal student loan had to be discharged when the primary student borrower died,[99] a private lender of a student loan could potentially require the cosigner to continue paying the loan.

### *Section 602—Certain Student Loan Debt in Credit Reports*

#### Provisions

Section 602 amends the FCRA to allow a consumer to request that information related to a default on a qualified private student loan be removed from a credit report if

---

[97] See U.S. Department of Housing and Urban Development, Office of Housing, *Servicemembers Civil Relief Act Notice Disclosure*, OMB Approval 2502-0584, December 31, 2017, at https://www.hud.gov/sites/documents/92070.PDF.

[98] U.S. Department of Housing and Urban Development webpage, "Questions and Answers for Reservists, Guardsmen, and Other Military Personnel," at https://www.hud.gov/program_offices/housing/sfh/nsc/qasscra1. See also, Office of the Comptroller of the Currency, U.S. Department of the Treasury, *Description: Extension of Time Period for Certain Protections*, at https://www.occ.treas.gov/news-issuances/bulletins/2016/bulletin-2016-20.html; and Federal Deposit Insurance Corporation, *FDIC Compliance Examination Manual, V. Lending—Servicemembers Civil Relief Act*, April 2016, at https://www.fdic.gov/regulations/compliance/manual/5/v-11.1.pdf.

[99] See U.S. Department of Education, Office of Federal Student Aid, "*If your loan servicer receives acceptable documentation of your death, your federal student loans will be discharged,*" at https://studentaid.ed.gov/sa/repayloans/forgiveness-cancellation/death.

the borrower satisfies the requirements of a loan rehabilitation program offered by a private lender (with the approval of prudential regulators).

Borrowers who default on some federal student loan programs (defined as not having made a payment in more than 270 days[100]) have a one-time loan rehabilitation option.[101] If the defaulted borrower makes nine on-time monthly payments during a period of 10 consecutive months, the loan is considered rehabilitated.[102] The borrower's credit report would then be updated to show that the loan is no longer in default, although the information pertaining to the late payments that led up to the rehabilitation generally would still remain on the report for seven years.[103] Students who default on private loans do not necessarily have a similar rehabilitation option.[104] Section 307 does not require banks to offer rehabilitations, but each bank has the discretion to do so in light of various business, accounting, and regulatory considerations. If a financial institution does choose to offer a rehabilitation program—after getting permission from its federal bank regulator—and the consumer completes the terms of the program, Section 307 allows for the exclusion of default information related to the rehabilitated loan from the consumer's credit report.

## Regulatory Relief for Large Banks

Title IV is intended to provide regulatory relief to certain large banks. In general, there is widespread agreement that the largest, most complex financial institutions whose failure could pose a risk to the stability of the financial system should be regulated differently than other institutions. However, identifying which institutions fit this description and how their regulatory treatment should differ are subjects of debate.

### Background

The 2007-2009 financial crisis highlighted the problem of "too big to fail" (TBTF) financial institutions—the concept that the failure of a large financial firm could trigger

---

[100] 34 C.F.R. §§682.200 and 685.102.

[101] See CFPB, "What Does It Mean to 'Default' on My Federal Student Loans?" press release, August 4, 2016, at https://www.consumerfinance.gov/ask-cfpb/what-does-it-mean-to-default-on-my-federal-student-loans-en-649/.

[102] See CRS Report R40122, *Federal Student Loans Made Under the Federal Family Education Loan Program and the William D. Ford Federal Direct Loan Program: Terms and Conditions for Borrowers*, by David P. Smole.

[103] See Experian, "I've Defaulted on My Student Loans. Should I Consider Loan Rehabilitation?" press release, October 18, 2016, at https://www.experian.com/blogs/ask-experian/defaulted-on-student-loans-should-i-consider-loanrehabilation/.

[104] CFPB, *Private Student Loans*, Report to the Senate Committee on Banking, Housing, and Urban Affairs, the Senate Committee on Health, Education, Labor, and Pensions, the House of Representatives Committee on Financial Services, and the House of Representatives Committee on Education and the Workforce, August 29, 2012, at http://files.consumerfinance.gov/f/201207_cfpb_Reports_Private-Student-Loans.pdf.

financial instability, which in several cases prompted extraordinary federal assistance to prevent their failure. In addition to fairness issues, economic theory suggests that expectations that a firm will not be allowed to fail create *moral hazard*—if the creditors and counterparties of a TBTF firm believe that the government will protect them from losses, they have less incentive to monitor the firm's riskiness because they are shielded from the negative consequences of those risks.

Enhanced prudential regulation is one pillar of the policy response for addressing financial stability and ending TBTF. Under this regime, the Fed is required to apply a number of safety and soundness requirements to large banks that are more stringent than those applied to smaller banks. Enhanced regulation is tailored, with the largest banks facing more stringent regulatory requirements than medium-sized and smaller banks. Specifically, under criteria set by Dodd-Frank and the Basel III accords, organizations were divided into the following three tiers that determine which enhanced regulations they are subject to

1. about 38 U.S. bank holding companies or the U.S. operations of foreign banks with more than $50 billion in assets;
2. a subset of 15 *advanced approaches* banks with $250 billion or more in assets or $10 billion or more in foreign exposure;[105] and
3. a further subset of *globally systemically important banks* (G-SIBs), designated as such based on a bank's cross-jurisdictional activity, size, interconnectedness, substitutability, and complexity. There are currently 8 G-SIBs headquartered in the United States out of 30 G-SIBs worldwide.[106]

Title I of the Dodd-Frank Act created a new enhanced prudential regulatory regime that applied to all banks with more than $50 billion in assets (unless noted below):

- Stress tests and capital planning ensure banks hold enough capital to survive a crisis.
- Living wills provide a plan to safely wind down a failing bank.

---

[105] The term "advanced approaches" comes from a Basel III rule that applies capital requirements to the activities undertaken primarily by large banks and is a more complex, sophisticated set of requirements than those applying to smaller institutions. Basel III is a nonbinding international agreement that the United States is currently implementing.

[106] Since 2011, the Financial Stability Board (FSB), an international forum that coordinates the work of national financial authorities and international standard-setting bodies, has annually designated G-SIBs. U.S. bank regulators have incorporated the advanced approaches and G-SIB definitions into U.S. regulation for purposes of applying the following regulations. In addition, several of the foreign G-SIBs have U.S. subsidiaries. Financial Stability Board, "Policy Measures to Address Systemically Important Financial Institutions," November 4, 2011, at http://www.financialstabilityboard.org/publications/r_111104bb.pdf. The identification methodology is described in Basel Committee on Banking Supervision, "Global Systemically Important Banks: Assessment Methodology," *Consultative Document*, July 2011, at http://www.bis.org/publ/bcbs201.pdf.

- Liquidity requirements ensure that banks are sufficiently liquid if they lose access to funding markets. These liquidity requirements are being implemented through three rules: (1) a 2014 final rule implementing firm-run liquidity stress tests,[107] (2) a 2014 final rule implementing a Fed-run liquidity coverage ratio (LCR) to ensure that banks hold sufficient "high quality liquid assets,"[108] and (3) a 2016 proposed rule that would implement the Fed-run net stable funding ratio (NSFR) to ensure that banks have adequate sources of stable funding.[109]
- Counterparty limits restrict the bank's exposure to counterparty default through a single counterparty credit limit (SCCL) and credit exposure reports.
- Risk management standards require publicly traded companies with more than $10 billion in assets to have risk committees on their boards, and banks with more than $50 billion in assets to have chief risk officers.
- Financial stability requirements mandate that a number of regulatory interventions can be taken only if a bank poses a threat to financial stability. For example, the Fed may limit a firm's mergers and acquisitions, restrict specific products it offers, terminate or limit specific activities, or require it to divest assets. Other emergency powers include a 15 to 1 debt to equity ratio; FSOC reporting requirements; early remediation requirements; and enhanced FDIC examination and enforcement powers.[110]

Most of these requirements were already in place at the time of enactment of P.L. 115-174, but some proposed rules had not yet been finalized. Some of these requirements had been tailored so that more stringent regulatory or compliance requirements were applied to advanced approaches banks or G-SIBs. For example, versions of the LCR, NSFR, and SCCL applied to advanced approaches banks are more stringent than those applied to banks with more than $50 billion in assets that are not advanced approaches banks. The SCCL as proposed also includes a third, most stringent requirement that applies only to G-SIBs.

Pursuant to Basel III, banking regulators have implemented additional prudential regulations that apply only to large banks. For these requirements, $50 billion in assets was not used as a threshold. The following requirement applies to advanced approaches

---

[107] Federal Reserve, "Enhanced Prudential Standards," 79 *Federal Register* 59, p. 17240, March 27, 2014, at https://www.gpo.gov/fdsys/pkg/FR-2014-03-27/pdf/2014-05699.pdf.

[108] The Office of the Comptroller of the Currency, the Federal Reserve System, and the Federal Deposit Insurance Corporation, "Liquidity Coverage Ratio: Liquidity Risk Measurement Standards," 79 *Federal Register*, October 10, 2014.

[109] The Office of the Comptroller of the Currency, the Federal Reserve System, and the Federal Deposit Insurance Corporation, "Net Stable Funding Ratio; Liquidity Risk Measurement Standards and Disclosure Requirements; Proposed Rule," 81 *Federal Register* 105, June 1, 2016.

[110] For a comprehensive list of these provisions, see CRS Report R45036, *Bank Systemic Risk Regulation: The $50 Billion Threshold in the Dodd-Frank Act*, by Marc Labonte and David W. Perkins.

banks, with a more stringent version applied to G-SIBs, and are affected by a provision in P.L. 115-174:

- Supplementary Leverage Ratio (SLR). Leverage ratios determine how much capital banks must hold relative to their assets without adjusting for the riskiness of their assets. Advanced approaches banks must meet a 3% SLR, which includes off-balance-sheet exposures. G-SIBs are required to meet an SLR of 5% at the holding company level in order to pay all discretionary bonuses and capital distributions and 6% at the depository subsidiary level to be considered well capitalized as of 2018.[111]

Large banks are also subject to other Basel III regulations that are not directly affected by P.L. 115-174. The *countercyclical capital buffer* requires advanced approaches banks to hold more capital than other banks when regulators believe that financial conditions make the risk of losses abnormally high. It is currently set at zero (as it has been since it was introduced), but can be modified over the business cycle.[112] The *G-SIB capital surcharge* requires G-SIBs to hold relatively more capital than other banks in the form of a common equity surcharge of at least 1% and as high as 4.5% to "reflect the greater risks that they pose to the financial system."[113] G-SIBs are also required to hold a minimum amount of capital and long-term debt at the holding company level to meet *total loss-absorbing capacity* (TLAC) requirements. To further the policy goal of preventing taxpayer bailouts of large financial firms, TLAC requirements are intended to increase the likelihood that equity- and debt-holders can absorb losses and be "bailed in" in the event of the firm's insolvency.[114]

## Provisions and Selected Analysis

### *Section 401—Enhanced Prudential Regulation and the $50 Billion Threshold*

#### Provision

Section 401 of P.L. 115-174 automatically exempts banks with assets between $50 billion and $100 billion from enhanced regulation, except for the risk committee

---

[111] Office of the Comptroller of the Currency et al., "Regulatory Capital Rules," 79 *Federal Register* 84, May 1, 2014, p. 24528, at https://www.gpo.gov/fdsys/pkg/FR-2014-05-01/pdf/2014-09367.pdf.

[112] Federal Reserve, "Regulatory Capital Rules: The Federal Reserve Board's Framework for Implementing the U.S. Basel III Countercyclical Capital Buffer," 81 *Federal Register* 180, September 16, 2016, p. 63682, at https://www.federalreserve.gov/newsevents/press/bcreg/20160908b.htm.

[113] Bank for International Settlements, *Basel III Summary Table*, at http://www.bis.org/bcbs/basel3/b3summarytable.pdf.

[114] Federal Reserve, "Total Loss-Absorbing Capacity, Long-Term Debt, And Clean Holding Company Requirements For Systemically Important U.S. Bank Holding Companies," 82 *Federal Register* 8266, January 24, 2017, p. 8266, at https://www.federalreserve.gov/newsevents/pressreleases/bcreg20161215a.htm.

requirements. Banks with between $100 billion and $250 billion in assets will still be subject to supervisory stress tests, and the Fed has discretion to apply other individual enhanced prudential provisions (except for most of those included in the "Financial Stability" bullet above)[115] to these banks if it would promote financial stability or the institutions' safety and soundness. Banks that have been designated as domestic G-SIBs and banks with more than $250 billion in assets remain subject to enhanced regulation. To illustrate how specific firms might be affected by P.L. 115-174, Table 2 matches the criteria found in the three categories created by the legislation to firms' assets as of September 30, 2017. The $250 billion threshold matches one of the two thresholds used to identify advanced approaches banks (it does not include the foreign exposure threshold).

Prior to the enactment of P.L. 115-174, foreign banking organizations that have more than $50 billion in *global* assets and operate in the United States were also potentially subject to enhanced regulatory regime requirements. P.L. 115-174 replaces that threshold with $250 billion in global assets (with Fed discretion to impose individual standards between $100 billion and $250 billion). All of the IHCs in Table 2 belong to a foreign parent with more than $250 billion in global assets.[116] During the period the threshold was set at $50 billion, the implementing regulations in practice imposed significantly lower requirements on foreign banks with less than $50 billion in *U.S.* nonbranch assets compared to those with more than $50 billion in U.S. nonbranch assets. Foreign banks with more than $50 billion in U.S. nonbranch assets must form intermediate holding companies (IHCs) for their U.S. operations, which are essentially treated as equivalent to U.S. banks for purposes of applicability of the enhanced regime and bank regulation more generally. The manager's amendment to P.L. 115-174 clarified that the increase in the $50 billion threshold to $250 billion would not invalidate the rule implementing an IHC, capital planning, stress tests, risk management, and liquidity requirements for banks with more than $100 billion in global assets and would not limit the Fed's authority to establish an IHC or implement enhanced prudential standards for banks with more than $100 billion in global assets. Thus, it remains at the discretion of the Fed how to tailor enhanced regulation for foreign banks with a smaller U.S. presence, including what IHC threshold to use.

---

[115] The Fed could only subject banks with $100 billion to $250 billion in assets to requirements found in Section 165 of the Dodd-Frank Act. Those include a 15 to 1 emergency debt to equity ratio. Most of the provisions covered by the bullet are found in other parts of Title I of the act, including FSOC reporting requirements; emergency powers to require block mergers, limit activities, and divestiture; approval of acquisitions; early remediation requirements; and FDIC examination and enforcement powers. For more information, see CRS Insight IN10877, *P.L. 115-174 and Enhanced Regulation for Large Banks*, by Marc Labonte.

[116] See Federal Reserve, "Enhanced Prudential Standards," 79 *Federal Register* 59, p. 17269, March 27, 2014, at https://www.gpo.gov/fdsys/pkg/FR-2014-03-27/pdf/2014-05699.pdf.

**Table 2. BHCs and IHCs with Over $50 Billion in Assets (as of September 30, 2017; dollar amounts in billions)**

| Institution Name | Assets |
|---|---|
| Banks With Over $250 Billion in Assets or G-SIBs | |
| JP Morgan Chase & Co. | $2,563 |
| Bank of America Corporation | $2,285 |
| Wells Fargo & Company | $1,935 |
| Citigroup Inc. | $1,889 |
| Goldman Sachs Group, Inc. | $930 |
| Morgan Stanley | $854 |
| U.S. Bancorp | $459 |
| PNC Financial Services Group, Inc. | $375 |
| TD Group U.S. Holdings LLC[a] | $374 |
| Capital One Financial Corporation | $361 |
| Bank of New York Mellon Corporation | $354 |
| HSBC North America Holdings Inc.[a] | $286 |
| State Street Corporation | $236 |
| Banks With $100 Billion to $250 Billion in Assets | |
| BB&T Corporation | $220 |
| Credit Suisse Holdings (USA), Inc.[a] | $220 |
| Suntrust Banks, Inc. | $208 |
| Barclays US LLC[a] | $175 |
| American Express Company | $169 |
| DB USA Corporationa | $165 |
| Ally Financial Inc. | $164 |
| MUFG Americas Holdings Corporation[a] | $155 |
| Citizens Financial Group, Inc. | $152 |
| UBS Americas Holding LLC[a] | $146 |
| BNP Paribas USA, Inc.[a] | $146 |
| Fifth Third Bancorp | $142 |
| RBC USA Holdco Corporation[a] | $138 |
| Keycorp | $137 |
| Santander Holdings USA, Inc.[a] | $132 |
| Institution Name | Assets |
| Northern Trust Corporation | $131 |
| BMO Financial Corp.[a] | $131 |
| Regions Financial Corporation | $124 |
| Institution Name | Assets |
| M&T Bank Corporation | $120 |
| Huntington Bancshares Incorporated | $102 |
| Banks With $50 Billion to $100 Billion in Assets | |
| Discover Financial Services | $98 |
| BBVA Compass Bancshares, Inc.[a] | $86 |
| Comerica Incorporated | $72 |
| Zions Bancorporation | $66 |
| CIT Group Inc.[b] | $49 |

Sources: CRS, using Federal Reserve data reported in Bank Holding Company Performance Report; S&P Global. Notes: Domestic G-SIBs are bolded. IHC = intermediate holding company. BHC = bank holding company. SVB Financial Group has had more than $50 billion in assets for less than four quarters. If its assets remain above $50 billion for four consecutive quarters, it will become subject to enhanced regulation, per 12 C.F.R. 252. [a]. IHC whose foreign parent has more than $250 billion in assets. [b]. CIT Group has had less than $50 billion in assets for less than four quarters. If its assets remain under $50 billion in assets for four consecutive quarters, it will no longer be subject to enhanced regulation.

P.L. 115-174 makes tailoring of the regime (e.g., imposing different compliance standards on different banks) mandatory instead of discretionary. For banks with less than $100 billion in assets, Section 401 took effect immediately. For banks with more than $100 billion in assets, the changes take effect within 18 months of enactment, although the Fed has discretion to alter any prudential standard for banks with $100 billion to $250 billion in assets before that date.

The legislation also makes changes to specific enhanced prudential requirements. Section 401 gives regulators the discretion to reduce the number of scenarios used in stress tests. It also gives regulators the discretion to reduce the frequency of company-run stress tests and supervisory stress tests for banks with $100 billion to $250 billion in assets. It increases the asset thresholds for company-run stress tests from $10 billion to $250 billion and for a mandatory risk committee at publicly traded banks from $10 billion to $50 billion. The bill makes the implementation of credit exposure report requirements discretionary for the Federal Reserve instead of mandatory. To date, the Fed has not finalized a rule implementing credit exposure reports.

Banks and thrifts with $50 billion to $100 billion in assets no longer must pay assessments to finance the cost of enhanced regulation, and any bank or thrift with $100 billion to $250 billion in assets will have its assessments adjusted to reflect changes in its regulatory status. Banks with $50 billion to $250 billion no longer pay assessments to fund the Office of Financial Research.

**Analysis**

Supporters and opponents of P.L. 115-174 generally agree that enhanced prudential regulation should apply to systemically important banks, but disagree about which banks could pose systemic risk. Prior to the enactment of P.L. 115-174, there had been widespread support for raising the $50 billion threshold, including from certain prominent regulators, but no consensus on how it should be modified.[117] In particular, critics of the $50 billion threshold distinguish between *regional banks* (which tend to be at the lower end of the asset range and, it is claimed, have a traditional banking business model comparable to community banks) and *Wall Street banks* (a term applied to the largest, most complex organizations that tend to have significant nonbank financial activities).[118] If there are economies of scale to regulatory compliance, the regulatory burden of enhanced regulation is disproportionately higher for the banks with closer to $50 billion in assets. Thus, if the legislation reduces the number of banks that are subject to enhanced regulation but are not systemically important, a significant reduction in cost could be achieved without a significant increase in systemic risk.

---

[117] See, for example, Daniel Tarullo, "Rethinking the Aims of Prudential Regulation," speech at the Federal Reserve Bank of Chicago, May 8, 2014, at https://www.federalreserve.gov/newsevents/speech/tarullo20140508a.htm.

[118] See, for example, Deron Smithy, testimony before the Senate Banking Committee, March 24, 2015, at http://www.banking.senate.gov/public/index.cfm?FuseAction=Files.View&FileStore_id=14d286e0-9c50-4b96-87cffe999112550f.

Definitively identifying banks that are systemically important is not easily accomplished, in part because potential causes and mechanisms through which a bank could disrupt the financial system and spread distress are numerous and not well understood in all cases. In addition, there is not an exact correlation between size and traditional banking activities.

Many economists believe that the economic problem of "too big to fail" is really a problem of firms that are too complex or too interdependent to fail. Size correlates with complexity and interdependence, but not perfectly. Size is a much simpler and more transparent metric than complexity or interdependence, however. As a practical matter, if size is well correlated with systemic importance, a dollar threshold could serve as a good proxy that is inexpensive and easy to administer. Designating banks on a case-by-case basis could raise similar issues that have occurred in the designation of nonbanks, such as the slow pace of designations; difficulty in finding objective, consensus definitions of what constitutes systemic importance; and legal challenges to overturn their designation.

P.L. 115-174 attempts to maximize the benefits and minimize the problems by using both approaches—an automatic designation for banks with assets of more than $250 billion and a case-by-case application of standards for banks with assets between $100 billion and $250 billion. This approach can mitigate the drawbacks inherent in both approaches, but cannot eliminate them. Any dollar threshold still potentially includes banks that do not pose systemic risk with assets above that threshold. Compared with a dollar threshold, any case-by-case application of standards would be more expensive, time-consuming, and subjective, and could potentially create opportunities for legal challenges.

Aside from the effects on financial stability, reducing the number of banks subject to enhanced regulation also reduces second-order benefits, such as protecting taxpayers against FDIC insurance losses. It could also worsen the "too big to fail" problem if market participants perceive the banks subject to enhanced regulation as officially too big to fail. This could lead to greater moral hazard—if the creditors and counterparties of a TBTF firm believe that the government will protect them from losses, they have less incentive to monitor the firm's riskiness because they are shielded from the negative consequences of those risks. One rationale for (1) setting the asset threshold low and (2) subjecting any bank above it to enhanced prudential regulation automatically is that this method would reduce the likelihood that banks in the regime would be viewed as having a de facto TBTF designation.

P.L. 115-174 makes tailoring of the regime mandatory instead of discretionary, and likely will result in more tailored regulation for banks with between $100 billion and $250 billion in assets because the Fed will likely consider the application of each provision separately. In contrast, systemic risk regulation may be less tailored overall, because the legislation mostly eliminates two existing tiers of regulations—those that apply at $10 billion and $50 billion in assets. However, expanding beyond systemic risk regulation, overall bank regulation will be more tailored because of the new size-based exemptions included in other titles of the legislation.

CBO estimated that Section 401 would increase the deficit by $114 million, for two reasons. First, CBO estimated that the probability of a large bank failing would be greater if fewer banks were subject to enhanced regulation, imposing losses on the FDIC insurance fund that would not fully be offset by higher deposit insurance premiums within the 10-year budget window. Although CBO believed a large bank failure would be a relatively large cost to the government (via the FDIC), the change in probability of failure under the legislation is small. Thus, CBO's estimate of the provision's budgetary effect was small. Second, CBO estimated that the reduction in banks paying fees to cover the costs of the Fed's duties under enhanced regulation would exceed the reduction in costs to the Fed of no longer subjecting those banks to enhanced regulation.[119]

### *Section 402—Custody Banks and the Supplementary Leverage Ratio*

#### Provision

Section 402 allows custody banks—defined by the legislation as banks predominantly engaged in custody, safekeeping, and asset servicing activities—to no longer hold capital against funds deposited at certain central banks[120] to meet the SLR, up to an amount equal to customer deposits linked to fiduciary, custodial, and safekeeping accounts. As discussed in the leverage section above, under leverage ratios, including the SLR, the same amount of capital must be held against any asset, irrespective of risk.

#### Analysis

Custody banks provide a unique set of services not offered by many other banks, but are generally subject to the same regulatory requirements as other banks. Custodian banks hold securities, receive interest or dividends on those securities, provide related administrative services, and transfer ownership of securities on behalf of financial market asset managers, including investment companies such as mutual funds. Asset managers access central counterparties and payment systems via custodian banks. Custodian banks play a passive role in their clients' decisions, carrying out instructions. Generally, banks must hold capital against their deposits at central banks under the leverage or

---

[119] Congressional Budget Office, Cost Estimate, P.L. 115-174, March 5, 2018, at https://www.cbo.gov/system/files/115th-congress-2017-2018/costestimate/s2155.pdf. CBO's score of the manager's amendment reduced the cost associated with this provision, but did not explain the source of the reduction. The manager's amendment changed both the number of banks subject to enhanced regulation and the number subject to fees. Congressional Budget Office, *Estimates of the Direct Spending and Revenue Effects of Amendment Number 2151*, March 8, 2018, at https://www.cbo.gov/system/files/115th-congress-2017-2018/costestimate/s2155amendmentnumber2151.pdf.

[120] The central banks that currently qualify for this exemption include all countries belonging to the Organization for Economic Cooperation and Development (OECD) except Mexico and Turkey. For a list, see OECD, Country Risk Classifications of the Participants to the Arrangement on Officially Supported Export Credits, January 26, 2018, at http://www.oecd.org/trade/xcred/cre-crc-current-english.pdf.

supplemental leverage ratio, but custody banks argue that this disproportionately burdens them because of their business model.[121] However, other observers argue that the purpose of the leverage ratio is to measure the amount of bank capital against assets regardless of risk, and to exempt "safe" assets undermines the usefulness of that measure.[122]

P.L. 115-174 leaves it to bank regulators to define which banks meet the definition of "predominantly engaged in custody, safekeeping, and asset servicing activities." Other large banks that offer custody services but do not qualify for relief under the "predominantly engaged" definition may be at a relative disadvantage under this provision. A CRS analysis of call report data[123] identified three banks that had a significantly greater amount of assets under custody than total exposures—Bank of New York Mellon, Northern Trust, and State Street.[124] If determined to be custody banks, Northern Trust (as an advanced approaches bank) would be able to reduce its capital by $3 for every $100 it deposits at central banks, and Bank of New York Mellon and State Street (as G-SIBs) would be able to reduce their capital by $6 for every $100 of banking subsidiary deposits at central banks. The FDIC reports that Bank of New York Mellon held $36 billion, Northern Trust held $23 billion, and State Street held $25 billion of deposits at the Federal Reserve at the end of December 2017.[125] The FDIC does not separately report bank deposits at foreign central banks, which will also receive capital relief under the legislation for some deposits, or custodial or safekeeping deposits, which could potentially limit the amount of capital relief. As mentioned earlier, whether banks in addition to the three identified here will also receive relief under Section 402 will be up to the regulators' discretion.

CBO estimated that Section 402 would increase the budget deficit by $45 million over 10 years because a reduction in capital held by custody banks would result in a greater likelihood that a custodial bank would fail, imposing losses on the FDIC insurance fund that would not fully be offset by higher deposit insurance premiums within the 10-year budget window.[126] Although CBO believed a large bank failure would

---

[121] Bank of New York Mellon, Northern Trust, and State Street, letter to the Honorable Mike Crapo and Honorable Sherrod Brown, April 14, 2017, at https://www.banking.senate.gov/public/_cache/files/1c835896-8b5e-4387-8431- b3c5c41810b9/AFC62A5DEEDEF3838A75891481F5471F.custody-bank-coalition-submission.pdf.

[122] Former Federal Reserve Governor Daniel K. Tarullo, "Departing Thoughts," Remarks at the Woodrow Wilson School, Princeton University, Princeton, NJ, April 4, 2017, pp. 11-13, https://www.federal reserve.gov/newsevents/ speech/files/tarullo20170404a.pdf.

[123] Federal Financial Institutions Examination Council, *Banking Organization Systemic Risk Report (FR Y-15), Fourth Quarter 2016*.

[124] Each of those three had at least 48 times as many assets under custody as total exposures. The bank with the next highest ratio, Charles Schwab, had more than 12 times as many. These are the same three banks that noted that they lead the custody banking business in a letter to the Senate Banking Committee requesting the provision. See Bank of New York Mellon, Northern Trust, and State Street, letter to the Honorable Mike Crapo and Honorable Sherrod Brown, April 14, 2017, at https://www.banking.senate.gov/public/_cache/files/1c835896-8b5e-4387-8431-b3c5c41810b9/AFC62A5DEEDEF3838A75891481F5471F.custody-bank-coalition-submission.pdf.

[125] Data from Federal Financial Institutions Examination Council, Consolidated Report of Condition and Income (FFIEC 031), Schedule RC-A and Schedule RC-T, Fourth Quarter 2017.

[126] Congressional Budget Office, Cost Estimate, P.L. 115-174, March 5, 2018, at https://www.cbo.gov/system/files/ 115th-congress-2017-2018/costestimate/s2155amendmentnumber2151.pdf.

be a relatively large cost to the government (via the FDIC), the change in probability of failure under the legislation is small. Thus, CBO's estimate of the provision's budgetary effect was small.

### *Section 403—Municipal Bonds and Liquidity Coverage Ratio*

#### Provision

Section 403 requires bank regulators to treat any municipal bond "that is both liquid and readily marketable and investment grade" as a level 2B high-quality liquid asset for purposes of complying with the LCR. Municipal bonds are debt securities issued by state and local governments or public entities. Prior to the enactment of P.L. 115-174, the Fed allowed banks to count a limited amount of municipal securities as level 2B assets, but the FDIC and the Office of the Comptroller of the Currency (OCC) did not. Half of the value of a level 2B asset may be counted toward fulfilling the LCR, and level 2B assets may not exceed 15% of total high-quality liquid assets (HQLA).

#### Analysis

To the extent that the LCR reduces the demand for bank holding companies to hold municipal securities, it would be expected to increase the borrowing costs of states and municipalities.[127] The impact of the LCR on the municipal bond market may be limited by the fact that relatively few banks are subject to the LCR. Finally, even banks subject to the LCR are still allowed to hold municipal bonds, as long as they have a stable funding source to back their holdings. CRS estimates that banks subject to the LCR held $187 billion in state and municipal bonds in the third quarter of 2017, compared with total outstanding municipal debt of $3.8 trillion.[128] CRS was unable to determine what portion of these bonds meet the "liquid and readily marketable and investment grade" criteria.

Arguments that municipal bonds should qualify as HQLA because most pose little default risk confuse default risk, which is addressed by capital requirements, with liquidity risk, which is addressed by the LCR. The purpose of the LCR is to ensure that banks have ample assets that can be easily liquidated in a stress scenario; a municipal bond may pose very little default risk, but nevertheless be illiquid (i.e., hard to sell quickly).

---

[127] For more information, see CRS Report R44146, *The Demand for Municipal Bonds: Issues for Congress*, by Darryl E. Getter and Raj Gnanarajah.

[128] Federal Reserve Y-9C data accessed on December 27, 2017, at https://www.chicagofed.org/applications/bhc/bhchome; Securities Industry and Financial Markets Association, U.S. Bond Market Issuance and Outstanding data, accessed on January 3, 2018, at https://www.sifma.org/wp-content/uploads/2017/06/cm-us-bond-market-sifma.xls.

## CAPITAL FORMATION

Title V of P.L. 115-174 is focused on providing regulatory relief to participants of *capital markets*. Certain provisions of Title V provide streamlined registration and disclosure requirements for certain securities issuers as well as market intermediaries (e.g., asset managers and stock exchanges). These provisions allow for reduced regulatory obligations in relation to selected aspects of capital formation.

### Background

Companies turn to a variety of sources to access the funding they need to grow, including by accessing capital markets. Capital markets are segments of the financial system in which funding is raised through issuing equity or debt securities.[129] Equity securities—also called stocks or shares—represent part ownership of a firm. Debt securities, such as bonds, represent indebtedness of a firm. Capital markets are the largest source of financing for U.S. nonfinancial companies, representing 65% of all financing for such companies in 2016,[130] significantly more than bank loans and other forms of financing. U.S. capital markets are considered the deepest and most liquid in the world. U.S. companies are generally more reliant on capital markets for funding than companies in other countries with developed economies, which rely more on bank loans.[131] The principal regulator of U.S. capital markets is the Securities and Exchange Commission (SEC).

Capital markets are often the focus of policy discussions. Access to capital allows businesses to fund their growth, to innovate, to create jobs, and to ultimately help raise society's overall standard of living. Capital formation also involves investor protection challenges, including the challenge to ensure that investors, such as less sophisticated retail investors, could comprehend the risks of their investments. Policymakers frequently debate the balance between these two potentially conflicting objectives: (1) facilitating capital formation and (2) fostering investor protection largely through mandatory disclosure and compliance. Proposals that reduce the regulatory compliance that a securities issuer or a market intermediary must comply with can decrease these market

---

[129] A more detailed definition of securities could be found through the Howey test. In *SEC v. W.J. Howey Co.*, 328 U.S. 293 (1946), the Supreme Court set forth the foundational test for whether a transaction qualifies as a form of security known as an *investment contract*. Under *Howey*, an investment contract is (1) an investment of money (2) in a common enterprise (3) with a reasonable expectation of profits (4) to be derived from the entrepreneurial or managerial efforts of others. See also SEC v. Edwards, 540 U.S. 389, 393 (2004). Rahul Mukhi and James Michael Blakemore, Cleary, Gottlieb, Steen & Hamilton LLP, "SEC Cyber Unit and Allegedly Fraudulent ICO," December 26, 2017, at https://corpgov.law.harvard.edu/2017/12/26/sec-cyber-unit-and-allegedly-fraudulent-ico.

[130] Data provided by SIFMA.

[131] SIFMA, *U.S. Capital Markets Deck*, September 2017, at https://www.sifma.org/wp-content/uploads/2016/10/USCapital-Markets-Deck-2017-09-11-SIFMA.pdf.

participants' compliance costs and increase the speed and efficiency of capital formation. However, this reduced regulation may also expose investors to additional risks. These risks could potentially include the reduction in information that is important to investment decisionmaking; and the lack of compliance that could hinder an intermediary's capacity to safeguard investor assets or act in the best interest of investors, among other investor protection concerns. In addition, investor protection can help contribute to healthy and efficient capital markets because investors may be more willing to provide capital, and even at a lower cost, if they have faith in the integrity and transparency of the underlying markets.

Many of the provisions in Title V involve some version of the policy debate mentioned above. On the one hand, some observers generally believe that capital markets require updated regulations to ensure that companies have adequate access to markets and that they are not unduly burdened by inefficient or outdated regulations with limited benefits. In particular, they argue that small- and medium-sized companies have more difficulty accessing capital relative to larger companies, and should be given regulatory relief. On the other hand, other observers generally believe that capital market regulations in place prior to the enactment of P.L. 115-174 strike an appropriate balance between capital access and investor protection, and that paring back protections unnecessarily exposes investors to risks, particularly among investors that may lack sophisticated knowledge or the ability to withstand unexpected financial losses.

## Provisions and Selected Analysis

### *Section 501—National Security Exchange Parity*

#### Provisions

Section 501 alters a criterion that exempts covered securities from state securities regulation under the Securities Act of 1933. Prior to the enactment of P.L. 115-174, "covered" securities were defined as securities that are listed on the New York Stock Exchange, the American Stock Exchange, and the National Market System of the Nasdaq Stock Market, or on an exchange that the SEC determines has securities listing standards that are "substantially similar" to those three.[132] If a security meets the definition of a covered security, then it is exempt from certain state regulations. Section 501 removes the substantially similar criterion and gives covered status to any securities listed on exchanges that are SEC-registered, which is generally required of all domestic exchanges.

---

[132] 15 U.S.C. §77r(b).

The provision's advocates claim that the substantially similar criterion was outdated, and as a result, the SEC could have been limiting the number of potentially innovative and competitive exchanges. Furthermore, they argue that some of these innovative exchanges could help alleviate the lack of access small companies have to secondary capital markets.[133] Critics, however, are concerned that eliminating the SEC's regulatory authority in this area could help spur the development of securities exchanges with lower listing standards and fewer regulatory requirements, and thus increase the opportunities for investor fraud.[134]

### *Section 504—Registration Requirements for Small Venture Capital Funds*

#### Provision

Section 504 creates a new subset of *venture capital funds* called *qualifying venture capital funds* (QVCFs) and exempts them from the definition of *investment company* under the Investment Company Act of 1940 (ICA; P.L. 76-768). No longer being classified as an investment company under the ICA reduces the qualifying fund's registration and disclosure requirements. Venture capital funds are investment pools that manage the funds of generally wealthy investors interested in acquiring private equity stakes in emerging small- and medium-sized firms and startup firms with perceived growth potential. The funds often take an active role in the businesses, including providing managerial guidance and occupying corporate board seats. The ICA requires certain pooled investments—including venture capital funds—to register with the SEC. Registration triggers certain reporting responsibilities, including disclosures about investment objectives, financial condition, structure, operation, and product offerings. In addition, registered investment companies are obligated to safeguard investor assets and act in the best interest of investors, among other requirements. Investment company registration and compliance are intended to (among other things) mitigate certain conflicts of interest that may arise, but impose compliance costs on funds. Under the ICA, an investment pool generally must register if it has more than 100 beneficial shareholders,[135] unless it otherwise qualifies for an exemption.[136] Section 504 allows a venture capital fund to qualify as a QVCF and avoid registration requirements if it has no more than 250 beneficial investors (up from 100 beneficial investors), provided it had no

---

[133] House Financial Services Committee, "House Passes Bill to Create an Equal Market Playing Field," press release, at July 12, 2016, https://financialservices.house.gov/news/documentsingle.aspx?DocumentID=400925.

[134] Minority Views on H.R. 5421: The "National Securities Exchange Regulatory Parity Act of 2016", at https://democrats-financialservices.house.gov/uploadedfiles/mv_hr_5421_signed.pdf.

[135] A beneficial shareholder is a shareholder in the investment pool who enjoys the benefits of ownership in the pool, even though the titular shareholder may be another entity such as a broker-dealer who is acting on behalf of the beneficial shareholder.

[136] 15 U.S. Code §80a–3(c).

more than $10 million in invested capital (no size threshold is currently in place) before triggering the ICA registration requirement.

Some observers argue capital access for small businesses could be improved by allowing venture capital funds to have a broader shareholder base before they are subjected to registration requirements.[137] However, others are concerned that limiting federal regulatory oversight of investment funds of larger size unnecessarily weaken protections for the underlying venture fund investors.[138]

### *Section 506—U.S. Territories Investor Protection*

#### Provision

Section 506 repeals the exemption available to mutual funds organized in domestic territories— including Puerto Rico, the Virgin Islands, and Guam—from compliance with the Investment Company Act of 1940 (P.L. 76-768; ICA). The ICA generally requires investment pools— including mutual funds—to register with the SEC. Registration subjects investment pools to SEC enforcement and regulatory oversight and triggers certain reporting responsibilities, including disclosures about the fund's investment objectives, financial condition, structure, operation, and product offerings. According to a congressional report,[139] when the ICA was enacted in 1940, Congress determined that it would be too costly for the SEC to travel to and inspect investment companies located beyond the continental United States. Subsequently, some areas lost the exemption (e.g., Alaska and Hawaii), but others (e.g., Puerto Rico, the Virgin Islands, and Guam) still retained it prior to the enactment of P.L. 115-174.[140] A general argument for Section 506 is that the earlier logistical challenges presented by noncontinental territories have diminished over time.

### *Section 507—Disclosure Requirements for Companies Paying Personnel in Stock*

#### Provision

Section 507 requires the SEC to increase the threshold amount of stock a company can sell to its corporate personnel without becoming subject to additional disclosure

---

[137] Representative Patrick McHenry, "McHenry Introduces Bipartisan, Bicameral Bill to Promote Investments in Businesses and Startups," press release, March 6, 2017, at https://mchenry.house.gov/ news/documentsingle. aspx? DocumentID=398484.

[138] Letter from Americans for Financial Reform and Consumer Federation of America to Chairman Jeb Hensarling, Ranking Member Maxine Waters, and Members of the House Financial Services Committee, June 14, 2016, at https://www.ourfinancialsecurity.org/wp-content/uploads/ ... /HFSC-Markup-AFR-CFA-Letter.pdf.

[139] U.S. Congress, House Committee on Financial Services, *U.S. Territories Investor Protection Act of 2017*, Report to accompany H.R. 1366, 115th Cong., 1st sess., May 1, 2017, H.Rept. 115-103, pp. 1-2.

[140] Senator Bob Menendez, "Senate, House Committees Advance Menendez Bipartisan Bill Protecting Investors in Puerto Rico, U.S. Territories," press release, March 9, 2017, at https://www.menendez.senate.gov/news-and-events/ press/senate-house-committees-advance-menendez-bipartisan-bill-protecting-investors-in-puerto-rico-us-territories.

requirements from $5 million over any 12-month period to $10 million over any 12-month period. A company that offers or sells its securities to the public is required to register them with the SEC, a process that requires the company to make certain disclosures about its business. This process imposes certain compliance costs, which potentially could be disproportionately burdensome to small- and medium-sized businesses and startups.[141] In 1988, the SEC adopted Rule 701 under the Securities Act of 1933. The rule created an exemption from certain registration requirements to nonpublic companies, including startups that offer their own securities (such as stock options and restricted stock) as part of formal written compensatory benefit agreements to employees, directors, general partners, trustees, officers, specified advisers, and consultants. Certain conditions must be met for eligibility, including a limit on the issuance of stock to the aforementioned corporate personnel during a 12-month period not to exceed the greater of $1 million, or 15% of the issuer's total assets, or 15% of all the outstanding securities of the class of securities being offered. In addition, prior to the enactment of P.L. 115-174, if the issuance of securities to corporate personnel exceeded $5 million during any 12-month period, the company was required to provide investors with additional disclosures on a recurring basis, including information on risk factors, the plans under which the offerings have been made, and certain financial statements.[142] Section 507 raises the $5 million threshold, which could result from one of the two aforementioned 15% asset or securities scenarios being triggered, to $10 million.

### *Section 508—Expanding Regulation A+ Access to Reporting Companies*

#### Provisions

Section 508 expands the SEC's Regulation A+ to allow certain "fully reporting" companies to be eligible for certain exemptions from disclosure requirements.[143] The offers and sales of securities must either be registered with the SEC (as a public offering) or be undertaken with an exemption from registration (as a private offering). A fully reporting company is a company that files registration statements and other reports with the SEC, either voluntarily or through public offering requirements. Regulation A+, a type of exemption from registration, is a private offering designed to facilitate capital access for small- to medium-sized companies by subjecting them to fewer disclosure requirements. Prior to enactment of P.L. 115-174, Regulation A+ applied to nonreporting companies only.[144] By broadening the base of eligible issuers of Regulation A+ offerings, thousands of SEC reporting companies qualify for a more streamlined registration and

[141] Rep. Randy Hultgren, "Hultgren Reintroduces Encourging Employee Ownership Act," press release, May 7, 2017, at https://hultgren.house.gov/newsroom/press-releases/hultgren-reintroduces-encouraging-employee-ownership-act.

[142] 17 C.F.R. §230.701.

[143] 17 C.F.R. §230.251 through §230.263.

[144] For information about private offerings in general, see CRS In Focus IF10747, *Private Securities Offerings: Background and Legislation*, by Eva Su.

disclosure approach under Regulation A+. That reduced disclosure will likely reduce costs for companies but also will likely reduce the information available to investors.

### *Section 509—Streamlined Closed-End Fund Registration*

#### Provisions

Section 509 directs the SEC to allow closed-end funds[145] to use certain streamlined reporting procedures available through the *well-known seasoned issuer* (WKSI) status.[146] A closed-end fund is a publicly traded investment company that sells a limited number of shares to investors in an initial public offering and the shares are traded on secondary markets.[147] The WKSI status has generally been granted to operating companies that produce goods and services, rather than investment companies such as closed-end funds. Prior to enactment of P.L. 115-174, registered investment companies, including closed-end funds, generally could not be granted WKSI status even when required conditions are met. Examples of distinct WKSI benefits include (1) certain simplified registration statements filed beforehand to automatically take effect without SEC review,[148] also referred to as *shelf registration*;[149] (2) communication with potential investors before and during the offering period; and (3) deliver of electronic instead of physical prospectuses (formal legal documents describing the details of the securities offerings).[150] Section 509 enables closed-end funds that meet WKSI requirements to partake of the benefits of such status. In addition, if the SEC fails to finalize the rules within one year of enactment, closed-end funds would be subject to the Securities Offering Reform of 2005, which

---

[145] Closed-end funds are registered investment companies under the Investment Company Act of 1940 (15 U.S.C. §80a-5) and listed on national stock exchanges. The provision could also include issuers that makes periodic repurchase offers pursuant to 17 C.F.R. §270.23c-3—*Repurchase Offers by Closed-end Companies*. More details see *Congressional Record—Senate (S1564)*, March 8, 2018, at https://www.congress.gov/crec/2018/03/08/CREC-2018-03- 08-pt1-PgS1529-7.pdf.

[146] A *well-known seasoned issuer* (WKSI) generally refers to an issuer that is eligible for Form S-3 for registration of a primary offering of securities and has at least $700 million shares available for trading, or has sold at least $1 billion in aggregate principal amount of registered debt in primary offerings for cash. For more on WKSI, see Westlaw, *Glossary: Well-known Seasoned Issuer*, at https://content.next.westlaw.com/Document/Ibb0a1321ef0511e28578f7ccc38dcbee/View/FullText.html?contextData=(sc.Default)&transitionType=Default&firstPage=true&bhcp=1.

[147] More on closed-end fund see SEC, *Closed-End Fund Information*, at https://www.sec.gov/fast-answers/answersmfclosehtm.html.

[148] For example, the provision proposes to allow eligible closed-end funds to incorporate registration statements through referencing information in other SEC shareholder reports or filings, instead of direct incorporation of information into the registration statements. As such, the simplified process is said to save time and associated costs.

[149] A primary advantage of shelf registration is that "a company fulfills all registration-related procedures beforehand, so that it can offer securities quickly when funds are needed or when market conditions are more favorable." For more details on shelf registration, see Westlaw, *Glossary: Shelf Registration*, at https://content.next.westlaw.com/Document/Ibb0a10cdef0511e28578f7ccc38dcbee/View/FullText.html?originationContext=document&transitionType=DocumentItem&contextData=(sc.DocLink).

[150] Congressional Budget Office, H.R. 4279, *Expanding Investment Opportunities Act*, January 16, 2018, at https://www.cbo.gov/publication/53475; and House Financial Services Committee, *Report 115-517*, January 16, 2018, at https://www.congress.gov/115/crpt/hrpt517/CRPT-115hrpt517.pdf.

provide regulatory relief for noninvestment companies and are currently not applicable to closed-end funds.[151]

The number of close-end funds has decreased in recent years from 662 funds at the previous peak in 2007 to 530 funds in 2016.[152] Some argue this is the result of unduly burdensome regulation.[153] However, isolating the effects of regulations across time in a dynamic market is difficult, and no consensus exists over what role various market forces have played in this decline.

## MISCELLANEOUS PROPOSALS IN P.L. 115-174

The Economic Growth, Regulatory Relief, and Consumer Protection Act contains a number of provisions that do not necessarily pertain directly to the issue areas examined above, including the following:

- Deposits in U.S. Territories. Section 208 extends the applicability of Expedited Funds Availability Act (P.L. 100-86) requirements (which relate to how quickly deposits, once made, are available to account holders) to American Samoa and the North Mariana Islands.
- Small Public Housing Agencies. Section 209 classifies public housing agencies administering 550 housing units or fewer that predominately operate in rural areas as *small public housing agencies* (SPHAs) and reduce administrative requirements faced by such agencies, including less frequent inspections and reduced environmental review requirements. In addition, Section 209 creates a process for corrective action to be undertaken for troubled SPHAs and an incentive program for SPHAs to reduce energy consumption.[154]
- Insurance. Section 211 creates an "Insurance Policy Advisory Committee on International Capital Standards and Other Insurance Issues" at the Federal Reserve made up of 21 members with expertise on various aspects of insurance. It requires an annual report and testimony from the Federal Reserve and the Department of the Treasury on the ongoing discussions at the International

---

[151] 17 C.F.R. §§200, 228, 229, 230, 239, 240, 243, 249, and 274.

[152] Investment Company Institute, *The Closed-End Fund Market, 2016*, April 2017, at https://www.ici.org/pdf/per2302.pdf.

[153] House Financial Services Committee, *Report 115-517*, January 16, 2018, at https://www.congress.gov/115/crpt/hrpt517/CRPT-115hrpt517.pdf.

[154] For more information on public housing, see CRS Report R41654, *Introduction to Public Housing*, by Maggie McCarty.

Association of Insurance Supervisors through 2022, and a report prior to supporting any specific international insurance standards.[155]

- National Credit Union Administration Budget. Section 212 requires the National Credit Union Administration to publish a draft of its annual budget in the *Federal Register* and hold public hearings on the draft.
- Federal Reserve Surplus. The Fed's capital comprises paid-in capital issued to member banks and retained earnings deposited in its surplus account. Section 217 reduces the statutory cap on the Fed's surplus account from $7.5 billion to $6.825 billion and requires funds in excess of that amount to be remitted to Treasury as general revenues. CBO estimated that this provision would increase revenues by $478 million on net over 10 years.[156] CBO assumed that the Fed would finance the transfer by selling Treasury securities, which otherwise would have earned $177 million in income that would have been remitted to the Treasury in the next 10 years. Thus, the provision can be thought of as shifting Fed remittances from the future to the present, as opposed to representing new economic resources available to the federal government.
- Remediating Lead and Asbestos Hazards. Section 305 directs the Secretary of the Treasury to use loan guarantees and credit enhancements to remediate lead and asbestos hazards in residential properties backing mortgages acquired by the Treasury.
- Family Self Sufficiency Program. Section 306 makes alterations to the Family Self Sufficiency Program (FSS), an asset-building program for residents of public and assisted housing. The changes are designed to harmonize separate FSS programs into one, unified program; expand the range of services that can be provided to participating residents; and make other technical changes to the program.
- Overpayments to the SEC. Section 505 permits national securities exchanges that have made overpayments to the SEC in excess of their required fees to offset those payments against future fees owed within 10 years of the overpayment.
- Studies and Best Practices. Section 216 requires a Treasury report on cyber threats to financial institutions and capital markets. Section 308 requires a Government Accountability Office (GAO) report on consumer reporting. Section 311 requires a GAO report on foreclosures in Puerto Rico. Section 312 requires a Department of Housing and Urban Development report on lead-based paint hazard prevention. Section 502 requires an SEC report on algorithmic trading in

---

[155] For more information on international insurance issues, see CRS Report R44820, *Selected International Insurance Issues in the 115th Congress*, by Baird Webel and Rachel F. Fefer, and CRS Report R44958, *Insurance Regulation: Legislation in the 115th Congress*, by Baird Webel.

[156] Congressional Budget Office, *Estimates of the Direct Spending and Revenue Effects of Amendment Number 2151*, March 8, 2018, at https://www.cbo.gov/system/files/115th-congress-2017-2018/costestimate/s2155 amendmentnumber2151.pdf.

capital markets. Section 503 amends the Small Business Investment Incentive Act of 1980 (SBIIA; P.L. 96-477) by requiring the SEC to release (1) a public assessment of the findings and recommendations of the annual Government-Business Forum on Small Business Capital Formation; and (2) a public report on what actions, if any, it will be taking to address those findings and recommendations. Section 603 directs the Financial Literary and Education Commission to establish best practices for institutions of higher learning regarding methods to teach financial literacy skills and to provide information to students at those institutions to assist them when making financial decisions.

## APPENDIX A. ASSET SIZE AND OTHER THRESHOLDS IN P.L. 115-174

Table A.1 lists provisions in P.L. 115-174 that create or change size-based threshold criteria that alter the regulatory treatment of certain institutions or activities.

**Table A.1. Asset Size and Other Thresholds in P.L. 115-174**

| P.L. 115-174 Section Number | New Size Threshold | Former Size Threshold | Provision Description |
|---|---|---|---|
| Asset Size Threshold | | | |
| 207 | $3 billion | $1 billion | BHCs below this threshold, subject to other requirements, are not subject to the same capital requirement as depository subsidiaries and are permitted to take on more debt to acquire other banks. |
| 210 | $3 billion | $1 billion | Banks below this threshold, subject to other requirements, are eligible for less frequent examination. |
| 205 | $5 billion | None | Banks below this threshold are eligible for reduced reporting requirements to federal regulators. |
| 101 | $10 billion | $2 billion | Mortgages originated and retained by banks or credit unions below this threshold, subject to other requirements, are considered "qualified mortgages" for the purposes of the Ability to-Repay Rule. |
| 109 | $10 billion | $2 billion | Banks or credit unions below this threshold, subject to other requirements, are exempt from certain escrow requirements. |
| 201 | $10 billion | None | Banks below this threshold, possibly subject to other regulatory requirements, are considered as meeting all capital and leverage requirements if they maintain at least a minimum Community Bank Leverage Ratio. |
| 203 | $10 billion | None | Banking organizations below this threshold are exempt from the Volcker Rule, provided their trading assets and liabilities are less than 5% of total assets. |
| 206 | $20 billion | None | Federal savings associations below this threshold, subject to other requirements, can opt-in to the national bank charter regulatory regime. |

| P.L. 115-174 Section Number | New Size Threshold | Former Size Threshold | Provision Description |
|---|---|---|---|
| 401 | $50 billion | $10 billion | Publicly traded BHCs below this threshold are exempt from certain risk committee requirements. |
| 401 | $100 billion | $50 billion | BHCs below this threshold are exempt from Dodd-Frank enhanced prudential regulation (except for the risk committee requirement). |
| 401 | $100 billion - $250 billion | $50 billion | Regulatory discretion to apply Dodd-Frank enhanced prudential regulation to BHCs in this range, except supervisory stress testing requirements to which these BHCs would still be subject. |
| 401 | $250 billion or G-SIB | $10 billion for company-run stress tests; $50 billion for others | BHCs above this threshold would be automatically subject to Dodd-Frank enhanced prudential regulation. |
| Other Institution Threshold | | | |
| 209 | 550-unit public housing agency | None | An agency of small size is subject to less frequent inspection, provided it predominately operates in a rural area. |
| 504 | $10 million in invested capital and 250 beneficial owners | 100 beneficial owners | The new threshold applies to when a qualifying venture capital fund must register with the Securities and Exchange Commission as an investment company. |
| 507 | $10 million in aggregate sales of company securities to employees | $5 million in aggregate sales of company securities to employees. | Certain companies that are exempt from registering their securities with the SEC are subject to a higher threshold before they would be required to give employee-investors additional investor disclosures. |
| Product/Activity Limitations | | | |
| 202 | Lesser of $5 billion or 20% of total liabilities | None | Reciprocal deposits below this threshold are not considered brokered deposits for the purposes of prohibitions from accepting brokered deposits facing banks that are not well capitalized. |
| 103 | $400,000 mortgage | $250,000 mortgage | Loans below this threshold, subject to other requirements, do not require an appraisal of the property in rural areas. |

Source: Congressional Research Service.

Notes: BHC = bank holding company. Some existing thresholds are statutory, whereas others are applied through regulation.

## APPENDIX B. SIMILAR POLICY ISSUES IN SELECTED HOUSE BILLS

P.L. 115-174 addresses a number of policy issues that are also addressed by the Financial CHOICE Act (H.R. 10), which was passed by the House on June 8, 2017, and other House bills that have seen legislative action in the 115th Congress. Table B.1 lists such policy issues and identifies the sections of P.L. 115-174, the sections of H.R. 10, and House bills that have seen action that propose changes in those areas. It should be noted, however, that while certain issues addressed in the various pieces of legislation are similar, how the bills address them may differ to varying degrees, some quite significantly. An examination and discussion of how the various proposals differ across the each piece legislation is beyond the scope of this chapter.

**Table B.1. Policy Issues Addressed in P.L. 115-174 and Selected House Legislation**

| Policy Issue | P.L. 115-174 Section | H.R. 110 Section | Other House bills (status in parentheses) |
|---|---|---|---|
| Additional criteria for mortgages to receive "Qualified Mortgage" status | 101 | 516 | H.R. 2226 (Passed by House, voice)<br>H.R. 2133, Sec 15 (Hearings held) |
| Charitable donations of home appraisals | 102 | 591 | H.R. 2255, Title I (Passed by House, voice) |
| Appraisal requirement exemptions for rural or low value mortgages | 103 | H.R. 2133, Sec 3 (Hearings held) H.R. 3221 (Ord. to be Rept., 32-26) | |
| Exemptions from certain HMDA reporting requirements | 104 | 576 | H.R. 2954 (Passed by House, 243-184) H.R. 2133, Sec 8 (Hearings held) |
| Loan originator grace period during license changes | 106 | 556 | H.R. 3978, Title V (Passed by House, 271-145) H.R. 2948 (Rept. by Comm., 60-0) |
| Mortgage rule exemptions for certain manufactured homes retailers | 107 | 501 | H.R. 1699 (Passed by House, 256-163) |
| Escrow requirements for mortgages exemptions | 108 | 531 | H.R. 3971 (Passed by House, 294-129) H.R. 2133, Sec 2 (Hearings held) |
| Mortgage waiting period requirement exemptions | 109 | H.R. 2133, Sec 12 (Hearings held) | |
| Bank leverage ratio criteria for exemption from other ratios and rules | 201 | 601-602 | |
| Reciprocal deposits restrictions exemptions | 202 | H.R. 2133, Sec 14 (Hearings held) | |
| Federal Reserve Small BHC Policy Statement asset threshold increase | 203 | 526 | H.R. 4771 (Passed by House, 280-139) H.R. 2133, Sec 4 (Hearings held) |
| Volcker Rule trading restriction exemptions | 204 | 901 | H.R. 4790 (Passed by House, 300-104) |
| Volcker Rule naming restriction exemptions | 205 | H.R. 3093 (Passed by House, voice)<br>H.R. 4790 (Passed by House, 300-104) | |
| Shortened "call report" in bank financial reporting requirements | 206 | 566 | H.R. 4725 (Passed by House, voice) |
| Alternative to charter changes for federal thrifts seeking to increase certain loan types | 207 | 551 | H.R. 1426 (Passed by House, voice) |
| Deposit availability time requirements in U.S. territories | 208 | 521 | |
| Reduced examination frequency for certain small banks | 210 | H.R. 5076 (Rept. by Comm., 60-0) | |

| Policy Issue | P.L. 115-174 Section | H.R. 110 Section | Other House bills (status in parentheses) |
|---|---|---|---|
| International insurance standards oversight | 211 | 1101-1102 | H.R. 4537 (Rept. by Comm. 56-4) |
| Public disclosure of NCUA budgets | 212 | 541 | |
| Scanned images of ID cards and online banking | 213 | H.R. 1457 (Passed by House, 397-8) | |
| High volatility commercial real estate exposures in capital requirements | 214 | H.R. 2148 (Passed by House, voice) | |
| Wait period before including veterans' medical debt in credit reports | 302 | H.R. 2683 (Rept. by Comm., 59-0) | |
| Whistleblower protection for identifying cases of defrauding seniors | 303 | 491-493 | H.R. 2255, Title III (Passed by House, voice)<br>H.R. 3758 (Rept. by Comm., 60-0) |
| Alterations to the Family Self Sufficiency program | 306 | H.R. 4258 (Passed by House, 412-5) | |
| Enhanced prudential regulation regime alterations | 401 | H.R. 3312 (Passed by House, 288-130)<br>H.R. 4292 (Passed by House, 414-0)<br>H.R. 4293 (Passed by House, 245 - 174) | |
| SLR central bank deposit exemption<br>for custodial banks | 402 | H.R. 2121 (Rept. by Comm., 60-0) | |
| Treatment of municipal debt under LCR | 403 | H.R. 1624 (Passed by House, voice) | |
| National securities exchange definition in exemption from state registration | 501 | 496 | H.R. 4546 (Rept. by Comm., 46-14)<br>H.R. 3978, Title IV (Passed by House, 271-145) |
| Exemptions from certain registration and disclosure requirements for certain venture capital funds | 504 | 471 | H.R. 1219 (Passed by House, 417-3) |
| Future SEC assessment offset after overpayment | 505 | 416 | H.R. 1257 (Rept. by Comm., 59-0) |
| Application of certain securities requirements to funds located in U.S. territories | 506 | H.R. 1366 (Passed by House, voice) | |
| Compensation disclosure requirement exemption | 507 | 406 | H.R. 1343 (Passed by House, 331-87) |
| Expanded Regulation A+ access to reporting companies | 508 | | H.R. 2864 (Passed by House, 403-3) |
| Streamlined closed-end fund registration | 509 | 499A | H.R. 4279 (Passed by House, 418-2) |

Source: CRS.

Notes: The table identifies bills that have passed the House or have otherwise seen legislative action as of May 14, 2018. "Rept. by Comm." refers to the House Financial Services Committee unless otherwise noted and includes bills that were ordered to be reported. The table does not include sections of the House appropriations bill (H.R. 3354) that passed the House on September 14, 2017, some sections of which do address certain policy issues listed in the table.

# INDEX

## A



## B

## C



## D

## E



## F

## W